Pathologies of Love in Classical Literature

Trends in Classics –
Supplementary Volumes

Edited by
Franco Montanari and Antonios Rengakos

Associate Editors
Stavros Frangoulidis · Fausto Montana · Lara Pagani
Serena Perrone · Evina Sistakou · Christos Tsagalis

Scientific Committee
Alberto Bernabé · Margarethe Billerbeck
Claude Calame · Jonas Grethlein · Philip R. Hardie
Stephen J. Harrison · Stephen Hinds · Richard Hunter
Christina Kraus · Giuseppe Mastromarco
Gregory Nagy · Theodore D. Papanghelis
Giusto Picone · Alessandro Schiesaro
Tim Whitmarsh · Bernhard Zimmermann

Volume 122

Pathologies of Love
in Classical Literature

Edited by
Dimitrios Kanellakis

DE GRUYTER

ISBN 978-3-11-127661-8
e-ISBN (PDF) 978-3-11-074794-2
e-ISBN (EPUB) 978-3-11-074806-2
ISSN 1868-4785

Library of Congress Control Number: 2021938905

Bibliographic information published by the Deutsche Nationalbibliothek
The Deutsche Nationalbibliothek lists this publication in the Deutsche Nationalbibliografie;
detailed bibliographic data are available on the Internet at http://dnb.dnb.de.

© 2023 Walter de Gruyter GmbH, Berlin/Boston
This volume is text- and page-identical with the hardback published in 2021.
Editorial Office: Alessia Ferreccio and Katerina Zianna
Logo: Christopher Schneider, Laufen
Printing and binding: CPI books GmbH, Leck

www.degruyter.com

Legerat huius Amor titulum nomenque libelli:
'Bella mihi, video, bella parantur' ait.

Love, having read the name and title on this book,
said: 'It's war, you declare against me, I see, it's war'.

                        Ov. *Rem.* 1–2 (transl. A. S. Kline)

Preface

The present collection sprang from a conference held at Oxford in June 2018. The enthusiastic participation of the audience and the stimulating discussions on that occasion motivated us to pursue this publication. All the contributors to this volume are deeply indebted to the colleagues who also offered their inspiring insights and expertise on the literary and visual representation of the topic: Angus Bowie, Christopher Faraone, Eleni Pachoumi, Thomas Mannack, Jane Masséglia, Amy Smith and Giacomo Fedeli. As the convenor, I am grateful to all the speakers for kindly accepting my invitation and for our excellent collaboration. Warm thanks are also due to everyone who supported the realisation of the conference: Emilia Savva, Paul Madden, Charles Crowther, Armand D'Angour, Stephen Harrison, Stephen Heyworth, Bill Allan, Malcom Davies, Gregory Kantor, Christopher Metcalf and Maria Stamatopoulou. The Board of the Faculty of Classics, the Craven Committee, The Queen's College, University College, Corpus Christi College and the Classical Association kindly offered generous funding and use of their facilities.

The COVID-19 pandemic, which occurred while the papers were being edited, has created an unfortunate yet significant context for this volume. When conceiving the title of the conference, I could not have imagined how relevant 'pathology' would become two years later, nor how bitterly literal the notion of 'pathology of love' would sound today. Having to practise 'social distancing' and 'self-isolation', to 'work from home' and 'study via synchronous e-learning platforms' essentially means that to meet the people we love is to put our health, or theirs, at risk. Love has somehow been equated to illness. At the same time, health experts have warned about the mental impact of those social restrictions, and the financial impact of the lockdown on the global economy will only cause further anxiety, depression, and isolation from beloved ones. This is not to start our book with a pessimistic tone – if anything, this collaborative project is a confident statement on the joy of working together – but to say that our current experience allows us to better perceive several of the paradoxes entailed in the notion of the 'pathology of love': it feels like a deadlock and a vicious circle in which the roles of victim and violator are not always discernible, and individual desires clash with social and political ethics. Moreover, we should remember that the ancient people were more vulnerable to epidemics – already recorded in the prologue of the *Iliad*, the first piece of western literature – and, therefore, disease as *a common experience* and *a public discourse* was a phenomenon more frequent than, but as vivid as, COVID-19 is for us today. For example, that the plague of 430 BCE killed at least a quarter of the

Athenian population means that we cannot interpret the nosologic imagery of the authors of the time related to *erôs*, or to any other concept, solely in terms of poetic tradition. Such vocabulary would inevitably elicit the readers' and spectators' emotional response, evoke their living memories and anxieties, and create a community of compassion. If the modern world is accustomed to reading ancient literature as monuments of timeless and universal wisdom, aesthetic magnitude, and historical knowledge, our contemporary pandemic is perhaps a reminder for us to also engage emotionally with our predecessors: to feel empathy for them and the human race as a whole. (At the same time, thinking outside the anthropocentric box of Classics, let us not forget other living beings: all the livestock and wildlife species whose exploitation is linked to corona-viruses, and those species used in the production and testing of our vaccines.)

DK
Athens, March 2021

Contents

Preface —— VII
List of Figures —— XI
Texts and Abbreviations —— XIII

Dimitrios Kanellakis
Introduction —— 1

Chiara Thumiger
The Ophthalmology of Lovesickness: Poetry, Philosophy, Medicine —— 23

Claude Calame
Performance and Pragmatics of Erotic Poetry in Archaic and Classical Greece: A Pathology of Sexualities? —— 47

Anastasia-Stavroula Valtadorou
Pathological *Erôs* in the Euripidean Fragments: *Aeolus*, *Cretans*, and *Protesilaus* —— 65

Thomas K. Hubbard
Pathological Heterosexuality and Other Male Anxieties —— 83

Ed Sanders
Xenophon and the Pathology of *Erôs* —— 101

Andreas N. Michalopoulos
The Pathology of Love in Ovid's *Metamorphoses* —— 119

Thea S. Thorsen
In Sickness or in Health? Love, Pathology, and Marriage in the Letters of Acontius and Cydippe (Ovid's *Heroides* 20–1) —— 135

Ioannis M. Konstantakos
Pathological Love in the 'Open' or 'Fringe' Novels —— 159

Dimitrios Kanellakis
Appendix: An Anthology of the Pathologies of Love —— 179

List of Contributors —— 195
Bibliography —— 197

Index Locorum —— 221
Index Nominum et Rerum —— 229

List of Figures

Fig. 1: Alexandre Cabanel, *Phèdre*, 1880. Oil on canvas 194x286 cm. Montpellier: Musée Fabre. —— 7

Fig. 2: Attic black-figure amphora by Exekias, ca. 530 BCE. British Museum 1836.2-24.127. © The Trustees of the British Museum. —— 17

Fig. 3: Attic red-figure kylix by Penthesilea Painter, ca. 460 BCE. Munich, Antikensammlungen 2688. Reproduced under CC BY-SA 4.0 (Wikimedia Commons). —— 18

Fig. 4: Gustave Moreau, *Pasiphaé*, 1880. Oil on canvas 195x91cm. Paris: Musée National Gustave-Moreau. —— 82

Fig. 5: Robinet Testard, *Cydippe writes a letter to Acontius*. Illustration from Octavien de Saint-Gelais' translation of Ovid's *Heroides*, Paris 1497. Bibliotèque Nationale de France, MS Fr.875 fol.124v. —— 158

Texts and Abbreviations

While primarily aimed at an academic readership, the book is accessible to anyone interested in classics and/or the subject of love, with all Greek and Latin texts translated into English and with a handy anthology in the appendix conceived for teaching purposes. Unless otherwise indicated, the ancient texts are quoted from the *Oxford Classical Texts* and each contributor specifies the translations used. Names of ancient authors and their works are abbreviated according to *The Oxford Classical Dictionary* (or Liddell-Scott-Jones' *A Greek-English Lexicon*, if missing from there) and journals according to *L'Année philologique*.

Dimitrios Kanellakis
Introduction

> *I have carefully collected whatever I have been able to learn of the story of poor Werther, and here present it to you ... To his spirit and character you cannot refuse your admiration and love: to his fate you will not deny your tears.*
>
> *And thou, good soul, who sufferest the same distress as he endured once, draw comfort from his sorrows; and let this little book be thy friend, if, owing to fortune or through thine own fault, thou canst not find a dearer companion.*
>
> — Goethe, The Sorrows of Young Werther, 1774: Preface [transl. R.D. Boylan]

Love and death are among the most prominent – arguably, the two most prominent – themes of literature across time and cultures. As a topic for investigation, the 'pathology of love' perfectly combines the two, as it connects *erôs* with disease, and synecdochically (or metaphorically) with death. Therefore, without exaggeration, the pathology of love could serve as an ideal standpoint for retelling the history of literature. The peak point in such a historiographical narrative would probably be the Romantic and Decadent movements of the nineteenth century, although most elements of this literary tradition derive from Greco-Roman antiquity.[1] Of course, as the contributors rightly emphasise (Thumiger: 24, Calame: 50), what we call *erôs* in the Greco-Roman context is not a transhistorical category; however, it is precisely the 'gaps, discontinuities, and fragility' of such cultural concepts, even within their contemporary frame, that provide us with 'a useful tool to think with' today (Hubbard: 84). In this volume there are indeed notable gaps in what a chronological history of the pathology of love in classical

---

[1] See, for example, Wack 1990 on the Middle Ages; Wells 2007 and Dawson 2008 on early modern English and Italian literature; Dye 2004 on Goethe; Small 1996 and Gilbert 1997 on the Victorian novel; Labbe 2000 and Béres Rogers 2019: 91–118 on Romanticism; Sobol 2009 on eighteenth- and nineteenth-century Russian literature. The reverse enquiry, i.e. what we might call 'the erotics of pathology', is pursued by Susan Sontag in her 1978 essay *Illness as Metaphor*, in which she explores various metaphors historically attached to tuberculosis and cancer (most important, their identification with death itself) through the popular mythology that has been built around these diseases. Of all metaphors, 'the most striking similarity between the myths of TB and of cancer is that both are, or were, understood as diseases of passion. [...With the Romantics,] TB was conceived as a variant of the disease of love. [...] As once TB was thought to come from too much passion, afflicting the reckless and sensual, today many people believe that cancer is a disease of insufficient passion, afflicting those who are sexually repressed, inhibited, unspontaneous, incapable of expressing anger.' (20–1). 'Having TB was imagined to be an aphrodisiac, and to confer extraordinary powers of seduction. Cancer is considered to be de-sexualizing' (13).

https://doi.org/10.1515/9783110747942-001

antiquity would present, such as the Homeric epics or Hellenistic poetry. (This introduction, as well as the appendix, aim to compensate for most gaps, suggesting further reading.) Instead, this book aspires to put forward, through appropriate case studies, a methodology for constructing such a history of literature. It does so, by visiting medical sources to understand 'pathology' in its synchronic epistemic dimension, acknowledging that medical authors have exercised an influence on literature and vice versa (Thumiger); by tracing how the poetic expression of the theme corresponds, potentially, to a pragmatic realisation, as far as the performative genres are concerned (Calame); by exploring what a given society considers a socio-pathological *erôs*, according to its moral and political standards, and how literature portrays that (Valtadorou, Hubbard); by deducing the narrative patterns of the experience of love, from 'infection' to 'symptomatology', from 'acute' to 'chronic condition', and so on (Sanders); by comparing the different manifestations of the theme within a single author's oeuvre to synthesise his/her poetic biography or programme (Michalopoulos) and by resorting to textual criticism to treat ill-preserved passages towards that purpose (Valtadorou, Thorsen); finally, by reading this key theme as a gauge of generic compliance or innovation (Konstantakos). The following sketch of a literary history of the pathology of love in Ancient Greece and Rome aims to help the reader contextualise the respective case studies.

A Long Love-Story Short

In her 1995 monograph *In Pandora's Jar: Lovesickness in Early Greek Poetry*, the only book-long treatment of the topic before our volume, Monica Cyrino explored the development of erotic malady in archaic literature. She argued that the Homeric epics introduced a repertoire of imagery and vocabulary connecting *erôs* to suffering, if only implicitly; subsequently, Hesiod specified that vocabulary as distinctly pathological; and finally, the lyric poets elaborated on the hexameter tradition by shifting from martial and mythological narrative to personal experience and by explicitly equating love with illness. Here I shall only cherry-pick the most characteristic manifestations of the theme, adding some of the more recent bibliography and extending the chronological scope to include Greek and Latin literature up to the imperial period. It should go without saying that my intention is not to reduce complex interpretative issues of individual works and passages to something simple and presumably obvious, but – what is more pertinent to an introduction – to summarise how each era and each genre shed light upon new *aspects* of the subject matter.²

The pathology of love became a crucial element in the narrative and the characterisation already in Homer, even though it is not explicitly and systematically presented there. Achilles' *mênis* is triggered by his loss of Briseis to Agamemnon, which hurt not only his pride but also his feelings for her (*Il*. 1.348–50, 9.342–3). It is not clear whether he truly loves *her*,³ or the prestige that her ownership entails,⁴ but in either case he is motivated by an obsessive desire. To close the circle, Achilles rejoins the war towards the end of the epic, in revenge for another, more painful and unambiguous loss: the murder of his beloved Patroclus. *Philia*, rather than aristocratic pride, is the explicit motivation here, leading to excessive mourning with suicidal tendencies (*Il*. 18.80–99). But Achilles is fantasising rather than actually considering death, as he is 'enamoured with the absolute', i.e. with a paroxystic, narcissistic, and sadomasochistic ideality.⁵ Rather similar is Penelope's wish for death while longing for Odysseus; she fantasises that Artemis will rescue her from the suitors and reunite her with her husband by killing her (*Od*. 18.201–5, 20.79–83).⁶ Homer also offers the first account of Helen's story, the Greek myth of erotic malady *par excellence*. Paris' heart was seized by *erôs* for her (*Il*. 3.441–6) and thus she infamously became the cause of the Trojan War; while Helen always appears conscious of her scandalous behaviour, she calls herself a victim of Aphrodite's will (*Od*. 4.259–64).⁷ Hesiod offered another myth propagating female blame: Pandora as the cause of all evils. This proto-woman was given

---

2 For other general, short accounts, see Toohey 1992 (with a focus on melancholia); Tallis 2004: 6–13 (on mental illness); Duffin 2005: 43–51; McNamara 2016: 309–16.
3 See Taplin 1992: 214–16; Fantuzzi 2012: 99–128.
4 Loden 2006: 133–4 asserts that Briseis serves 'a typical function', a companion dear to Achilles, as much as Phoenix does.
5 Evzonas 2017. On Achilles' characterisation see de Jong 2018: 43–5 with further bibliography.
6 Felson-Rubin 1994: 34–6. For Katz 1991: 149, Penelope's wish 'is ambiguous, since the wish to maintain virginity forever and the sorrow at its impending loss is a regular prelude to marriage for women in archaic poetry'.
7 Ebbott 1999 analyses Helen's regret and awareness of her notoriety and Roisman 2006 presents her 'as a suffering figure with a good mind'. Lesser 2019, on the contrary, reads the Iliadic Helen as an archetypal unfaithful wife contrasted to loyal Penelope, both female figures thus exemplifying the intertextual rivalry of the two epics. For the Homeric canonisation and later transformations of the myth, up to Euripides, see Austin 1994. Blondell 2013, who considers texts and archaeological artefacts alike, argues that Helen is a figure that embodies ambiguous roles (e.g. object *vs* agent, lure *vs* threat) and each author deliberately elides some of her aspects to give his own stance on gender, sex, violence etc.

as a trap-gift from Zeus to men, in revenge for Prometheus stealing the fire. Pandora was adorned with 'grace and painful desire and limb-devouring cares' by Aphrodite, thus becoming an object of the male gaze, but at the same time she bore deadly diseases for mankind in her jar – probably a metaphor for the vagina (*Theog.* 585–9, *Op.* 57–8, 65–6, 90–104). Therefore, sexual attraction appears as a prerequisite to physical destruction.[8] 'Sexual desire is exclusively and intensely negative in value [and] whenever women make an appearance it is as a dire threat to the hardworking male farmer' of the Hesiodic world; that womankind arises from Pandora without the involvement of Eros, i.e. without a genealogical/reproductive connection, in contrast to most of Earth's descendants in *Theogony*, might account for the ill-minded female race.[9] In terms of nosologic vocabulary, Hesiod used more descriptive terms than Homer, for example calling *erôs lusimelês*, 'limb-loosening' (*Theog.* 121), which was followed by Archilochus and Sappho.

Whereas the epics sporadically and implicitly narrated events of pathological desire, the lyric poets repeatedly and vividly confessed their own experience as victims of *erôs*' attacks: '*I am* in the throes of desire, miserable and lifeless, pierced through my bones' (Archil. 193 W), 'Eros pours sweetly down and warms *my* heart' (Alcm. 59a *PMG*), 'limb-loosening Love makes *me* tremble' (Sappho 130 L-P), 'Love has struck *me* like a smith with a great hammer' (Anacr. 68 *PMG*), and so on.[10] Apart from the suffering lyric 'I', the poems often include the addressee of the confession, whether a sympathetic listener (e.g. Archil. 196 W: 'But, *my friend*, limb-loosening desire overwhelms me'), or the very object of desire (e.g. Sappho 31 L-P: 'For when I look at *you* for a moment, then it is no longer possible for me to speak'). Whether the addressees are fictional characters or real persons in the audience or the performing team (fellow symposiasts or *choreutai*) is neither possible to tell nor vital for our emotional engagement.[11] Moreover, in the case of choral poetry, it is often ambiguous whether the 'I' voice expressing erotic sentiment, for example praising

---

[8] See Cyrino 1995: 50–4.
[9] Most 2013: 169–71, 173. Further bibliography in Lye 2018, who analyses Pandora as 'a commodity constructed for visual pleasure' (182) and interprets Hesiod's misogyny as part of his self-identification: women threaten the male hierarchy, Hesiod feels politically powerless in his society, therefore women – and males of a different status from his own – receive his attacks. For a psychoanalytic reading of the jar/vagina, see Blum 2007.
[10] All translations here are from the Loeb series. On Archilochus' erotic language see Swift 2019: 34–6 and Swift 2016b. On Anacreon's metaphors of erotic domination see Williamson 1998.
[11] Cazzato 2013: 274-5 argues, for example, that in the love poem Ibycus 286 *PMG* the symposiastic setting might simply be an aesthetic *locus* and we do not have to assume an *actual* sympotic performance.

the beauty of a male patron in encomiastic poetry, is representative of the individual narrator or the chorus, or both.¹² The poems thematise a wide range of pathological erotic conditions, from unrestrained passion in Archilochus to retirement in Mimnermus, from romantic jealousy in Sappho to sexual jealousy in Theognis, and so on, employing language and imagery from a vast array of bodily and mental diseases.¹³ Confessions of erotic suffering contribute to male bonding in the context of the symposia, whether the singer and his beloved (male or female) are specified individuals or generic personas; by assuming such a traditionally male narrative standpoint, Sappho challenges the hierarchy of subject and object of desire, and claims a distinctly female authorial voice.¹⁴ Her famous poem 31 L-P (φαίνεταί μοι κῆνος... 'He seems to me...') is the first milestone towards the standardisation of the pathology of love, being the first *ekphrasis* of the symptomatology, combining physical and mental conditions in a cohesive narrative, where the gaze is the starting point – the first word indeed.¹⁵

In the context of Athenian democracy, the connection of love with disease enters the political sphere. Orators and historians adjust the metaphor to common affairs, conceiving the city-state as a unified body, as an *erastês* or *erômenos* of a particular politician, military project, proposed policy etc. A notable occasion is the public debate on the Sicilian expedition (415 BCE); advising against the expansionist project, Nicias urges the Athenians to resist their 'morbid desire for what is absent', i.e. impossible to obtain (Thuc. 6.13.1: δύσερως τῶν ἀπόντων), yet the Athenians 'were all struck by love' for the enterprise (Thuc. 6.24.3: ἔρως ἐνέπεσε τοῖς πᾶσιν, cf. Plut. *Per.* 20.4). For them, Sicily was a cure against the shame of *malakia*, 'softness', which was viewed as a threat to Athenian prestige. And given that 'softness' is a male anxiety in particular, 'the necessity that drives Athens to rule others or be ruled itself, the cruel binarism that translates any failure of mastery into slavery' has been rightly labelled as 'the pathology of Athenian masculinity'.¹⁶ A second notable occasion is Isocrates' speech *On Peace*, written in view of Athens' imminent defeat in the War of the Allies (357–355 BCE). The orator characterises the specific war, and any war indeed, as a madness (8.8,

---

12 Rawles 2011.
13 For 'bittersweet' *erôs* striking various organs first (*kardia, phrenes, thumos, stêthea, psukhê*), see Calame 1999: 14–23. For analytical discussion of passages, Cyrino 1995: 71–90 (Archilochus, Alcman), 91–132 (Alcaeus, Ibycus, Anacreon), 133–64 (Sappho).
14 Stehle 2009: 66–71.
15 'The archetype of erotic affection in Western poetry', Thumiger 2017: 374. For bibliography see Thumiger p. 26 nn. 5–9 in this volume and, additionally, Budelmann 2018: 132–7 for a commentary, D'Angour 2013 and Livrea 2016 for reconstructions of the missing stanza(s).
16 Wohl 2002: 190.

8.17: ἄνοια, μανία) which the *dêmos* supported, misled by politicians who speak for their pleasure (8.9: ἡδονή). Isocrates warns his fellow citizens that 'while many treatments of all kinds have been discovered by physicians for the ills of our bodies, there exists no [easy] remedy for souls which are ignorant of the truth and filled with base desires' (8.39: πονηρῶν ἐπιθυμιῶν).[17]

Greek tragedy, with its notoriously nefarious love stories, pushed the limits of lovesickness, portraying 'sickness' not only in its medical sense – on which psychoanalytic criticism elaborated, using Oedipus' myth as its constitutional paradigm – but also as ethical disgust and socio-political disorder. The nexus between civil and personal/familial malady is a key theme in the *Oresteia*, where Clytaemnestra's coup against, and murder of, Agamemnon is presented as an act of maternal and marital retribution. Even though the sexual motivations remain subtle for the most part, in a single revealing moment Clytaemnestra's gazing at her husband's and Cassandra's corpses explicitly becomes a necrophiliac fantasy.[18] *Oedipus Rex* starts with the description of a civil *nosos* (60, 61, 150, 170, 217, 303, 307) which is slowly and painfully revealed to be caused by Oedipus' murder of his father and incest with his mother. Jocasta feels sickened as she starts perceiving the appalling truth (1061) and eventually commits suicide, whereas Oedipus chooses to live with this unbearable 'disease' for the rest of his life (1293), self-blinded and exiled from Thebes so as not to cause any further *miasma*.[19] While the political aspect is not absent from Euripidean lovesickness, the focus is on the detailed psychography of the suffering individual. Medea's pathological jealousy of Jason for his new wife leads her to a momentous, and 'textually pathological', i.e. corrupt, monologue which portrays her emotional instability, in which her pride seems to outdo her love for her children (1021–80).[20] 'Sickened by her dear ones' since the opening of the play (16), she finally slays the children in revenge of her husband's betrayal, yet insisting that it was *his nosos* that killed them (1364). However, if we had to single out one tragedy as the most 'pathologically erotic', that would doubtlessly be *Hippolytus*, with more occurrences of *nosein-* and *nosos-*forms than any other play. Struck by Aphrodite with the *mania*

---

[17] For medical language in oratory, see Das 2015 (14–19 on Isocrates, for whom see also Wohl 2002: 178–9).
[18] Kanellakis 2020: 45.
[19] See Lloyd 2003: 85–8 and Ryzman 1992. Of all Sophoclean plays, the pathology of love has been studied mostly with regard to *Trachiniae*: see Wender 1974; O'Connor 1974: 102–24; Holt 1981. On Sophocles' medical thought and language see Mitchell-Boyask 2012 and Allan 2014 with further bibliography.
[20] On her sexual jealousy, see Sanders 2013; Allan 2021: 31–4; Cairns 2021: 22–5. On the textual issue, Mossman 2011: 314–18 and Mastronarde 2002: 388–97.

of *erôs* (38–40, 241, 764–6, 1274),²¹ Phaedra falls in love with her son-in-law Hippolytus and suffers in silence for this shameful passion; physically exhausted and mentally weak, she lies in bed refusing to eat and wishing for death. Thus her suicide, upon the revealment of her secret, seems no more pathetic than her illness. Phaedra is the personification of the pathology of love in the most literal/medical sense possible. This should be seen in connection with the rise of Hippocratic medicine and the Plague of Athens that appeared the year before the play was staged.²²

Fig. 1: Alexandre Cabanel, *Phèdre*, 1880. Oil on canvas 194x286 cm. Montpellier: Musée Fabre.

---

21 On the connection between erotic drive and madness in tragedy, see Thumiger 2013; on *erôs*' maddening sting in *Hippolytus* in particular, Padel 1992: 122 (and 116–37 for more metaphors). Seneca too describes the heroine's lovesickness as a total *furor* (17 occurrences in *Phaedra*).
22 Jouanna 2012 (see 61–5, 76–7 on *Hippolytus*) demonstrates that late Sophocles and Euripides were influenced by Hippocratic treatises, as evidenced in their nosologic terminology and descriptions of epileptic fits, even though tragedy entails a less rational and more ritualistic conception of illness; this is due not only to the mythological content of the genre, but also to the rise of the cult of the healer god Asclepius in late 5th century. Kosak 2004: 131–92, who is more sceptical about Euripides' or his audience's technical knowledge and specific influences, offers a detailed medical reading of *Orestes*, *Heracles*, *Phoenician Women* and *Bacchae*. On the implications of the Plague and the cult of Asclepius for tragedy, see Mitchell-Boyask 2008.

Political and medical ideas also permeate Aristophanes' pathology of love, which serves both the *geloion* and the didactic strain of his comedies.²³ For example, and narrowing down to sexual pathology, the unsettling erections of the men in *Lysistrata*, which are indeed compared to disease (1085–8), are 'hardly' anything but an opportunity for obscene jokes and comic business. On the other hand, the representation of Demos as *kinaidos* in *Knights*, and of Paphlagon and the Sausage-Seller as his *erastai-kolakes* who yet have been sexually compromised – a total reversal of the pederastic hierarchy – may be seen as a critique on Athenian democracy, both on the leaders' egotism and the people's compromise with corruption.²⁴ Various social and political (mis)behaviours and phenomena are described in medical *and* erotic terms, such as Philocleon's jury-mania in *Wasps* (87–9), which is actually an 'epidemic' of the entire city (651),²⁵ or the unfair distribution of wealth in the eponymous play, which is personified by Plutus, initially blinded by Zeus who 'envies the people' (87–92) and eventually cured by Asclepius who 'loves the city' (726). While comic fantasy momentarily provides the remedies for pathological love, by bringing the sexual strike to an end, rejuvenating Demos, sending Philocleon to parties instead of trials, healing Plutus, and so on, the ironic readings of the plays – for example, *Lysistrata*'s happy ending requires the rape of Reconciliation – undermines the suggested 'treatments', pointing at the ever-pathological human state.²⁶

Such philosophical implications in the poetic treatments of the pathology of love should be read, of course, in connection with contemporary philosophy. Plato addresses romantic love and sexual desire as a malady, trying to align this *topos* with his wider conceptual system. Pursuing a political usage of the theme in characterising *erôs* a tyrant of the soul (*Resp.* 573d), he attributes *hêdonê* – as opposed to the philosophers' idealised passion for knowledge – to the lowest part of the soul, the *epithumêtikon*, which hosts all forces arising 'through afflictions and illness' (439d). The two Erotes in the *Symposium*, Heavenly *vs* Vulgar (180d–

---

23 The degree of influence of Hippocratic medicine upon the comic dramatist, for example whether his medical vocabulary is technical or not, is debated. On the receptive side, see Byl 2006, Jouanna 2000, Zimmermann 1992; on the sceptical side, Willi 2003: 79–87, Soleil 2010. In an excellent thesis, Hobe 2018 deals with Aristophanes' representations of the body and disease that match with Hippocratic ideas, as well as with his literary treatment of more abstract medical issues, such as causation, responsibility, accountability, distinction between experts and laymen etc.
24 Scholtz 2007: 58–70.
25 See Hobe 2018: 120–36.
26 For a detailed discussion of sexual/political pathology in *Peace*, see Kanellakis (forthcoming).

e) or 'love in the healthy body' *vs* 'love in the unhealthy body' (186b), exemplify the familiar Platonic distinction between forms and everyday experience; the former are traditionally compared to health and the latter to disease (*Resp.* 515c). In *Phaedrus*, Socrates identifies *erôs* as a form of divine *mania*, alongside prophetic, ritual, and poetic madness (249d–257b). However beneficial, as it eventually enables the lovers' souls to remember the Form of Beauty, this process is painful for the male lover, who suffers when not seeing his handsome boyfriend, the only 'healer of his woes' (253b).[27] In his late writings Plato changes his mind, and in *Laws* he condemns homosexuality, male and female, as something 'unnatural' (636b-c). For Aristotle, sex between men is not only unnatural but also pathological in the literal/medical sense; in *Nicomachean Ethics*, desire for anal penetration is attributed to physiological anomalies or sexual abuse during childhood, and discussed alongside excessive, and thus avoidable, moral behaviours (1148b).[28] The problematisation of homosexuality, and indeed pederasty, in the course of the classical era – also evidenced in Aristophanes' homophobic jokes – has been explained as the reaction of the rising democratic middle class in Athens against the culture of the elite; even 'the chaste, non-physical love which is praised in both Xenophon's and Plato's *Symposia* [...] should perhaps be understood as a sanitized version of elite pederasty for public consumption'.[29]

The Hellenistic poets, with their philological expertise and mastery of the short but stylistically dense form of the epigram, rediscovered the pathology of love as a personal experience, as it was in archaic lyric, but often in a more confessional style. The amatory-heterosexual and pederastic epigrams of the *Greek Anthology*, Books 5 and 12 respectively, include many depictions of *erôs* as suffering, and indeed as a disease. Asclepiades, for example, asserts that the god Eros overcomes Zeus' cataclysmic storms, since even Zeus himself suffered from passion for the prostitute Danae (5.64). Posidippus too insists that 'not even the fire

---

[27] Gazing upon the beautiful youth is thus not only the starting point for this disease, as it was for Sappho, but also a sedative. On 'bad *erôs*' in Plato and its connection to tyranny see Kraut 2008: 302–6 and Arruzza 2018: 139–83. Kahn 1987 is a fine account of the development of, and potential inconsistencies in, Plato's conception of desire. For *erôs* in individual works see, more recently, Schindler 2007, Obdrzalek 2010, Foley 2010 (*Symposium*), Ludwig 2002 (*Republic*), Cairns 2013 (*Phaedrus*). The latter provides a very useful and rich taxonomy of the metaphors for *erôs*, including disease: 240 n. 13.
[28] In Ps.-Arist. *Pr.* 879b–80a, the supposed anatomical anomaly is specified as an internal connection between a man's genitals and his anus, where the semen is channeled to and collected, thus requiring release by penetration. See Thornton 1998: 103–5.
[29] Hubbard 1998: 69–70.

sent by Zeus wears out the man fainting with desire and tamed by love' (5.168).[30] The erotic gaze, especially in Meleager's pederastic poems, is again at the epicentre of the erotic pathology, whether as its starting point (12.127: 'And double rays burnt me, the rays of love from the boy's eyes'), a symptom (12.106: 'I know but one beauty in the world; my greedy eye knows but one thing, to look on Myiscus, and for all else I am blind'), or even a cure (12.159: '[Myiscus'] eyes can speak even to the deaf').[31] In his characteristically playful tone, Callimachus says that there are only two remedies for love, namely poetry and poverty, and as a poet he has both (12.150=*Epigr.* 46).[32] In a less romantic conception of *erôs*, naughty Strato, the compiler of the *Musa Puerilis*, writes about 'playing the doctor' with a group of young boys (12.13): 'I once found some beardless doctors, not prone to love, grinding a natural antidote for it. They, being lovesick, besought me to keep it quiet, and I said, "I am mum, but you must cure me"'.[33] In contrast to the epigrams' focus on single episodes and achronic impressions, epic poetry allowed more room for a detailed aetiology and a developing narration of pathological *erôs*, most notably in Medea's passion for Jason in Apollonius Rhodius' *Argonautica*, Books 3 and 4. From her initial shooting by Eros under the instructions of Hera and Aphrodite to murdering her brother in support of Jason, Medea experiences increasingly violent physical and mental symptoms, ranging from speechlessness and agony to suicidal behaviour and madness.[34] Yet, the most explicitly and consistently medical description is Simaetha's account of her passion for Delphis in Theocritus' second *Idyll*, arguably the most important milestone after Sappho fr. 31: 'I saw him, I got mad, my heart was lit on fire (82) ... a fiery disease changed me, ten days and ten nights I stayed in bed (85) ... my colour was fading yellow, all my hair dropping, I was only skin and bones (88–90)... Please go, Thestiles, find a remedy for my terrible disease (95)'. While Theocritus elsewhere presents poetry as the only *pharmakon* for lovesickness (*Id.* 11.1–3), here copulation is the solution.[35]

In the Greek novels of the imperial period, somaticised lovesickness proves not only a persistent literary *topos*, but one which unites the entire genre:

---

30 Anagnostou-Laoutides 2015: 563–4.
31 On the pederastic gaze see Fountoulakis 2013. The symptoms of love often coincide with those of drunkenness; Fantuzzi/Hunter 2004: 338–41.
32 See Faulkner 2011. See also Rynearson 2009 and Kazantzidis 2014, on *Aetia*.
33 The *double entendres* are clear: 'not prone to love'='virgin', 'grinding a natural antidote'='masturbating', 'being lovesick'='having an erection', 'cure me'='fuck me'.
34 See Toohey 1992: 275–8=2004: 59–64, also on Valerius Flaccus' *Argonautinca*. Sanders 2021 examines the interplay between Medea's *erôs* and other emotions: grief, fear, and shame.
35 See Griffiths 1979, Giangrande 1990 (also on Ov. *Ars am.*), Hunter 1999: 220–4.

Chaereas and Callirhoe in Chariton (1.1), Clitophon and Leucippe in Achilles Tatius (1.9), Daphnis and Chloe in Longus (4.27–8), Habrocomes and Anthia in Xenophon of Ephesus (1.5), Charicleia, and to a lesser degree Theagenes, in Heliodorus (3.5, 3.10–11, 4.5), all suffer from it.[36] The narrative value of the pathology of love is more or less fixed: the protagonists see each other and immediately fall ill/fall in love, then suffer further symptoms because their *erôs* is being frustrated, and are finally cured once (sexually) united in marriage. The symptomatology initially deceives the enamoured youths and their parents, who suspect an actual disease; a priest diagnoses Charicleia as having the 'evil eye' before a doctor confirms her condition, which is *erôs*. As for the *pharmakon*, the common principle in all five novels is that 'there is no remedy for Love, none to drink, to eat, or chant in songs, except kissing, embracing, and lying down together with naked bodies' (Longus 2.7.7).[37]

The pathology of love, both in the sense of lovesickness and deviant sex, 'infected' Latin literature from its very beginnings, i.e. starting with drama, through the stock character of the *adulescens*, the young man who is madly in love – often suicidally so – with a prostitute or slave girl, and the stock theme of him raping a virginal girl who, although born a citizen, has lost her identity. Inherited from Greek New Comedy, these two elements became trademarks of comic plots, which were now revolving around domestic themes rather than the political affairs of Old Comedy. For the *adulescens*, who depends on his slave's machinations in order to approach his beloved girl, lovesickness is 'a powerful affliction that undermines [his] performance of adult masculinity. [...] the young man will only achieve adult masculinity on marriage to a woman who can produce legitimate heirs'.[38] That woman is none other than the girl he has raped (once her true identity, and thus eligibility for marriage, has been restored) and, in that way, the crime is morally whitewashed.[39] Menander and his Roman successors focus on

---

36 The young lovers are suffering for each other, except for Leucippe; her 'lovesickness episode' is that she suffers a stroke of madness when a love potion is given to her by a rival lover (Ach. Tat. 4.9).
37 See Cummings 2009: 60–99. It is particularly argued that madness is more a metaphor/metonymy for *erôs* than a symptom. The translation is from Loeb.
38 Foley 2013: 267–8. Two notable cases of lovesick young men are Charinus in Plautus' *Mercator* 471 ff. and Thraso in Terence's *Eunuch* 1026 ff. See Duckworth 1971: 237–41 for an overview, Preston 1916: 3–14 on Plautus and Fantham 1972: 82–91 on Terence. On lovesickness as *melancholia* in Menander, see Cusset 2014.
39 'We may recoil at this feature of rape, rather than seduction, but the latter would probably have prejudiced the audience irremediably against the girl, while they seem to have found rape a human error, when mitigated by darkness, drink, and youthful desire. [...] for the girl to achieve

the emotional contentment of the sympathetically portrayed *adulescens* and no interest is shown in the psychological trauma of the girl.⁴⁰

In philosophy, the Stoics and the Epicureans view *erôs* as an irrational passion of the soul which must be cured to achieve tranquillity. Lucretius (*DRN* 4.1030–287) and Cicero (*Tusc. Disp.* 4) portray the lovesick as totally ill, submissive, and deceived. In sharp contrast to Plato's conception in *Phaedrus* of the erotic gaze as a mutual optical and metaphysical penetration between the *erastês* and the *erômenos* which leads them to self-improvement, Lucretius condemns vision as a force of self-deception. The latter is evidenced, for example, in the wet dreams that adolescents have when dreaming of idealised bodies (4.1030–6) and in how love-struck men describe their ugly, in reality, girlfriends as beautiful (4.1153–70). The lover's eyes are therefore misguiding and hinder him from truly, i.e. romantically, possessing his beloved.⁴¹ In his dialogue *On Anger*, Seneca argues that love, like a disease or bodily injury, may cause anger (2.20.1) and anger, in its turn, is an *insania* which 'conquers the most ardent love, and so in anger men have stabbed the bodies that they loved' (2.36.5–6); in a letter to his friend Lucilius, he calls love *insanam amicitiam*, 'a friendship run mad' (*Ep.* 9.11). The philosophers' remedy for this illness of the soul is to present the lovesick with arguments against his passion, i.e. to appeal to his logic so that he consciously embarks on the course of therapy.⁴² The elegists, on the other hand, prescribe the writing of poetry as a sedative (e.g. Catullus 65–8 and Propertius 1.10.14–20). Lovesickness is an inherent trait of the elegiac lover who experiences *servitium amoris*, 'slavery to love', who neglects his career and friends, wastes several nights outside his mistress' house (e.g. Tibullus 1.1.55–8) and desperately hopes to unite with her both in love and in death. Towards such men, the elegists show a more compassionate attitude than the philosophers, advocating the relief from suffering through poetry, rather than the rejection of *erôs* itself.⁴³ Yet, a cure for the madness of love is impossible to find in elegy.

---

security and happiness in marriage it was legally essential that she should have been kept chaste, and comedy invariably emphasizes her decency of character and sexual innocence', Fantham 1975: 53–4, 57.

40 Pierce 1997: 178 and Rosivach 1998: 43–5, who draws a comparison with Euripides' focus on the perspective of the female victim in *Augê*.

41 Bartsch 2006: 72–6. She further argues that the rejection of the Platonic model betrays the Romans' 'pathophobic' bias, i.e. their prejudice against passive male sex, 4–5.

42 The rational character of Lucretius' therapeutic argument, despite its poetic 'coating', is analysed in detail by Nussbaum 1989.

43 Caston 2006. Propertius is radical in handling the love-and-death *topos*: going beyond 'love until death' and 'death because of love', he creates erotic death fantasies; Papanghelis 1987. He

This elegiac *topos* is also alluded to by Vergil in connection to Dido's fate in the *Aeneid*. Contrary to the historiographical sources, which presented Dido as a chaste queen who prefers death over forced marriage, in the *Aeneid* she is eroticised, madly in love with Aeneas (4.65: *furentem*), feeling her bones aflame (4.66: *flamma medullas*), wounded like a deer (4.67: *vulnus*), and eventually committing suicide 'in the heat of sudden frenzy' when he abandons her (4.697: *subitoque accensa furore*). It has been suggested that the deer simile, in particular, implies Dido's unsuccessful search for an antidote to her maddened love, a *medicina furoris* like the one that love-stricken Gallus pursues in vain in *Eclogue* 10.55–61.[44] Horace, on the other hand, in trying to distance himself from neoteric and elegiac poets, challenges his predecessors' pathological obsession with a *puella* and projects a more rational approach to *erôs*. He thus recommends sex with freedwomen, rather than adulterous relationships with married ones, as a means of avoiding emotional tortures (*Sat.* 1.2; 2.7). In recounting his own past affair with Inachia, however, he seems to have experienced that bad wound (*Epod.* 11.17: *malum vulnus*) in a very 'elegiac' manner; indeed, he was hoping that writing poetry would soothe his pain, but he no longer does (11.1–2), and in his mature work, the uselessness of elegy against lovesickness is taken for granted (*Carm.* 1.33.1–4).[45]

No other Roman poet exercised such an impact as Ovid, whose *Remedia Amoris* upgraded the pathology of love from a literary *topos*, as it was in archaic lyric, and a generic marker, as it was for New Comedy or the novel, to an autonomous work. Ovid focused on the healing process, drawing much from Lucretius and Cicero. His recommendations to the lovesick, mostly boys but girls too (49), on how to overcome their crushes or breakups include: distraction through physical labour or travelling, avoiding aphrodisiac foods, spending time with friends and family, recalling the negative traits of the beloved person, throwing away all reminders of them, and stopping reading poetry (757) – but ironically, the very reading of the *Remedia* violates that rule. Despite the elegiac form of the poem, Ovid satirically remodels the elegiac *puella*, as he 'displays an ugly female body to an audience of men and suggests the appropriate response: revulsion and

---

is also radical in the motif of the erotic gaze: 'the *puella*'s perception of desire in the lover's objectifying gaze is one key to the elegiac destabilization of traditional Roman gender hierarchy, which constructs the woman as unable to intercept the man's gaze'; O'Neill 2005: 245.
44 O'Hara 1993. For the historiographical tradition on Dido see Gildenhard 2012: 244–55.
45 Fedeli (forthcoming).

laughter'.⁴⁶ To reach that point, however, he had first exhausted the *topoi* of elegiac lovesickness in his early *Heroides*, consisting of fictional epistles sent from plaintive mythical heroines to their absent husbands or lovers (and some paired epistles). Among the imaginary senders are some of the figures we have already discussed: Penelope, Medea, Phaedra, Dido are all heroines coming from genres other than elegy and yet Ovid 'successfully negotiated the transfer of the elegiac voice' to characters other than the poet's own persona.⁴⁷ Ovid's early experimentation with the boundaries of genres and the possibilities of mythological collage led to his mature masterpiece, the hexametric *Metamorphoses*, whose Books 5–11 have been identified as the 'Pathos of Love' section.⁴⁸ One of the most renowned pathological love stories of western literature found in this work is Narcissus' self-erotic gaze that led him drown in the waters mirroring his beauty.⁴⁹

In a more cheerful tone, the satirists transfer the pathology of love from its high-register-poetic and philosophical realm to the comically bitter reality of common relationships. Thus Martial warns any gold-digging gigolo not to wait for his phthisical old woman to die, because the latter is only faking her symptoms to get sexual services (2.26);⁵⁰ Juvenal in his notorious *Satire* 6 advises his friend to commit suicide rather than get married;⁵¹ and Petronius in *Satyrica* parodies the male anxiety of sexual impotence.⁵² His anti-hero Encolpius tries everything to achieve an erection and satisfy the nymphomaniac Circe, from praying to Priapus, the god of fertility, to sleeping apart from his boyfriend Giton, resorting to aphrodisiac foods and magical cures, even rebuking his penis – all in vain (*Sat.* 126–35).⁵³

All this literary tradition, Greek and Latin, of the pathology of love has both influenced and been influenced by the medical tradition. Rather surprisingly, given the prominence in literature of the *erôs-as-nosos* motif since the archaic period, the Hippocratic corpus lacks an explicit discussion of lovesickness or even

---

46 Brunelle 2005: 154.
47 Knox 2002: 138–9.
48 Otis 1970: 83, 85.
49 See Bartsch 2006: 84–102.
50 See Hejduk 2011.
51 Braund 1992 argues that the perspective is that of a misogamist, not a misogynist.
52 And Ovid's impotence in *Am.* 3.7; Hallett 2012.
53 On the hilarious scene of Encolpius addressing, and threatening with an axe, his uncooperative penis, and the latter's reaction (*Sat.* 132), see Murgatroyd 2000 and Hawkins 2015: 53–5.

sexual desire as an emotion.⁵⁴ Instead, it only focuses on the physical aspect of sexual activity, warns against excessive intercourse (mostly for men) or abstinence (mostly for women), advises on the timing of intercourse, even recommends sex to cure some physical and mental disorders. More important for later approaches to *erôs*, the Hippocratics established humoural theory, according to which four fluids dominate the human body – blood, phlegm, yellow bile and black bile – and determine whether a person is healthy, when these exist in balance, or sick, if unbalanced. Indeed, the peripatetics linked *erôs* to melancholy, i.e. the superfluity of black bile, the physician Aretaeus (1st century CE) noted their similar symptoms,⁵⁵ while Galen (2nd century CE), who unlike the Hippocratics turned his interest to lovesickness, alongside sex, tried to avoid the confusion. A notable casualty is Justus' wife, who was agitated and insomniac, and for whom Galen first diagnosed that '*either* she was dispirited because of black bile, *or* she was aggrieved at something she did not want to admit to'; after days of behavioural observation and pulse checking, the doctor's final diagnosis was *erôs* for a dancer named Pylades.⁵⁶ Even though Galen does not identify lovesickness with melancholia, he also rejects, with evident irony, the traditional/poetic conception of Eros as a god; people who believe in myths 'think they are led to this condition [*pathos*, i.e. love] by a small, new-born god [*daimon*] carrying burning torches'.⁵⁷ To the other extreme, the pagan physician Oribasius of Pergamum (4th century CE) and, much later, Paul of Aegina (7th century CE) treated lovesickness as a real disease *sui generis* – they both wrote a chapter on it – rather than as a severe condition *similar to* disease. As a remedy, they suggested 'frightening' the lovesick (as if *erôs* were hiccups) and other practices a charlatan would apply.⁵⁸

A genre which should not be omitted from this account is a kind of pragmatic, i.e. enacted in real life, pathology of love: the erotic spells (*agôgai*) of the magical papyri from Greek and Roman Egypt. In those charms we typically find lovesick men, 'beset with torments … with tears and bitter groans …, distressed at heart because of her' (*PGM* IV.1405–13), casting curses upon their female love-targets, such as 'may she, in fear, seeing phantoms, sleepless because of her passion for me and her love for me, come to my consecrated bedroom' (*PGM* VII. 886–9). Here

---
54 Perhaps, the reason was that *erôs* was 'too closely associated with folk practices from which the Hippocratics are keen to distance themselves in the classical period', McNamara 2016: 308, 322.
55 Ps.-Arist. *Pr.* 30.1 (954a32–4); Aret. *CD* 3.5.4–11.
56 Gal. *Praecog.* 14.631–2 Kühn, transl. Mattern 2008: 135.
57 Gal. *Hipp. Progn.* 18b.19 Kühn, transl. Hägg/Utas 2009: 159.
58 Duffin 2002: 49–50; for the verdict on Oribasius, see Thompson 1947: 134.

erôs is conceived as an unwanted and ideally reciprocal disease, already inflicted on the man/performer of the spell, and hopefully also induced onto the woman/victim. A standard formula of the erotic spells is that the man curses the woman not to have sex with anyone else: 'Let her not be had in a promiscuous way, let her not be had in her ass, nor let her do anything with another man for pleasure, just with me alone' (*PGM* IV.352–4).[59] These charms present close affinities with curse spells, both in their language, such as using conditional clauses, and ritual practices, such as throwing a wax effigy of the enemy/victim in the fire: 'burn her guts, her breast, her liver, her breath, her bones, her marrow, until she comes to me' (*PGM* IV.1530–1).[60]

Apart from literature, philosophy, medicine and magic, the pathology of love also became a popular theme in iconography;[61] we recall for example the plethora of representations on vases of the abduction of Helen – an erotic malady which infected Greece and Troy with war.[62] Even though literary imagery does not have the technical restrictions, and on the other hand the sensorial immediacy, of material iconography, the two spheres of creation exercised a great influence upon each other. And while the archaeological attestations of the subject matter fall outside the scope of this book, we must emphasise that authors elaborated on the same motifs as artists. As already pointed out, the most characteristic motif of the pathology of love is the erotic gaze, and a prime example in iconography is the myth of Penthesilea. In an episode of the Trojan War the mighty Achilles slays the Amazonian queen, but the moment he wounds her he falls in love with her; as she is pierced by his spear, he is struck by *erôs*.[63] Achilles' astonished eyes and Penthesilea's plaintive eyes became an iconographic *locus* (Figs. 2–3),[64] and when this *locus* is absent, it becomes clear that the artist aimed at the war narrative, rather than the love story.[65]

---

[59] Bain 1991: 57, 59.
[60] Transl. Betz. See Faraone 1999: 49–55; Pachoumi 2012.
[61] For general accounts and anthologies of Greek and Roman erotic iconography, see Brendel 1970, Johns 1982, Kampen 1996 and Clarke 1998. On Greek erotic and homoerotic vase-paintings, in particular, see Kilmer 1992 and Lear/Cantarella 2008.
[62] ἀνθρώπινον νόσημα according to Gorg. *Hel.* 19. For the iconography see Masters 2012.
[63] Quint. Smyrn. 1.891–922; Apollod. *Epit.* 5.1, and perhaps in Arctinus' *Aethiopis* (arg. 1 West).
[64] Same in sculpture, e.g. Antikenmuseum Basel BS 214 and 298 (Penthesilea's and Achilles' heads from a group of 250–200 BCE; https://artdaily.com/v2/PhotoGalleries.aspx?GalleryId=41).
[65] On the erotic gaze in art, see Frontisi-Ducroux 1996. On the iconography of Penthesilea's story, see Galoin 2015: 123–36. In the case of an Attic stamnos by Syleus Painter which portrays no eye contact (http://www.beazley.ox.ac.uk/record/49CC9C6F-3F16-407A-9C32-9052C8435BE4), Galoin notes that 'the love of the hero for his victim is not suggested by the painter', 129.

Fig. 2: Attic black-figure amphora by Exekias, ca. 530 BCE. British Museum 1836.2-24.127. © The Trustees of the British Museum.

Fig. 3: Attic red-figure kylix by Penthesilea Painter, ca. 460 BCE. Munich, Antikensammlungen 2688. Reproduced under CC BY-SA 4.0 (Wikimedia Commons).

Patholog-*ies* of Love

This short but inclusive overview demonstrates that 'pathology' is a salient ingredient of the erotic discourse of classical antiquity and an ingredient which provides a useful gauge for evaluating the authors' swinging between tradition and innovation, on which potential I rest my case for a literary history with this theme. Indeed, the recognition since antiquity of this theme as a *locus* is evidenced by the vocabulary, by frequently invoked paronyms such as *pothos-pathos*, *erôs-eris*, *cupio-capio*, *amor-mors* and polysemous words such as *thumos* (desire/anger) and *contingere* (to touch/to affect, discussed by Thorsen: 153–5). Similarly, the designation of the 'pathology of love' is based on two polysemous terms and so it can describe a variety of phenomena – hence the plural form has been preferred in the title of this collection. 'Pathology' may be understood as a literal (i.e. biological, medical) disease or as a literary (i.e. poetic, metaphorical) one; as a mental, emotional, or bodily disorder; and as a description of the different stages (causes, symptoms, cures) of an illness. 'Love' in its turn may be understood as sexual desire, intercourse, romantic attraction, friendship, familial affection, humanitarian spirit, religious devotion, self-esteem, or even as the passion for money, power, food and drinking. Of all possible combinations of these nuances, this book focusses on the conception of *erôs* as a physical-emotional-mental disease, a social-ethical disorder, or a literary unorthodoxy. Specifically, the reader will encounter two broad categories of 'pathology':
a) lovesickness as/similar to disease, in the contributions by Thumiger, Calame, Sanders, Michalopoulos, and Thorsen;
b) deviant sexuality, described in nosologic terms, in the contributions by Hubbard, Valtadorou, and Konstantakos.

These two threads are not examined separately, i.e. I have not structured the book into two corresponding sections, and their coexistence in the same volume should not be seen as a symptom of the inconsistency that often characterises conference proceedings. On the contrary, the very purpose of the chronological order I have chosen is to demonstrate that the tropes involved in these *parallel traditions* are similar, building on one another over time, thus suggesting that lovesickness could be perceived as a form of improper *erôs* (as it is by Horace) or, conversely, that deviant sex could be romanticised (as it is by Propertius).

Chiara Thumiger (Chapter 1) treats 'the sexual and passionate side of love ... as a pathology with a precise repertoire of triggers and symptoms'. This repertoire derives from a long and dynamic tradition, where poetic, philosophical, and medical literature inform each another. Central to this tradition is the motif of the erotic gaze, as already pointed out; the author provides an ensemble of concepts and practices subtending the visuality of attraction and obsession. **Claude Calame** (Chapter 2) considers the pragmatic physiological, psychological, and emotional effects of *erôs* in the context of archaic melic poetry. He too emphasises the role of the gaze and *deictics*, in arguing that those poems realise and ritualise, during their performance, the amorous relationships of which they sing, i.e. between the poetic 'I' and his/her addressee. This poetic diction does not essentially differentiate 'heterosexual' and 'homosexual' relationships; what is common is the asymmetry of the protagonists' age. **Anastasia-Stavroula Valtadorou** (Chapter 3) reads pathological, in the sense of deviant, *erôs* in three fragmentary plays by Euripides, tracing the nosologic vocabulary, where preserved, and the attitudes of the dramatist and his audience, where possible, towards these stories: incest in *Aeolus*, bestiality in *Cretans*, and sex with a statue in *Protesilaus*. Despite the unambiguously problematic nature of such relationships, Euripides provides his characters with the chance to explain their motivations. **Thomas K. Hubbard** (Chapter 4) introduces the concept of 'pathological heterosexuality', that is, the social stigma – often expressed in medical terms such as *gynaimanês*, 'woman-crazy' – placed upon Greek men who were excessively dependent on, or passionate about, women. His typology of such pathological behaviours, drawing on mythological and historical evidence, especially from comedy and oratory, supports the argument that pederasty appeared as 'a less risky alternative'. **Ed Sanders** (Chapter 5) explores the narrative patterns of the experience of *erôs* in Xenophon, especially in his *Symposium* and *Cyropaedia*, discussing the 'pathological episodes' of this 'script'. The Xenophontic corpus is a very balanced source – more than tragedy or Plato, for instance – as it represents both the homo- and heterosexual (male) experience, in a surprisingly similar way indeed. In both cases, 'love develops from its early acute stage into a chronic form' of disease, i.e. from sexual attraction to love. **Andreas N. Michalopoulos** (Chapter 6) draws the story of love in Ovid's move from elegy and elegiac didactic on to epic. Specifically, he analyses the pathological – in medical terms – love stories of Apollo-Daphne and Iphis-Anaxarete in the *Metamorphoses*, and argues that Ovid's earlier teaching in the *Remedia Amoris*, that love is curable, is not realised here: not even Apollo, the god of medicine, can heal himself. On a metaliterary level, the mythological characters seem not to have read their *Remedia* yet. **Thea S. Thorsen** (Chapter 7) offers a close reading of the paired Acontius' and Cydippe's letters in Ovid's *Heroides*, from the perspective of pathological love. Through a network of implications, such as the incompatible characters of the protagonists, the inherent inclination of Acontius towards *hubris*, the sickness rather than lovesickness of Cydippe, and the textually corrupt (hence 'open') closing couplet, Ovid undermines the 'happy ending' of the story as delivered by Callimachus. The 'pathology of love' has been replaced by a 'love for pathology'. Finally, **Ioannis M. Konstantakos** (Chapter 8) surveys the pathological eroticism in a group of novelistic biographies (*Lives* of Aesop, Alexander, Apollonius, and Secundus) which scholars have termed as 'open/fringe novels', in counterpoise to the 'ideal' erotic novels of the imperial period. In the latter group, an 'orthodox' romantic story is the epicentre of the narrative, whereas the 'open' novels feature 'deviant sex: exhibitionism, nymphomania, adultery, necrophilia, bestiality, rape, incest'. This socially/ethically anomalous *erôs* epitomises the generic deviation of the texts.

The reader will easily spot the common premises and directions of analysis across the chapters, such as the emphasis on the erotic gaze (Thumiger, Calame, Sanders), the pragmatic and historical contextualisation (Calame, Hubbard, Valtadorou), the collapsing of the difference between homo- and heterosexual *erôs* (Calame, Sanders), the concept of textual and generic 'openness' (Thorsen, Konstantakos) and the need for textual criticism (Thorsen, Valtadorou), the metaliterary and poetological investigation (Michalopoulos, Konstantakos) and the role of, and departure from, tradition (Thumiger, Sanders, Thorsen, Konstantakos). Through this methodological plurality we hope to offer a seminal work, able to 'infect' the reader with desire for further research, or, to appropriate a common literary paronym, to offer *mathos* through *pathos*.

Chiara Thumiger
The Ophthalmology of Lovesickness: Poetry, Philosophy, Medicine

Abstract: From the beginning of the Western literary tradition, one particular representation of *erôs* emerges clearly: love as dangerous or even pathological in a literal, concretely medical sense, love as disease: 'Lovesickness', 'Mal d'amore', 'Liebeskummer', 'Mal de amores', and so on. Challenging the obviousness of such a conception, this chapter explores the *topos* as the situated product of a specific tradition, with its own origins, elements of variation, and specific developments. The idea that human *erôs* could become a true and proper disease, and that this disease is caused and triggered by vision, offered a formidable point of conjunction and an interface between otherwise separate environments: poetry, medicine, and philosophy. Hallucination, dreaming, and even affection of the eyes emerge as key markers of the 'disease of lovers', also recognised by doctors. This ophthalmological aspect allows us to reappraise the traditional references to erotic viewing, perceived beauty, and longing as matter of desired – and lost – images of the beloved in a more concrete, medical light. The topic of lovesickness displays thus a persistent hybridity, suspended between seriousness and *ludus*, while a repertoire of bodily symptoms of *erôs* appears to remain largely consistent through centuries of ancient and early Medieval history, literary and medical.

An earlier version of this study was published in German in N. Reggiani and F. Bertonazzi (eds.), *Parlare la Medicina: fra lingue e culture, nello spazio e nel tempo* (Thumiger 2018), and was delivered before that as a *Habilitationsvortrag* at the Humboldt-Universität zu Berlin (11.01.2017). I would like to thank Philip van der Eijk, Glenn Most, and Anna Maria Kanthak for their help and feedback on that occasion, as well as my other colleagues in Berlin, and Innocenzo Mazzini for further suggestions. The revised study benefitted immensely from the questions and criticism offered at the conference on 'The Pathology of Love in Greek and Roman Art and Literature' organised by Dimitrios Kanellakis and Emilia Savva, whom I wholeheartedly thank for the invitation. In particular, I am grateful to Claude Calame for his thoughtful advice and for forwarding me his contributions on topics relevant to my argument here; to Ed Sanders for comments and suggestions on the final draft; to Martin Müller for editorial help, and to S. Douglas Olson for his careful reading – while all the shortcomings remain, of course, my own. I thank the Wellcome Trust for its sponsorship of my research.

The representation of love – more precisely, of the sexual and passionate side of love, what the Greeks called *erôs* – is an interesting topic in cultural studies of the ancient world. But it also has a history that engages precisely with the role of medicine in society and its influence on ancient cultures generally. This topic offers us, as historians, a unique opportunity to explore the contacts between technical and non-technical literatures, medical and philosophical approaches to the care of the self and, within medicine, the development and evolution of psychopathological models.[1]

There are of course important methodological challenges and pitfalls in such an enterprise: first, the well-known difficulty of identifying emotions trans-historically and cross-culturally;[2] second, the very meaning of the terms *love* or *erôs*, even when synchronically intended, for us as community of readers, as much as for the ancients; third, the constructedness and conventionality of love as a subject of reporting and reflection – socially, culturally, and (for the purposes of this inquiry) literarily. All these considerations cause the subjective experience of love to remain in large part impenetrable. Of all the emotions, *erôs* appears to be especially difficult for the historian to grasp – its discourse, as Barthes remarked, is today *of an extreme solitude ... warranted by no one ... completely forsaken by the surrounding languages*'.[3]

From the beginning of the Western literary tradition, one particular representation of sexual love, of *erôs*, nonetheless emerges clearly: love as dangerous or even pathological in a literal, concretely medical sense, love *as disease*, 'Lovesickness', 'Mal d'amore', 'Liebeskummer', 'Mal de amores', and so forth. This *topos* is immediately recognisable in literature and culture, as much as in everyday language. I propose here to challenge this self-explanatory quality of the connection, and with it the obviousness – even banality – of the model. I argue that it would be a mistake to reduce the motif of 'love-sickness' to a natural, immediate, and merely universal human experience of intense passion, as some might be inclined to do, and as analogies with narratives of erotic suffering with deadly consequences in other, non-Western traditions might suggest.[4] The lovesickness

---

[1] Regarding this popular topic in ancient literature, see Amundsen 1974; Cyrino 1995; Mazzini 1990 and 2012; Carson 1986; McNamara 2016; Toohey 1992 and 2004.
[2] See Cairns 2004: 11–15 for methodological remarks, and Lloyd 2007: 58–85 for a discussion of idealisation, 'metalanguage' (65), and the question of the universality of the emotions.
[3] Barthes 1978: 2.
[4] The topic of lovesickness is very common in Chinese literature, for example, where it is represented as a longing for something vanished and unattainable, rather than as personal affection between the two parties (an example is offered by *The Peony Pavilion* 牡丹亭 by Tang Xianzu 湯顯祖 in the late Ming, or in the so-called legend of the 'butterfly lovers'). The analogies of these

I will explore is the situated product of a specific tradition, with its own origins, elements of variation, and specific developments. This *erôs* is concretely (and even medically, as we shall see) discussed as illness, as a pathology with a precise repertoire of triggers and symptoms.

On my reading of the evidence, the model of *erôs* as disease has been strong and persistent in our culture because it combined two key factors: first, an embodied interest in the somatic symptoms of the erotic emotion, and second, the prominence of the visual sense (and of the images that accompany visual appraisal) as a cause or trigger of this intense experience. These two factors can be found already in Archaic literature and are extremely productive in naturalistic as well as philosophical/metaphysical reflections on human psychology.

The Poetic Account

If we wish to specify a beginning for this story, an easy choice is the well-known Sappho fr. 31 L-P:

> φαίνεταί μοι κῆνος ἴσος θέοισιν
> ἔμμεν' ὤνηρ, ὄττις ἐνάντιός τοι
> ἰσδάνει καὶ πλάσιον ἆδυ φωνεί-
> σας ὐπακούει
> καὶ γελαίσας ἰμέροεν, τό μ' ἦ μὰν   5
> καρδίαν ἐν στήθεσιν ἐπτόαισεν,
> ὠς γὰρ ἔς σ' ἴδω βρόχε' ὤς με φώναι-
> σ' οὐδ' ἒν ἔτ' εἴκει,
> ἀλλ' ἄκαν μὲν γλῶσσα †ἔαγε λέπτον
> δ' αὔτικα χρῶι πῦρ ὐπαδεδρόμηκεν,   10
> ὀππάτεσσι δ' οὐδ' ἒν ὄρημμ', ἐπιρρόμ-
> βεισι δ' ἄκουαι,
> †έκαδε μ' ἴδρως ψῦχρος κακχέεται† τρόμος δὲ
> παῖσαν ἄγρει, χλωροτέρα δὲ ποίας
> ἔμμι, τεθνάκην δ' ὀλίγω 'πιδεύης   15
> φαίνομ' ἔμ' αὔται·

... He seems as fortunate as the gods to me, the man who sits opposite you and listens nearby to your sweet voice and lovely laughter. Truly that sets my heart trembling in my breast. For when I look at you for a moment, then it is no longer possible for me to speak; my tongue

---

examples with Western tales of lovesickness are an interesting reminder of the universality of certain embodied human experiences, which must be left aside in the present chapter. (I thank MinChih Sun for his advice on this topic.)

has snapped, at once a subtle fire has stolen beneath my flesh, I see nothing with my eyes, my ears hum, sweat pours from me, a trembling seizes me all over, I am greener than grass, and it seems to me that I am little short of dying ... [Transl. Campbell]

In this fragmentary poem, the lyric *I* of the poetess imagines herself observing a young couple she knows, who are sitting together, laughing and chatting and – we are made to imagine – expressing mutual pleasure and enchantment in each other's company. The poetess focuses on the girl as she smiles sweetly at the boy, and describes in detail her own feelings and physical reactions to this scene, the first detailed bodily and psychic 'autopathography' to reach us from antiquity. What are the manifestations and experiences of the lyric subject? What constitutes her *suffering*? As she catches sight of the couple, her heart suffers a spasm; she can no longer speak; her tongue is paralysed; and all her senses (vision, hearing, touch) are blocked. She has the feeling that a fire (*pur*) 'has stolen beneath her flesh'; as a consequence, it seems, she sweats and trembles, and her complexion alters; she is close to death. All these reactions arise as the erotic scene is *seen*, 'as I saw'. The words '*erôs*' and 'disease' do not appear, but they are clearly implied by the context, by the intense and in large part unpleasant feelings directed towards one particular individual: the meeting between a young woman and a young man, both of them known, it seems, and the stirring and passion this sight causes.[5]

The bodily manifestations of the emotional experience are so intense and plausible that already in antiquity these lines were praised for their realism by the anonymous author of *On the Sublime,* who preserved them.[6] This is so much so, that some readers have interpreted this text, through an exercise in retrospective diagnosis, as a form of panic attack.[7] The unique combination of traditional words and elements,[8] and the imitations and elaborations of them – more or less subtle and aural – became one of the most powerful and influential models, both

---

5 The interpretation of the feelings expressed in these verses and their causes are one of the most extensively discussed topics in classical scholarship; see Most 1995 for an illuminating discussion of this theme as a mode of reception of the fragments and of the figure of Sappho.
6 On the Sublime 10.
7 Devereux 1970; Di Benedetto 1985; Ferrari 2001 and 2007.
8 The elements found in Sappho fr. 31 are in part, if not entirely, traditional (Turyn 1929; Lanata 1966; Bonanno 2002). This core repertoire of somatic symptoms can be found also in the *Homeric Hymn to Pan* (the 'wet desire', πόθος ὑγρός, of the god, *h.Pan* 33), and (apart from the πῦρ, 'fire') are widespread in Homeric descriptions of war panic. West analyses parallels as far back as Biblical and Semitic literatures in which the Sapphic selection of symptoms is found, almost literally, in non-erotic, military contexts (West 1997: 527–8; to bridge the discussion to the idea of 'love as battlefield', see Winkler 2002).

in content and in form, in later European literature whenever *erôs* was at the centre of the discussion (and not only then, as we shall see). To trace back all the instances of influence, reception, quotation, and imitation of these lines would be impossible;[9] let it suffice to mention the Latin translation and interpretation in Catullus 51 and the reworking by the Hellenistic poet Theocritus in his poem about magic spells and love potions (*Id.* 2.76–110).[10] Key to the erotic experience described by Theocritus are again vision, madness, and a general pathological turmoil with bodily consequences. The importance of the motif of seeing emerges clearly, as do the disturbing symptoms. There can be no doubt that Theocritus is explicitly referring to Sappho in his choice of details and words, and that a tradition is here created and consolidated. More precisely, the syntagma 'when I saw ...' (ὡς ἴδον, ὡς ἰδέν, *ut vidi* ...), which is found already in Homer in a similar connection, becomes a formula for erotically charged situations – almost standard language.[11]

It is also clear, however, that these connections and patterns go beyond mere literary mimesis and cannot be dismissed as neutral instances of intertextuality of the sort that abound in any traditional literature. A similar pathological representation is found, in fact, already in fifth-century tragedy, where the experience of *erôs* is always negative and unfulfilled.[12] This is evident in the portrayal of erotic suffering in Euripides' *Hippolytus*, as well as in many other plays,[13] with the element of seeing as trigger or cause of illness returning again and again. It is significant that in the Euripidean tragedy the actual confrontation between Hippolytus and his father's wife is avoided precisely because its effect would have been both dramatically too intense and ethically repulsive.[14] It is not by chance that the most famous ancient story of destructive *erôs*, that of Paris and Helen, is constructed in Euripides by means of a focus on the image, the phantom of the

---

9 See again Turyn 1929; Lanata 1966; Bonanno 2002.
10 Cf. Acosta-Hughes 2010: 20; Bonanno 1990 and 2002.
11 Cf. for instance Verg. *Ecl.* 8, 41 *ut vidi, ut perii, ut me malus abstulit error*; and so forth. The structure is first attested in Homer, in the episode of the *Dios apatê*, at *Il.* 14.294 (ὡς δ' ἴδεν, ὥς μιν ἔρως πυκινὰς φρένας ἀμφεκάλυψεν). Cf. Calame 2016a on the topic of the 'amorous gaze' in lyric poetry.
12 As explored in Thumiger 2013.
13 For instance, Sophocles' *Trachiniae* or Euripides' *Andromache*.
14 A famous anecdote describes the first version of the Euripidean play, a *Hippolytus Veiled* (*Kalyptomenos*) in which Phaedra openly confessed her feelings to Hippolytus. This was deemed so outrageous by the public that the playwright had to change the text to appease his scandalised audience – a story we can take as confirming the power of erotic sight, both as lovers directly facing each other and, voyeuristically, for a (poetic or theatrical) audience.

beloved: only Helen's *eidôlon* travels to Troy, where the empty image keeps Paris' love alive throughout the years. Without sight, there can be no *erôs*, as Aeschylus already said, again with reference to Helen and her betrayed husband Menelaus (*Ag.* 414–19):

> πόθῳ δ' ὑπερποντίας
> φάσμα δόξει δόμων ἀνάσσειν· 415
> εὐμόρφων δὲ κολοσσῶν
> ἔχθεται χάρις ἀνδρί,
> ὀμμάτων δ' ἐν ἀχηνίαις
> ἔρρει πᾶσ' Ἀφροδίτα.

> Because of his longing for her beyond the sea,
> a phantom will seem to rule the house.
> The charm of beautiful statues
> has become hateful to the husband:
> in the absence of eyes,
> all Aphrodite's powers are lost. [Transl. Sommerstein, with adjustments.]

The list of relevant poetic examples could be extended[15] at much too great length for this chapter, and the topic has been well discussed by others. As we consider this mass of material as a whole, however, one point must be stressed again. Several, if not all of the parallels mentioned could be read as forms of intertextuality, literary homage, or even simple quotation. All these operations might be of interest and offer relevant material for the traditional inquiry of 'Quellenforschung', in which the perpetuation of an influential theme – lovesickness as disease – and the weight of a literary authority – Sappho and her successors – mutually reinforce one another. But literary tradition or poetic fashion alone cannot guarantee or explain this long survival of key ideas about human erotic experiences and their physiology. We must turn instead to the philosophical and medical material to frame the relevance of vision and embodied manifestations beyond the appeal of conventional poetic expressions and the power of traditional imagery.

---

15 Dido's doomed love for Aeneas in Verg. *Aen.* 4, elaborating on all these, and itself the pivot of a rich poetic reception, is of central importance. In the poet's representation of her physical pathology imagination, fantasy and vision, and ultimately death are key elements.

Erôs as Philosophical Problem

A key premise to be borne in mind as we explore the scientific discourses behind associations of vision and emotional turmoil in Greek culture, epistemology, and medicine is a concept of the sense of vision that is sometimes labelled 'active sight' and can take various forms. This concept is based on the idea that vision is a kind of exchange, a two-way traffic between the perceived object and the perceiving subject. Vision is not passive reception, then, but a form of communication channelled by a flow from the perceived object to the eye of the observer. On this view of things, the image produced by the object can persist even after the object itself has vanished or departed. Philosophers elaborated on this theory of vision in different ways, exploring its effects on body-mind interaction. These epistemological developments play a role in the representation of pathological *erôs*, as they do in its association with vision.[16]

Perhaps the most well-known discussions of the forms that *erôs* can take, of its physiology, and of the possibility of pathological deviations caused by intense passion must have been a well discussed *topos* where literary examples offered much material to philosophical and ethical reflection, more playfully in Gorgias' *Encomium of Helen* (D 24),[17] but of course not only so – notably in Plato. Plato

---

16 Cf. Pl. *Ti.* 45b–d, 67c–d, where the act of viewing is depicted as an encounter between an emanation from the eye of the perceiver and daylight; Aristotle (*De an.* 2.7, 418a27–419b4, *Sens.* 3.439a6–440b25) speaks instead of an alteration in the medium between eye and object, while the Stoics conceived of a modification in the base of the cone-shaped pneuma emanating from the eye via contact with the viewed object, a theory that influenced Galen's view, which was also based on the emission of pneuma (*UP* 8.6.464–5 Helmreich = III.640–1 K.); cf. Sedley 1992; Ierodiakonou 2014 on Galen, 25–38 for the background. See Sassi 1978 on theories of perception in Democritus, 96–109 on vision; Padel 1992: 42 for a summary of pre-Socratic material. On various models of emissionist and interactionist viewing in ancient Greek culture, see Cairns 2005: 138–9; Calame 2016a, especially 288–91, regarding the physiological correspondences between ancient Greek philosophy of nature and lyric representations of erotic seeing.

17 See especially D24 (4. Love), 180–2 Laks-Most: 'by means of sight the soul is shaped even in its basic ways of being' (διὰ δὲ τῆς ὄψεως ἡ ψυχὴ κἂν τοῖς τρόποις τυποῦται). The example brought in justification of Helen's reckless choice is that of fear: 'for the truth of [one's] thought establishes itself within them as forceful by the fear that comes from sight, which, when it arrives, makes people neglect both what is fine as judged by the law and what is good as produced by justice ... many have fallen victim of groundless suffering, terrible diseases, and incurable madnesses. Thus, *sight* inscribes within *thought* the images of things seen (πολλοὶ δὲ ματαίοις πόνοις καὶ δειναῖς νόσοις καὶ δυσιάτοις μανίαις περιέπεσον· οὕτως εἰκόνας τῶν ὁρωμένων πραγμάτων ἡ ὄψις ἐνέγραψεν ἐν τῶι φρονήματι).'

thematises explicitly for the first time what in other sources had remained implicit: that seeing and pathos (and pathology) are closely connected in erotic contexts. This notion is famously found in *Phaedrus* and the *Symposium*, where *erôs* is seen as potentially pathological, but also in *Timaeus*, where Plato introduces a physiological description of erotic-sexual disturbance as a kind of disease of the soul (*Ti.* 86c3–d1). In *Phaedrus* 251a–c, first of all, it is through vision and the action of *erôs* that the 'wings of the soul' are made to grow via physical suffering, famously represented by means of somatic symptoms:

> But he who is newly initiated, *who beheld many of those realities* (ὁ τῶν τότε πολυθεάμων), when *he sees* (ὅταν … ἴδῃ) a godlike face or form which is a good image of beauty, shudders at first, and something of the old awe comes over him. Then, *as he gazes* (προσορῶν), he reveres the beautiful one as a god, and if he did not fear to be thought stark mad, he would offer sacrifice to his beloved as to an idol or a god. And as he looks upon him (ἰδόντα … αὐτόν), a reaction from his shuddering comes over him, with sweat and unwonted heat; for as the effluence of beauty enters him *through the eyes* (διὰ τῶν ὀμμάτων), he is warmed … Now in this process the whole soul throbs and palpitates … [Transl. Henderson, slightly adapted.]

At the beginning, we have the glimpse of the beloved (ἰδόντα αὐτὸν …); the consequences are intense and physiologically concrete. Not only confusion, but also fear, unrest, frustration, weakness, trembling and shivering, and a rapid pulse follow. Psychological and physical disturbances that arise from seeing the image of the beloved object (… 'for as the effluence of beauty enters him through the eyes, … the quills of the feathers swell and begin to grow') are also mentioned. An interpretation of *erôs* as a powerful alteration (μεταβολή), which could be as much a dissolution as a form of healing or blossoming for the person affected, is more than a poetic metaphor: it expresses an archetypal model for the interaction between body and soul in general that will remain active throughout the Graeco-Roman tradition and beyond. In Plato, this is strongly linked to the philosopher's own ethical and epistemological system, in which *erôs* plays a central role in stirring the soul towards true knowledge; others will use the model for different, non-metaphysical purposes. From a radically different angle, for instance, Aristotle in his *De Insomniis* elaborates on physiology and on the senses and their ability to grant access to reality, in particular *vis-à-vis* the persistence of images after the disappearance of the object. He explains how strong emotions such as anger or specifically *erôs* can induce a person to mistake the vague suggestion of a resembling image for its original.[18] This happens, for example, when a person thinks he is confronting his enemy, or in the case of a lover his beloved, ὁ δ' ἐρωτικὸς ἐν ἔρωτι (*Insomn.* 460b1):[19]

> ... the sensation still remains perceptible even after the external object perceived has gone (ἀπελθόντος τοῦ θύραθεν αἰσθητοῦ), and moreover that we are easily deceived about our perceptions when we are in emotional states, some in one state and others in another; e.g. the coward in his fear, the lover in his love; so that even from a very faint resemblance the coward thinks that he sees his enemy, and the lover his loved one. [Transl. Hett.]

These are patently not casual parallels; instead, they illustrate the different ways in which philosophical authors have shared these traditional views on intense emotions and elaborated them in theoretical and allegorical (the passage in *Phaedrus*), as well as physiological and biological (Aristotle) form. The next example, Lucretius, combines both in his own unique take on the motif '*erôs* through vision', effectively bringing an ethical-eudaimonistic critique of human flaws and weaknesses into intersection with a naturalistic-philosophical discussion of the senses in human subjects.

In *De Rerum Natura* 3, first of all, Lucretius discusses the combination of soul (or reason: *animus, mens* – the distinction is irrelevant here), on the one hand, and body (through the *anima*, which is dispersed throughout the body), on the other. In particular, he considers the case of 'strong commotions' as causes in our intellect or our senses (... *caput aut oculus temptante dolore* ..., 3.147–8), for instance in the case of fear (*vehementi metu*).[20] When these disturbances occur, the body suffers along with the soul, and the following symptoms are experienced (3.154–6):

> *sudoresque ita palloremque existere toto*
> *corpore et infringi linguam vocemque aboriri,*
> *caligare oculos, sonere auris, succidere artus*
>
> sweating and pallor thus arising all over the body,
> the tongue stumbling and voice fading,
> the eyes darkening, the ears ringing, the knees buckling ...
> [Here and below, transl. Rouse]

---

18 See, in this volume, Sanders on Xen. *Symp.* 4.22: Critobulos constantly 'sees' the image of his beloved Clinias, and vision plays a key role in his infatuation.
19 Similar theories about the persistence of images in dreams are found in Hippoc. *Vict.* and Arist. *Somn. Vig.* See Thumiger 2017: 299–300.
20 Fear and *erôs* are often associated by philosophers as examples of emotions which can strongly affect the mind: see Arist. *Rh.* 1370b19–29, and again Gorgias, n. 17 above.

These verses show how closely *animus* and *anima* are tied together. (Here *animus* and *corpus*, body, are in an important sense equivalent, since the *anima* is found *throughout* the body.) It is in this connection that Lucretius uses the erotic words of Sappho (whether consciously or not, is of no interest for our purposes) to pose a philosophical question about the relationship between mind and body, and more generally about the experience of suffering through emotion. The classical symptoms of *erôs* are directly understood by him – and plausibly by his public – as the archetype of a reactive mechanism triggered by vision. When Lucretius speaks directly about love and sex, in *De Rerum Natura* 4, *erôs* is explicitly made a paradigm for psycho-pathological disturbance (4.1058–72):

> *Haec Venus est nobis; hinc autemst nomen Amoris,*
> *hinc illaec primum Veneris dulcedinis in cor*
> *stillavit gutta et successit frigida cura;* 1060
> *nam si abest quod ames, praesto simulacra tamen sunt*
> *illius et nomen dulce obversatur ad auris.*
> *sed fugitare decet simulacra et pabula amoris*
> *absterrere sibi atque alio convertere mentem*
> *et iacere umorem coniectum in corpora quaeque* 1065
> *nec retinere semel conversum unius amore*
> *et servare sibi curam certumque dolorem;*
> *ulcus enim vivescit et inveterascit alendo*
> *inque dies gliscit furor atque aerumna gravescit,*
> *si non prima novis conturbes volnera plagis* 1070
> *volgivagaque vagus Venere ante recentia cures*
> *aut alio possis animi traducere motus.*

This is Venus to us; this is where Love derives its name; this is where that drop of Venus' sweetness came from which first dripped into our heart, to be succeeded by icy anxiety. For if the subject of your love is not there, the images are still to hand and the sweet name rings in the ears. The right thing to do is to run away from the images, to scare off those things that feed love, to direct the mind elsewhere, to ejaculate the build-up of fluid into bodies indiscriminately rather than hold on to it, obsessed with with the love of one person only and thus saving up love-sickness and inevitable pain for oneself; for the sore quickens and turns chronic if it is nourished, the madness gets worse day by day, the trouble becomes more depressing if you do not confound the original wounds with new blows, treating them in time while they are still fresh by roaming about in sexual promiscuity or else transferring the movement of the mind in another direction.

Haec Venus est nobis: this is our human, mortal form of *erôs*, a bodily and physiological need above all. Like Sappho, Lucretius places the physical symptoms in the middle; then come the images, even the sound of the name. When the beloved is absent, his/her *simulacra* and *nomen* follow the lover, and a wound, *vulnus*, and a kind of suffering, *dolor*, arise as a consequence. In this case, of course, an important role is played by Epicurean materialistic epistemology (images are formed material objects, made of atoms, which fluctuate before our sensory organs). The same idea returns as in the other examples, however, even if it is formulated differently: images (in the extended sense of visual and auditory perceptions, 'memories' of a person) are key in the experience of *erôs*.

A repertoire of elements has now emerged as shaping the poetic, especially lyric conventions from Sappho onwards, but also as influencing and inviting engagement in philosophical reflections in Graeco-Roman culture. Physiologically, we find overheating, fire; a wound that is hidden and festers beneath the surface; sensory disturbance; an inability to speak; sweating; trembling. All these symptoms, moreover, arise from seeing and imagining, and *imaging* the beloved person – a form of phantasmagoria that can extend to a hallucinatory experience. The beloved is, first and foremost, an *image* in the lover's mind.[21]

The Medical Perspective

Since we are dealing with alterations in fundamental physiological functions and faculties, the contributions of medical authors are central, although the interactions of this evidence with non-technical literatures have mostly been overlooked; the general tendency in scholarship is to consider the bulk of medical literature (be it the texts of the Hippocratic corpus, the more literarily crafted treatises of Galen, or the important works of Late Antique nosology) a world apart from the conventions, genres, occasions, and fruition modes of 'high literature'. When points of contact have been noted, this has mostly involved recognising the specific, active interest of a literary author in medicine, for example in the overt cases of Euripides[22] or Plutarch.[23] Such segregation of domains makes no cultural/historical sense, as the case of *erôs* makes particularly clear. The medical evidence has nonetheless been mostly ignored up to this point, although there has been no shortage of scholarship on *erôs*.[24]

Erôs as a subject of medical interest becomes visible for the first time in the early centuries CE. This is in itself interesting and partially explains the mutual

---

21 See Thorsen 2020 for a discussion of literary and visual sources vis-a-vis optical viewing and intellectual, emotional 'insight' in erotic love, especially in Roman poetry.
22 See for example the important work by Guardasole 2000; Craik 2001; Kosak 2004.
23 See for example the discussion of diseases, especially *phrenitis*, in Thumiger (forthcoming).
24 In the 2013 volume I edited with Ed Sanders *et al.*, only Rosen discussed Galen (Rosen 2013). See Thumiger 2017: 2–12 for discussion of this trend.

neglect of each other's material by modern scholars of ancient medicine and literature in connection with our topic. Notably, the *Hippocratic Corpus* mostly eschewed questions of personal life and subjective emotions, as I demonstrate in depth elsewhere.[25] This avoidance of the private sphere of human well-being, which later doctors, by contrast, do include among their interests and sphere of action, has to do with the specific history of Graeco-Roman medicine, its self-definition, and its dialogue with philosophy in regard to ethical and personal themes. Classical medicine (Hippocratic and coeval) omits ethical or private questions from its exploration of health; topics like the legitimacy of pleasures and desires, how to approach flaws of character, and the need to gain control over strong emotions such as anger and grief first emerge in the interest and awareness of the physicians in texts of the early CE centuries, and especially in Galen.

As far as the erotic sphere is concerned, the older texts contain some references to sexual activity as physiologically relevant, for example in recommendations about the suitable age of women for sexual intercourse and,[26] symmetrically, the invitation to male patients to avoid sexual excess, since it can have pathological consequences.[27] Such is the case of the melancholic patients described in the (admittedly exceptional) pseudo-Aristotelian *Problem* 30.1, *On Melancholy*, which clearly states that a kind of lovesickness can be linked to melancholy[28] – the beginning of a long tradition in the representation of the suffering lover. But the personal, emotional, and subjective level – the psychology of the phenomenon and its existential dimension implicating relationships, family complications, and social negotiation – is excluded from medical discussions until the beginning of the Imperial era.

The richest information for a medical psychopathology of *erôs* is found in the works of Galen. From the point of view of pathology, as Roselli points out with great clarity, the seminal acknowledgement of a form of erotic sickness in Galen falls under the larger category of types of worry or anxiety (φροντίς).[29] According

---

25 Thumiger 2017: 419–22; see also McNamara 2016.
26 The short fragment *On the Diseases of Virgins* is most clear in this respect (Lami 2007): women of reproductive age who remain unmarried and do not have sexual intercourse suffer from a deadly disease with strong psychological disturbances, especially of the hallucinatory kind, where 'frightening images' play a central role.
27 See Thumiger 2017: 239–51.
28 *Pr.* 30.1 (954a32–4).
29 Roselli 2008: 392–3. On anxiety as pathogen in Galen, see Mattern 2015.

to the physician, these emotions can cause physiological disease, especially fevers, as discussed in *De Crisibus* 13 (162.4 Alexanderson = IX.696.16ff. K.).³⁰ Conditions of emotional turmoil manifest themselves in intense thoughts, hollow eyes, and paleness; in a physiognomic spirit, Galen also mentions the special condition of the eyes, from whose affect the different kinds of worry can be distinguished. Alongside this, the explicit description of cases of a true and proper illness caused by *erôs* (as by other kinds of mental distress) also feature in the Galenic corpus, where the physician elaborates medically on a topic already circulating in a number of stories in the first centuries CE: patients suffering from lovesickness would waste away, with doctors sitting impotently at their side, until the crucial bit of evidence is discovered.

Three cases are especially notable. In his treatise *On Prognosis*, first of all, Galen mentions the wife of Justus, who was ill because she was secretly in love with the dancer Pylades.³¹ The patient could not sleep and lay sadly in bed, weak but restless, with her head and body wrapped in a blanket. Once, *as the name of the dancer was mentioned by chance*, Galen noticed that 'her glance and her appearance were altered, and her pulse became irregular'; in this way, he discovered the truth and correctly diagnosed the woman's lovesickness (102.15). Another famous anecdote that was popular at the same time presents a similar case, this time in a royal context: that of Antiochus, the son of King Seleucus I, and the famous Alexandrian doctor Erasistratus. Erasistratus diagnosed and was able to cure the illness of the young man, who was secretly in love with his father's wife. Galen mentions this story a number of times,³² and a version can also be found in Plutarch's *Life of Demetrius* 38.³³ The latter version, coming from a non-medical source, is particularly interesting, since it offers evidence of a traffic and dialectic between medical discourses (which Plutarch often uses in a competent and sophisticated manner in his writing) and poetic/philosophical traditions. Here the young man is ashamed to admit that he is madly in love with his father's wife Stratonice, but Erasistratus nonetheless intuits his condition: 'when any one else came in, Antiochus showed no change; but whenever Stratonice came to see him,

---

30 As well as *Ad Glauconem De Methodo Medendi* 2 (XI.10.16–14, 9 K.)
31 *Praecog.* 5, 94.20–4 (XIV.625–6 K.); *Praecog.* 6 (XIV.630–3 K.), 7 (XIV 640 K.), 13 (XIV 669 K.).
32 Antiochos und Erasistratos: *Praecog.* 5 (XIV 625–6 K.), 6 (XIV 634–5 K.); *In Hipp. Progn. Comm.* 1.8 (XVIII b40 K.). The sources for this story are all Late Antique: apart from Galen, the anecdote is elaborated by Valerius Maximus, Appian, Lucian, and Julian. The dates in these stories are contradictory – Erasistratus was born in 300 BCE and could thus hardly be already active and famous around 294 BCE, when Seleucus was a young man. On these stories, see also Roselli 2008: 394 n. 13.
33 See also Heliod. *Aeth.* 4.7.

as she often did, either alone or with Seleucus, *those tell-tale signs of which Sappho sings were all there in him* – stammering speech, fiery flushes, darkened vision, sudden sweats, irregular palpitations of the heart, and finally, as his soul was taken by storm, helplessness, stupor, and pallor'.[34] For this fictional doctor, the checklist of symptoms described by Sappho is straightforwardly recognisable as typical of love suffering. As readers we too can easily compare these patients to those described by Galen as objects of his clinical observation.[35]

If we are looking, however, for a full acknowledgement of love-sickness as disease entity, only two Late Antique medical authors, Oribasius and Paul of Aegina, include it in their nosological lists. Oribasius, the famous doctor and author of the fourth century CE, describes 'lovers' as patients in his *Synopsis* (*Syn*. 8.8, 249–50 Raeder):

> *On Lovers* (Περὶ τῶν ἐρώντων)
>
> Some fail to recognise those patients who are despondent and insomniac because of love sickness, and cause their condition to become weaker by (prescribing) abstinence from bathing, fasting and a light diet. Instead, having recognised (the nature of) erotic suffering, we divert their mind with baths, wine drinking, strolls, images and sounds, in some cases even causing fear; for those who enjoy too much leisure suffer from the disease in a more severe form [...] Those affected by love sickness show the following symptoms: hollow but tearless eyes; they appear to be full of lust;[36] and their eyelids flutter frantically. While all other body parts are affected, only these (the eyes) are not.[37] [My transl.] (ὀφθαλμοὶ κοῖλοι καὶ οὐ δακρύουσι, φαινόμενοι δ' ὡσὰν ἡδονῆς πεπληρωμένοι εἰσίν· κινεῖται δ' αὐτοῖς καὶ τὰ βλέφαρα θαμινά, τῶν τε ἄλλων τοῦ σώματος μερῶν συμπιπτόντων, μόνοι οὗτοι τοῖς ἐρῶσιν οὐ συμπίπτουσιν.)[38]

Intriguingly, the eyes of these patients are a prominent *locus affectus*:[39] 'hollow, but tearless', in line with the Galenic description of those oppressed by types of φροντίς. Therapy should take place through strong impressions, like terror

---

34 Transl. Perrin (ὡς οὖν τῶν μὲν ἄλλων εἰσιόντων ὁμοίως εἶχε, τῆς δὲ Στρατονίκης καὶ καθ' ἑαυτὴν καὶ μετὰ τοῦ Σελεύκου φοιτώσης πολλάκις ἐγίνετο τὰ τῆς Σαπφοῦς. ἐκεῖνα περὶ αὐτὸν πάντα, φωνῆς ἐπίσχεσις, ἐρύθημα πυρῶδες, ὄψεων ὑπολείψεις ἱδρῶτες ὀξεῖς, ἀταξία καὶ θόρυβος ἐν τοῖς σφυγμοῖς, τέλος δὲ τῆς ψυχῆς κατὰ κράτος ἡττημένης ἀπορία καὶ θάμβος καὶ ὠχρίασις).
35 Zadorojnyi 1999 on the reference to Sappho fr. 31 in Plutarch.
36 Roselli 2008: 397–8 rightly emphasises this detail as a novel element in Oribasius.
37 See Roselli 2008: 297 n. 23 on a variant to this passage on the unaffected eyes of the lovers in the Latin tradition.
38 The chapter is reproduced word for word in Ps.-Polemo, *Phgn*. 81, 1–5 (Foerster).
39 Biesterfeldt/Gutas 1984: 22 say that these authors 'merely reproduce traditional lists of symptoms', disregarding the important ophthalmological development.

(φόβος), and through diversion of the mind by means of 'images and sounds' (θεάματα καὶ ἀκούσματα).⁴⁰ In this way, in these more somber medical contexts too one can identify contacts with the elements foregrounded by poetic narratives, here localised with anatomical precision: the eyes are exhausted, we are made to think, by lack of sleep, lust, and a desperate addiction to images and obsessive thoughts.

The second text, by Paul of Aegina, the medical compiler from the seventh century, repeats more or less the same observations, but also inserts some further details (Paul of Aegina III.17, 160 Heiberg). First, Paul firmly categorises these patients as suffering from a disease of the brain, akin to other forms of φροντίς; second, he adds that the key symptoms arise whenever a memory is evoked through seeing or hearing (ὁπότε δὲ εἰς ὑπόμνησιν ἔλθοιεν τοῦ ἐρωμένου ἤτοι δι' ἀκοῆς ἢ ὁράσεως), especially when this happens suddenly (ἐξαίφνης). For this reason the therapy, as Oribasius had also said, must include images and sounds – forms of *divertissement* for the intellectual faculties.⁴¹

We can now begin to place the physical suffering described by poets in dialogue with the medical interpretations of our topic. The eyes as organs of seeing are central. The imaginative, fantastic element in the medical version has nothing romantic or frivolous about it, nor anything 'Platonic' (unlike what a modern reader might think at first glance: the breathtaking beauty of the beloved, or the like). On the contrary, the emphasis on vision belongs to a highly influential idea in ancient psychology, which is that different kinds of images (*phantasiai*, to use the *terminus technicus*) can have a direct influence on physical health: the appearance (through an image or evoked by name) of the beloved, especially when sudden, plays a central role as a trigger or aggravating factor. In the latest ancient stages of the medical tradition surveyed here, these kinds of *idée fixe*, obsessive thinking, and hallucinations are categorised as diseases of the brain as centre of

---

40 The resort to 'diversion of the mind' through artistic offerings among other things is a recurring element in psychotherapeutic approaches in this period (compare Lucretius' recommendations in *DRN* 4, above, p. 32); see Thumiger 2020. The antecedent to these recommendations in the specific case of the lovesick (as well as those offered by Paul in his section *On Lovers*) is the Galenic discussion in *Comm. Hipp. Epid.* VI (494.10–30 Wenkebach-Pfaff) surviving in the Arabic translation: Galen criticises the prohibitions offered by other doctors to those who 'im heisser Liebe erbrannten', and proposes instead 'dass sie häufig baden, Wein trinken, reiten und alles, was Vergnügen macht, sehen und hören sollten'. Cf. Roselli 2006: 401 n. 35.

41 My translation. On this point, the obsessive thinking triggered by the beauty of the beloved, see the explicit commentary in the footsteps of Galen by Theophilus/Stephanus (cap. 47 Sicurus p. 34, 17 ff. = Daremberg 607 ff.) quoted by Roselli 2008: 398–9 (D. Sicurus, *Theophili et Stephani Atheniensis de febrium differentia ex Hippocrate et Galeno*, 1862).

thinking and judgement[42] (framed, as we have seen, under the umbrella of φροντίς). This categorisation provides historians with a fine illustration of how Late Antique and early Medieval receptions of the Graeco-Roman psychopathological tradition re-organised a vast repertoire of embodied observations towards a simplified localisation, in the case of affections involving the mental sphere, largely around the brain.[43]

If a conceptualisation of lovesickness was absent from classical medicine, the psychology of images and vision in its concrete relation to sexual arousal and physiology, which I am arguing was central to the history of lovesickness, had long been noticed by ancient physicians and biologists. The most materialistic and concrete aspects of this process are described in detail as early as the Hippocratic treatise *De Genitura*, dated to the fourth century BCE. At issue here is not the psychological, affective experience of *erôs*, or even the ideal one, but an aesthetic response in the most literal sense, with a definite, material consequence: the production of sperm in the male body. This physiological point is portrayed with rich detail in its association with sexual desire and bodily stimulation, involving touching, moving, and rubbing: 'The matter is as follows: vessels and cords from the whole body lead to the penis, and these, as they are gently rubbed, warmed, and filled, and experience a kind of tickling sensation, and from this pleasure and warmth arise in the whole body. As the penis is rubbed and the man moves, the moisture in his body is warmed, turns to liquid, is agitated by his movement, and foams up, just as all other liquids foam when they are agitated ...' According to this author, a similar process happens in the case of wet dreams, which are especially relevant to our topic due to the analogy with images: 'Furthermore, persons who have nocturnal emissions do so for the following reason: ... visions of intercourse appear in his dreams, and his moisture *is in the same state* as that of a person having intercourse ...'[44]

Sexual desire is a unique experience, insofar as it challenges and stresses the body in the highest degree and, most of all, since it can occur by proxy, without the intervention of actual bodily interaction, meaning that it can happen through images, not just on a psychological level, but with bodily consequences. Doctors are aware of this detail: Caelius Aurelianus, the Late Antique author of a treatise

---

[42] As in Paul of Aegina III.17, 160.10–11 Heiberg; see Roselli 2008: 399–401 on the Galenic passage.
[43] Likewise in Ibn al-Jazzar's *Viaticum*, also quoted by Roselli 2008: 400, where lovesickness is clearly labelled a 'disease of the brain' characterised by intense thoughts and affections of the eyes (as well as by humoral unbalances); a general disturbance of the soul that destroys the body in turn (Ch. Daremberg and Ch. E. Ruelle (eds.), *Oeuvres de Rufus d'Éphèse*, 582.1–583.5).
[44] *De Genitura* 1.1, 146.3–148.10 Giorgianni = 7.470.1–472.4 L. Transl. Potter.

Acute and Chronic Diseases, at *CD* 5.7 (902.4–906.19 Bendz) devotes a chapter to wet dreams as pathology, *De Somno Venerio*. This illness consists precisely of involuntary ejaculation caused by *inania visa*: 'patients are afflicted by emission of semen during sleep triggered by vain images' (*per somnos inanibus visis adfecti aegrotantes semini lapsu vexantur*). The pathologisation of this relatively common experience is in itself interesting;[45] the affection is, in most cases, 'a consequence of what the person sees (*visis*) while he sleeps (Greek *phantasia*), and results from a longing for sexual enjoinment (*ob desiderium veneris voluptatis*) ...' Even more technical are the references to the role of the eyes in various medical theories of semen production and fertility in ancient medicine collected and commented on by Laskaris:[46] Aristotle and others regarded the area around the eyes as most productive of generative semen (*Gen. an.* 747a14–20: ὅ τε γὰρ περὶ τοὺς ὀφθαλμοὺς τόπος τῶν περὶ τὴν κεφαλὴν σπερματικώτατός ἐστιν)[47] and thus considered the functioning, receptivity, and state of health of the eyes to be associated with an individual's sexual capabilities.

In sum, the technical account of the noso-pathology of lovesickness is closely linked to the psychology of images and its physiological consequences, and has a number of points of contact with the poetics of erotic suffering. With Galen, these narratives are strongly shaped by the model of φροντίς and are brought back to a largely encephalocentric account and handed over as such to his successors. The importance of images and sense perception, however, retains its relevance and persists in the eyes as pathological focus.

Lovesickness at the Crossover

The medical/biological points surveyed, material and technical as they are, constitute one side of the story, which shows continuities from the early Classical phases of the surviving medical tradition to the Late Antique. The psychological and cultural construct of lovesickness as a broader phenomenon, on the other hand, as a discourse bringing together physiological exploration, personal experience, and social event, is a product of the Imperial era.

---

45 And presented as such from early on: see Thumiger 2017: 243 on the Hippocratic material.
46 Laskaris 2016; the folk belief (or moralistic myth to the purpose of chastising sexual instincts) about masturbation causing blindness in young men comes to mind.
47 Compare, with Laskaris, Hippoc. *Nat. Mul.* (99 Potter; 7.416 L.) for a similar association of eyes with fertility in women.

It is in this period, as we have seen, that *erôs* is first thematised in a medical perspective, in two symmetrical ways: literary representations incorporate medical details and narratives, on the one hand, while erotic emotion surfaces within the medical and nosological systems, on the other. Nonetheless, lovesickness does not become a central nosological category, and although its captures the attention of physicians, it somehow retains an anecdotal quality, with a hint of *divertissement* – more an extreme example or a parodic instance than an assimilated medical item.[48] On the whole, the topic displays a persistent hybridity, suspended between seriousness and *ludus*, medical and novelistic, and medical and philosophic.

Attention to *erôs* as pathology, in fact, raises fundamental questions about the role of the medical art and the boundaries of its territory. If medicine since Galen had appropriated the right to express views on ethical problems such as self-control and anger,[49] erotic emotions and sexual behaviours remained too complex and intimate, and at the same time both too highly socialised and too private a sphere to be regulated by clinical advice. As a topic for technical writing, moreover, it had already been the province of other genres (lyric, tragedy; but also the novel, epic, and comedy) for too long to be a comfortable choice for somber medical discussion.

A clear example of this hybrid status is offered by a remarkable Arabic source on lovesickness discussed by Biesterfeldt and Gutas in an article from 1984.[50] In this text, preserved in different versions of varying lengths that emerged between 850 and 1000 CE, lovesickness is presented as a type of melancholic pathology and, in contrast to the general tendency in its medical predecessors, it is a pathology centred on the heart. This sickness produces emotional turmoil and distress for the lover, up to the point of a genuine mental disorder accompanied by physical weakness; in some cases, it can even cause sudden death, when the patient unexpectedly catches sight of the beloved. Biesterfeldt and Gutas connect the text to the confluence of Aristotelianism and humoral medicine that characterises the Late Antique Alexandrian *Problemata Physica*, and consider it a medical source.[51] In this case, however, the dominant features seem rather to be the non-technical use of medical jargon and concepts, and its hybridisation with *topoi* from poetic

---

48 Such as the mentions by Aretaeus (see below, p. 43) or the Galenic cases (above, p. 35).
49 In Galen: see Singer 2014 and 2017; Gill 2013 and 2018.
50 Cf. Biesterfeldt/Gutas 1984: 52–3, 41–5 for the translation; p. 23 n. 22 for information about the text and its variants.
51 Biesterfeldt/Gutas 1984: 48 mention 'literary tradition' to explain a contamination in one of the versions, but on the whole consider the text 'the most systematic and consistent account of the malady of love given in humoral medicine'.

genres. In particular, one version of the text dramatises a fictional encounter, in the form of dialogue, between Aristotle and his pupils as they discuss the topic of love as illness, a setting that evidently owes much to popular genres (not least, ludic refractions of the model of the Platonic dialogue).[52] The replies offered by the philosopher blend physiological notions akin to those of the Aristotelian *Problemata* with classical nosological elements and stock features from ancient poetics of *erôs*.[53] Love 'is a desire born in the heart'; once it grows, it includes 'elements of yearning/irresistible desire';[54] the yearning takes the patient to 'disquieting grief, continuous insomnia, infatuation, sorrows, depression, brooding, loss of appetite, impaired reasoning'. Physiologically, 'relentless desire burns the blood ... [which] ... changes into black bile'. Black bile, in turn, 'creates a disposition for excessive thinking', and as the patients' plans and desires turn hopeless, 'heat flares up, the yellow bile is inflamed, and then it burns ... [and later] it mixes with the black bile'. These rather confusedly exposed patterns of humoral imbalance aggravate the illness and the patient's cognitive impairment.

This source too considers vision to be central to the pathology; in fact, it brings the theme of the beloved's image as trigger of malaise to a medical (and dramatic) peak, culminating with the death of the lover. One of Aristotle's disciples asks him: 'Tell us, master, why the lover faints when he looks at his beloved and why he dies suddenly because of it'. He said: 'Sometimes he looks at his beloved and dies of joy and distress. Sometimes he moans heavily, causing his spirit to remain concealed for twenty-four hours. When his spirit is concealed, he faints until he is taken for dead, and he is then buried while still alive ... Sometimes he heaves a deep sigh when he looks at his beloved, and his soul is stifled in his pericardium, the heart then closes in on the soul and does not release it until he dies ... Sometimes he yearns to have a look, and he suddenly sees the person he loves – and his soul departs suddenly in one stroke and he dies'. Further discussion concerns the change in the lover's complexion when he sees the beloved, how he turns yellow as his blood drains, and so forth, in a blend of novelistic

---

52 Compare the 'Platonic' *locus amoenus* that hosts the conversation between Democritus and Hippocrates in the pseudepigraphic letters, especially *Ep*. XVII, on which see Kazantzidis 2018: 74–8; see also Amundsen 1974 and Pinault 1992: 61–71 on the figure of the physician as presented in literary and cultural models.
53 I quote here from Biesterfeldt/Gutas 1984: 41–3.
54 Biesterfeldt/Gutas 1984: 41 translate the Arabic *ḥirṣ* as 'avidity', although what is at stake here is really immoderate desire (as dictionaries show: Wehr: 'greed', 'cupidity', 'aspiration'; Kazimirski: 'désirer ardemment, convoiter quelque chose'). I thank Simon Swain for this clarification regarding the Arabic text.

elements, humoral medical principles, and accounts of the physiology of the emotions in line with Aristotelian physiology.

There are many parallels from the Late Antique period to which one might turn to exemplify this hybrid product of the encounters between medicine, philosophy, and literary modes. One that stands out is the anonymous verses of the 5th-century *epyllion Aegritudo Perdiccae*, which thoroughly exploits the many strands and cultural implications of lovesickness at the end of the ancient world. Perdicca's story, like that of Erasistratus, circulated widely in Late Antiquity: he was the son of Alexander I Philhellenos, who lived in the late fifth century (450– 413) BCE, and his fate was very similar to that of Antiochus. Perdicca fell in love with his mother-in-law, Phila, and became ill; Hippocrates visited him (an episode recounted also in Soranus' *Vita Hippocratis*), but was unable to effect a cure. He ultimately died of suicide.

In the version offered by the *Aegritudo,* Perdicca is in love not with his stepmother, but with his own mother Castalia – which is, of course, a more extreme dilemma – and the blame is placed on Eros, *Cupidus*, the child-god: Perdicca has failed to bring offerings and sacrifices to Cupid's mother, the goddess Venus, and Cupid is seeking revenge. The *topoi* of the neglected goddess to be appeased, and of the rivalry with another deity are here reworked with a touch of parody and in an allegorical key: the young Perdicca has just returned from Athens, where he has been focusing on his – philosophical? – studies (19–20: *studiis animos praebebat et aures*) when the erotic punishment hits, producing an illness that only suicide will resolve.

First comes the maddening image, the *imago*, produced upon the encounter between mother and son.[55] Perdicca sees his mother (... *ut vidit* ...) and immediately becomes ill. The replacement or displacement of this image and the ensuing emotions play a key role in this erotic pathology, as the poet speaks of the *mutata ... figura* of the mother in Perdicca's displaced desire (*somnia tristia*). The ensuing symptoms are the typical ones, with strong Vergilian colouring (Dido is the obvious model for lovesickness in the text): fire and burning, a kind of inflammation (113–14: *nam fulmine tactus | ardebat miser*; 188: *plus uris amantem*; 195–6: *et tecum vigilat per noctis tempora longa | intorquens dira assiduis incendia flammis*); weakness, overheated humours, and lack of appetite (134: *deficient iuveni paulatim fortia membra*); and madness (104–7). In particular, it is the eyes of the lover that are affected by burning: *sola tibi dulci nunquam, Perdica, quieti | tradidit assiduis ardentia lumina flammis* (104–5). He cannot sleep or eat (113–14, 134–6); he falls prey to a *furor* (200, 216, 276); he is *demens* and burns (188, 196, 206).

---

[55] Transl. Hunt.

As in the cases of Justus' wife and Antiochus, the doctor is called, this time Hippocrates himself. But, unlike in the other cases, he cannot be of help. At first, 'medicine remains silent', *medicina tacet* (155): the doctor cannot understand where Perdicca's illness is based. As the mother enters the room, however, the young man's pulse is suddenly altered (166–70), and Hippocrates formulates his diagnosis: Perdicca is in love and is suffering from an illness of the soul, a *labor animi* (174). Crucially, this means that the duties of medicine end at this point (*munera medicinae cessant*) and that the doctor *par excellence*, Hippocrates, must give up (173–4).

The helplessness of medicine in the case of *erôs*,[56] here honed down to an 'illness of the soul', symbolises – and, in this case, banalises – a key theme in the intellectual life of the early CE centuries: which are the fields of competence of medicine, which of the philosophers, and which, with increasing relevance, should be those of religion?[57] Medical authors also took part in the discussion regarding boundaries and categorisation *vis-à-vis* lovesickness and medicine. Aretaeus, in his *Chronic and Acute Diseases*, denied that *erôs* should be regarded as a real disease: he mentions the case of a 'false melancholic', a young man who was not really melancholic, and who would be cured when he finally managed to win the love of his woman.[58] On the other hand, we have seen how Galen stresses that lovesickness can be a disease, but like any other pathological anxiety (φροντίς), one that doctors could handle therapeutically.[59] Caelius Aurelianus is more open, but still sceptical when he discusses lovesickness in his *Chronic Diseases* 1.5, describing *mania* (*De Furore*, 536.2–13 Bendz): he underlines the apparent similarities between *furor* and pathological *erôs*, and at the same time heavily criticises doctors who prescribe erotic satisfaction, *amor*, as therapy for those affected by *mania*. Such patients are stirred even more by the sight of their object of desire, and sexual intercourse is no help to them whatsoever. Curiously, and a bit inconsistently, he also doubts the ability of manic patients to fall in love at all,

---

56 A parallel to this scene, and a further illustration of the cultural relevance of the theme, is offered by Heliod. *Aeth.* 3.10.4, where the young Chariclea lies ill with lovesickness and the doctor Acesinus is summoned; the most extensive treatment of the passage is offered in Robiano 2003.
57 See Polito 2016, in particular on the rivalry between medicine and philosophy expressed by the text of Caelius Aurelianus.
58 Aret. *CD* 3.5.3 (41 Hude).
59 Galen denies, for instance, that a particular 'pulse of the lovers' exists. Likewise Paul of Aegina: 'the pulse of the lovers is in no way remarkable, unlike what some think, but is like that of other patients who are oppressed by worry', Paul of Aegina 3.17 (160 Heiberg), my translation; see Roselli 2008: 395.

insofar as they are *iudicio carentes*, i.e. unable to appreciate the beauty they see (*pulchritudinem probare*) due to their mental impairment.

To conclude, a rivalry, if not an open conflict emerges, in several forms in various genres and literary works, between kinds of self-care: medicine, which in different ways claims control over mental illnesses; the opposite idea, both popular and medical, that these disorders 'of the soul' belong to another category altogether; and finally, the religious mission to devise a 'true medicine' for the soul.

Conclusions

We have by now established a repertoire of bodily symptoms of *erôs* that remains largely consistent through centuries of ancient and early Medieval history, literary and medical. A look at the *Canon* suffices to confirm this; this medical text, compiled at the turn of the first millennium by *Ibn Sīnā* (Avicenna), became standard in medical education in Europe and greater Islamic world for centuries, in Arabic and in Latin. Here, a version of love-madness ('*ishq*') is handed over for the use of generations of physicians, largely elaborated on the Greek medical sources we have surveyed: it is a 'delusionary' illness, characterised by 'obsession with the loved one', by 'hollow, dry eyes except when crying, and continuous movements of the eyelid', and by laughter, withdrawal, much sighing, insomnia.[60]

We can follow these trajectories into the Early Modern period: at central moments in the cultural afterlife of classical antiquity when thinkers have tried to reflect on the functions of our body and soul, or on the deepest human experiences, they have often returned to *erôs* as bodily affection and alteration associated with the senses and anchored to the experience of *seeing*, extended to signify

---

[60] See Dols 1992: 84–6; 484–5 for the full text of Avicenna. The Persian doctor mentions the following therapeutic possibilities (always directed, of course, to a male patient): to allow marriage with the beloved, or to buy slave girls and increase the patient's sexual activity; to turn the patient's interests in other directions; to offer sincere advice and rebukes from the doctor, if the person is reasonable; in addition, with an interesting Lucretian touch, to use old women, who can most effectively 'malign the beloved and display part of their bodies in a shameful parody of the beloved's attributes' (Dols 1992: 85, with his translation and summary). On the motif of love madness in a variety of legends and texts from the Islamic East, see Dols 1992: 320–48 on Majnūn and Laylā and other examples.

a radical existential challenge that goes far beyond the personal sphere of sentiments and private life. The *De amore* by Andreas Cappellanus, a text that exercised enormous influence on high-Medieval poetry, addressing the question 'What love is', opens as follows:

> *Capitulum I: Quid sit amor. [1] Amor est passio quaedam innata procedens ex visione et immoderata cogitatione formae alterius sexus, ob quam aliquis super omnia cupit alterius potiri amplexibus et omnia de utriusque voluntate in ipsius amplexu amoris praecepta compleri.*
>
> 1. Love is an inborn suffering that results *from the sight* of and *uncontrolled thinking* about the beauty of the other sex. This feeling makes a man desire before all else the embraces of the other sex and to achieve the utter fulfilment of the commands of love in the other's embrace by their common desire. [Transl. Walsh; my italics.]

The persistence and ubiquity of this representation, literary and anthropological, cannot be exaggerated; one need only think of the long tradition of lyric poetry (notably Cavalcanti, Dante, and Petrarch).[61] In 1623, Jacques Ferrand wrote a treatise *On Lovesickness* (*Traité de l'essence et guérison de l'amour*), gathering a vast selection of traditional examples (some of them mentioned above) and interpreting them as forms of melancholy.[62] In his much-read discussion of the 'Language of *erôs*' and its various *Figures* which the 'discourses of *erôs*' encounter in our tradition and culture, Roland Barthes illustrates perhaps most fully the endurance of the nexus *erôs*-imagination-vision-suffering. In his Modes of an 'erotic subjectivity', we find elements such as 'absence', 'image', 'the echo' of the beloved, 'the exile from the imaginary', 'the sadness of the image', along with 'the heart', 'Angst', 'Suicide' – all fundamental components of the history of body and mind relationships tentatively sketched out above.[63] In yet another perspective, Giorgio Agamben in his *Stanzas* focuses on the 'phantasms of *erôs*' in the Western tradition ('a doctrine that, many centuries previously, has conceived of *erôs* as an essentially phantasmatic process and had prepared a large place in the life of the spirit of the phantasm' (1.5)[64] and speaks of the Medieval reception of ancient theories of sensory appraisal and memory as key to understanding the recurrent representation of *phantasia* and *erôs* in this period as an '*erôs* at the mirror' (3.2).[65]

---

61 See Tonelli 2015 for an exploration of medical cultures in the themes and language of lyric poetry in Italian in the 13th/14th centuries.
62 Other modern, even contemporary readers have returned time and again to the diagnosis of melancholy; the motif has remained a *topos*. See Mazzini 1990 and 2012; Toohey 1992 and 2004.
63 Barthes 1977.
64 Agamben 1993: 23.
65 Agamben 1993: 73–89.

The triad *erôs*, sickness, and vision returns again and again, despite travesties, elaborations, and attempts at scientific reduction.

The idea that human *erôs* could become a true and proper disease, and that this disease and erotic suffering are caused and triggered by vision, thus offered a formidable point of conjunction and an interface between otherwise separate environments. First, poetry and art: vision can be seen as a primary creative step and as the initial, most immediate moment of the production of artistic beauty. Second, medicine: the professional observation of and response to the suffering of a patient, as well as of the emotionally charged vision that can trigger physical suffering. Finally, philosophy and the epistemological role of *phantasia*: vision symbolises our potentially deceptive grasp on reality and is a metaphorical moment of appraisal and learning. In an ethical and spiritual sense, the sublimation and contemplative liberation from the slavery of sexual drives and needs is also a way of negotiating kinds of 'vision'. Accordingly, the construct 'lovesickness' offered an ideal arena for a competition between these major players – medicine and philosophy, or religion – for control over man's soul and the responsibility for its healing and salvation. These are deep and lasting human preoccupations, far removed from trite romantic clichés of the kind a modern audience might more readily expect from this long, diverse tradition of erotic texts.

Claude Calame
Performance and Pragmatics of Erotic Poetry in Archaic and Classical Greece: A Pathology of Sexualities?

Abstract: The different forms of Greek melic erotic poetry outline what we could call a 'pathology of love' (in the literal meaning of the word), that is, a description of the physiological, psychological, and emotional effects that *erôs* has on men and women according to the ancient Greeks. At the same time, the song performance of those erotic poems, as it is inscribed in their enunciative development, points to the realisation of the amorous relationship which those poems portray, between the poetic *I* (or *we*) and his/her addressee. Our very fragmentary tradition of Greek erotic poetry attests the existence of a formulaic language – with 'pathology' as a salient ingredient – that is adapted to every single situation, regardless of the monodic or choral delivery of a poem, regardless of the melic or elegiac form chosen, regardless of the metrical pattern adopted for the poem as an act of singing, and regardless of the sex of the protagonists of the erotic relationship. Yet, those poems regularly stage an asymmetrical relationship in terms of age, between an adult person (male or female) and an adolescent (male or female). This chapter offers a close reading of selected fragments, and a more detailed analysis of the new 'Kypris Poem' by Sappho, under the rubric of pathological love.

'Once again limb-loosening Eros makes me tremble, the bitter-sweet, irresistible creature' sings the woman believed to be the poetess Sappho; 'Again Eros, looking at me meltingly from under his dark eyelids, hurls me with his manifold enchantments into the boundless nets of Cypris' sings the man delivering the lines composed in the same period by the poet Ibycus.

As far as the expression of love incarnated in the divine power of winged Eros is concerned, the different forms of Greek melic erotic poetry outline what we could call a 'pathology of love' in the literal sense of the word: that means a description of the physiological, psychological, and emotional effects (with their ambiguities) that the power of Eros has on men and women according to the ancient Greeks. We will also have to take into account the dynamics of the song performance of those erotic poems, as it is inscribed in their enunciative development; the latter points to the realisation of the amorous relationship which those poems portray. These are the potentialities of the formulaic and pragmatic language of Greek melic poetry in general. Crossing the boundaries which we traditionally attribute to gender categories, crossing also the line we are used to drawing between 'homosexual' and 'heterosexual' relationships, Greek erotic melic songs of the archaic and classical periods weave, in their very performance, a web of ritualised social relationships.

To begin with, let us take for granted the now generally accepted opinion about what we persist in calling 'Greek lyric poetry': Greek lyric poetry not as a poetic and written expression of the personal and intimate feelings of a poet perceived as sole author (according to the Romantic definition of 'lyric' accepted throughout the 20th century); but Greek melic poetry as a class including an extreme variety of rather short poetic compositions corresponding to the Greek, original and 'native', category of *melos* – i.e. poems which, as texts, offer us enunciative forms of the *I/we* and of the *you*; verbal performative forms such as 'I sing' (ἀείδω) or 'we are about to dance' (χορεύσομεν); deictic forms pointing to the 'here' and 'now' of the performance of the poem; and strophic or triadic metrical forms. An illustrative example is the short initial line of a probable *partheneion* by Alcman:[1]

Μῶσα Διὸς θύγατερ λίγ' ἀείσομαι ὠρανίαφι

Muse, heavenly daughter of Zeus, I shall sing clearly ...

[Transl. Campbell]

Therefore melic poems offer enunciative strategies, rhythmical patterns, and linguistic performative verbal forms making of them real and developed speech acts; this means a poetic delivery referring to a sung and generally choral performance – to a musical and ritualised performance – as an aesthetic, emotional, ritual and collective practice of the voice and the body.[2]

Thus Greek melic poems are (a) poetic forms referring, through deictic markers, to the *hic et nunc* of a precise situation of enunciation and performance: a ritual, institutional, and political situation in a broader historical, religious, eco-

---

[1] Alcm. fr. 28 *PMG* = 85 Calame, preserved by the sch. Hom. *Il.* 13.588 (III, p. 512 Erbse) which presents the poet Alcman as a μελοποιός.
[2] On many occasions, I have had the opportunity to insist on these various dimensions of Greek melic poetry; see for instance Calame 2005: 1–16 and 2019a. *Captatio benevolentiae*: as in previous contributions, I will have to quote in an immodest self-referential way some of my own studies consecrated to the melic lines I will bring as examples. There one can find the references to the numerous articles and monographs I am relying on.

nomic and cultural context; (b) poetic forms corresponding, through performative verbal markers, to ritual acts of song with their intellectual and emotional pragmatics (i.e. with what would be for us their psychological, physiological, pathological and social effects); (c) poetic forms partly understood, already in the pre-classical period, as depending on what we may call poetic genres: religious and cultic forms of choral poetry (like the paean addressed to Apollo or the dithyramb to Dionysus); (d) ritual forms of poetry (the *hymenaios* for marriage ceremonies and the *thrênos* for funerals); (e) more narrative forms (as the citharodic *nomos*, close in its diction and delivery to epic poetry).

Besides the various forms of *melos*, the different forms of elegiac poetry, composed in elegiac dimeters, and of iambic poetry are also to be considered. These very different forms of sung and performed poetry are reshaped and recreated on every single occasion by a poet. In Greek terms, these poets are presented (for us in a contradictory way) both as craftsmen (as in Hom. *Od.* 17.386, along with the seer, the physician, and the carpenter) and as inspired by a divine power generally represented by the Muses (as the aoidos of the *Odyssey* himself in the first line of the poem: 'Tell me, Muse, of the man of many resources, who …'). Divinely inspired like the epic poet, they are called ποιηταί, 'creative makers', i.e. poets in the etymological meaning of the word. Moreover, they assume the role of διδάσκαλοι, 'trainers', for the choral groups singing and dancing their poetic compositions, and the communities that hire them.

The geographical and institutional space of their poetic practices is the set of the small civic Greek communities developing from the 8th to the 6th century BCE around the Aegean and spreading out through colonial settlements in Southern Italy and Sicily (Syracuse, Agrigento, Himera, and so on), Libya (Cyrene), Egypt (Naucratis) and the Black Sea (Olbia), each with its own political regime, its own 'pantheon', its own constellation of gods and heroic figures (having their own cultic attributes), its own 'song culture' base for its social and religious life. These communities are informally organised in a vast network of poetic culture, animated by wandering poets, and have their local dialectal and formal distinctive features; they rely on a shared tradition of multiple poetic forms and on a common polymorphic poetic diction with its rhythmical and linguistic variations.

The Greek Pathology of Love and the Pragmatics of Erotic Poetry

Around the theme of 'the pathology of love', I would like to propose a linguistic and anthropological confrontation with some fragments of Greek erotic melic poetry of the pre-classical period. Despite the enormous lacunae in our tradition, particularly around the so-called Greek 'lyric' poetry, the perspective of linguistic anthropology and of ethnopoetics proposed here requires us to go back to the contemporary (ancient) categories, using modern notions as instruments in a project of transcultural translation. In fact, our modern concepts of love and sexuality are inappropriate for grasping the nature of the πάθη, the experiences and emotions the ancient Greek melic poets considered as the effects of a force incarnated in the divine figures of Eros and Aphrodite. And we must add that our modern concept of literature is inadequate for grasping the pragmatics of those poets' compositions, i.e. the net of amorous and erotic relationships that their poems, in their very musical and ritualised performances, were able to weave and realise for the protagonists of the songs.

Back to *melos* and to the divine power of Eros. What we could call a 'pathology of love' in Ancient Greece is based on anthropology, i.e. a general conception of the human being that is both physiological and religious, a conception of his/her mind and his/her body with the forces that animate them, a conception of his/her psychology and physiology with emotions and actions influenced by divine powers (as expected in a polytheistic system).[3] This is particularly the case for the Greek notion of what would be for us – in our modern, shared anthropology – the libido, i.e. the sexual impulse. In Ancient Greece, the emotional and practical expression and realisation of what we grasp as forces of the libido are particularly dependent on the physiology of the gaze. As I have tried to show in two previous studies, the (amorous) gaze in Ancient Greece is understood as the vehicle of a material flow. Sometimes seen in atomistic terms, this flow is provoked by the beauty of the beloved person: it emanates from his/her body, and particularly from his/her eyes, to hit and penetrate the lover (male or female); it thus establishes a relationship between beloved and lover. Even in Hippocratic

---

[3] On the ancient Greeks' conception of emotions, see particularly Konstan 2006a: 12–27, on pathos and passion.

medicine, this material and fluid force is considered divine: it is embodied by and represented as the very young Eros, a cupid, the winged assistant of Aphrodite.[4]

To be able to grasp the 'pathology' of the erotic relationships portrayed in the melic poems through their very musical and ritual performances, we have to understand the relationships between their protagonists: on the one hand, the speaker who verbally appears as the poetic *I* (or *we*) and on the other hand his/her addressee, appearing as *you*. This means that the love relationships are inscribed in the enunciative web of the poem; linguistically speaking this enunciative web is realised by the markers we have already mentioned: the *I/we* and the *you*, the deictic markers of the *hic* and the *nunc*, and the performative verbal markers making of the poem in ritual performance a real speech act and then an act of song.

The Gaze as Vehicle for *Erôs* and its Physiological and Pathological Effects

In pursuit of what would be for us the psychological, physiological, and thus pathological pragmatics of erotic melic poetry, we need to examine the descriptions of the gaze as a vehicle for *erôs*. Here the so-called 'first' *partheneion* by Alcman (fr. 1 *PMG* = 3 Calame) is particularly meaningful. Let us note that, though composed by a male poet, the poem was sung and performed by a chorus of young girls, most probably on the occasion of a ritual with initiatory purpose, in the context of a heroic cult celebrated in 7th-century Sparta in honour of Helen as a heroine in her growing beauty.[5]

The complex web of enunciative and erotic relationships woven by the choral utterance of the *partheneion* is supported mainly by the erotic gaze. First, after the (probably double) narrative account of Dioskouroi's struggle against the Hippokoôntidai (their probable rivals in love), the poetic *I* looks at Agido and sings of her brightness in a performative way, comparing her to the sunrise (39–43):

---

[4] On the Greek emotional physiology of the erotic gaze, see Calame 1999: 4–5, 19–23, as well as 2016a, and for the 'native' theories, see Cairns 2011; for Pindar, see Fearn 2017: 92–104. On the materialistic conceptions of vision by the *sophoi* called pre-Socratics, see, among others, Rudolph 2016. For the iconography of the erotic gaze, see Frontisi-Ducroux 1996.

[5] See my commentary on both *partheneia* in Calame 2019b: 502–30 and 1983: 311–49 and 393–420, both with many bibliographical references to other proposals for the identification of the goddess to whom the 'first' *partheneion* of Alcman alludes. On the problem of visual perception and deixis in these poems, see Peponi 2004.

> ἐγὼν δ' ἀείδω
> Ἀγιδῶς τὸ φῶς· ὁρῶ
> ϝ' ὥτ' ἄλιον, ὅνπερ ἇμιν
> Ἀγιδὼ μαρτύρεται
> φαίνην·
>
> And so I sing
> of the brightness of Agido.
> I see her like the sun,
> which Agido summons
> to shine on us as our witness.
>
> [Transl. Campbell]

The following strophe begins with a question addressed to a generic *you*: 'but don't you see?' (50). The choreutai are invited to direct their gaze towards the light coming from Hagesichora's hair and the sparkle of her face – she is their choregos. To the seduction provoked by the erotic gaze, the effect of a melodious voice is then added, that is, the song of the swan.

Third, when the choreutai name themselves in a form of *praeteritio*, their wish is that some of them (three specific ones) may cast a look (75: ποτιγλέποι) on their fellow-singers. Of those who stand out, Vianthemis inspires erotic desire (76: ἐρατά).

The role played by the gaze as a vehicle for erotic desire is also apparent in the so-called 'second' *partheneion* by the same poet (fr. 3 *PMG* = 26 Calame). Again in a self-referential and performative way, the choreutai state their intention to toss (9: τινάξω) their blond hair in the context of performing a beautiful song (5: μέλος). Singing, first, of their choregos Astymeloisa, 'the darling of the people' (74: μέλημα δάμωι), the choreutai describe her looks; it is 'more melting than sleep and death' (61–2: τακερώτερα δ'ὕπνωι καὶ σανάτωι ποτιδέρκεται). The poetic context is explicitly an erotic one. At the same line, probably the *I*-speaker herself sings that she is animated, physiologically and emotionally speaking, by some 'limb-loosening desire' (61: λυσιμελεῖ πόσωι). The form ποτιδέρκεται (62: 'she looks [at me?]') recalls, of course, the gaze as a vehicle for erotic desire expressed by the form ποτιγλέποι in the other *partheneion* (75).

But there is more. On the one hand the adjective τακερός, 'melting', is used directly as an epithet for Eros in a poem by Anacreon (fr. 459 *PMG*).[6] And in a famous poetic fragment by Ibycus (fr. 287 *PMG*), the *I*-speaker describes and indirectly addresses Eros who is 'again (1: αὖτε) looking at me meltingly from under

---

[6] The expression is preserved by sch. Ap. Rhod. 3.120 (p. 221 Wendel), which describes Eros as μάργος, an adjective explained by the scholiast as '(Eros) who makes the men mad'.

his dark eyelids' (2: τακέρ' ὄμμασι δερκόμενος). In the following lines the poet, or whoever is singing the poem, describes the effect provoked by that erotic gaze: he is hurled 'by the enchantments' (3: κηλήμασι) of Eros into the boundless nets of Kypris. Again, the gaze of Eros is 'melting' – a material and physiological effect expressed in a frequent metaphor of melic poetry.[7]

On the other hand the comparison between the impressions aroused by Eros and the effect of sleep and death, or better, the (physiological, emotional, and pathological) equivalence between sleep, death, and love as an 'altered state of consciousness' is frequent in Greek erotic poetry. Consider, for example, the famous expression concluding the poem by Sappho that lists and describes the physiological effects of love – a poem we will return to (fr. 31 L-P): 'It seems to me that I am little short of dying' (15–16). We recall the poetic enumeration in this song of the various pathological manifestations of the erotic power on the subject's body and on her mind, provoked precisely by the gaze upon the beloved person, i.e. the *you* of the poem and then the indirect addressee of the song (7: ἐς σ' ἴδω).

Moreover, in Alcman's 'second' *partheneion*, πόθος, which can be considered as the equivalent of *erôs*, is described as λυσιμελής (61): 'limb-loosening desire'. This corresponds to the qualification of πόθος in a line by Archilochus (fr. 196 W): 'But, my friend, limb-loosening desire overwhelms me'. The same qualification is to be found about Eros himself as a cosmogonic force in Hesiod's *Theogony* (120–1): 'Eros, the most beautiful among immortal gods, the limb-loosening, the one who in the breasts of all gods and all men subdues their reason (ἐν στήθεσσι νόον) and prudent will (βουλήν)' – a claim which is affirmed at the very beginning of the narration of the entire cosmogonic and theogonic process developed in the poem. *Erôs* is also limb-loosening in an anonymous poem (*carm. pop.* fr. 873 PMG) sung by the best men of the cities of Chalcis and addressed to the παῖδες, inviting them to offer the graces of their beauty. As I tried to show for the description of the role of gaze in transmitting the erotic power, here too we have, as far as the Greek physiology and pathology of love is concerned, a formulaic language which is adapted to every single situation and to different forms of poetry in different contexts of performance.[8]

---

[7] On these different poems and on this physiology of the erotic desire, see further remarks in Calame 1999: 14–27.
[8] See further examples in Cairns 2001 and Calame 2016a, along with Swift 2016a (focussed on Alcman's and Pindar's *partheneia*).

Performative Turns in the Poetic Expression of *Erôs*

As just mentioned, melic poetry is not only narrative (as epic poetry mainly is); it is not only descriptive; it is also a practical poetry, not to say a 'performative' one – a term which should be limited to its linguistic meaning in the domain of the realisation of speech acts through the enunciative use of language. As such, melic poetry offers enunciative turns and enunciative strategies which make of the entire poem in performance, as already indicated, a 'speech act', and specifically an act of song, a ritual act of song.

In an earlier study of the pragmatic dimension of the formulaic language of erotic melic poetry, I focused attention on the use by different poets, with variations depending on the metre and the poetic form they choose, of the deictic expression δηὖτε, 'Here once again'.[9] With the spatial and temporal demonstrative reference implied by δή and with the idea of re-enactment expressed by αὖτε, this deictic implies the manifestation of *erôs hic et nunc*, once again, in the space and time of the musical performance of the poem, and with its aesthetic and pragmatic effects.

> σὺ δ', ὦ μάκαιρα,
> μειδιαίσαισ' ἀθανάτῳ προσώπῳ
> ἤρε' ὄττι δηὖτε πέπονθα κὤττι   15
> δηὖτε κάλημμι
>
> κὤττι μοι μάλιστα θέλω γένεσθαι
> μαινόλᾳ θύμῳ· τίνα δηὖτε πείθω
> βαῖσ' ἄγην ἐς σὰν φιλότατα; τίς σ', ὦ
> Ψάπφ', ἀδικήει;   20

But you, O holy one,
smiling with your immortal looks,
kept asking what is it once again *this* time [*deûte*] that has happened to me
and for what reason once again *this* time [*deûte*] do I invoke you,

and what is it that I want more than anything to happen
to my frenzied heart? Whom am I once again *this* time [*deûte*] to persuade,
setting out to bring her to your love?
Who is doing you, Sappho, wrong?

[Transl. Nagy]

---

9 See the various references given in Calame 2016b in response to Nagy 2015, on the basis of Calame 1997; see also Calame 2009.

The song is by Sappho (fr. 1.13–20 L-P). This so-called *Hymn to Aphrodite*, the text of which opened the Alexandrian edition of her poems, attributes the different sentences deictically marked by δηὖτε to the goddess Aphrodite; and it does so, first in indirect speech and then in direct speech with questions addressed directly, in *I*-forms, to Sappho, the *you*.

But δηὖτε is also used for making the power of Eros present in and through the poem itself. So it is in these two lines attributed to the Spartan poet Alcman (fr. 59(a) *PMG*):

Ἔρως με δηὖτε Κύπριδος ϝέκατι
γλυκὺς κατείβων καρδίαν ἰαίνει.

At the command of the Cyprian, Eros once again
drips sweetly down and warms my heart.

Then in a fragment by Anacreon (fr. 413 *PMG*), the context of which is also completely unknown:

μεγάλῳ δηὖτέ μ' Ἔρως ἔκοψεν ὥστε χαλκεὺς
πελέκει, χειμερίῃ δ' ἔλουσεν ἐν χαράδρῃ.

Once again Eros has struck me like a smith
with a great hammer and doused me in the wintry torrent.

And finally, in two lines by Sappho herself (fr. 130.1–2 L-P), again quoted just for their particular metrical form:

Ἔρος δηὖτέ μ' ὁ λυσιμέλης δόνει,
γλυκύπικρον ἀμάχανον ὄρπετον.

Once again limb-loosening Love makes me tremble,
the bitter sweet, irresistible creature.
[Transl. Campbell]

In each case, the lines quoted correspond to the beginning of an erotic melic poem. What is provoked by the deictic and enunciative turn of these lines is the presence of Eros from the outset, at the very beginning of the musical and ritual performance of the melic song.

We should add two elegiac distichs from the 'pederotic' book of the *Theognidea* (1249–53). The four lines are addressed to an anonymous someone who has come back to 'our stables' (or quarters), back to the nice meadow with a fresh fountain and shadowy groves: a green meadow, flowing fresh water, the shade of the trees – these are the parameters of the space, ritual and poetic, emotionally and physically inviting for the expression and realisation of love.[10]

The Tradition of Greek Melic Love Poetry and Gender

Considering the variations owed to different metrical schemes and shapes, we find here a confirmation of the formulaic character of the language of pre-classical erotic poetry; that means not only a narrative formulaic language, as in the various forms of epic and Homeric poetry, but also an enunciative formulaic language supporting the pragmatics of the poem in its sung and ritualised performance.

What is particularly interesting to point out in the poetic uses of this descriptive/narrative *and* enunciative formulaic language is that, despite the extraordinarily fragmentary character of our tradition, the sung poem weaves a 'crossing' of sex and gender relationships between the different protagonists of its utterance and performance. These fragmentary lines may sing and stage: (a) the love of a male (probably adult) poetic *I* for a young girl, or an adolescent in the case of Anacreon's poems, or just for a young boy in the *Theognidea*; (b) the love of a choral poetic *I* or *us*, referring to a group of young girls and choreutai, for a more mature young woman with the role of the choregos in the *partheneia* composed by Alcman; (c) the love of a female and adult melic *I* for younger women or girls in the case of the poems by Sappho.

Regardless of the monodic or choral delivery of a poem, regardless of the melic or elegiac form chosen, regardless of the metrical pattern adopted for the poem as an act of singing, and above all, regardless of the sex of the protagonists of the erotic relationship supported by the gaze (with its psychological and physiological effects) and woven into the performance of the poem, our very poor and very fragmentary tradition – from a lexical and enunciative point of view – of Greek erotic poetry on the one hand, attests the existence of a formulaic diction for the poetic expression of *erôs* animated by Kypris, with the 'pathology' im-

---

10 On the different settings and roles of the gardens of love, see Calame 1999: 165–74. Notice that two other lines from the second book of the *Theognidea* (1353–4) describe Eros as πικρὸς καὶ γλυκύς, on the model of γλυκύπικρος in Sappho or in a very fragmentary threnos by Pindar (fr. 128b Snell/Maehler).

plied. This formulaic diction spread across a network of melic traditions developed in the various small civic communities of the pre-classical period with their mainly aristocratic institutions, their polis-cults, and their peculiar song cultures.[11] On the other hand, these poems regularly stage an asymmetrical relationship, in terms of age, between an adult person (male or female) and an adolescent (male or female). And as far as the focalisation of these erotic relationships is concerned, the erotic desire is, generally speaking, aroused by the beauty of a younger person and transferred through the gaze to the adult poetic *I* (Anacreon, Sappho, Theognis or whoever is singing the poem), who expresses the corresponding (physiological and pathological) feeling; and the same erotic emotion may be aroused by an almost adult woman and expressed chorally by a group of girls, as is the case of the *partheneia* composed by Alcman.

It looks as if the song, in and by the effect of its very musical and ritual performance, would (at least provisionally) fill up this kind of 'décalage', this constant erotic asymmetry. Whatever the answer to the question of the pathological pragmatics of the Greek erotic songs may be, the very use of a lexical and enunciative diction for establishing various love relationships, in different contexts, makes our modern concepts of heterosexuality and homosexuality irrelevant.[12]

The Pragmatics of Erotic Songs: Sappho

Let us go a step further with the new papyrological poems recently published under the name of Sappho. And let us move from the formulaic character of the physiological, psychological, and pathological language of love, and from the modes of enunciation of erotic melic poetry, to the question of the pragmatics of their various practical uses.

First, let us briefly recall the fragment by Sappho on old age (fr. 58 Voigt), recently reshaped into an almost complete poem by the combination of a fragmentary text from an anthology of poems by Sappho in a Cologne papyrus, small scraps of an Oxyrhynchus papyrus, and an incomplete quotation of two lines by Athenaeus.[13] After an initial evocation of the Muses, the poetic *I* complains about

---

11 For a first sketch of such a poetic and melic network, see Calame 2014.
12 On the irrelevance of our modern concepts of homo- and heterosexuality, see in particular Boehringer 2019; Skinner 2005: 45–78.
13 *P. Oxy.* 1787, frr. 1 and 2 and *P. Köln* inv. 21351 + 21376 with the complements by Ath. 15.687b, who refers, at the two final lines of the poem, to Clearchus fr. 41 Wehrli. See the new edition of

the physiological effects of old age: withered skin, white hair, a heart weighed down, shaking knees, no more ability to dance like a fawn. The (pathological) affirmations are supported, as is frequent in melic poetry, by a narrative paradigm drawn from the heroic world, i.e. a 'myth': the famous erotic narrative of the abduction of the young Tithonus by Eos, 'Dawn with rosy arms'. Compared to the version of the story found in the *Hymn to Aphrodite*, Sappho's very short narrative is focused on the beauty of the young man, on the erotic desire (ἔρῳ) which seizes Dawn, and probably on the eternal musical voice of Tithonus who is condemned to age in perpetuity in contrast to his spouse's eternal youth (and beauty):

> ἀλλὰ τί κεν ποείην;
> ἀγήραον ἄνθρωπον ἔοντ' οὐ δύνατον γένεσθαι.
> καὶ γάρ π[ο]τα Τίθωνον ἔφαντο βροδόπαχυν Αὔων
> ἔρῳ φ . αθεισαν βάμεν' εἰς ἔσχατα γᾶς φέροισα[ν,
> ἔοντα [κ]άλον καὶ νέον, ἀλλ' αὖτον ὔμως ἔμαρψε
> χρόνῳ πόλιον γῆρας, ἔχ[ο]ντ' ἀθανάταν ἄκοιτιν.

> But what to do?
> No being that is human can escape old age.
> For people used to think that Dawn with rosy arms
> and loving murmurs took Tithonus fine and young
> to reach the edges of the earth; yet still grey age
> in time did seize him, though his consort cannot die.

[Transl. West]

After two entirely fragmentary and syntactically incoherent verses, we reach the final lines of the poem,[14] which are not found in the version of the anthology, but which certainly conclude the song with the usual return to the actual situation of enunciation. These final lines may be understood and translated in two different ways:[15]

> ἔγω δὲ φίλημμ' ἀβροσύναν,]τοῦτο καί μοι
> τὸ λά[μπρον ἔρος τὠελίω καὶ τὸ κά]λον λέ[λ]ογχε. ⊗

---

the text by Gronewald/Daniel 2007; it has been re-examined by Yatromanolakis 2008 (with abundant bibliography), and Obbink 2009.
14 i.e. 'Continuation 2' in Obbink 2009.
15 References on both these translations are to be found in Calame 2013: 58–60. For the meaning of ἀβροσύνη under the authority of Aphrodite, see the comment by Ferrari 2010: 66–71, who proposes the translation: 'to me the love for the sun has allotted [this] splendour and [this] beauty'.

> But I love the graceful delicacy (of youth) ...] that, and
> Eros gave me a share in the splendour of the sun and its beauty.

Or:

> But I love the graceful delicacy (of youth) ...] that, and for me
> the desire for the sun obtained a share in splendour and beauty.

In either case, it is essential for the definition of a Greek poetic pathology of love that the erotic desire is here attached to the light and the beauty (of the sun); and that, in relation to the particular version of the myth offered by Sappho in the preceding lines: Eos, the divine incarnation of the light of dawn, is explicitly seized by Eros as she abducts the young and handsome Tithonus. Moreover, from an enunciative point of view, the poem with its apparently personal conclusion is addressed to a group of παῖδες (1), i.e. young girls in pursuit of 'the violet-laden Muses' handsome gifts' and with 'the loud-voiced lyre so dear to song' (transl. West). This address not only confirms the collective and musical, if not choral, performance of the song; but it also shows that a 'heterosexual' relationship staged in a narrative of the heroic past can be exemplary for a homoerotic one; and even though the heroic example chosen is for us 'heterosexual' compared to the effective 'homosexual' relationship staged in the poem, from the point of view of *erôs* it is focussed on the female protagonist, Dawn, rather than on the male, as is the case in most Greek myths of abduction. The physiological, psychological, and emotional effects of old age in the myth are replaced at the end of Sappho's song by the erotic desire for the light and the beauty (of the sun?): that is felt and poetically expressed by a woman.

A Psycho-physiological Pathology of *Erôs*: The New 'Kypris Poem'

As far as the pathology of love is concerned, we finally have to consider the second of the two new poems by Sappho known to us through the mysterious *P. Sapph. Obbink*, of dubious origin.[16] The poem begins with an address to Aphrodite, calling on the presence of the goddess in the *hic et nunc* of the performance of the song.

---

16 As far as the papyrological text of the new poem is concerned, the fragmentary lines of *P. Sapph. Obbink* are to be completed by the small fragments of the old *P. Oxy.* 1231 fr. 16; they were

⊗ πῶς κε δή τις οὐ θαμέως ἄσαιτο,
   Κύπρι, δέσποιν', ὄττινα δὴ φίλ[ησι
   κωὐ] θέλοι μάλιστα πάθος χάλ[ασ]σ[αι
       τῶ γ'] ὀνέχησθα;

πᾶ σάλοισί μ' ἀλεμάτως δαΐσδ[ης   5
ἰμέρῳ λύσσαντι; γόνωμ', ἄνασ[σα.
πόλλ' ἀπά(μ)μαι μ'· οὐ προτέρ' ἦσ[θα – x
    οὔτ' ὀνεέρξαι

[– ⏑ – x –] σέ, θέλω[⏑ – x
[– ⏑ – x τοῦ]το πάθη[ν ⏑ – x   10
[– ⏑ – x –] ˳αν, ἔγω δ' ἔμ' ˳αὔτᾳ
    τοῦτο σ˳ύνοιδα

How can someone not be seized by vertigo, again and again,
Kypris, Mistress – whomever they love –
and not really want to be delivered from the sufferings
    you impose?

Why pierce me with shivers and nausea
through desire that makes one mad? I beseech you, mistress.
You inflict on me many pains. In the past you were not [
    and you did not turn me away.

            ] you, I wish [
            ] to suffer that [
            ] for myself I am fully
    conscious of that.
                [My transl.]

Here we find a real pathology, in the Greek meaning of the word πάθος, which is indeed used twice in the poem. Despite the considerable lacunae of the papyrological text, the general movement of the poem is clear: an appeal to Aphrodite, in the vocative, and her divine power; justification for this address to the goddess by reference to a general situation first, and then to the particular situation of the poetic *I*. This is a pathological experience: impetuous erotic desire which drives

---

edited as fr. 26 L-P and, because of their composition in Sapphic strophes, modern editors included them in Book I of Sappho's Alexandrian edition: see Obbink 2016a: 26–8, 33, and 2016b. More recently, Burris 2017, one of the editors of *P. Sapph. Obbink*, has inserted into the very fragmentary lines of the second strophe of the 'Kypris poem' a small fragment of the *P. GC.* inv. 105 (fr. 4). Here I follow the text and comments proposed by Neri 2017, with a few deviations in lines 2 and 7–8.

one mad, and thus provokes first vertigo and suffering, then nausea and a feeling of being pierced, followed by the wish to be finally liberated. After referring to a past situation in which the poetic *I* was not rejected by the goddess, a new appeal to her comes, with the *persona cantans* finally expressing her wish (the object of which is yet unknown), her awareness (of the power of Aphrodite?), and the sufferings she is undergoing (most likely because of the effects of *erôs*).

Of course, as already indicated by the editio princeps of the papyrus,[17] the state of suffering, of dizziness and vertigo (1: ἄσαιτο), mentioned in the indefinite mode at the beginning of the poem, coincides with the state of the poetic *I* at the beginning of the Sapphic *Hymn to Aphrodite* (fr. 1 L-P). There, the fictional *I* asks the goddess not to overpower her heart (4: θυμός) with the feeling of nausea and longing (3: ἄσαισι) or with grief and distress (3: ὀνίαισι). In the hymnic poem this sense of loss, combined with pain, is the subject of the initial prayer by the poetic *I*; by her presence, by coming here and now, Aphrodite will dispel this feeling and this grief. In the new poem, the same condition is also linked to an absence (real or felt), namely that of the beloved person. Invoked in this context, Kypris with her divine power is implicitly likely to alleviate this suffering (3: πάθος χάλ[ασ]σ[αι), perhaps by bringing about the presence of the person whose absence the *I* is feeling. Moreover, the 'passion' of love (3: πάθος / 10: πάθην) is attested both in the *Hymn to Aphrodite* (15: πέπονθα) and in another poem by Sappho, in an appeal in direct speech (fr. 94.4 L-P: πεπόνθαμεν) which a young girl addresses to Sappho using the vocative (5: Ψάπφ').

The feeling of being pierced as if by an arrow, and the shivers and nausea which the poetic *I* says that she is seized by, recall the numerous physiological and psychological symptoms provoked by the power of *erôs* at the hands of Aphrodite, as they are sung in the famous fr. 31 L-P.[18] Without going back to every single bodily or mental symptom of the person seized by *erôs* in this real physiopsychological pathology of love designed by the poem,[19] we should just point out that this well-known poem provides confirmation of the contradictory feelings also expressed in the Kypris song.

The kind of passion which Aphrodite is asked (in the song and by means of it) to liberate the poetic *I* from, in the Kypris poem, is the erotic desire which 'makes one mad'. Thus it is particularly significant to underline the use in this

---

17 Obbink 2014b: 46–7. On the erotic synaesthesis in the poem see Briand 2021.
18 Text and translation quoted on pp. 25–6 in this volume.
19 See the study by Burnett 1983: 231–43 and the fine commentary by Hutchinson 2001: 168–77, without forgetting the important study devoted to this poetic language of pathological love by Lanata 1966, and Thumiger in this volume: 26–8.

context of the word ἵμερος (6). The respective adjectival form is used in fr. 31 to qualify the sensual smile of the young woman (5: ἱμέροεν) which arouses the passion felt by the feminine (14: παῖσαν) poetic *I*. The term also appears in one of the 'poems of remembrance', to describe the effect caused on the heart of a woman consumed by desire by recalling the youthful Atthis (fr. 96.15–17 L-P). And in the Sapphic *Hymn to Aphrodite*, the verbal form describes the strong desire animating the poetic *I*; the goddess is asked to take it away: 'Come to me now again and deliver me from oppressive anxieties: fulfil all that my heart longs (or: strongly desires) to fulfil' (fr. 1.26–7 L-P; transl. Campbell).

We should recall here that in Plato's *Cratylus* (420a–b), the etymology that Socrates attributes to the term ἵμερος (ἱέμενος ῥεῖ, 'it flows boosting') corresponds to the etymology he attributes to ἔρως (ἐσρεῖν, 'flowing in'). The fluid and dynamic aspect of both terms is emphasised, referring to a moving force – an impulse. Socrates highlights the strength of a current (τὴν ἔσιν τῆς ῥοῆς) which pulls (ἕλκοντι), attracts (ἐπισπᾷ), and moves.

Seized by the current of Eros, the *I* uttering the Kypris poem is aware that she is literally transformed by shaking (5: σάλοισι), a phenomenon which Sappho describes as 'trembling' in the poem 'He seems to me' (fr. 31.13 L-P).[20] In other poems, verbal forms also express the power of Eros to cause shivers and nausea. The short fr. 130 L-P, already mentioned, reads 'Once again here (δηὖτε) limb-loosening Eros makes me tremble (δόνει)' – using the same verb which Homer uses to describe the effect of the wind (*Il.* 12.157, 17.55). And in fr. 47 L-P, the shaking effect of Eros on the heart of the *persona cantans* is explicitly compared to the effect of strong winds on alpine trees: 'Eros shook (ἐτίναξε) my heart like the wind in the mountains falling on the oaks'. Likewise, in the Kypris poem the person in love is stirred up like a tree shaken by the wind in a vain and mad movement, as the adverb ἀλεμάτως (5) indicates.

But the body and the mind of the fictional *I* are not completely overwhelmed by the physiological and psychic power of erotic desire. In terms of enunciation, the adverb θαμέως in the first line of the Kypris poem indicates that the pathological symptoms of love do not correspond to a brutal shock or an acute ache, but to a persistent psycho-physiological state.[21] And faced with this persistent state of vertigo and grief, the *I* is not entirely passive but affirms, in a sort of speech

---

20 D'Alessio 2017 proposes a different reading of this line: πασσάλοισί μ'ἀλεμάτως δαΐϲδ[- (translated as 'tear me asunder with nails in vain').
21 See the new occurrence of this adverb in fr. 58 L-P; for the verbal form στεναχίσδω, 'I persistently complain' (7), see Boehringer 2013: 33–4.

act, her will (9: θέλω) – unfortunately this verb occurs in a hopelessly fragmentary line – and her full consciousness (11–12: ἔγω δ' ἔμ' αὔτᾳ τοῦτο σύνοιδα). Furthermore, through the common use of the form ἔμ' αὔτα, 'for myself', here and in fr. 31 L-P in which the feeling of death is expressed as a symptom of *erôs* (15–16), the new poem seems to add a clear awareness, perhaps, of this passionate state.

Finally, again in terms of enunciation, the double initial interrogative of the Kypris poem is marked by the recurrence of the Greek *demonstratio ad oculos* particle *par excellence*, namely δή, 'here and now', i.e. under the eyes of the *persona cantans*.[22] In combination with θαμέως, 'again and again', it recalls the deictic δηὖτε, 'here again', which marks the beginning of the erotic poems we have seen, both in enunciative and performative terms, with the corresponding pragmatics. δή crystallises the whole process of the ritual performance of the poem with its vocal power, its choreographic rhythm, and the emotions it arouses for the poetic *I* and her/his addressees. Once again (!) the melic poem in its very musical performance not only expresses, but corresponds to the emotions and sufferings felt by the *persona cantans* in his/her mind and body under the force of *erôs*, which emanates from the beloved person and is transmitted through the gaze. Let us thus conclude with the rhetorician Gorgias, who at the end of the 5th century analysed the effects of Helen's beauty on Paris (*Encomium of Helen*, 18):

> Πολλὰ δὲ πολλοῖς πολλῶν ἔρωτα καὶ πόθον ἐνεργάζεται πραγμάτων καὶ σωμάτων, εἰ οὖν τῷ τοῦ Ἀλεξάνδρου σώματι τὸ τῆς Ἑλένης ὄμμα ἡσθὲν προθυμίαν καὶ ἅμιλλαν ἔρωτος τῇ ψυχῇ παρέδωκε, τί θαυμαστόν;

> Many things (that we see) create in many people love and desire of many actions and bodies. So if Helen's eye, pleased by Alexander's body, transmitted in eagerness and striving of love to her mind, what is surprising?[23] [transl. MacDowell]

How better to illustrate, almost in modern terms, the physiological, emotional, and psychological effects of *erôs*, according to a real 'pathology of love'?

---

22 On the *demonstratio ad oculos* as a deictic procedure in Greek, using demonstratives in *-dê* to denote both a proximate reference in the text and what the audience has in mind, see references in Calame 2004: 415–23.
23 On that passage, see Spatharas 2019: 52–6.

Anastasia-Stavroula Valtadorou
Pathological *Erôs* in the Euripidean Fragments: *Aeolus*, *Cretans*, and *Protesilaus*

For little Sophia

Abstract: Even though it has been well documented that Euripides was *au fait* with contemporary medical thought and love is often presented as a medical condition in his extant works, little attention has been paid so far to examples of pronounced pathological *erôs* in his fragments. This chapter explores some forms of erotic passion or sexual intercourse that could be labelled 'pathological', both from an ancient and a modern perspective, focusing on three fragmentary dramas whose plots revolve around relationships well beyond the bounds of the ordinary, even abnormal: (1) male desire and sexual intercourse between full siblings in *Aeolus*, (2) female desire towards, and sexual intercourse with, a bull in *Cretans*, and (3) female desire towards, and possibly intercourse with, a male statue in *Protesilaus*. Whereas these cases are quite dissimilar to each other and the study of fragmentary plays involves much scholarly speculation, a common poetic stance is evidenced. In all cases, Euripides seems to have offered his characters the opportunity to explain their actions, emotions, or motivations, thus preferring to present an ambiguous picture to his audience, even when the desire in question exceeds what his contemporary spectators would have considered normal and socially appropriate.

I wholeheartedly thank Douglas Cairns, Patrick Finglass, Mark Huggins, Michael Lloyd and Richard Rawles for many helpful suggestions. I am also grateful to Dimitrios Kanellakis for the invitation, his comments, and for helping me obtain bibliographical sources amidst the 2020/2021 lockdowns. All errors are my own.

†διπλοῖ γὰρ ἔρωτες ἐντρέφονται χθονί†
ὁ μὲν γεγὼς ἔχθιστος εἰς Ἅιδην φέρει,
ὁ δ' εἰς τὸ σῶφρον ἐπ' ἀρετήν τ' ἄγων ἔρως
ζηλωτὸς ἀνθρώποισιν, ὧν εἴην ἐγώ.[1]

For there are two loves bred on earth:
one, which is most inimical, leads to Hades,
but the love which leads towards morality and virtue is something
men may envy – among whose number I wish I may myself be!

Eur. Sthen. fr. 661, 22–5

The speaker of these lines, Bellerophon, son of Poseidon and Eurynome, draws an important distinction as regards human *erôs*.[2] According to him, there are two kinds of love.[3] As he states in the lines that precede this passage, he has been the witness and recipient of the first kind, the one that brings sickness and disorder to the *oikos* – it literally makes a house diseased (20: νοσοῦντας δόμους).[4] This is the sexual longing that a married woman, in this case Stheneboea, feels for a man other than her husband. The type of extramarital, hence improper, desire that wives may experience permeates Euripides' oeuvre to such an extent that Aeschylus attacks his fellow tragedian in Aristophanes' *Frogs* (1043–56) for that very reason.[5] Euripides' *Hippolytus* provides a well-

---

[1] The first line of this passage is corrupt, while the following ones have been suspected to be inauthentic by some scholars. See Kannicht 2004: 651. However, I choose to start with this passage because it nicely summarises the double nature of *erôs* often found in Euripides' oeuvre. Translations of passages are taken from Collard/Cropp 2008a–b, sometimes slightly adapted. References to ancient testimonia and fragments are according to Kannicht 2004, whose text I follow, while for the production dates I follow Cropp/Fick 1985.
[2] For the word *erôs* and its difference from 'love' in English, see Konstan 2018: 33 and Sanders in this volume.
[3] For this differentiation cf. Eur. *Theseus* fr. 388: ἀλλ' ἔστι δή τις ἄλλος ἐν βροτοῖς ἔρως | ψυχῆς δικαίας σώφρονός τε κἀγαθῆς. | καὶ χρῆν δὲ τοῖς βροτοῖσι τόνδ' εἶναι νόμον, | τῶν εὐσεβούντων οἵτινές τε σώφρονες | ἐρᾶν, Κύπριν δὲ τὴν Διὸς χαίρειν ἐᾶν ('But there is another kind of love amongst mortals, belonging to a soul that is just and temperate and good. And indeed it would be better if this were their rule, to love those who practise piety and temperance, and leave Zeus' daughter Cypris well alone.'), Eur. *Med.* 627–42; *Hipp.* 525–33; *IA* 553–7.
[4] Again, see Eur. *Sthen.* fr. 661, 6: τοιᾷδε Προῖτος γῆς ἄναξ νόσῳ νοσεῖ ('such is the affliction besetting Proetus'). On the point that *erôs* can inflict disease, esp. on those who experience it improperly, see Eur. *Hippolytus Veiled* fr. 428.
[5] This does not mean that tragic *erôs* always leads to chaos and death in Euripides. For a (possibly) positive portrayal of heterosexual youthful *erôs* in his fragmentary *Antigone* and *Andromeda*, see Valtadorou 2020. For the more complicated picture that his fragments offer with regard to heterosexual bonding, see also Foley 2020, 73.

known example of this motif;⁶ yet the same pattern is found in his fragmentary plays. Apart from *Stheneboea*, a married woman unsuccessfully tries to seduce a virtuous young man both in *Hippolytus Veiled* (where Phaedra makes advances on her stepson, Hippolytus)⁷ and *Peleus* (where Acastus' wife makes an effort to seduce the young Peleus).⁸ Except for Acastus' wife, for whom the ancient evidence is slight, the seduction scheme did not end well for the other women involved: the Phaedra of the fragmentary drama probably commits suicide after the horrendous injury or death of the young hero (test. *iic.1 and *iic.2),⁹ whereas Stheneboea is killed by Bellerophon after her husband's second attempt on his life is revealed (test. iia.22–4, frr. 670 and 671). Therefore, this kind of *erôs* that is ethically and socially unacceptable, since it challenges the hierarchies and values within the *oikos* of the tragic universe (and within the real-life Athenian *polis*), often leads to destruction and death for the characters who experience it on the Euripidean stage.

However, extramarital yearnings or dalliances do not constitute the most extreme aberrant forms of sexual desire or activity one can find in Euripides' oeuvre. In this chapter I explore some forms of erotic passion or sexual intercourse that could be labelled 'pathological' – both from an ancient and a modern perspective – focusing on three fragmentary dramas whose plots revolve around relationships well beyond the bounds of the ordinary, even abnormal: (1) male desire and sexual intercourse between full siblings in *Aeolus*, (2) female desire towards, and sexual intercourse with, a bull in *Cretans*, and (3) female desire towards, and possibly intercourse with, a male statue in *Protesilaus*. My two inquiries here are whether vocabulary and imagery of sickness and pathology appear in these plays, and how Euripides and his characters comment on such sexual activities that reach the limits of, or even exceed, what his audience would have considered normal. The reason I have chosen to focus on his fragmentary oeuvre is that, though it has been well documented that (1) Euripides was *au fait* with

---

6 Phaedra's illicit passion is referred to as *nosos* in that play. Cf. e.g. 40, 176, 184, 203, 279, 292–3, 394, 462, 476, 478–9, 597, 698, 730, 1306 (with Cairns 2017: 250 and Kanellakis and Thumiger in this volume).
7 On Eur. *Hippolytus Veiled*, see Barrett 1964: 11–12, 13–15, 18–22, 26; Reckford 1974: 309–13; Collard/Cropp 2008a: 466–89. Due to a comment found in an ancient hypothesis, it is often assumed that the fragmentary play preceded the surviving *Hippolytus*, the so-called *Stephanephoros*. Doubts concerning this assumption have been expressed by Gibert 1997.
8 Unfaithful wives also feature in plays by Aeschylus (Clytaemnestra in *Ag.*) and Sophocles (in his fragmentary *Phaedra* and, perhaps, *Nauplius Sails in*). On the Sophoclean Phaedra, see Sommerstein 2020: 64–5.
9 With Collard/Cropp 2008a: 467–8.

contemporary medical thought and (2) *erôs* is often presented as a medical condition in his extant works,¹⁰ little attention has been paid so far to examples of pronounced pathological *erôs* and how they are portrayed in his fragments.

Falling in Love with One's Sister: *Erôs* and Disaster in *Aeolus*

Euripides' *Aeolus* (between 455 and 423 BCE) may have well been an 'erotic tragedy', as Evangelia Mimidou concludes in her commentary.¹¹ The story of Aeolus,¹² son of Hippotes and master of the winds, first appears in the *Odyssey*, where we hear about the idyllic life he leads with his family. Aeolus has six sons and six daughters whom he has married to each other and they all live happily together (Hom. *Od.* 10.1–12).¹³ In his distinctive fashion, Euripides has taken this family story lacking intrigue or pathos and turned it into an illegitimate love affair that leads to destruction and death.¹⁴ *P. Oxy.* 2457 (= test. ii) provides the plot, preserving an important part of the play's ancient Hypothesis. There we learn that in Euripides: (1) Aeolus' youngest son Macareus has fallen in love, and had intercourse, with one of his sisters (24–5: νεώτατος Μακαρεὺς μιᾶς τῶν ἀδε[λφῶν ἐ]ρασθεὶς διέφθειρεν); (2) during an *agôn*, he convinces his father to intermarry his children (27–8), without however revealing his own sexual misconduct, and the persuaded Aeolus allots his daughters to his sons by lot (28–9: συνκα[λεσά]μενος κλῆρον τοῦ γάμου); (3) the girl in question is, unfortunately, bestowed to another brother (31–3: τὴν γὰρ ὑπὸ τούτου ἐ[φθαρ]μένην ὁ κλῆρος πρὸς ἄλλου συμβίωσ[ιν ἐνυμ]φαγώ[γ]ει). We cannot be certain about the final scenes of this tragedy, since the papyrus breaks after line 34. Aeolus somehow finds out that the illicitly impregnated girl, Canace, has already given birth – perhaps line 34 refers to the cries of the baby that a nurse tries to conceal: τὸ μὲν γεννηθὲν ἡ τροφός – and sends her a sword, by which she is expected to commit

---

10 On Euripides' frequent use of medical language, cf. Ferrini 1978; Craik 2001; Kosak 2004; Cairns 2017, while on erotic desire as sickness in *Hippolytus*, see Cairns 2017 with n. 6.
11 Mimidou 2013: 173. Cf. Xanthaki-Karamanou/Mimidou 2014: 51–2.
12 There is more than one mythological figure with this name, hence the ensuing confusion; see Gantz 1993: 167–70; Magnani 2018.
13 On this episode, see Hom. *Od.* 23.314–7. A famous brother-sister incestuous couple that unproblematically figures in the Homeric epics is Zeus and Hera. For their famous sex-scene, see Hom. *Il.* 14.160–351.
14 See Jouan/van Looy 1998: 17; Xanthaki-Karamanou/Mimidou 2014: 51.

suicide. There is no direct evidence of her suicide in the fragments or in the Hypothesis. Yet in all versions of the myth Canace dies,[15] so it can be assumed that this was her fate in Euripides too. Macareus also possibly kills himself over her dead body,[16] as some later sources attest.[17] Last, it has been suggested that a *deus ex machina* (Athena? Apollo?) perhaps appears at the end, predicting that their baby will survive and prosper.[18]

With respect to the pathological symptoms of erotic love that this volume sets out to explore, Macareus is the one who experiences the effects of *erôs*.[19] However, apart from fr. 26 that is perhaps delivered by the female chorus and refers to the dual nature of *erôs* (τῇ δ' Ἀφροδίτῃ πόλλ' ἔνεστι ποικίλα· | τέρπει τε γὰρ μάλιστα καὶ λυπεῖ βροτούς· | τύχοιμι δ' αὐτῆς, ἡνίκ' ἐστὶν εὐμενής, 'Aphrodite is very fickle; she brings men the greatest delights and the greatest pains. I wish I may meet with her when she is kind!'), most fragments deal with the debate between father and son,[20] while there are no textual traces of any description of *erôs* as pathology regarding Macareus. It is thus very probable that the Euripidean *Aeolus* starts when the erotic relationship has already been consummated and the couple now deals with its consequences, especially the illicit late pregnancy and birth of the bastard child. Unfortunately, we are not given any specific information about the emotions that Canace experiences for her brother. In contrast to the Ovidian version in *Heroides*, where the young woman is going through the usual (literary) symptoms of erotic love (burning, lack of appetite and wasting away, difficulty sleeping, moaning),[21] we do not know whether her Euripidean counterpart united with him willingly or was forced to sleep with her brother.[22]

---

15 Cf. test. iiia, viib and ixb with Jouan/van Looy 1998: 21.
16 Thus Lloyd-Jones 1963: 444; Webster 1967: 159; Collard/Cropp 2008a: 14 (*pace* Jäkel 1979: 118).
17 See e.g. Sostratus *FGrH* 23 fr. 3; Hyg. *Fab.* 242.
18 Cf. Webster 1967: 159; Lloyd-Jones 1963: 444; Mülke 1996: 52; Jouan/van Looy 1998: 26; Collard/Cropp 2008a: 14.
19 Cf. *P. Oxy.* 2457, 24–5 (ἐρασθεὶς διέφθειρεν); Stob. 4.20.72 (ἐρασθεὶς ἐβιάσατο); Plut. *Parall. Min.* 28a (ἔρωτι ἔφθειρε); all these expressions constitute paraphrases, not direct quotations of the Euripidean text.
20 See Eur. *Aeolus* frr. 19–24.
21 See Ov. *Her.* 11.27–32. Casali 1998: 703 notes that these symptoms of lovesickness can also be symptoms of early pregnancy.
22 See the discrepancy between the verbs used to describe this union in n. 19; διαφθείρω may mean 'corrupt' or 'seduce' (e.g. Lys. 1.16), while βιάζομαι may well connote rape.

However, a discussion (or onstage representation) of physical sickness was certainly part of the plot as a means to conceal the late pregnancy and delivery of the baby, as we learn from *P. Oxy.* 2457 (26–7).[23]

What is particularly interesting is the possibility that the unmarried Canace may have been briefly envisaged as a bride in this play. *Aeolus*, in all likelihood, included a double reversal of fortune, similar to the one we witness, for instance, in Euripides' *Heracles Mainomenos*.[24] At the beginning of the drama, the two siblings find themselves in a very difficult position, since the birth of the incestuous child forebodes trouble and punishment. As we have seen above, the Euripidean Macareus then succeeds in convincing Aeolus to intermarry his children. Therefore, for a small period of stage time, Canace could have been projected in the play – and thought of by the audience – as a bride-to-be, as she is in Ovid's *Heroides* (61–2), when Macareus' encouraging words about a prospective wedding may allude to Aeolus' consent.[25] Maidens of marriageable status, being on the verge of marrying or having just married, are often presented as brides of death in Greek drama,[26] usually when a tragic turn of events is anticipated or realised: e.g. Andromeda, Antigone, Cassandra, Iphigenia, Creusa, Jason's bride, and Polyxena.[27] Indeed, the situation will be reversed for Canace as well; because of bad fortune, she will be allotted to another brother and thus the expected and desired marriage to Macareus, which would smoothly guarantee (among other things) the survival of the incestuous baby, is cancelled. Therefore, despite the hopes for a wedding, Canace will die unwedded and disgraced.

Another interesting aspect of this plot must have been the manner in which Canace commits suicide, i.e. with a sword.[28] Several tragic wives kill themselves in this fashion in Greek dramas.[29] So does Deianira, for example, upon realising

---

23 The delivery of the baby, Neoptolemus, by the unmarried daughter of the king Lycomedes, Deidameia, is also described as a grave sickness in Eur. *Scyrians* fr. 682.
24 Cf. Jäkel 1979: 113–4; Jouan/van Looy 1998: 25.
25 Thus Lloyd-Jones 1963: 443; Labate 1977: 584–5; Jäkel 1979: 112; Philippides 1996: 438–9.
26 See Rose 1925; Guépin 1968: 141; Foley 1982; Redfield 1982; Jenkins 1983; Armstrong/Ratchford 1985: 7–10; Seaford 1987; Rehm 1994.
27 See Eur. *Andromeda* fr. 122; Soph. *Ant.* 814–5, 876, 891, 917–8; Eur. *Tro.* 319, 354; *IT* 214–7, 364–71; *IA* 457–64; *Med.* 978–9; *Hec.* 416, 418. Cf. Persephone (or Kore) as the bride of Hades in the *Hymn Hom. Dem.* 79–80.
28 See above, pp. 68–9 and test. iiia, vi, viib, viiib, ixb.
29 Cf. Loraux 1987: 14–17.

that her fatal mistake will cost the life of her spouse, Heracles, in Sophocles' *Trachiniae* (813–91). Similarly, in a perhaps spurious passage of Euripides' *Medea*,[30] the nurse is afraid that Medea will commit suicide with a dagger (37–41). As we shall see below, Laodamia too possibly commits suicide with a blade in Euripides' *Protesilaus*.[31] Piercing the female torso with a sword usually connotes tragic pathos, uxorial dedication, and desperation, while it can call to mind the fact that these characters have been transformed to full women (and mothers, as regards Medea and Deianira) through their sexual relationships with their husbands.[32] In the case of Canace, this motion can remind us of the penetration she experienced during intercourse with her brother: a union, however, that was not only out of wedlock, but also with a quite unsuitable partner.

This leads me to a final point. Why is Canace's fate similar to these tragic wives-to-be, or wives, and so different from what we encounter in the Homeric vignette? Christoph Mülke has convincingly argued that the precise relationship of these siblings must have played a considerable role in the way Euripides chose to present it and also in the way his contemporary audience would have approached it.[33] In classical Athens, for instance, it was not infrequent for first cousins to intermarry in order to secure the continuation of the paternal fortune.[34] What might be surprising to modern readers is that even marriage between siblings was, under specific circumstances, socially and legally acceptable: half-siblings from the father's side, that is, ὁμοπάτριοι but not ὁμομήτριοι, were allowed to marry, as is suggested by the evidence found in the orators (e.g. Dem. 57.20) and later authors, such as Philo of Alexandria, Plutarch, and an ancient scholiast on Aristophanes' *Clouds*.[35] Of course, we should always be alert to the difference between the mythical world presented on stage and real life in contemporary Athens, a difference of which the ancient audience was aware. It seems, nonetheless, that Euripides intended to present this story of full siblings having illicit sexual

---

30 The entire passage is defended by Pratt 1943 and Seaford 1987: 122–3. Cf. the doubts over authenticity expressed by Müller 1951; Mastronarde 2002; Mossman 2011.
31 See below, p. 78.
32 There is sharp contrast between these wives and the Sophoclean Haemon who commits suicide with a sword (Soph. *Ant.* 1231–9), thus being the one who bleeds, while Antigone remains unpenetrated, even in death (with Cairns 2016: 106).
33 See Mülke 1996. Cf. Kannicht 1995: 28–9.
34 See Thompson 1967.
35 See Philo *On the Special Laws* 3.22–3; Plut. *Vit. Them.* 32.2; Schol. Ar. *Nub.* 1372d Holwerda (ἐπειδὴ παρὰ Ἀθηναίοις ἔξεστι γαμεῖν τὰς ἐκ πατέρων ἀδελφάς 'because it is possible for Athenians to marry their agnatic/paternal sisters', my translation) with Dover 1968 on Ar. *Nub.* 1372; Sommerstein 1982 on Ar. *Nub.* 1372.

relationships and trying to secure marriage as problematic, thus reflecting Athenian norms. It has been rightly suggested that Macareus uses deceit to convince Aeolus and his words reveal 'sophistic relativism',[36] and the sense of aversion is evident when Aristophanes in *Clouds* 1371–2 insists on the exact nature of their kinship: ὡς ἐκίνει ἀδελφός ... τὴν ὁμομητρίαν ἀδελφήν ('that a brother would screw his own sister from the *same* mother!').[37]

All in all, even though this couple's fate was possibly presented with some sympathy by the dramatist – Macareus is stricken by bad luck at the last minute, after having successfully convinced his father, while Canace, the innocent party, loses her life in a tragic way – this drama seems to indicate that an erotic relationship which *spectacularly* disrupts social norms and moves into the realm of what the audience would label as pathological tends to end disastrously on the Euripidean stage.

It's Not What You Think! Erotic Union between a Woman and a Bull in *Cretans*

Euripides' *Cretans* (between 455 and 428 BCE) dealt with an aspect of pathological human desire, one that led to sexual intercourse with an animal, in this case, a bull. Our knowledge of this lost drama was very limited until the beginning of the 20th century, thus scholarly reconstructions were necessarily based on evidence provided by various mythological or literary sources.[38] According to Apollodorus' summary of the myth in his *Library* (3.1.3–4), when the Cretan king Asterius died, Minos, son of Zeus and Europa, wanted to prove that he alone had the divine right to reign after his stepfather's death. So he boasted that the gods would materialise whatever he wished for. While sacrificing to Poseidon, he prayed for a bull to rise from the sea in order to sacrifice. The god sent a magnificent bull but Minos did not keep his promise and sacrificed another animal instead; this reckless action naturally provoked Poseidon's punishment, which took the form of inflicting desire for the bull upon the king's wife. This abnormal passion was not left unfulfilled. Pasiphae managed to have sex with the bull thanks to the aid of Daedalus, who built a hollow wooden cow, from inside which

---

36 See Xanthaki-Karamanou/Mimidou 2014: 50, 58, and *passim*.
37 My translation and emphasis.
38 Sources that provide details about this myth: Hes. fr. 145 (MW) = fr. 93 (Most); Bacchyl. *Od.* 17; Isoc. 10.27; Diod. Sic. 4.77.1–5; Apoll. *Bibl.* 3.1.3–4; Paus. 1.27.9–10; Hyg. *Fab.* 40.

the queen received the animal. As Apollodorus continues his narration, a monstrous half-man, half-bull was born, whom Minos confined in the famous Cretan labyrinth.

P. Berlin 13217 (= fr. 472e), published in 1907, shed important light on the plot of *Cretans* and on the episodes of the constituent myth.[39] We now know that *Cretans* included the birth of the Minotaur; the papyrus also confirms that the play revolved around the sexual union of the queen and the bull that led to this unnatural offspring, by preserving part of a dialogue between Minos and Pasiphae upon the discovery of the truth. This scene seems to belong approximately to the middle of the drama, possibly constituting 'the play's central episode'.[40] Moreover, as fr. 472b (= *P. Oxy.* 2461) indicates, Minos was not aware of that sexual union at the beginning of the play, and so he summoned the chorus of old priests of Idaean Zeus (fr. 472)[41] to explain to him the reasons behind the monstrous birth. As regards other details of the plot, it can be assumed that an onstage role was assigned to Daedalus and his son Icarus,[42] although it is difficult to determine exactly what form this took. Finally, a *deus ex machina* perhaps delivered the prologue (Poseidon? Aphrodite? both of them?),[43] while the same or another deity possibly made an appearance at the end of the tragedy,[44] plausibly determining Pasiphae's fate and informing the audience of the aftermath of Daedalus and Icarus' flight.

With regard to Pasiphae's bestial desire that Euripides brings to the centre of attention, it is important that, apart from Pasiphae, the bull imagery is intrinsically interwoven with the fate of this family. The perpetually desire-stricken Zeus had sexually united with Europe in the form of a bull, whence Minos was born. Moreover Phaedra, daughter of Minos and Pasiphae, alludes to her mother's *erôs*

---

39 See Schubart/Wilamowitz-Moellendorff 1907: 73–9.
40 Collard/Cropp 2008a: 530.
41 This fragment has generated much scholarly discussion because the priests refer to their religious practice by combining elements from different cults: 1) the worship of Idaean Zeus, 2) Dionysus-Zagreus, 3) the Mountain Mother, and 4) the cult of Orpheus. See Cantarella 1964: 63–9; Collard/Cropp/Lee 1995: 69–70; Cozzoli 2001: 83–93; Collard/Cropp 2008a: 539; Bernabé Pajares 2016; Tralau 2017.
42 On Daedalus, see fr. 472g (= Schol. Ar. *Ran.* 849); fr. 988; fr. 472e, 17–18. For Icarus' appearance, see Schmidt 1992; Jouan/van Looy 2000: 316–7; Simon 2004; Collard/Cropp 2008a: 531–2.
43 Aphrodite: Webster 1967: 87, 89; Collard/Cropp/Lee 1995: 54; Sabatakis 2007: 23, n. 17. **Poseidon:** Jouan/van Looy 2000: 310; Collard/Cropp 2008a: 530. **Both:** Cantarella 1964: 113. Schmid 1940: 411, on the other hand, argues that the prologue was delivered by Minos.
44 Cf. Kappelmacher 1909: 33; Croiset 1915: 233 (Zeus, the god worshipped by the Chorus?); Schmid 1940: 412; Webster 1967: 87, 91–2 (Helios or Poseidon?); Jouan/van Looy 2000: 314; Sabatakis 2007: 25; Collard/Cropp 2008a: 531.

towards the bull while trying to conceal her own illicit desire (Eur. *Hipp*. 337–8) and later on in the same drama a different bull, again sent by Poseidon, makes its appearance in the description of Hippolytus' fatal injury (1213–48), an appearance alluding, as Charles Segal argues, to the element of sexual attraction that the virginal hero has so arduously rejected.[45] Consequently, bovine imagery seems to be associated with an overwhelming and intractable passion throughout this family's history.

Of interest here is to see in what terms the Euripidean Pasiphae describes her own eccentric desire for, and sexual encounter with, this animal and how the other characters react to that description. The queen endeavours to present her case as inherently different from the normal experience of love, yet she refers to the usual metaphorical symptoms used to portray *erôs* in Greek literature (NB: the same symptomatology is present in the description of Phaedra's desire in *Hippolytus*).[46] Specifically, Pasiphae treats her passion and the congress itself as a physical pain, a sting, a blow, and a disease six times, thus trying to stress its pathological and aberrant character: (1) 10: **ἀλγῶ** 'I suffer'; (2) 12: **ἐδήχθην** θυμὸν **αἰσχίστῃ νόσῳ**; 'I had my heart bitten by a most shaming affliction?'; (3) 20: τί δῆτα **τῇ[δ**' ἐμαι]νόμην **νόσῳ**; 'Why then was I [maddened] by this affliction?'; (4) 26: ἐς δ' ἔμ' ἔσκηψ[εν **νόσον** 'but launched [the affliction] upon me'; (5) 30: **πληγὴν** δαίμονος θεήλατον 'the god's stroke launched by heaven'; and (6) 35: ἐκ σοῦ **νοσοῦμεν** 'you are the cause of my affliction'. Another point that she makes is that this abnormal union cannot even be considered proper adultery, as it did not involve a young and desirable man (6, 16) – a relationship that she would also disapprove of (8). Again, it should be stressed that Pasiphae uses standard language of the pathology of the erotic vision,[47] though her point remains that her desire was utterly unnatural and unique. That is, she argues that she could not possibly be attracted to the bull by looking at him, as could have happened if the bull were a man. She thus uses a description that refers to the normal ways that *erôs* is usually inspired and enters someone's heart, i.e. by looking at his beautiful eyes, red cheeks, and shiny beard (13–16), yet she does so in order to negate the fact that she could experience desire due to the rather strange identity of her object of desire. Last, her accusations are repeatedly directed towards Minos (22–26, 28, 34–5, 41) and not against the god in charge (Poseidon), as Helen does, for

---

45 See Segal 1965: 145. On the bull as a sex symbol in this myth and in Eur. *Bacch*., see Sabatakakis 2007: 15, n. 4, while on the word ταῦρος and its use for the male genitals, see LSJ ταῦρος III. On Hippolytus' problematic attitude towards sex, see Valtadorou 2018.
46 See Cairns 2017: 248–54.
47 On the erotic vision in Greek literature, see Cairns 2011.

instance, when blaming Aphrodite for her relationship with Paris (Eur. *Tro.* 929–31).⁴⁸ Pasiphae certainly underlines the role played by the god in her own affliction (21–6), yet does not put the blame on Poseidon,⁴⁹ but on her husband who did not keep his oath to sacrifice the bull (23–4).

The fragmentary nature of Pasiphae's speech and the loss of Minos' preceding input create difficulties in interpretation. On a wider scale, it is risky to evaluate, based on Pasiphae's words alone,⁵⁰ how her character would have been portrayed throughout the play, especially since we lack knowledge of her final fate:⁵¹ did Pasiphae die from being buried alive in compliance with Minos' order, or was she saved by the intervention of a god?

All the same, there are some indications that Minos was presented as mistaken in condemning Pasiphae so quickly, and his manner might recall Theseus' swift condemnation of his son in the surviving *Hippolytus* (935–1088) or Creon's similar stubborn unwillingness to listen to his son Haemon in Sophocles' *Antigone* (635–765). In particular, we saw in Apollodorus' account that Minos is to blame for his wife's passion according to the standard narrative of the myth, and some points in the Euripidean text seem to confirm its compliance with that pattern. First, fr. 472e discussed above probably constitutes part of an *agôn* between Minos and Pasiphae: he speaks first, she voices her countercharge, and as Guido Paduano reminds us,⁵² the second position is the one usually reserved for the stronger argument in a tragedy.⁵³ In addition, the chorus do not seem to align themselves with Minos' general behaviour, but rather side with Pasiphae.⁵⁴ First, during the debate preserved by fr. 472e, the old priests advise the king thrice to act with prudence (2–3, 42–3, 50–1), before and after he delivers his harsh verdict (45–9, 52); provided that the speculative reading is correct, the chorus in this scene also supports Pasiphae's claim that her desire has been sent from the gods (42): πολλοῖσι δῆλον [ὡς θεήλατον] κακὸν τόδ' ἐστίν ('It is clear to many that this trouble [was launched from heaven]'), as she herself had claimed earlier (30). Second, in some damaged lyric lines sung by the chorus (fr. 472b) there are two points where the reconstructed text, if correct, reveals their agreement with Pasiphae's claim that her passion was a nemesis inflicted by the gods: (1) νέμ?]

---

48 *Pace* Dolfi 1984 and Holmes 2008: 244, n. 41, who maintain that these two speeches are analogous to each other.
49 Also stressed by Croiset 1915: 223–4.
50 Similarly Collard/Cropp/Lee 1995: 57.
51 Thus Jouan/van Looy 2000: 314.
52 See Paduano 2005: 135–6. For similar claims by other scholars, see Lloyd 1992: 17, n. 36.
53 *Pace* Lloyd 1992: 17.
54 Cf. Croiset 1915: 231; Rivier 1975: 45–6; Paduano 2005: 135.

εσις ὅτ᾽ ἐπιπνεῖ 'when [retribution?] blasts', fr. 2 col. 1, 1 and (2) θεοῖσι προσβολὴν 'with the gods' ... onslaught', fr. 1, 25.

In conclusion, *Cretans* is a tragedy that explored a sexual encounter that well exceeds both what its ancient audience and its modern readers would consider normal. As we have seen above, however, Euripides includes in his play the queen's pointed defence, with which the chorus of old priests seems to agree to a considerable degree; both she and the priests recognise divine involvement in her experience of *erôs*. It could therefore be argued that her passion, presented as godsent, was comparable to proverbial god-directed sufferings of other tragic characters, such as that of the Sophoclean Ajax and the Euripidean Heracles.[55] If this argument is correct, it seems likely that Euripides aligned himself with the chorus' sympathy towards Pasiphae, by (1) giving her the opportunity to draw the audience's attention to Minos' breach of a promise towards a god, and to the subsequent godsent nature of her passion, and (2) by substantiating her accusations via Minos' onstage presentation as impulsive and irascible.

Laodamia's Unwavering Love for her Husband: Female Desire and the Statue in *Protesilaus*

Euripides' *Protesilaus* (between 455 and 425 BCE) dealt with the power of marital love and its unique potential to transcend death. As is the case with *Aeolus*, Euripides seems to take a passing reference from the Homeric epics and expand it into a full drama. In particular, the first mention of Protesilaus is found in the *Iliad* (2.698–702), where the ancient audience heard of him being the first Greek to die in the Trojan War and of the grieving wife he left back home:

> τῶν αὖ Πρωτεσίλαος ἀρήϊος ἡγεμόνευεν
> ζωὸς ἐών· τότε δ᾽ ἤδη ἔχεν κάτα γαῖα μέλαινα,
> τοῦ δὲ καὶ ἀμφιδρυφὴς ἄλοχος Φυλάκηι ἐλέλειπτο
> καὶ δόμος ἡμιτελής· τὸν δ᾽ ἔκτανε Δάρδανος ἀνήρ
> νηὸς ἀποθρώισκοντα πολὺ πρώτιστον Ἀχαιῶν

'Of these in turn warlike Protesilaus was leader, while he was still alive; but by that time the black earth already held him fast. His wife, her cheeks torn in wailing, was left in Phylace

---

55 Thus Paduano 2005: 139.

and his house but half completed, and him a Dardanian warrior killed as he leapt from his ship by far the first of the Achaeans'

[transl. Murray, rev. Wyatt.]

The information that Protesilaus was the first Achaean to perish also appears in the *Cypria*,[56] where the Trojan prince Hector is named as his killer.[57] His death also seems to be linked in the mythological and poetic tradition to an oracle (that is, the first Greek to step onto Trojan soil will be the first to die).[58]

Protesilaus is even more fragmentary than *Cretans*, so care is needed in interpreting its fragments and the information provided by the indirect tradition of ancient scholars and poets. A scholium on Aelius Aristides 3.365 (= test. ii) refers to this play, thus offering valuable evidence: Protesilaus (1) was married for only one day when he went to Troy (γαμήσας καὶ μίαν ἡμέραν μόνην συγγενόμενος), (2) was the first to disembark and first to die (πρῶτος ἐπιβὰς τῆς Τροίας ἐτελεύτησεν), and (3) was granted by the gods of the underworld his wish to return to life and consort with his wife for a single day (συνεγένετο τῇ γυναικὶ ἑαυτοῦ).[59] Given that no earlier poet mentions this love-stricken hero's brief resurrection, it is probable that Euripides was the first to present Protesilaus' return to life, which signified his great love for his spouse.

Other ancient writers offer different details of this story, some of which certainly reflect the Euripidean drama. For instance, several sources, including Ovid, Apollodorus, Eustathius and Tzetzes, mention a statue that the (equally) love- and grief-stricken Laodamia builds in the shape of her husband.[60] This part of the narrative is confirmed to derive from Euripides by Ps.-Dio Chrysostom, who preserves a verse of the play (fr. 655): οὐκ ἂν προδοίην καίπερ ἄψυχον φίλον, 'I shall not forsake a loved one, even though he is lifeless'. By talking about an ἀνδριάς ('statue') right before he quotes this line, the ancient scholiast makes clear that fr. 655 refers to an effigy that a dramatic character (almost certainly, Laodamia) is reluctant to abandon – a statue that, according to some versions, receives

---

56 See arg. 10; fr. 22 West. In fr. 22 (West) Protesilaus' wife is called Polydora, daughter of Meleager.
57 For Hector as Protesilaus' killer, cf. Soph. *Poimenes* fr. 497; Apollod. *Epit.* 3.30. On the alternative versions that present other heroes as Protesilaus' slayers, see Mayer 1885: 103.
58 This is something that his name also alludes to: he is the first (πρῶτος) of the people (λαός). See the primary sources assembled by Ruiz de Elvira 1991: 139–43.
59 The scholium on Luc. 26.1. is quite similar to this one.
60 Ov. *Rem. am.* 723–4; Stat. *Silv.* 2.7.124–35; Apollod. *Epit.* 3.30; Eust. *Il.* 2.700–2, p. 325; Tzetz. *Chil.* 2.52.772–3.

(pretended?) ceremonial rites from her.⁶¹ Most scholars maintain that this fragment probably comes from an exchange between Laodamia and her distressed father Acastus,⁶² who disagrees with her extreme attachment to the effigy and possibly urges her to remarry.⁶³ I am inclined to believe that in the Euripidean version the construction of the statue and any debate over it must have preceded Protesilaus' brief return to earth (in contrast to what we find in Hyginus' *Fabula* 104).⁶⁴ In this way, the importance attached to the statue by Laodamia at the beginning of the play vividly underscores her uxorial fondness and dedication, a dedication that, as Louis Séchan argues,⁶⁵ is mirrored and scenically answered by the supernatural arrival of her equally devoted and love-stricken husband.

Another piece of information that is attested by later authors (e.g. Apollodorus, Hyginus, and Eustathius) but must be of Euripidean origin is Hermes' onstage appearance as Protesilaus' divine escort, as fr. 646a, quoted by Photius, proves: ἕπου δὲ μοῦνον ἀμπρεύοντί μοι, 'just follow me as I guide you'. Laodamia's death, also present in later versions, must have been part of Euripides' drama as well. I agree with scholars who maintain that her death, following Protesilaus' exchange with her father (fr. 647), the hero's return back to Hades, and her onstage deliberation on how to kill herself (fr. 656), probably took the form of committing suicide with the sword;⁶⁶ as noted above with reference to *Aeolus*, this sort of death is often perceived as a suitable way for a tragic wife to take her own life when her marriage goes wrong.⁶⁷ Moreover, as regards the beginning of *Protesilaus*, it has been suggested that Aphrodite delivers the prologue;⁶⁸ according to this reading which is based on the information provided by Eustathius, Aphrodite has been offended by the couple (who presumably neglected to bestow upon her the appropriate wedding offerings) and either punished Laodamia by

---

61 See Hyg. *Fab.* 104. We know that Protesilaus was venerated both in Thrace and his homeland, Phylace. On the various cults dedicated to him and his tomb, cf. Pind. *Isthm*. 1.58–9; Hdt. 9.116; Strabo 13.1.31. See Mayer 1885: 123–5; Herzog-Hauser 1937: 471–2, 474–5; Séchan 1953: 4–5; Jouan 1966: 330–1; Burkert 1983: 244–7; Jouan/van Looy 2000: 571–2.
62 See Herzog-Hauser 1937: 477; Séchan 1953: 10; Jouan/van Looy 2000: 579, 587; Collard/Cropp 2008b: 107–8.
63 See Mayer 1885: 107; Jouan 1966: 323; Oranje 1980: 171; Jouan/van Looy 2000: 578.
64 Thus Mayer 1885: 116; Séchan 1953; Jouan/van Looy 2000: 578–9; Collard/Cropp 2008b: 107 (*pace* Schmid 1940: 353; Webster 1967: 97; Lyne 1998: 202).
65 Séchan 1953: 15.
66 Thus Mayer 1885: 111–4, 121; Jouan 1966: 327; Jouan/van Looy 2000: 583; Collard/Cropp 2008b: 108.
67 See above, pp. 70–1.
68 See Séchan 1953: 12–13; Jouan 1966: 319; Jouan/van Looy 2000: 576 (with reference to earlier scholarship in n. 30).

causing her to feel unending desire for her deceased husband, or Protesilaus by making his love for his wife persist even after death. Unfortunately, no fragment contains any information that implies Aphrodite's participation in the play, which thus only remains a plausible speculation.

Some scholars have argued that, for a short period of dramatic time during which the separated couple happily reunites, their marriage is somehow renewed onstage,[69] perhaps through nuptial songs or celebratory exclamations. This would be comparable to the symbolic marriage-renewal in Euripides' *Helen* between Menelaus and his recently found innocent wife (639–41, 722–5). A sexual union could also perhaps be implied as taking place in *Protesilaus*,[70] given the spouses' mutual feelings and the probability that Protesilaus comes back to life as a virile strong man,[71] driven by his love and desire (cf. the ambiguous verb συγγίγνομαι employed in the above-discussed scholium that often denotes sexual intercourse and ἐράω which is, time and again, used by later authors in order to stress the erotic component of his marital love).[72] It is crucial to repeat that there is no concrete evidence to support these hypotheses, yet we can perhaps entertain the idea of Euripides presenting a marriage-gone-bad, symbolically renewed with the accompaniment of nuptial songs and the implied union of the couple, and tragically annulled once again by the final departure of the husband. (As is well studied, references to wedding rituals occur repeatedly in Greek dramas when things end up taking a turn for the worse and the characters involved die tragically.)[73] Besides, Laodamia herself, the dedicated bride of a dead man, could have well been presented as a 'bride of Hades',[74] both at the beginning and the end of the play.

So how could Laodamia's uxorial love fit into what I call 'pathological' in this chapter, especially since there is no indication in the fragments that *erôs* was presented as a disease in her case? It may be true that in fr. 653, 4 a speaker (Acastus?) speaks of a woman's bed that should be common to all men: κοινὸν γὰρ] εἶναι χρῆν γυναι[κεῖον λέχος. Yet when we take the fragment as a whole, we understand that this verse could constitute a gnomic negative assessment about women and their supposedly insignificant role in marriage, not a comment on

---

69 See Mayer 1885: 117; Jouan 1966: 324; Jouan/van Looy 2000: 579–80.
70 Thus Ruiz de Elvira 1991: 151–2.
71 As he was when he was a bridegroom: οἷος ἦν ἐκ τοῦ παστοῦ, Luc. *Dial. mort.* 28.3. Cf. Séchan 1953: 16; Collard/Cropp 2008b: 108.
72 See LSJ συγγίγνομαι II.3. Cf. Luc. *Dial. mort.* 28.1–2; Philostr. *Her.* 662.
73 For the intertwinement of marriage- and death-rituals in Greek tragedy, see, above all, the excellent study by Seaford 1987.
74 Cf. Mayer 1885: 117; Herzog-Hauser 1937: 476.

supposed sexual misconduct on Laodamia's part (although this cannot be wholly excluded).⁷⁵ The reason why I have chosen to include this play in my discussion of pathological desire is because some sources use ambiguous language in their description of Laodamia's treatment of the statue before Protesilaus' arrival: αἱρούμενη τὴν πρὸς τὸν τεθνεῶτα **συνουσίαν** 'choosing the company of the dead man', ἀνειδωλοποιουμένης ... τὸν ἄνδρα καὶ **συνεῖναι** δοκούσης αὐτῷ 'making an effigy ... in the shape of her husband and thinking that she would consort with him' (Eustathius), τούτῳ **προσωμίλει** 'she would consort with him' (Apollodorus), **συνεκοίταζεν** αὐτῇ ... τῷ πόθῳ τοῦ συζύγου 'she was sleeping with this form ... because of her desire for her husband' (Tzetzes).⁷⁶ Depending on the context, the words in bold could have a general meaning, e.g. 'being together', 'to consort', 'to spend time with', 'to lie with', but often connote sexual intercourse, especially when applied to the relations between men and women.⁷⁷

No ancient source provides us with *direct* evidence that any sort of sexual activity took place between this grieving widow and the effigy, as happens with other cases where some sort of sexual intercourse with, or desire for, a statue is reported in plain terms.⁷⁸ It seems probable, however, that Euripides may have used strong *eroticised language* in order to describe Laodamia's attachment to this man-sized statue,⁷⁹ especially given that this is what he does in his surviving *Alcestis* for the statue of the eponymous dead heroine (348–54).⁸⁰ Laodamia's desire may well have been expressed towards the statue, as an indication of her strong passion for what that statue represents, i.e. her untimely deceased husband. Therefore, this motif could have been used to underline her uxorial desire and devotion, rather than connote pathology *per se*. That Laodamia caresses, hugs, and kisses this statue, overwhelmed by her desire for Protesilaus, is not of course what a Greek father would expect and want, and could even be perceived as problematic from a social point of view. As Helene Foley notes,⁸¹ this attitude

---

75 In Hyg. *Fab.* 104, for instance, a servant mistakes the statue for a lover. We do not know whether such a scene was part of Euripides' play or not.
76 My translations.
77 See, for example, LSJ σύνειμι II.2; LSJ συνουσία I.4; LSJ προσομιλέω I.2.
78 On the case of a man who ejaculated on the statue of Aphrodite of Knidos, see Luc. *Am.* 15–16; Val. Max. 8.11.4; Plin. *HN* 36.4.21; Clem. Al. *Protr.* 4.57.3; Luc. *Im.* 4.; Philostr. *V A* 6.40. Cf. Pygmalion, who falls in love with his own work of art: Clem. Al. *Protr.* 4.57.3; Ov. *Met.* 10.243–97.
79 References to statue imagery are frequent in tragedy, esp. when it comes to lovers and their loved ones. See e.g. Aesch. *Ag.* 416–9; Eur. *Andromeda* fr. 125; Men. *Dys.* 677. Cf. the eroticised language used for the statue of Peace in Ar. *Pax* 535–8, 582–5.
80 I intend to thoroughly discuss statue imagery in Eur. *Alc.* elsewhere.
81 Foley 2020: 76.

would not correspond to the social (Athenian) expectations concerning widows, given that women of marriageable status were often expected to remarry after the death of their spouse.[82]

All in all, Euripides must have intended to make *Protesilaus* a pronounced drama about mutual *erôs*, marital love, and devotion that continues even after the advent of death. As we have seen above, both spouses (almost certainly) feel *erôs* for each other. Yet Laodamia's behaviour goes beyond what the social norms would dictate about a young *nymphê* who has not yet become a full woman through the birth of her first child. Nonetheless, it is possible that her out-of-the-ordinary devotion to her husband, similar to Evadne's or Alcestis', was not overall negatively presented by Euripides, as fr. 657 suggests: ὅστις δὲ πάσας συντιθεὶς ψέγει λόγῳ | γυναῖκας ἑξῆς, σκαιός ἐστι κοὐ σοφός· | πολλῶν γὰρ οὐσῶν τὴν μὲν εὑρήσεις κακήν, | τὴν δ' ὥσπερ ἥδε λῆμ' ἔχουσαν εὐγενές ('Anyone who puts all women together and blames them indiscriminately is foolish and not wise. There are many of them, and you will find one bad while another is of noble character, as this one is/was'). We do not know with certainty who expressed this opinion (perhaps a slave or a messenger?) or under what circumstances (before or after her suicide?), yet it is clear that unwavering dedication to a lawfully married spouse, even expressed in extreme ways, may be regarded as highly commendable in the Euripidean universe.

Conclusion

The study of fragmentary dramatic material (sadly) involves much scholarly speculation and, therefore, any conclusions must be drawn carefully and cautiously; only the discovery of new papyrological material could prove or disprove some of the suggestions made above. Having said this, I would tentatively argue that an interesting and complex picture emerges when we examine cases of erotic desire which border on the pathological in the fragmentary Euripidean oeuvre. The cases I have explored above are quite dissimilar to each other. Laodamia's extraordinary and ideologically laden dedication to a lawful, prematurely deceased husband and her expression of desire towards his effigy is different from Macareus' illicit and incestuous passion and seduction, or rape, of his own sister.

---

[82] On remarriage in classical Athens, esp. regarding widows, see Thompson 1972; Hunter 1989. For evidence in the orators, see Antiph. 1; Lys. 32; Hyp. *Lyc.* 5; Dem. 27.5; 40.6–7; 45.28; Isae. 7.5–7; 9.27.

Moreover, in two (*Aeolus*, *Protesilaus*) of the three plays the situation almost certainly ends with the death of the dramatic characters involved; Canace and Macareus, Protesilaus and Laodamia do not get a happy ending on stage. Pasiphae's fate, on the other hand, is more uncertain, since it is possible that she was saved by a *deus ex machina* at the very last minute (could this perhaps vividly illustrate her passionately argued innocence?). Yet, as I have argued, Euripides seems to have offered his characters the opportunity to explain their actions, emotions, or motivations, thus preferring to present an ambiguous picture to his audience, even when the desire in question exceeds what his contemporary spectators would have considered normal and socially appropriate, whether this be erotic passion for a full sibling, a deceased husband, or an animal.

Fig. 4: Gustave Moreau, *Pasiphaé*, 1880. Oil on canvas 195x91cm. Paris: Musée National Gustave-Moreau.

Thomas K. Hubbard
Pathological Heterosexuality and Other Male Anxieties

Abstract: Women's esteem mattered little to most Greek men and they regarded as effeminate any man whose heterosexual desires put him in a position of dependency or passionate devotion to women, a phenomenon that may be called 'pathological heterosexuality.' While heterosexual desire had a proper place and appropriate forms in Classical Athens, excessive attention to women was seen as blameworthy and un-masculine incontinence. Greek anxieties in this regard pertained to at least five issues: (1) being overly influenced in one's actions by a wife or concubine, (2) allowing oneself to be manipulated by a courtesan, especially if it involved waste of resources, (3) rape, (4) seduction of an unmarried girl, and worst of all, (5) adultery with an already married woman. Although pederasty became a ground of suspicion against elite opponents in late 5th and 4th century democratic discourse in Athens, none of these five manifestations of sexual excess were particularly pertinent to that practice. This chapter examines each of these five pathologies of heterosexual desire in detail, first from the symbolic perspective of Greek myth, and then with evidence from the era of recorded history, particularly as yielded by the textual genres of Greek oratory and comedy.

As a teacher of ancient gender and sexuality, one faces the challenge of explaining to young students the wide gulf between Greek notions and modern social constructions of what is masculine. One of the most fundamental divergences manifests itself in how modern heterosexual men in the West define their masculine prowess and self-worth primarily in terms of success with the opposite sex, whether that success is quantified through the seducer's notches on his bedpost or by a socially ambitious family man's public display of an exceptionally accomplished or beautiful trophy-wife. Recently, the winners in this arena of masculine competition have been belatedly called to account for their predatory and unconscionable behaviour, as we learn from the public disgrace of once powerful American media figures like Harvey Weinstein and Bill Cosby. The losers have taken to calling themselves 'incels' (short for 'involuntary celibates') and have responded to their plight with heinous acts of violence, whether in the form of individual murder and abuse of women who rejected them or random slaughter of crowds, as illustrated in April 2018 by a 25-year-old Toronto man who used a van to plow down pedestrians, killing ten and wounding another thirteen. Alek Minassian

https://doi.org/10.1515/9783110747942-005

made it clear that he viewed his act as one of 'incel rebellion' against hostile women, and invoked the memory of an affluent but troubled 22-year-old California student named Elliot Rodger, who killed six and wounded fourteen because he was traumatised over still being a virgin and resented other men's success with the attractive girls who avoided him.[1] This motivation also appears to have been an under-reported subtext in the wave of high school shootings that have recently plagued the US.[2] This ingrained sense of heterosexual entitlement and its resulting spasms of violence have engendered the concept of 'toxic masculinity', which has now become an unfortunate staple of gender studies courses at American universities.

Classical scholars have tended to appropriate this concept in their interpretation of ancient men, under the rubric of what they call 'Mediterranean masculinity', influenced by anthropologists and the *Annales* school of historiography in France, with its insistent focus on the concepts of honour and shame as essential motivations for all male behaviour.[3] While it may describe a system of values held by some Greek males in some cities of a certain era (even as it may be held by some, but not most, Southern European, Muslim, or Latin American males today), this generalisation is far too reductive and schematic to provide an adequate global understanding of all, or even most, Greek men in the totality of their social roles. I would argue that what is most interesting in historical societies, especially as heterogeneous a cultural space as classical Greece, is not the fact of male dominance, but precisely its gaps, discontinuities, and fragility: that is, those points where masculine performance diverges the most from our stereotypical expectations are the most useful for helping us imagine alternative formulations of masculinity even within contemporary cultures. In this sense, the Greeks can become a useful tool to think with.

My argument is that the Greeks are fundamentally different from the other cultures of antiquity in that, for most of their history, they set rather little value on women or on procreating a large number of children. Greek men married much later in life than most ancient Mediterranean peoples, more commonly sought non-procreative sexual alternatives, and limited childbirths to safeguard against the ever precarious carrying capacity of their unreliable natural environment.[4]

---

1 Beauchamp 2018.
2 See Rosen 2018.
3 For more on this view, see the references in Hubbard 2011: 189–90. For a critique on anthropological grounds, see de Pina-Cabral 1989.
4 Sallares 1991, demonstrates the plasticity of population growth in age-class societies like that of ancient Greece, where normative age of male marriage can be subject to variation in response to state policy.

The truly consequential social relationships for them were those with other men. Most ancient Greek males would have found our modern barometer of masculine success or failure in terms of female conquests utterly incomprehensible. Women's esteem mattered little to most Greek men, and they regarded as un-masculine and effeminate any man whose heterosexual desires put him in a position of dependency or excessively passionate devotion to women, a phenomenon that I will call 'pathological heterosexuality'.

Heterosexual desire had a proper place and appropriate forms. At least in the classical period, wives were seldom chosen based on beauty or talent, but a man's social relationship to the girl's father, and they were most often married in their mid-teenage years.[5] *Pornai* were a legitimate safety-valve for younger unmarried men. As solemn a lawgiver as Solon is said to have provided for low-cost state brothels,[6] and the sexually continent Socrates of Xenophon's *Memorabilia* (2.2.4) praised their use. Slave girls were available, even metic women as concubines, although a husband's attention to them could provoke domestic discord with his wife.[7]

However, excessive attention to women was seen as blameworthy and unmasculine incontinence. Greek anxieties in this regard pertained to at least five issues: (1) being overly influenced in one's actions by a wife or concubine, (2) allowing oneself to be manipulated by a courtesan, especially if it involved waste of resources, (3) rape, (4) seduction of an unmarried girl, and worst of all, (5) adultery with an already married woman. Although I have elsewhere argued that pederasty became a ground of suspicion against elite opponents in late 5th and 4th century democratic discourse in Athens,[8] none of these five manifestations of sexual excess were particularly pertinent to that practice.

Let us begin our examination of pathological heterosexuality by quickly surveying the evidence of Greek myth, which always provided the Greeks a useful tool to think with. Aeschylus' Agamemnon (*Ag.* 895–950) came to destruction by allowing himself to be coaxed by a manipulative wife to tread luxurious carpets

---

5 Flacelière 1965: 56–9; Lacey 1968: 105–8; Pomeroy 1994: 268–9. Ischomachus' wife was 14 when she married (Xen. *Oec.* 7.5); Hesiod (*Op.* 696–8) recommends 16 as the best age for a wife. Ingalls 2001 reviews previous studies and argues that early marriage of girls was more common among the elite classes (where substantial dowries were involved), but girls of the lower classes were often married in their late teens.
6 Philem. fr. 3 K-A; Nicander of Colophon 271/2F9 *FGrH* (= F125 Ruschenbusch). Whether Solon actually established such brothels in the archaic period is not as important as that he could be credibly believed to have done so. See Halperin 1990: 100–1; Frost 2002.
7 Euphiletus in Lys. 1.12 says his wife accused him of such attentions to the serving girl.
8 Hubbard 1998 and 2015.

he initially detested as oriental extravagance.⁹ Theseus killed his virtuous son by too readily believing his wife's false claims of rape (Euripides' *Hippolytus*). Heracles' subjugation to Omphale represents the ultimate effeminisation of a hero.¹⁰ Heracles' later extra-marital desire to appropriate Iole, who had previously been denied him in legitimate marriage, led to his tortured death at the hands of his subsequent wife (Sophocles' *Trachiniae*). The *Odyssey* is of course centred upon themes of self-destructive male desire outside marriage, whether in the suitors' collective obsession with Penelope, lonely sailors' succumbing to the sweet allure of the Sirens, Odysseus' men making pigs of themselves by too ready acceptance of Circe's hospitality, or Ares' embarrassment when caught *in flagrante* by Aphrodite's husband. Odysseus recuperates his masculinity and humanity only by escaping the extra-marital wiles of Calypso and returning to his proper wife. Mortal men who don't escape the clutches of a dominant goddess, such as Anchises, Tithonus, Endymion, and Adonis, always wind up enervated by the relationship.

Rape is of course a common *topos* in Greek myth, and as long as it is committed by a male god, there is no negative sanction. But it is a prerogative of only the gods. Mortals who try it always come to a bad end, whether Nessus, drunken centaurs attending weddings, Ajax son of Oïleus at the altar of Athena, Peirithous coming to Hades to rape Persephone, or Ixion coming to Olympus and raping a cloud he thought was Hera, thereby spawning the race of incontinent centaurs and earning himself eternal punishment on a spinning wheel in Hades (Pind. *Pyth*. 2.21–48). Even the suspicion of rape caused Theseus to disown and curse his own son. Orion's involvement with the daughter of King Oenopion of Chios appears to be a case of seduction rather than rape, but it earns him blinding by the offended girl's father.¹¹

---

9 For a discussion of the weakness of character evident in Agamemnon's dealings with his wife in this scene, see Simpson 1971. By bringing a Trojan concubine back home with him, Agamemnon does indeed assimilate himself to the polygamous Priam, whose city was destroyed due to excessive female attachments.

10 Although Sophocles (*Trach*. 248–78) mentions Heracles' year of slavery to Omphale, his effeminisation by exchange of clothing with Omphale is likely the product of comic treatments, such as Ion of Chios' satyr play *Omphale*. Plutarch (*Per*. 24.9) says that comedies in Pericles' time characterised his relationship with Aspasia as like Heracles' with Omphale. The first certain artistic evidence of an effeminised Heracles with a spindle while Omphale holds his club is a fourth-century Lucanian vase (Paris K545), likely illustrating a scene from Attic drama.

11 The part of the story about Oenopion and Orion's blinding is common among the standard mythographers (Apollod. *Bibl*. 1.4.3; Hyg. *Poet. astr*. 2.34.1–2; Parth. *Amat. narr*. 20; Serv. *ad Aen*. 10.763), with minor additions or variations. The story may well go back to Hes. fr. 148a MW. That Sophocles wrote a *Cedalion*, possibly satyric, also suggests that this story was well-established

Thyestes' adultery with his brother's wife leads to generations of family conflict, and is famously recapitulated in his son Aegisthus' adultery with the wife of Atreus' son, Agamemnon. Aegisthus is consistently portrayed as an unsavoury character who attains power through a woman: in his brief and inconsequential appearance at the end of Aeschylus' *Agamemnon*, the chorus calls him a 'woman' for staying at home with a woman rather than serving in the army (1625–7).

Of course, the most odious and destructive male adulterer in all of Greek mythology is Paris, a man of such baneful fate that his birth gave nightmares to Hecuba, and Cassandra called for him to be destroyed as an infant (Eur. *Andr*. 293–300). Although the full story of the Judgment of Paris appears in the *Cypria*, the *Iliad* acknowledges Paris as Aphrodite's favourite, saying that her reward to him was grievous lust (24.28–30). In Book 3.39–45, Hector calls him *gynaimanês* ('woman-crazy') and contrasts his beautiful appearance with his uselessness in combat, possessing neither *biê* nor *alkê*, neither physical strength nor valour; Aphrodite notoriously sweeps him off the battlefield to inhabit Helen's bedchamber instead. Attic red-figure vase painting always renders Paris as a beautiful youth, and Cratinus' comedy *Dionysalexandros* says Aphrodite bribed him with the gift not of Helen, but of being both handsome and desirable to women (*P. Oxy.* 663.17–18: κάλλιστόν τε καὶ ἐπέραστον), in other words the powers of a master seducer. All manner of discreditable legends accumulate around the figure of Paris: Parthenius (*Amat. narr.* 34) attributes to the fifth-century historian Hellanicus (4F29 *FGrH*) the story that Paris killed Korythos, his son by Oenone, because the boy was even more beautiful than he was and Helen felt pedophilic desire for him. The scholia to Lycophron (134) relate that he and Deiphobus were rival lovers of Antenor's son Antheus, whom Paris ultimately killed. Dictys of Crete (1.5) says he murdered the King of Sidon, who welcomed him as a host even as Menelaus had. Paris combines all of the worst traits Greek morality imputed to adulterous males: personal attractiveness and charm, combined with excessive libido, violation of hospitality, treacherous envy, and utter indifference to the social instability caused by his actions (i.e. an ideal 'metrosexual' in modern terms).

Let us now turn to the historical record of pathological heterosexuality, where the genres of comedy and forensic oratory are especially useful. In sequence, I would like to discuss our evidence for each of the five types of heterosexual excess I identified at the outset of my paper. (1) Being excessively subject

---

by the classical period. As Fontenrose 1981: 9 notes, Servius (*ad Aen.* 10.763) preserves a version of the story in which a group of satyrs deliver a drunken Orion to Oenopion to punish. This must have come from a satyr play, whether Sophocles' or another's.

to a woman's influence often came to be an issue when it led to a man's adopting a woman's relative as his legitimate heir. The complex inheritance cases of the orator Isaeus are not often read these days, but they provide a fascinating window into just how often wealthy men died without living issue of their own, and how tangled and dysfunctional family dynamics could then become. Isaeus' speech *On the Estate of Menecles* concerns an aging man who adopted his ex-wife's brother as heir. Menecles' own brother challenged the legitimacy of the adoption under a putatively Solonic law, which is quoted in one of Apollodorus' speeches against Stephanus.[12] The law provided that such adoptions were legally valid only if a man 'is not out of his mind (παρανοῶν) in virtue of being mad, old, under the influence of drugs or disease, or *obeying a woman* (γυναικὶ πειθόμενος)'. The adopted heir who delivers Isaeus' oration denies, no less than five times in the speech, that his adoption was a case of γυναικὶ πειθόμενος. He insists that his sister was at the time of his adoption already long married to a second husband and that his adoption was more a matter of Menecles' esteem for their late father Eponymus.

Even more complicated is the oration *On the Estate of Philoctemon*, which really revolves around the actions of Philoctemon's father Euctemon, who outlived his son and died at the age of 96. Late in life, he took up with a woman of servile origin who managed one of his tenement buildings, including a brothel. He eventually moved in with her and claimed as his own offspring her two sons, who the speaker claims were actually children of another man. Again, the claim is that *he was persuaded by her* (6.21: ἐπείσθη ὑπ' αὐτῆς) and the legitimacy of these offspring should therefore be rejected.

Apollodorus claims that Neaera and her daughter Phano resorted to the same persuasive guile, inducing the seriously ill Phrastor to claim Phano's son as his own legitimate offspring ([Dem.] 59.55–8), and later duping the guileless and inexperienced Theogenes, who held the office of *archôn basileus*, with their seductive charms and false claims of Phano's own legitimacy as daughter of Stephanus (59.72–84). Even in cases where the bastard offspring of a courtesan or concubine were indeed those of her wealthy lover, they disrupted his legitimate family unit by creating potential rival heirs and a separate outside family to consume resources that should properly be reserved for the estate.[13]

---

12 [Dem.] 46.14 = [Dem.] 44.68 = F49a Ruschenbusch, also cited by Plut. *Sol.* 21.3.
13 For the most careful diachronic study of Greek laws pertaining to the rights of bastard offspring to inherit, see Ogden 1996: 32–82. He concludes that bastard children may in the archaic period have had the right to inherit if no genuine children survived, although the law was later changed to privilege more distant relatives in a man's birth family; some extension of rights to

Although not the central issue in Andocides' speech *On the Mysteries*, Andocides (1.124–9) uses his opponent Callias' susceptibility to female wiles as evidence of the man's moral unfitness to claim the hand of an *epiklêros* granddaughter. Callias married the daughter of Ischomachus, but within a year of that marriage he made the girl's mother his mistress, and the two of them are alleged to have driven the daughter out; he then married the mother and subsequently tired of her, publicly denying that the son to whom she gave birth was his own. Later, she returned into his favour and he eventually did present the previously disavowed boy as his own legitimate offspring.

My concern is not with the truth claims in any of these cases, but with the acute anxiety evinced in Greek legal discourse over the excessive influence of women with whom men enjoyed carnal intimacy and their ability to manipulate men into adoptions or false claims of legitimate children, or even into bad business decisions, as when the procuress Antigone convinced the plaintiff of Hyperides' speech *Against Athenogenes* into purchasing what turned out to be a debt-ridden perfume business. One of the most notorious claims of outsized feminine influence pertained to Pericles' long-term mistress Aspasia, whose son Pericles attempted to legitimate (Plut. *Per.* 37.2–5) despite his own strict law on citizenship requiring both parents to be Athenian. While we have no extant comedies from the period of Pericles' life, we do possess a fragmentary testimonium of Cratinus' *Dionysalexandros* (*P. Oxy.* 663), which presents Pericles as Dionysus impersonating the sexually obsessed Paris; Eupolis (fr. 267 K-A) compares Aspasia to Helen. Even five years after Pericles' death, Aristophanes' *Acharnians* (526–34) could imply that her influence had spurred Pericles' war policy, and Plutarch (*Per.* 24.2, 25.1–2) gives credence to the charge that Pericles' war on the Samians was at the Milesian Aspasia's urging, as do some modern historians.[14] Plato's *Menexenus* (236b) even asserts that it was Aspasia who wrote Pericles' famous funeral oration. Plutarch's *Life of Pericles* is full of quotations from comedy, including authors who were active long after Pericles' death: Aspasia is repeatedly attacked as a brothel-keeper (Aristophanes) and even a prostitute herself (Cratin. fr. 259 K-A); Plutarch (24.9) says other comedies call her an 'Omphale' or

---

bastard children may also have occurred at the end of the fifth-century due to Athens' severe manpower needs after major losses due to war and plague. See also Carey 1995: 416–17. Even during periods when bastards could not inherit, they might be falsely claimed as legitimate offspring (as in the cases Isaeus treats, including *On the Estate of Pyrrhus*) and might benefit from a father's generosity prior to his death.

14 Stadter 1989: 233.

'Deianeira'. Hermippus (fr. 47 K-A) designated Pericles a 'satyr king' and supposedly indicted Aspasia for impiety and supplying Pericles with freeborn women for sexual purposes (*Per.* 32.1), although this more likely refers to attacks in his comedies rather than a formal legal proceeding.[15] Pericles' addiction to philandering, even with his own son's wife, was a *topos* of contemporary attacks and later gossip (see Ath. 13.569f–570a, citing Stesimbrotus, Antisthenes, and Clearchus).

The idea of taking women's advice on matters of war and peace was so ridiculous in the eyes of most Greek men that it could only be imagined in a comedy. And that of course is the comedy Aristophanes wrote in *Lysistrata*, where the flowers of Athenian hoplite courage are so sex-addled and uxorious that they appear pathetic and unmanly. The men of the later *Ecclesiazusae*, where their wives assume control of the economy and state apparatus, come off no better. Although these plays have been recently popularised as proto-feminist statements, that is not the way most Greek men would have received them, particularly amid the oligarchic revolution of 411 that surrounded *Lysistrata*.

(2) The usual complaint against male obsession with courtesans was not that they were too politically influential, as in Aspasia's case, but that they manipulated men out of too much money, which in turn caused men to commit other immoral and dishonest acts. Edward Cohen and Konstantinos Kapparis have recently surveyed the evidence for just how expensive such company could be.[16] Lucian's *Dialogues of the Courtesans*, from the 2nd century CE, gives us some information about high-end practitioners: Demophantus offers a talent (perhaps equal to €5,000,000 in modern spending power) for an eight-month relationship with Ampelis, and the courtesan Krokale demanded twice as much. These prices reflect the extravagance of the Roman imperial period and may well have been exaggerated for literary effect. Closer to the classical era is what we hear from New Comedy: in Menander's *Epitrepontes* (136–7), Charisius spends 12 drachmas per night (perhaps €1,000) on Habrotonon, and the extravagant prostitute in Menander's *Flatterer* (117 ff.) demanded 300 drachmas a night (€25,000). The earlier comic poet Theopompus (fr. 22 K-A) says a prostitute of middling rank could earn four drachmas a night, and two drachmas per act seems to have been a minimum for most women of quality. This corresponds rather closely to contemporary prices in the US and Europe. Perhaps the most reliable evidence is that of oratory, where we learn that the slave-prostitute Neaera was purchased for 30 minas

---

15 For a fuller review of Aspasia's treatment in comedy, see Henry 1995: 19–28.
16 Cohen 2015: 155–79; Kapparis 2017: 112, 302–13.

(about €250,000); New Comedy tells us that long-term contracts with free courtesans could run anywhere from 20 to 60 minas. The capacity of such prices to exhaust even a wealthy man's estate is evident. Experienced courtesans knew how to assess a client's eagerness and ability to pay: the notorious Laïs charged the hedonist philosopher Aristippus extravagantly for the same acts that she gave free to the penniless Cynic Diogenes (Ath. 13.588e).

The 4th-century comic poet Amphis (fr. 23 K-A) presents the god Wealth paralysed at home, surrounded by various entrapping hetaeras. Aeschines (1.115) accuses Timarchus of having accepted a bribe of 20 minas to prosecute an innocent man, and then spending the money on the courtesan Philoxene. In his speech *On the False Embassy* (19.229), Demosthenes accuses Philocrates of taking bribe money from Philip to feed his addiction to *pornai*. The historian Theopompus (115F213 *FGrH*) criticises the mercenary general Chares for spending all of his war spoils on prostitutes and musicians. The fabulously wealthy general Callias, whom we have discussed before, was known as πορνομάνης ('whore-mad') and consumed his vast estate in dissipation, as portrayed in Eupolis' *Flatterers*. His extravagance became a *topos* of later comic and rhetorical satire.[17]

Families not infrequently objected to relatives who wasted their patrimony on prostitutes, a complaint as old as Sappho's criticism of her brother Charaxus for his extravagance with the courtesan Rhodopis of Naucratis.[18] Sophocles' son sued his father for squandering his estate after he took up with the hetaera Archippe.[19] Olympiodorus ([Dem.] 48.53–5) is attacked for never taking a lawful wife and having children, but spending lavishly on a hetaera he freed, while neglecting his sister and niece (the speaker's wife and daughter); the speaker effectively contrasts their poverty with the fine robes and jewelry that enable the proud hetaera's public swagger. The speaker of Demosthenes' *Against Boeotus* (40.51) says his father spent far more money on Plangon than he ever did on his son.

Aristophanes reserves the distinction of the 'lowest' human being to one Ariphrades (*Eq.* 1280–9), who is so devoted to giving women pleasure that he goes down on all his female partners, even whores whose private parts have been exposed to all and sundry: 'He soils his tongue with filthy pleasures, | Licking the most loathsome dew in brothel-houses, | Sliming his beard and stirring up the

---

17 On Callias, see Cohen 2015: 176 n. 116.
18 Hdt. 2.134; cf. Sapph. fr. 15b.9–12 L-P. For comment on Sappho's condemnation of excess rather than the relationship itself, see Page 1955: 48–51.
19 Ath. 13.592b cites the 2nd-century-BCE Hellenistic historian Hegesander of Delphi (fr. 27, *FGH* IV, 418–19) as the source of this anecdote, not the most reliable authority. For other references, see Kapparis 2017: 141.

hearths …' His problem is not the expenditure of money, as he uses cheap brothels, but that his taste for women is so intense as to put him in a subordinate position relative to even the lowliest of them; brothel whores should be gratifying him orally, not the other way around.

A similar inversion of masculinity may be involved in the cases of young men who take up with wealthy older women for support, as we hear about from the Alexandrian comic poets Machon of Sicyon (frr. 6–7 Gow) and Lynceus of Samos (Ath. 13.584b). Gryllion, a member of the Areopagus, was supported by Phryne, and Satyrus by Pamphila (Ath. 13.591d–e). Plutarch's *Amatorius* revolves around such a case, where the handsome teenager Bacchon of Thespiae, pursued by many men, winds up being kidnapped by the wealthy widow Ismenodora. Although we know nothing about the relative ages of Stephanus and Neaera, Apollodorus alleges that Stephanus largely supports himself off Neaera, using her liminal status as courtesan-turned-wife to extort money from naïve young men who fall into her clutches by threatening to charge them with adultery ([Dem.] 59.41–2); he employs the same set-up to extort money from Epaenetus of Andros when he is caught with Neaera's daughter Phano ([Dem.] 59.64–70). As an Athenian citizen, Stephanus was Neaera and Phano's ticket to some measure of respectability and could provide them legal representation as their *kyrios*, but he was, according to Apollodorus, basically a pimp monetising their beauty and sexual allure.

(3) Forcible rape is certainly a serious manifestation of pathological heterosexuality that could have grave consequences even beyond the damage done to the immediate victims. As we all remember, Herodotus begins his history of the East-West conflict by narrating a series of mythological rapes leading up to that of Helen (1.1–5);[20] most interesting (and troubling) is the Persian contention that no woman can be raped without somehow consenting to it and the Greeks are to be blamed for taking such matters so seriously. In a previously discussed passage from the *Acharnians* (524–37) that likely alludes to Herodotus, Aristophanes reduces the origins of the Peloponnesian War to a similar quarrel between Athens and Megara over young scapegraces ravishing women he calls 'prostitutes', including two who belonged to Aspasia; the tone of the passage is trivialising.[21]

Rape of besieged civilian populations in wartime was an atrocity that became increasingly common in the 4th century, as Kathy Gaca's careful studies have

---

20 On this passage, see Walcot 1978. Cole (1984: 98 n. 9) objects that these are termed acts of plunder, not rape, but the women are in every case taken for sexual reasons.
21 For a catalogue of women whose possession became the nominal cause of war, see also Ath. 13.560b–c, and Doblhofer 1994: 23–4.

documented.[22] However, her work also shows that Greek authors generally condemned it as an outrage worthy of divine punishment, whether in Athena's shipwreck of Ajax son of Oïleus after he raped Cassandra in her Trojan precinct or in the supposed thunderbolt of Zeus that Clearchus (fr. 48 Wehrli = Ath. 12.522e) says confounded the Tarentines after their mass rape of Messapian women and girls, leading to a Messapian sack of Tarentum visiting the same punishment on Tarentine women. Lucian's *Toxaris* (39) tells us of men being forced to watch women of their own family being raped after defeat in war as a form of ritual humiliation, but it is unclear whether this was actually common in classical times. Alexander the Great was praised for protecting noble women from outrage by his troops,[23] but it is unclear that he could prevent it altogether.[24] Mass war-rape is a paradigmatic example of the feminist contention that rape is a crime of power rather than lust.

Equally paradigmatic are the many stories of tyrants who commit outrageous acts of sexual violation, often leading to their overthrow. Among these we can name Agathocles and Dionysius the Younger of Syracuse, Hegesilochus of Rhodes, Tartarus of Melite, Aristomelidas of Orchomenos, Clearchus of Heraclea, and Aristotimus of Elis.[25] Most familiar is the story of the Peisistratids: the events leading to their eventual overthrow began with Hipparchus' making sexual advances on Harmodius, who feared rape (according to Thuc. 6.54.3–4), and Pausanias (1.23.2) further reports that Hippias raped Leaena, Aristogeiton's favourite hetaera. The foundational legend for Roman overthrow of the Etruscan monarchs, originating in the same era, was the rape of Lucretia. My concern is not so much with the historicity of these stories, many of which became focal points for legendary elaboration, but how the motif of raping citizen women (and in some cases boys) became almost a defining characteristic of the tyrannical personality in ancient thought, but also the culminating act of *hubris* that awakens popular morality into revolutionary action. So common was the association of rape with the behavior of tyrants that Otanes, in the debate of the Persian statesmen over the best constitution, uses it as a key argument against monarchy (Hdt. 3.80.5).

What is puzzling is that outside of war and tyrant legends, we find so little evidence of rape of citizen women in our vast archive of literary and legal evidence from ancient Athens, despite the ubiquity of rape as a theme in mythology

---

22 See especially Gaca 2011 and 2015. Gaca 2014 shows that this treatment was visited specifically on women and female children, but not commonly on boys, who were either enslaved or killed.
23 Plut. *Mul. Virt.* 259f–260d; *Alex.* 21; Arr. *Anab.* 7.13.2–3.
24 On Alexander's policies in this area, see Doblhofer 1994: 28–31.
25 For the primary sources on these various tyrant legends, see Doblhofer 1994: 35–40, 64–5.

and visual art. Where allegations of rape come up in Athenian oratory, it always concerns women who were not Athenian citizens and were thus viewed as more vulnerable.[26] But even in the case of non-citizen women, rape was considered a serious enough offense that men were put to death for it, as Dinarchus (1.23) tells us Themistius of Aphidna was for raping a Rhodian lyre-girl at the Eleusinia or Euthymachus for forcing an Olynthian slave girl into a brothel. Demosthenes charged the Athenian ambassadors in Macedon with mistreating a free Olynthian woman at a drinking party (Dem. 19.196–8), but the remote location of the alleged incident made verification difficult and Aeschines (2.153–5) accuses Demosthenes of having suborned testimony; equally unverifiable are Aeschines' own claims about Timarchus raping free women while a magistrate on Andros (1.107). That the Athenian law on *hubris* protected even slaves from rape is beyond doubt and was a *topos* of Athenian self-praise (Dem. 21.46–50; Aeschin. 1.15–7); raping someone else's slave was damage to their property, and even abusing one's own slave could form a basis of prosecution by another family member (as in the case of Plato's *Crito*) or a personal enemy. Rape of a citizen woman was so serious that anyone murdering a rapist of his wife, daughter, sister, mother, or concubine was absolved of punishment (Dem. 23.55–6); Plato even incorporates this absolution as a fundamental law in his ideal state (*Leg.* 874c). Historical anecdotes tell of such murders even long after the rape going completely unpunished (Paus. 2.20.2; Plut. *Parallela* 19). Nor was the abhorrence of rape unique to Athens: Pausanias (8.5.12) tells of an Arcadian king's son being stoned to death after raping a priestess of Artemis. However, punishment by death was probably not the norm; payment of a fine to the victim's family is also well-attested in both a law attributed to Solon (Plut. *Sol.* 23.1 = F26 Ruschenbusch) and the Gortyn Code.[27]

One of the few clear examples where a free Athenian woman is raped can be found in Menander's *Epitrepontes*, where the irresponsible young Charisius had raped an unidentified girl attending the Tauropolia festival a few months before his marriage. But even this case is washed away with the happy ending typical of New Comedy, when he learns that the girl he had raped was actually his new wife, whom he had previously left after discovering that she was prematurely pregnant. Young girls attending a nocturnal festival like the Tauropolia were certainly

---

26 This conclusion is confirmed by Cohen 1991: 134 n. 1, on the basis of his perusal of the corpus.
27 For the fines prescribed by the Gortyn Code, which varied depending upon the social class of both the victim and perpetrator, see Willetts 1967: 8–17 and Cole 1984: 108–10. Much higher fines are attested in later sources of the Roman period (Cole 1984: 104–5), but these may be exaggerated for rhetorical effect and are unlikely to reflect common practice in the classical era.

in a position of vulnerability.[28] Eva Keuls has argued, based mainly on artistic evidence, that unaccompanied women bringing water from the local well-house were also subjected to male sexual harassment and assault, although these scenes might be depicting slave women.[29] The question nevertheless remains why we do not hear of a forcible rape of a free Athenian woman anywhere in the corpus of Attic oratory. Could it be because families usually settled such matters with a cash payment or a New-Comedy-style marital arrangement, to spare their women the public humiliation and embarrassment a case at law would inevitably bring?[30] Or was private vengeance of the sort the law explicitly excused the more common recourse? Or could it be that forcible rape of free women was genuinely rare, due to the ready availability of slaves and prostitutes?

(4) Adolescent girls were generally protected against any type of pre-marital sexual approach, and this was doubtless one of the reasons they tended to be married in their early or mid-teen years, especially if from a respectable family. Failing to protect a daughter's purity would constitute a failure and dereliction of responsibility on the part of any family patriarch, just like inability to provide a dowry; hence, Archilochus found it a useful strategy to humiliate Lycambes for breaking off his marriage to Neoboule by pretending to have had free sexual relations with her sisters in the Cologne Epode (196a W). This illicit relation was one more manifestation of antinomian spirit for the Archilochian persona, which elsewhere boasts of casting his shield away in battle and other immoral acts. It should not be construed as normative male bravado.

Aristophanes' *Ecclesiazusae* features a scene (877–1111) in which a young Lothario named Epigenes tries to visit a girlfriend with whom he has had previous assignations. She is apparently a not-yet-married girl of citizen status living with her mother, who is not currently present in the house (912–13); her father is either

---

28 Not only were women unprotected because of the absence of males at female-only festivals, but they could not recognise assailants in the dark. See Lape 2001: 92–3 and Bathrellou 2013, who notes that the festivals tend to be associated with girls' maturation and initiation into adulthood.

29 Keuls 1985: 235–40. Ar. *Lys.* 327–35 may suggest that citizen women would also carry water from the fountain, but this would surely not have been true of all classes.

30 This is the conclusion of Scafuro 1997: 212–16, with regard to almost all types of sexual cases involving free women. See also Pierce 1997 and Rosivach 1998: 13–50, for an even wider range of examples. Lape (2001: 105–12) treats the numerous New Comic plots where a rapist/seducer from a wealthy family winds up having to marry a girl from a poor family whom he violated, and sees these as a positive movement toward democratic class-levelling. However, Cole 1984: 107 warns that the happy marital endings of New Comedy may not be an accurate reflection of how such events usually turned out.

dead or invisible and ineffective, like most of the men in this play. That their meetings are sexual is implied by both the girl (914) and the old hag she tries to chase away from her window, who in turn accuses her of eagerness to give her boyfriend oral sex (919–20). Critics have faulted this scene as disgusting, because three repulsive old women proceed to rape the boyfriend under the new laws of sexual communism, but from the perspective of a Greek audience, Epigenes gets exactly what he deserves. Seducing an unmarried girl, no matter how willing, was only slightly less serious than adultery, as it potentially leaves the girl unmarriageable.[31] Indeed, Solon specifically exempted her from the protection of his law against prostituting one's children (Plut. *Sol.* 23.2 = F31a Ruschenbusch), so this must have seemed an appropriate destiny to some parents of wayward girls.[32]

(5) Adultery was of course the worst offense, because it threatened the legitimacy of offspring.[33] Unlike rape, it also undermined a wife's loyalty and emotional allegiance to her husband, which may have already been fragile due to the relatively large age difference and the arranged nature of Greek marriages.[34] An attentive and enthusiastic young lover close to her own age might indeed tempt a wife whose husband was 15–20 years older and had never really needed to court her romantically. The strict policing of girls by their parents prior to marriage gave them little contact with boys of their own age, so the greater independence a young wife might have after marriage afforded ample opportunity to stray and explore new affections, particularly if her husband were away due to business or affairs of state. For their part, fashionable young rakes might prefer married women because they did not have to be bought and they need not worry about

---

31 See Hyperides 1 (*In Defense of Lycophron*), fr. 4b.12–13, where the speaker defends himself against the accusation that he has made many girls either unmarriageable or married to poor husbands.

32 Scafuro (1997: 273–4) argues that this law was no longer operative in the 4th century BCE, when forced marriage or fining the seducer would be more common ways of keeping the matter quiet.

33 For defence of this traditional view, see Carey 1995: 416 and Ogden 1997: 32–4. A one-time rape created less risk of pregnancy than an ongoing love affair. Harris (2006: 283–95) questions the credibility of Euphiletus' contention in Lys. 1.32–3 that death was the usual penalty for adultery, whereas rape merely earned a fine. However, Harris (2006: 299–305, 328) also acknowledges that rape of an unmarried girl was often resolved through marriage to the victim and its seriousness was highly dependent on context and intention. Adultery could not be resolved so easily. Similarly, seduction of an unmarried girl could also be remedied through marriage. Although Carey (1995: 408) and Scafuro (1997: 474–8) think the term *moicheia* included seduction of unmarried girls, Cohen (1991: 100–9) argues that it was an altogether different (and lesser) offense in both Greece and most other societies.

34 Xen. *Hie.* 3.6 asserts the universality of the death sanction for adulterers among Greek states for just this reason.

being forced into marriage with them, if the woman should become pregnant.[35] The risk and gamesmanship in the enterprise may have also added an element of challenge and excitement.

The Draconian law that one could kill or otherwise torment any man caught *in flagrante* with one's wife appears to have been virtually universal among Greek city states, as David Phillips (2018) shows. However, a wealthy man could buy his way out of such trouble, as Chremylus observes in Aristophanes' *Wealth* (168), since money is always more useful to a victim than violent revenge and adultery seems to have been a rich young man's hobby.[36] A weak or poor husband might prefer to cover the matter up out of shame and the need to divorce his wife and return her dowry if he went public.[37] Cratinus (fr. 81 K-A) says Callias paid three talents to compensate his seduction of Phocus' wife, and in Aristophanes' *Birds* (285–6), his feathers are pulled out by a succession of women. The women of *Thesmophoriazusae* fault adulterers as liars and men who financially exploit older women (343–5). When a comic character endorses adultery as an exquisite self-indulgence, it is always in the service of moral anomy, whether the appeal of the sophistic Lesser Argument to the spoiled Pheidippides in *Clouds* (1079–82) or as part of the ultimately dystopian dream-world of Cloudcuckooland (*Av.* 793–6). As we have seen, Stephanus and Neaera made their living from extortion of frightened young men who had been lured into adultery with what they supposed was a courtesan.

Any exceptionally attractive man was considered either a potential adulterer or a *kinaidos*, or both. Cratinus is ridiculed for sporting 'an adulterer's haircut' (*Ach.* 848–9), presumably a luxuriant mane of long hair, incongruous for a man whom Aristophanes' next play identifies as senile and decrepit. Aristotle presents as a common inference that a *kallôpistês* or *katharios* man must be an adulterer.[38] *Katharios* merely connotes cleanliness, tidiness, and care about one's habit, but the more marked term *kallôpistês* literally means 'beautified in the face', implying a certain artifice, such as a very neatly trimmed beard or even a clean-shaven, youthful appearance, as Alcibiades cultivated for his entire life. Lucian makes

---

35 On the motivations for both men and women, see Cohen 1991: 168–9.
36 Aristotle (*Rh.* 1372a23–4) says a poor man is unlikely to be charged with adultery, and (*Rh.* 1391a15–19) that adultery is a crime especially characteristic of *nouveaux riches* who behave badly out of insolence or self-indulgence. See also [Pl.] *Eryx.* 396e–397a.
37 On shame as grounds for silence in this matter, see Arist. *Rh.* 1373a34–5 and Aeschin. 1.107. That a husband has to separate from his wife if he makes the accusation public is commonly asserted (Cole 1984: 100; Carey 1995: 414; Ogden 1997: 28–9; Kapparis 1999: 354–5; Fisher 2001: 336), based on [Dem.] 59.86–7, but the law as quoted there may not be authentic.
38 Arist. *Soph. Elench.* 167b8–12; *Rh.* 1401b23–4 and 1416a22–3. See Davidson 1998: 164–5.

Charicles of Corinth, the enthusiastic young advocate of heterosexuality in the sexual preference debate of the *Amores*, not only conspicuously handsome, but skilled in applying cosmetics to enhance his appeal even more (*Am.* 9); in contrast his pederastic opponent was an athletic man 'of straightforward ways'. Given the characteristic beauty of the young adulterer (taking Paris as his model), it is not surprising that a common punishment was to turn the seducer into a sexually passive object. Any man who likes women too much deserves to be treated as one through anal rape or other forms of sexual abuse.[39]

Of course a man who takes such care of maintaining a beautiful appearance may as well be a woman, surrounded by jars of perfume and facial ointments, and holding a mirror in hand. Alcibiades was well-known as a ladies' man, such that Eupolis implies he is always among a crowd of women (fr. 171 K-A); a character in Pherecrates (fr. 164 K-A) says, 'Although he isn't manly, it looks like Alcibiades is man enough for all our wives'. Shortly before his assassination in Phrygia, Alcibiades supposedly had a dream in which the courtesan Timandra dressed him in her own clothes, dandled his head in her lap, and applied make-up to his face (Plut. *Alc.* 39.1–4); Plutarch also tells us that she in fact did cover his corpse in her own garments and paid for his burial.

The ultimate nightmare of what happens to a man who submerges himself eternally in the company of women is found in an account of the late 5th-century Ctesias of Cnidus (688F1.23 *FGrH*): the Persian King Sardanapalus never emerged from his harem, and when the Mede Arbaces finally obtained access to him, Sardanapalus was found among his concubines dressed in a woman's robe, combing wool, and his clean-shaven face covered in white lead. Too much heterosexual attention to women was perceived as effeminising and properly the domain of the Oriental Other, like Sardanapalus or the last days of Alcibiades, the very antithesis of proper Greek notions of masculinity.

*

None of these five areas of potential heterosexual excess and loss of control was at issue in the case of pederasty, or at least not to the same extent. By definition, adultery was not a problem, because there was no homosexual marriage and no threat to legitimacy of offspring. For the same reason, sex before marriage was not at issue. Boys, who were by definition much younger and less experienced

---

39 This punishment is the point of the *euruprôktos* joke in Ar. *Nub.* 1083–6. For other sources, see Roy 1991; Cohen 1991: 116 n. 56; Ogden 1997: 37 n. 23. However, Cohen 1985 expresses doubts about the historicity of the practice.

than their lovers, are not accused of exerting undue influence over their lovers' decision-making in matters of inheritance or business: it is interesting that Hyperides' speech against Athenogenes does not blame the boy whose freedom the speaker was trying to purchase, but the female procuress who suggested that the best way to do so was to buy the whole perfume business of which the boy and his father were a part. We have no historical examples of homosexual rape aside from contexts of warfare or tyrannical behaviour, or at least theoretically as punishment of an adulterer caught in the act; all three are symbolic assertions of dominance rather than motivated primarily by lust. Lust was the motive in Euripides' dramatisation of Laius' rape of Chrysippus, but as I have argued elsewhere, Euripides was introducing a radical innovation into the myth with this play, which was produced during a period of radical democracy when pederasty was out of fashion.[40]

The one area of overlap between heterosexual and homosexual anxiety is with regard to prostitution. Male prostitution certainly did exist in classical times. We hear of one Diophantus suing his partner for four drachmas (Aeschin. 1.158), presumably the price of a single night, which does not much differ from what we hear middling female prostitutes charged. On the other hand, our one piece of evidence about a long-term contract for company concerns the Plataean youth Theodotus in Lysias' *Against Simon*, who charged his partner 3 minas, perhaps not much different from middling female prostitutes, but modest in comparison with the 20 minas or more that we hear about high-class courtesans costing. The speaker of Isaeus' oration *On the Estate of Aristarchus* (25), accuses his cousin of wasting money on boys, but no amounts or details are given. We never hear about boys being set up in lavishly furnished houses of their own as courtesans were: even the demanding party boy Timarchus simply moved from one man's house to another whenever he took on a new lover. The fleeting attractiveness of their beardless youth made boys less of a long-term threat to a man's financial stability, and most teenage boys lacked the experience or social graces that made mature courtesans so successful in manipulating large sums out of their enamoured clients, although some upper-class youths like Timarchus or those ridiculed in Aristophanes (*Plut.* 155–7) could be costly.

As such, pederasty may be seen to have evolved within the sexual economy of ancient Greece as a less risky alternative to the potential pitfalls of heterosexual excess. This is not to say that pederasty was universally accepted or without moral criticism; as I have argued elsewhere, it did come to be problematised especially in the context of Athens' radical democracy in the second half of the 5th

---

40 Hubbard 2006.

century, as pro-natalist attitudes encouraged male marriage at younger ages.[41] However, the relatively high age of male marriage for most of Greek history did create an inherently unstable situation in which sexually needy young men in their late teens and twenties had a limited range of legitimate outlets. The Medieval historian Jacques Rossiaud has noted the similar demographic contours of 15th century France, where men did not marry until their mid- to late twenties: here there was no homosexual alternative, so the result was widespread gang rape of peasant and working-class women.[42] Together with the threat of adultery, this phenomenon led both civil and clerical authorities to tolerate low-cost brothels, even in the face of theological objections. The pressure was of course even greater in Ancient Greece, where marriage did not regularly occur until men were in their thirties, and their brides were even younger than in late Medieval France.

What these two historical examples teach us is the elasticity of sexual mores in response to demographic and environmental factors. When economic and environmental carrying capacity are under pressure, marriage and large families become less attractive options, and alternative non-procreative forms of sexuality need to evolve as outlets for the pent-up sexual energies of the young. This gives us food for thought in the 21st century, as we in the Western world confront the twin anxieties of economic stagnation and environmental limitations, as young people postpone or completely renounce marriage and as birth rates of even the world's wealthiest populations plummet. It should not surprise us that we see within this context liberalisation of sexual morality to accommodate recognition of non-procreative same-sex relationships and toleration of sex work, overtly in some European cities, more covertly in others. But what the Greek example teaches us, in addition, is the fluidity of sexual preference, open to same-sex options when expedient but also opposite-sex when necessary. For too long, the gay and lesbian movement in the modern West has ghettoised itself with rigid essentialising categories of 'either/or', which today's youth deconstruct in favour of a 'non-binary' or 'pan-sexual' alternative in which the individual is valued for their qualities regardless of gender, which is itself articulated as a false dichotomy. Recognising this fluidity of sexual and gender options may help resolve whatever crisis we suffer today with what has been deemed 'toxic masculinity' or the rebellion of the 'incels' (involuntary celibates) with whom we started.

The Greeks had figured this out long before us. We should listen to their wisdom.

---

[41] Hubbard 2015.
[42] Rossiaud 1984.

Ed Sanders
Xenophon and the Pathology of *Erôs*

Abstract: Scholarship on love in the Classical period frequently concentrates on Plato or tragedy. However, the former's focus is idealist, homosexual, but sex-free; the latter usually heterosexual, and tending towards violent death. The Xenophontic corpus provides a corrective: Xenophon is interested in both homo- and heterosexual love and he provides a number of vignettes portraying what we might call the 'experience' of being in love. Using a psychological methodology, the 'emotional episode', this chapter approaches the experience of *erôs* by breaking it down into its pathological components: causes; psychological feelings; physiological responses; verbal, physical and attitudinal reactions (or 'symptoms'); defences; and resolutions. In the *Symposium* we find *erôs* as a response to beauty, perceived through the eyes, and enhanced by other senses. Symposiasts react in words, deeds, and thoughts; to erotic stimuli, nascent and long-lasting love; and to beloveds both present and absent. 'Socrates' introduces a characteristic twist – but one that reflects Xenophon's pedagogic concerns rather than Plato's. And the whole is imbued with rich humour and irony. In the *Cyropaedia* we find love that is unrequited, requited, and avoided, as different men respond to the extraordinary beauty of Pantheia, the Lady of Susa.

Your eyes meet someone else's. You cannot stop looking at their face. You are fascinated by their smile, their laugh, their voice. You talk and flirt, then go on a date, or leap straight into bed. The flirtation and sex continue, you begin to miss them when apart, and spend ever more time together. You smile when you think of them, your heart pounds when you see them ... a relationship forms. As time rolls forward, excitement wears off. Sex becomes perfunctory, their companionship is taken for granted, and you slip into a trusting friendship (perhaps marriage) or drift apart.

In this story of a sexual romance, we can debate where 'love' starts and ends. The English term is broad, including feelings for family and friends, abstracts and

---

I am grateful to Fiona McHardy and Chiara Thumiger for their comments on this chapter.

inanimate objects. Romantic love can, but need not, include sexual attraction.¹ Greek *erôs*, however, is more straightforward. It encompasses scripts of both sexual desire and sexual love – scripts we might distinguish semantically as 'lust' and 'love', but which Greeks saw merely as aspects of *erôs*, or more precisely, as different stages of the same narrative arc.² *Erôs* starts at the beginning of the above story, and continues until sexual attraction ceases – after which other words might be used: *philia, storgê, agapê*.³

In exploring *erôs*, I use a theoretical approach I have found fruitful with Greek emotions – especially those whose boundaries differ from their English language equivalent, or for which there is no name in Greek.⁴ *Erôs* cannot be categorised unambiguously as an emotion. Aristotle, for example, says that emotions (*ta pathê*)⁵ are such things as affect our judgments, and are accompanied by pain or pleasure.⁶ This definition sees emotions as cognitive: we perceive something, we judge what the perception means, it makes us feel pain/pleasure, and we interpret that feeling as a specific emotion, which lasts until our judgement changes.⁷ *Erôs* is not generally included in Classical-period lists of emotions.⁸ This is reasonable, since it responds primarily not to what someone does, but to

---

1 On the distinction between sexual desire and romantic love in English, see Diamond 2014: 314–16. For further psychological scholarship on love, see Sternberg/Weis 2006; Weis/Sternberg 2008.
2 On differing scripts included in the same emotion term, see Kaster 2005; Cairns 2008; Sanders 2014.
3 On these, especially *philia*, see Konstan 2006a: 169–84.
4 Such as *phthonos* and sexual jealousy – Sanders 2014.
5 The closest Greek word to 'emotion' is *pathos*, though their usage is not identical. On translating *pathos*, see Grimaldi 1988: 12–15. For Greek philosophical views of emotion, from Plato onwards, see Wisse 1989; Knuuttila 2004; Konstan 2006b.
6 *Rh.* 1378a19–21: ἔστι δὲ τὰ πάθη δι' ὅσα μεταβάλλοντες διαφέρουσι πρὸς τὰς κρίσεις οἷς ἕπεται λύπη καὶ ἡδονή.
7 E.g., if we perceive we have been slighted, we feel a pain which we interpret as *orgê* (anger), the appropriate response to a slight (*Rh.* 1378a30–2). If we achieve revenge for the slight, we no longer feel *orgê*. Most modern theories of emotions take a cognitivist perspective – i.e. that psychological and physiological reactions follow cognitive stimuli. For an introduction to modern theories of emotion, see Shiota/Kalat 2018; Niedenthal/Ric 2017. Griffiths 1997 is an in-depth and accessible study.
8 Arist. *Rh.* 2.2–11 discusses anger, calming down, friendship and hatred, fear and confidence, shame and shamelessness, gratitude and ingratitude, pity, indignation, envy, emulation and scorn. These are ostensibly the emotions relevant to rhetoric (1388b29–30), though Aristotle omits hope, pride and desire, all regularly seen in deliberative oratory – Sanders 2016. The list of emotions at *Eth. Nic.* 1105b21–3 also excludes *erôs*, but includes *epithumia* (desire/appetite) and *pothos* (longing). Note Plato includes *erôs* within a short list of emotions at *Philebus* 47e1–2.

who they are, and does not end after any specific action. Aristotle includes *erôs* within *epithumiai*, 'desires' or 'appetites' (*Rh.* 1385a23: τοιαῦται δὲ αἱ ἐπιθυμίαι, οἷον ἔρως), or connects it with *epithumia* as a near synonym (*Rh.* 1392a23: ὧν ἢ ἔρως ἢ ἐπιθυμία φύσει ἐστίν). Elsewhere he refers to *epithumiai* shared by everyone, including for dry and wet nourishment, and sex (*eunê*; *Eth. Nic.* 1118b8–11); or says the *alogoi epithumiai* – irrational desires/appetites for bodily pleasure – include hunger, thirst, sexual pleasures (*aphrodisia*) and sensory stimulations (*Rh.* 1370a16–25).[9] Modern lists of emotions also rarely include *erôs* (or equivalent), as noted by the psychologist Nico Frijda.[10]

Some psychologists prefer to talk not of emotions, but of emotional episodes.[11] These are described by the psychologist Gerrod Parrott as 'the story of an emotional event',[12] and begin with antecedent or eliciting conditions: i.e. elements physically present in a scenario, and our perception and interpretation of those elements. These arouse psychological feelings, and stimulate physiological changes. Verbal expressions and physical actions may follow, as may attempts to regulate (or cope with) the emotion. Eventually, there is resolution. In simple English, we have causes or triggers, feelings, bodily symptoms, things we say and do, and the emotion ending. In literary descriptions, we might add similes, metaphors and imagery used to describe the feelings and symptoms. This methodology can fruitfully be used for analysing *erôs* episodes, which can be considered 'pathological' in the sense that *erôs* proceeds like – and is sometimes explicitly described as – a disease, with a discernible and predictable progress and prognosis.[13]

Erôs has been explored and portrayed in many genres and authors, each of which has its own style, emphasises certain aspects, or examines certain types of relationship. Archaic lyric poets vividly depict erotic episodes, which this theoretical approach can help us explore. Many such attractions are one-sided. In Sappho 31 L-P, there are three triggers for *erôs*: seeing the girl, hearing her soft voice, and her lovely laughter (1–5). No fewer than nine symptoms follow: heart leaping, tongue paralysed, fire beneath skin, eyes blinded, ears drumming,

---

9 Soble 2008: 37 disagrees with the comparison of sexual desire with hunger and thirst, since (as individuals, if not as a species) we can live without sex, but die without food or water.
10 Frijda 2007: 227.
11 See e.g. Fehr/Russell 1984; Shaver *et al.* 1987; Parrott 1991; Sharpsteen 1991; Russell/Lemay 2000; Gross 2007. They are sometimes labelled emotional experiences, events, concepts or processes, and can be considered specific instances of the general 'scripts' referred to above.
12 Parrott 1991: 4.
13 Plut. *Demetr.* 38.2–7 and Heliod. *Aeth.* 4.7 show the 'disease' of *erôs* diagnosed and treated.

sweating, shaking, pallor, and feeling as if dying (5–16).[14] Ibycus fr. 287 *PMG* talks of the horse-yoke (6: φερέζυγος) and hunting nets (4: δίκτυα) – metaphors for being controlled and unable to escape. Archilochus fr. 196a W describes an erotic encounter, from the man's initial attraction, through attempted verbal seduction of the girl, to her rape.

Classical-period poetry gives us the priapic lust of Old Comedy,[15] and many erotic relationships in tragedy.[16] In prose, historiography and oratory provide brief examples of *erôs*,[17] but insufficient to be considered comprehensive authorial or generic views on the topic. *Erôs* is frequently explored through the writings of Plato – especially *Symposium* and the erotic speeches of *Phaedrus*, on which vast amounts have been published. I single out Douglas Cairns' recent analysis of Socrates' second speech (*Phdr.* 244a–257b), which notes no fewer than twenty symptoms, metaphors, behaviours etc.[18] However, Plato focuses almost exclusively on homosexual relations; he shows a marked distaste for physical consummation of erotic love; and his approach to pederastic *erôs* is highly idiosyncratic,

---

14 The poem is quoted on pp. 25–6. On the symptoms etc. of *erôs* in Archaic lyric poetry, see Calame 1999: 13–37.
15 Most obviously in *Lysistrata*, but also the final scenes of *Acharnians* and *Thesmophoriazusae*, the symposium and its aftermath in *Wasps*, and (in female equivalent) the competition for sex with a youth in *Assemblywomen*. See Robson 2013a on Aristophanic 'languages of love'.
16 Sanders 2014: 130–56 explores Medea's, Deianeira's and Hermione's erotic desires for their husbands, each leading to sexual jealousy and (attempted/actual) violence. Thumiger 2013 connects tragic *erôs* and madness, frequently within marriage. Goldhill 1995: 149 refers to the necessarily disastrous end of female desire in Classical literature. See also Kaimio 2002 on marital love in tragedy, from an ethical perspective; P. Brown 1993 on marital love in New Comedy.
17 Lysias has two men in love with a boy (3.5), and two others with a girl (4.8), both instances leading to alleged attempted murder. Herodotus comments on the unusualness of a husband falling in love with his wife (1.8), and mentions the political consequences of Ariston's love (6.62) – see Harrison 2003 on *erôs* as motivation in Herodotus. In Thucydides, *erôs* impels violence against a tyrant (6.54 ff.), or is a rapacious political force (6.13, 6.24). Xenophon regularly uses *erôs* in a metaphorical sense: e.g. *Hell.* 5.2.30 for war; *Cyn.* 12.10 for hunting; *Ages.* 10.4 for glory; *Hell.* 7.5.16 for ancestral glory; *Cyr.* 1.5.12 for praise; *Mem.* 2.6.4 and *Oec.* 12.15 for making money/profit; *Mem.* 1.4.7 for begetting and rearing children; *Symp.* 4.62 for philosophy; *Hell.* 5.2.28 for life; *Ana.* 3.1.29 for death to end suffering.
18 Cairns 2013: 240 n. 13: 'A list of traditional poetic metaphors, symptoms, expressions, typical behaviour patterns, metonymies, etc. used of *erôs* in the *Phdr.* would include at least the following: (a) gaze as expression/cause of *erôs*; (b) consumption of food or drink; (c) hunting (pursuit); (d) warmth, fever; (e) shuddering; (f) sweating; (g) softening, melting; (h) disease; (i) madness; (j) force; (k) pain (stings, goads, etc.); (l) near-death experience; (m) burden; (n) bitter-sweet; (o) slavery; (p) wrestling; (q) other contests; (r) fluttering (of heart, etc.); (s) beloved as *agalma*; (t) forgetting family' [references and cross-references removed].

sometimes almost mystical. This is no more a guide to *erôs* as normally experienced by Classical Greeks than tragedy's exclusive focus on heterosexual *erôs*, usually within marriage, with its frequent accompanying psychoses and resolutions in violent death.

Thus I turn to Xenophon not merely because he is under-explored on the topic, though he is. There has been, so far as I can determine, no comprehensive exploration of homo- and heterosexual erotic *experience* across the Xenophontic corpus. While Clifford Hindley has extensively discussed homosexuality in Xenophon,[19] his perspective is ethical – the types and instances of homosexual activity Xenophon (and Socrates) thought acceptable. Simon Goldhill examines Socrates' encounter with the hetaera Theodote (*Mem.* 3.11), in a discussion of Athens' viewing culture,[20] but goes no further into erotic experience than this. So there is ample work still to be done on Xenophontic erotics. But as important as filling this lacuna is for its own sake, the widely differing works and types of erotic relationships depicted in Xenophon's corpus provide a more useful guide to 'normal' *erôs* in the Classical period – i.e. *erôs* as experienced in 'real life' – than any other single author or genre, and a more balanced view to set alongside theirs. Throughout a heterogeneous corpus, Xenophon depicts a surprisingly unified view of the experience of being in love; and in particular his works include some charming vignettes that showcase what we might call the 'pathology' – i.e. the causes, progression, and outcomes – of that experience.[21]

I ground this exploration in a reading of *Symposium*, because of its rich variety on the topic, but refer to other works where relevant, and in particular end with some episodes from *Cyropaedia*.[22] The focus of conversation in *Symposium* is not formally *erôs* (or the god Eros) as in Plato's *Symposium*, but things that make one proud. Nevertheless, the topics of erotic attraction and love recur so often, that *erôs* can be considered its real principal theme,[23] even if mostly treated in a light-hearted way.[24] And by including the presence of women amongst the entertainers, Xenophon provides a more realistic depiction of a symposium than

---

19 Hindley 1994, 1999 and 2004. Huss 1999a also explores the normative aspect of Socrates' speech in *Symp.* 8.
20 Goldhill 1998.
21 These are, unfortunately, almost entirely male experiences. In literature of the Classical period, we must largely turn to tragedy for women in love – see note 16.
22 Of 124 *erôs*-words in Xenophon, 47 appear in *Symp.* and 28 in *Cyr*. Most of the rest occur in *Mem.* (some referred to in this chapter) and *Hier.* (see n. 36). See also those in note 17.
23 As noted by Waterfield 1990: 224.
24 On the mixture of serious and playful that characterises the entire dialogue, see Huss 1999a, esp. 391.

Plato – notwithstanding that the conversation remains at a more elevated level than was probably typical.[25]

The Erotic Gaze, and Other Senses

Erotic attraction begins from seeing the beloved,[26] and the erotic gaze is a *leitmotif* in *Symposium*. We are introduced to Autolycus, a boy (*pais*) Callias is in love with (1.2: ἐρῶν). Autolycus has just won the prize in the boys' pankration wrestling contest at the Great Panathenaia, and Callias invites him – with his father as chaperone – for dinner, along with various others including Socrates. As Autolycus sits for dinner, Xenophon says in his own voice (*Symp.* 1.8–10):

> εὐθὺς μὲν οὖν ἐννοήσας τις τὰ γιγνόμενα ἡγήσατ' ἂν φύσει βασιλικόν τι κάλλος εἶναι, ἄλλως τε καὶ ἂν μετ' αἰδοῦς καὶ σωφροσύνης, καθάπερ Αὐτόλυκος τότε, κεκτῆταί τις αὐτό. πρῶτον μὲν γάρ, ὥσπερ ὅταν φέγγος τι ἐν νυκτὶ φανῇ, πάντων προσάγεται τὰ ὄμματα, οὕτω καὶ τότε τοῦ Αὐτολύκου τὸ κάλλος πάντων εἷλκε τὰς ὄψεις πρὸς αὐτόν· ἔπειτα τῶν ὁρώντων οὐδεὶς οὐκ ἔπασχέ τι τὴν ψυχὴν ὑπ' ἐκείνου. οἱ μέν γε σιωπηρότεροι ἐγίγνοντο, οἱ δὲ καὶ ἐσχηματί- ζοντό πως. πάντες μὲν οὖν οἱ ἐκ θεῶν του κατεχόμενοι ἀξιοθέατοι δοκοῦσιν εἶναι· ἀλλ' οἱ μὲν ἐξ ἄλλων πρὸς τὸ γοργότεροί τε ὁρᾶσθαι καὶ φοβερώτερον φθέγγεσθαι καὶ σφοδρότεροι εἶναι φέρονται, οἱ δ' ὑπὸ τοῦ σώφρονος ἔρωτος ἔνθεοι τά τε ὄμματα φιλοφρονεστέρως ἔχουσι καὶ τὴν φωνὴν πραοτέραν ποιοῦνται καὶ τὰ σχήματα εἰς τὸ ἐλευθεριώτερον ἄγουσιν. ἃ δὴ καὶ Καλλίας τότε διὰ τὸν ἔρωτα πράττων ἀξιοθέατος ἦν τοῖς τετελεσμένοις τούτῳ τῷ θεῷ.

An observer of the scene would at once have reflected that beauty has something naturally regal about it, especially if it is combined with modesty and self-discipline in the possessor, as it was then in Autolycus. In the first place, his beauty drew everyone's attention to him, as surely as a light draws all eyes towards it in the night; and secondly, there was not a man there whose soul was not moved at the sight of him. Some became more silent, and the behaviour of others underwent a sort of transformation. All those possessed by one of the gods are worth observing. Those who are influenced by other gods tend to become more intimidating in their appearance, more truculent in their speech and more aggressive in their conduct; but those who are inspired by discreet Love have a kindlier expression in their eyes, speak in a gentler tone and behave in a way more befitting a free man. Such was

---

25 Cf. Ar. *Vesp.* 1299 ff., which describes a symposium at a similar period to Plato's and Xenophon's.
26 I shall use this word for the object of erotic attachments, in Greek the *erômenos*/*erômenê*; the erotic pursuer, or 'lover' is an *erastês* (pl. *erastai*). The hetaera Theodote is another Xenophontic beauty men gaze at (*Mem.* 3.11) – see Goldhill 1998. Hindley (2004: 139 n. 54) also compares Autolycus to Theodote.

the effect that Love had upon Callias on this occasion, as was duly noted by those who were initiates of this god.

[Transl. Tredennick/Waterfield, amended.]

This passage contains several points of interest. First, beauty (κάλλος) draws everyone's eye, and moves their soul (ψυχήν). We should note this is not a matter of having a 'type': everyone is drawn (as to light in the night, in Xenophon's vivid simile), and everyone experiences feelings on seeing him. The verb used for 'feeling' is *paschein*, cognate with *pathos*. This is, as we have seen, the closest Greek word to our 'emotion'; but the word also translates as 'suffering', being acted upon.[27] So while the gaze goes towards the beloved, something must come back from him to have a psychological effect on viewers.[28] It also stimulates other reactions in them, which Xenophon identifies as falling silent (an effect that continues throughout dinner – 1.11), and changing behaviour.

Callias, who is in love with Autolycus (1.2), is described as possessed (κατεχόμενος) by the god Eros. He is further along in the *erôs* script than the others, and his reactions, including changes in appearance and behaviour, are depicted more explicitly: his eyes look more kindly (φιλοφρονεστέρως ἔχουσι), his voice becomes gentler (πρᾳοτέραν), and his gestures (σχήματα) become more like those of a free man. When Callias later makes a joke, he glances towards Autolycus (1.12), presumably hoping to see him smile. Callias is not the only attendee in love: we later hear that Critobulus loves his near-age friend Clinias (4.12 ff., see further below; 8.2: ἐπιθυμεῖ); Socrates cannot say when he was not in love (ἐρῶν) with someone; Charmides has felt desire (ἐπιθυμήσαντα) for some of his many erotic pursuers (ἐραστὰς); Antisthenes is, perhaps jokingly, in love (ἐρᾷς) with Socrates; and Niceratus is in love (ἐρῶν) with his wife (8.2–3) – one of Xenophon's several reminders that *erôs* is not exclusively homosexual.[29]

In the following scene, a Syracusan brings in entertainers: a female aulos-player, a female dancer skilled in acrobatics, and a male (*pais*) dancer and cithara-player. No comment is made on the girls' appearance, but the *pais* is described as very handsome (2.1: πάνυ γε ὡραῖον) – the Greek word implying the

---

27 Hence 'passions', via the related Latin verb *patior, pati, passus*. In English, the category 'emotions' gradually replaced 'passions', 'affections' etc. over the course of the 18th/19th centuries – see Dixon 2003.
28 See Cairns 2011 on emanations from the *erômenos* affecting the gazing lover. On the connection between *erôs* and sight more generally, see Squire 2016: 25–6.
29 Cf. Waterfield 1990: 221.

attractiveness of youth.³⁰ After the musicians play, Socrates comments on the very pleasant sights and sounds (2.2: καὶ θεάματα καὶ ἀκροάματα ἥδιστα). He then refuses Callias' suggestion of bringing perfume into the room, as he prefers the smell of those exercising wearing unperfumed oil – which, just before the acrobats start dancing, can only be referring to them.

The acrobat girl dances while juggling hoops, then performs somersaults over upright swords – the only comments made are on her ability and bravery. Yet when the boy simply dances, Socrates comments again on his looks: that he is handsome (καλός) at rest, and even more so (καλλίων) when dancing (2.15) – comments later echoed by the company as a whole (2.22). Socrates continues by complimenting the boy's neck, legs, hands, and rather vigorous (2.16: εὐφορώτερον) body. When the boy plays and sings, Charmides comments that the youthful beauty (ὥρα) of *paides*, combined with music, awakens Aphrodite (3.1) – the goddess of sexual love, whose name is a euphemism for sexual desire. The Syracusan later says that everyone who sees the boy wants to sleep with (συγκαθεύδειν) him, and that he himself does so every night (4.53–4). While left inexplicit, this scene is threaded throughout with an eroticism – the beautiful boy, the dancing, the rapt viewers – which is closely tied not just to sight, but also sound and smell. Later, Socrates jokes that even touching the handsome Critobulus gave him a sting in his heart (4.28: ἐν τῇ καρδίᾳ ὥσπερ κνῆσμα) – linking yet another sense to erotic arousal.³¹

Shortly before his long speech, Socrates asks the Syracusan to have the acrobats perform a dance, so they might all most exceedingly enjoy watching them (7.2: ἡμεῖς δ' ἂν μάλιστ' ἂν εὐφραινοίμεθα θεώμενοι αὐτούς). He wants to watch the attractive youths (7.3: τοὺς καλοὺς καὶ ὡραίους θεωρεῖν), but believes that seeing them dance will be more pleasing by far (7.5: πολὺ ἐπιχαριτώτερον) than the music and acrobatics, which are described as less pleasurable (7.3: οὐδὲ ... ἥδιον).

In the final scene, this request is fulfilled: the boy and girl act Dionysus meeting Ariadne.³² All see how happy (9.3: ἀσμένη) Ariadne is when she hears the Bacchic music, so that she can barely keep still. Dionysus kneels before her most lovingly (9.4: φιλικώτατα) and kisses her, which she returns also affectionately (φιλικῶς) – he handsome (9.5: καλόν), she in youthful bloom (ὡραίαν). The

---

30 The word *pais* here is ambiguous, as later both acrobats are called *ho pais* and *hê pais* respectively (7.2), so it could simply mean a 'slave' (of any age) – however, *hôraios* shows he is young.
31 On Classical synaesthesia in general, see Butler/Purves 2013. For an instance in Latin literature where all five senses are connected to erotic desire, see Keilen 2013: 159 ff.
32 Autolycus and his father leave the room before this rather racy scene.

spectators watch their gestures as they kiss and caress each other (9.5: φιλούντων τε καὶ ἀσπαζομένων ἀλλήλους σχήματα παρῆν θεάσασθαι), not playacting, but genuinely kissing with their mouths (ἀληθινῶς τοῖς στόμασι φιλοῦντας), until the spectators are themselves aroused (ἀνεπτερωμένοι). The dancers continue to swear their love and desire for each other, until they head off to their bed – for implied consummation. At this, the unmarried men swear to get married, and the married men leap onto their horses to get home to 'encounter' their own wives (9.7: πρὸς τὰς ἑαυτῶν γυναῖκας, ὅπως τούτων τύχοιεν). This extraordinary voyeuristic scene – pornography as marital aid – is all the more intriguing at the end of a dialogue that has largely featured homosexual *erôs*, suggesting that Xenophon did not see a *pathological* distinction between erotic feelings for boys and those for women.[33]

Our methodological approach allows us to appreciate the richness of Xenophon's depiction of the early stages of *erôs*. Erotic attraction is triggered visually: i.e. caused by seeing the (usually youthful) beauty of another. This attraction can be heightened by other senses: sounds, smells, touch. It engenders a psychological feeling – a suffering in the soul – and sexual arousal, and leads to a number of behavioural changes: in facial expression, tone of voice, physical gestures, and actions. Sexual arousal can be heightened by visual erotica, and can lead one to seek satiation even with someone other than the person who has caused it, if someone (such as a wife) is available.[34]

A Young Man in Love

The most detailed depiction in *Symposium* of someone in love does not appear in this final scene, nor in the opening comments about Callias, but involves Critobulus – another of the guests, and a young man. Critobulus appears a number of

---

[33] On increasing depictions of hetero- instead of homosexual *erôs* in the fourth century, see Fisher 2013; Stafford 2013. Thesleff 1978: 168 suggests a purpose for this episode was to defend heterosexual/marital love, in response to Plato's *Symposium*'s exclusive concern with homosexual *erôs*. Regarding their relative chronology, Thesleff argues persuasively that Xen. *Symp.* 1–7 pre-dates, but 8–9 post-dates, Plato's version. See also Huss 1999b: 13–15, which summarises the debate on relative chronology; Danzig 2005.
[34] In *Vesp.* 1342–7, Philocleon prefers the more direct approach of kidnapping the sexy aulos-player, and encouraging her to give him a hand-job.

times in Xenophon's Socratic dialogues,[35] and is elsewhere consistently portrayed as having an eye for handsome youths and a desire to kiss them.[36]

In *Symposium*, he goes beyond a desire simply to kiss, to being completely love-struck with Clinias (4.23: ὑπὸ τοῦ ἔρωτος ἐκπλαγέντα) – a love that has apparently lasted some years: from the time they met at school,[37] through and past Critobulus' marriage.[38] In those early days, Socrates says teasingly, Critobulus was strongly 'on fire' (4.23: ἰσχυρῶς προσεκαύθη) for Clinias, staring at him unblinkingly as if turned to stone, but after years of Socrates' ministrations is now able to blink (4.24).[39] Socrates speculates that Critobulus had kissed Clinias, as nothing is a more terrible fuel for *erôs* (4.25) – using a second burning metaphor. A kiss provides sweet hopes (4.26: ἐλπίδας τινὰς γλυκείας).

Socrates' teasing follows Critobulus' own earnest self-description of his infatuation.[40] The sight (4.22: ὄψις) of Clinias has the power εὐφραίνειν – to gladden his mind/heart (*phrên*) or senses (*phrenes*) – though imagining Clinias' image only brings longing (πόθον). He looks with more pleasure (4.12: ἥδιον μὲν θεῶμαι)

---

35 As Socrates' interlocutor in *Oeconomicus* (esp. chs 1–6); as one of the party in *Symposium*; and in two places in *Memorabilia* (1.3.8–14 and 2.6). Waterfield 1990: 284 puts *Oeconomicus*' dramatic date between 401 and 399 BCE, and (226) *Symposium*'s in 422 BCE. Critobulus is portrayed as mature and married in the former (3.12–13), young and newly married in the latter (his wife is described as a *numphê*, 2.3; and his beard has not yet reached his chin, 4.23 and 28) – though nevertheless in love with his male age-mate Clinias. His interest in the son of Alcibiades (*Mem.* 1.3.8–14) must dramatically post-date *Symposium*, as Alcibiades could not have had a son of pursuable age by 422; *Mem.* 2.6 does not have a discernible dramatic date, though as Critobulus is seeking moral improvement the implication is that he is still young. These presentations of Critobulus are consistent and plausible.
36 *Mem.* 2.6.30–3, handsome youths in general; 1.3.8–14, the son of Alcibiades. At *Symp.* 4.18 he challenges Socrates to a beauty contest, with kisses from the acrobat boy and girl as prizes – though he apparently does not collect his winnings (6.1). *Ages.* 5.4–5 also combines handsomeness with a desire to kiss (twice resisted by Agesilaus). The tyrant Hiero wishes to do a lot more than kiss his beloved Daïlochus, but restrains himself even from that, as he would not know if Daïlochus reciprocated willingly (*Hier.* 1.31–8). Cyrus does grant two kisses to his handsome admirer (*Cyr.* 1.4.27–8), though more likely for political reasons than desire.
37 *Symp.* 4.23 – an unusual example of a near-age homosexual attraction, their respective ages signified by extent of hair growth. On near-age homosexual relationships, see further Robson 2013b: 64; also 40, referencing a scholarly debate on whether the depiction of increasingly near-age couples on fifth-century vases is merely aesthetic or reflects real life.
38 See n. 35. Robson 2013b: 16–18 argues that Athenian men typically married between their late twenties and mid-thirties – though it was not unknown to marry younger.
39 At *Cyr.* 1.4.28, the youth in love with Cyrus says that a blink of an eye takes much more than a little time, when it deprives him of looking at such a (sc. beautiful) one as he. Cyrus teasingly replies that when he returns, the young man can stare at him unblinkingly, if he chooses.
40 And perhaps aims to lighten the mood.

at Clinias than anyone else. He would rather be blind to all but Clinias, than to him alone. He is vexed (ἄχθομαι) at night or sleep for depriving him of his view, but feels the greatest gratitude (τὴν μεγίστην χάριν) towards day and the sun for returning it. Once again *erôs* is bound up closely with vision – actual rather than imagined, even if the image is always present.

A range of claimed attitudinal effects follow. Though owning money is pleasant (4.14: ἡδυ), it would be pleasanter (ἥδιον, three times) to give his to Clinias than to get more, to be Clinias' slave than to be free, and to put himself at risk for Clinias than to live risk-free; it would also be easier to work for him than to rest. He says that beloveds (*erôtikoi*) not only make one more free with money, toil-loving and glory-seeking, but also more modest and self-controlled (4.15: αἰδημονεστέρους τε καὶ ἐγκρατεστέρους) – the qualities we saw earlier combined with beauty (1.8). Critobulus would even go through fire with Clinias (4.16: ἐγὼ γοῦν μετὰ Κλεινίου κἂν διὰ πυρὸς ἰοίην).[41] He is on his mind (με ... μεμνῆσθαι) the whole time, whether mentioned or not (4.21).

Though perhaps hyperbolic, nothing in this description sounds particularly odd to us, evidencing how diachronic and cross-cultural is the experience of *erôs* (or 'being in love').[42] Yet we should note the variety of details Xenophon includes, as his picture of *erôs* gets ever richer. We have the metaphors of fire, sweetness, and pleasure; love leads one to hope; it induces the behaviour of staring fixedly at the object of one's affections; and it generates a range of attitudes or intentions, including the willingness to do things no sane person would. We might thus call it a mania,[43] a type of illness. In pathological terms, these attitudinal effects can be termed 'symptoms', and follow the involuntary physiological and behavioural changes we saw earlier,[44] as love develops from its early acute stage into a chronic form.

'Socrates' on Love When Beauty Fades

The effects of *erôs*, as we saw, begin from gazing at beauty. Through all the years of Critobulus' love for Clinias, the latter has remained beautiful. Callias likewise has fallen for Autolycus' beauty. But what happens when beauty fades? Socrates'

---

[41] Cf. the Spartan Episthenes, willing to die in place of a beautiful late-teenage boy (παῖδα καλὸν ἡβάσκοντα ἄρτι) that he has only just set eyes on (Xen. *An.* 7.4.7 ff.).
[42] Notwithstanding the ethical acceptability of an adulterous homosexual passion.
[43] As Plato does at *Phaedrus* 245B and 249D ff.
[44] 'Script' theory notes emotions make us say and do things; *erôs* also makes us think things.

speech, 'in the presence of' the *daimôn* Eros (8.1), aims to guide Callias' love away from obsession with Autolycus' physical beauty, and an assumed concomitant desire for sex with him, towards a different set of goals. This speech does not have the philosophical rigour of those in Plato's *Symposium*, though it borrows some themes,[45] but Xenophon's Socrates' concerns are generally moral rather than philosophical: to encourage his pupils towards *kalokagathia*.[46] To this end he aims to guide Callias (and Autolycus) away from the physical expression Xenophon knew Callias' love would in reality take.[47]

Socrates is depicted by both Plato and Xenophon as being, for an Athenian, unusually hostile to physical homosexual sex acts.[48] Xenophon has him compare Critias' inability to refrain from sex with his beloved, to pigs rubbing themselves against stones (*Mem.* 1.2.30). He tries to deter his pupils even from kissing boys they find beautiful (*Mem.* 1.3.8–11, 2.6.32),[49] since trying makes one beggarly (*Symp.* 8.23: ὥσπερ πτωχός), and succeeding fires up erotic desire and makes one a slave (*Symp.* 8.23: ἀνελεύθερος; cf. *Mem.* 1.2.29: ἀνελεύθερον; 1.3.11: δοῦλος μὲν εἶναι ἀντ' ἐλευθέρου). He compares kissing to being bitten by a poisonous spider, which drives one out of one's mind with pain (*Mem.* 1.3.12: οὐκ οἶσθ' ὅτι τὰ φαλάγγια οὐδ' ἡμιωβελιαῖα τὸ μέγεθος ὄντα προσαψάμενα μόνον τῷ στόματι ταῖς τε ὀδύναις ἐπιτρίβει τοὺς ἀνθρώπους καὶ τοῦ φρονεῖν ἐξίστησι;), but says the man who is *kalos and hôraios* is even more dangerous, because he inflicts his bite at a distance, and even just looking can drive one mad (1.3.13: οὐκ οἶσθ' ὅτι τοῦτο τὸ θηρίον, ὃ καλοῦσι καλὸν καὶ ὡραῖον, τοσούτῳ δεινότερόν ἐστι τῶν φαλαγγίων, ὅσῳ ἐκεῖνα μὲν ἁψάμενα, τοῦτο δὲ οὐδ' ἁπτόμενον, ἐάν τις αὐτὸ θεᾶται, ἐνίησί τι

---

45 E.g. the twin Aphrodites, Celestial and Common; love of soul being greater than love of body; the beloved more likely to reciprocate the former; etc. For similarities between the *Symposia*, see Thesleff 1978: 158–63; Huss 1999b: 449–53; Danzig 2005: 334 n. 11. Cf. n. 33 on chronology.
46 On the 'mission' of Xenophon's Socrates compared to Plato's, see Waterfield 2004. Roscalla 2004 on guidance towards *kalokagathia* as a central concern of Xenophon's writings.
47 Huss 1999a: 399–400: 'Xenophon of course must have known that historically this relationship was far from being chaste: the fragments of Eupolis' *Autolykos*, a drama which because of its great success was performed twice, do not permit any doubts on that, even discounting comic exaggeration. The affair of Kallias and Autolykos obviously was wild and known all over Athens!' Cf. *Symp.* 8.7.
48 Xen. *Lac.* 2.12–13 comments on homosexual customs in various Greek states (without mentioning Athens), and says that in Sparta relationships are forbidden when *erastai* love the body, but accepted when they love the soul. Cf. *Symp.* 8.35.
49 On one occasion, Xenophon responds that he himself would have taken the kiss (*Mem.* 1.3.10). On the distinction between Socrates' and Xenophon's views on homosexuality, see Hindley 1999 and 2004, who rightly presents Xenophon's views as the more nuanced.

καὶ πάνυ πρόσωθεν τοιοῦτον ὥστε μαίνεσθαι ποιεῖν;).⁵⁰ He accordingly advises Xenophon to run away from attractive people (1.3.13: ἀλλὰ συμβουλεύω σοι, ὦ Ξενοφῶν, ὁπόταν ἴδῃς τινὰ καλόν, φεύγειν προτροπάδην).

In *Symposium*, Socrates' aversion to 'love of body' leads on to some hostile observations that cast what we have already seen in a different light. He relabels it 'being hung up on the body' (8.19: τὸν δὲ ἐκ τοῦ σώματος κρεμάμενον), and says the lover is drunk with desire (8.21: μεθύοντα ὑπὸ τῆς Ἀφροδίτης). The lover always follows his beloved closely behind, begging and entreating for a kiss or some other caress (8.23: ἀεὶ γάρ τοι προσαιτῶν καὶ προσδεόμενος ἢ φιλήματος ἢ ἄλλου τινὸς ψηλαφήματος παρακολουθεῖ) – behavioural symptoms not mentioned by Critobulus. The lover is like a tenant farmer in only trying to maximise his harvest while in possession, rather than increase the value of the land (8.25: … μεμισθωμένῳ χῶρον ἐοικέναι. οὐ γὰρ ὅπως πλείονος ἄξιος γένηται ἐπιμελεῖται, ἀλλ' ὅπως αὐτὸς ὅτι πλεῖστα ὡραῖα καρπώσεται). In seducing, he is even more detestable than someone who uses force, because he does not just show his own baseness, but corrupts the soul of the one he persuades (8.20: καὶ μὴν ὅτι γε οὐ βιάζεται, ἀλλὰ πείθει, διὰ τοῦτο μᾶλλον μισητέος. ὁ μὲν γὰρ βιαζόμενος ἑαυτὸν πονηρὸν ἀποδεικνύει, ὁ δὲ πείθων τὴν τοῦ ἀναπειθομένου ψυχὴν διαφθείρει).⁵¹ Disparaging symptoms appear in Xenophon's other Socratic works too. In *Memorabilia*, Socrates says those involved in love affairs are less able to take care of their needs and resist what they do not need, and even those careful with money waste it (sc. on their beloveds), then do not hesitate to make more in ways they had previously considered disgraceful (1.2.22). In *Oeconomicus*, Ischomachus – a cypher for Socrates – warns one not to employ as farm-managers those sick with love of sexual pleasure (12.14: οἱ τῶν ἀφροδισίων δυσέρωτες), as they are unable to think of anything else.

Socrates notes further problems with body fixation. A beautiful body can disguise a soul that is otherwise, and so many body-lovers censure their beloveds' habits and come to hate them (*Symp.* 8.13: τῶν δὲ τοῦ σώματος ἐπιθυμούντων πολλοὶ μὲν τοὺς τρόπους μέμφονται καὶ μισοῦσι τῶν ἐρωμένων). As with any appetite, such as eating, there comes a point at which one's enjoyment of the beloved's body is sated (8.15: καὶ μὴν ἐν μὲν τῇ τῆς μορφῆς χρήσει ἔνεστί τις καὶ κόρος). Finally, the bloom of youth will pass its prime,⁵² and then the body-lover's friendship for his beloved must wither away (8.14: τὸ μὲν τῆς ὥρας ἄνθος ταχὺ

---

50 Cf. *Mem.* 1.3.13: lovers are called archers, because they wound from a distance (square-bracketed as an interpolation in the Loeb edition).
51 A similar sentiment regarding wives can be found at Lys. 1.32–3.
52 Critobulus has already disagreed with this point (4.17).

δήπου παρακμάζει, ἀπολείποντος δὲ τούτου ἀνάγκη καὶ τὴν φιλίαν συναπομαραίνεσθαι).

The solution, Socrates argues, is to pursue love of soul, even if what has first attracted one to the beloved is his beauty. He says that love of soul is much greater than love of body (8.12: πολὺ κρείττων ἐστὶν ὁ τῆς ψυχῆς ἢ ὁ τοῦ σώματος ἔρως),[53] as it does not have these downsides: the soul does not lose its beauty; in pursuing it the lover augments rather than diminishes the character of the beloved, which will increase his love; and the resulting *philia* can last forever (8.13–15). This *philia* will be mutual, since love of soul persuades the beloved to love in return (8.16: εἰκὸς καὶ ὑπὸ τῶν παιδικῶν τὸν τοιοῦτον ἐραστὴν ἀντιφιλεῖσθαι, καὶ τοῦτο διδάξω). Elsewhere, Socrates boasts that he himself is a good lover, because when he loves, yearns, and desires someone's company, he strives his utmost to be loved, yearned for, and desired for his in return (*Mem.* 2.6.28: δεινῶς γὰρ ὧν ἂν ἐπιθυμήσω ἀνθρώπων ὅλος ὥρμημαι ἐπὶ τὸ φιλῶν τε αὐτοὺς ἀντιφιλεῖσθαι ὑπ' αὐτῶν καὶ ποθῶν ἀντιποθεῖσθαι καὶ ἐπιθυμῶν συνεῖναι καὶ ἀντεπιθυμεῖσθαι τῆς συνουσίας). Socrates anticipates the change from sexual to friendly love with which I opened this chapter, a change which is obscured in Greek due to their two separate labels, *erôs* and *philia*. He thus provides two pathways that lead to two possible endings for *erôs* episodes: a withering away into indifference, due to the lover's fixation solely on the physical; or its metamorphosis into *philia*, as the lover increasingly cares for his beloved's soul.

Cyrus, Araspas, Adrabatas and Pantheia

We have finally exhausted what *Symposium* has to tell us; but another collection of *erôs* stories, all interrelated and heterosexual,[54] appear in *Cyropaedia*. After the defeat of the Assyrians, the captives include Pantheia, the Lady of Susa, whose husband Adrabatas is away on an embassy (*Cyr.* 5.1.3). Pantheia is allotted to Cyrus, since she is reputed to be the most beautiful woman in Asia (4.6.11: ἣ καλλίστη δὴ λέγεται ἐν τῇ Ἀσίᾳ γυνὴ γενέσθαι), distinguished by her height, virtue, and grace (5.1.5: διήνεγκε δ' ἐνταῦθα πρῶτον μὲν τῷ μεγέθει, ἔπειτα δὲ καὶ τῇ ἀρετῇ καὶ τῇ εὐσχημοσύνῃ). However, surpassing Socrates' usual determination not to kiss

---

53 In *Memorabilia*, Xenophon says Socrates clearly loved people because their souls were inclined to virtue, not their bodies to youthful beauty (4.1.2: πολλάκις γὰρ ἔφη μὲν ἄν τινος ἐρᾶν, φανερὸς δ' ἦν οὐ τῶν τὰ σώματα πρὸς ὥραν, ἀλλὰ τῶν τὰς ψυχὰς πρὸς ἀρετὴν εὖ πεφυκότων ἐφιέμενος).
54 Though still mostly focused on the male lover's *erôs*.

beautiful people, Cyrus agrees with his even stronger advice: to run away. He forbears even to look at Pantheia, since he has heard she is beautiful (καλή), and having gazed at her once fears he will keep returning to gaze again, and neglect his duties through gazing (5.1.8, repeatedly using the verb θεάσθαι). He therefore self-centredly asks his friend Araspas to be her guardian.[55]

Araspas is sceptical that beauty (κάλλος) causes love, since everyone would love the same people, just as fire burns all equally; instead, we love some beautiful people but not others (5.1.9–10: τῶν δὲ καλῶν τῶν μὲν ἐρῶσι τῶν δ' οὔ, καὶ ἄλλος γε ἄλλου). Even beautiful people cannot compel one's love; rather it is worthless men, incontinent in all their desires, who put the blame on love (5.1.14: καὶ οἱ καλοὶ οὐκ ἀναγκάζουσιν ἐρᾶν ἑαυτῶν ..., ἀλλὰ τὰ μοχθηρὰ ἀνθρώπια πασῶν οἶμαι τῶν ἐπιθυμιῶν ἀκρατῆ ἐστι, κἄπειτα ἔρωτα αἰτιῶνται). He has seen Pantheia and found her beautiful, but it has not affected the performance of his duties (5.1.15).

Cyrus disagrees, saying Araspas had merely not been sufficiently exposed, since *erôs* takes a while to seize hold of a man (5.1.16: ἴσως γὰρ θᾶττον ἀπῆλθες ἢ ἐν ὅσῳ χρόνῳ ἔρως πέφυκε συσκευάζεσθαι ἄνθρωπον). Copying Araspas' comparison, Cyrus says we can touch fire briefly without being burned, and a log takes a while to kindle. He would neither touch fire, nor look upon the beautiful (οὔτε τοὺς καλοὺς εἰσορῶ), and – ignoring that he is about to hand Pantheia over to him – advises Araspas to act likewise. To be burned by fire one must touch it, but – as Socrates also points out (*Mem.* 1.3.13, above) – beautiful people inflame those gazing even from afar, so that they burn with love (οἱ δὲ καλοὶ καὶ τοὺς ἄπωθεν θεωμένους ὑφάπτουσιν, ὥστε αἴθεσθαι τῷ ἔρωτι). As in *Symposium* and elsewhere in Xenophon, *erôs* is caused by seeing beauty, and is likened to fire.

Araspas believes that he is immune, but his pride goes before a falling in love, as Xenophon proleptically tells us: seeing her beauty and good character, he was conquered by love (5.1.18: ἅμα μὲν ὁρῶν καλὴν τὴν γυναῖκα, ἅμα δὲ αἰσθανόμενος τὴν καλοκἀγαθίαν αὐτῆς ... ἡλίσκετο ἔρωτι). Importantly, though, it was not simply exposure to her beauty that caused this love, but additionally – in the '...' above – Araspas spent time with Pantheia, took care of her and thought he gratified her, perceived she was not ungrateful, and (through her servants) she took care of him in return (ἅμα δὲ θεραπεύων αὐτὴν καὶ οἰόμενος χαρίζεσθαι αὐτῇ, ἅμα δὲ αἰσθανόμενος οὐκ ἀχάριστον οὖσαν, ἀλλ' ἐπιμελομένην διὰ τῶν αὐτῆς οἰκετῶν ὡς καὶ εἰσιόντι εἴη αὐτῷ τὰ δέοντα καὶ εἴ ποτε ἀσθενήσειεν, ὡς μηδενὸς

---

55 On Cyrus' manipulation of Araspas, Adrabatas and Pantheia for his own benefit, see Whidden 2007a: 551–3; also Whidden 2007b: 150–2. The latter examines Cyrus' deceptions and manipulations throughout *Cyropaedia*.

ἐνδέοιτο). It was out of *all* these things that he fell in love (ἐκ πάντων τούτων ἡλίσκετο ἔρωτι).

This is important because it explains why everybody does not simply fall in love with the same people, i.e. the beautiful ones. We saw in *Symposium* that everyone responded to Autolycus' beauty with the first stages of erotic attraction. But it was only Callias who had fallen in love with him, and that was – reading between the lines – because Callias had spent time with Autolycus, and had been given reason to believe Autolycus was happy with Callias paying suit to him. On more than one occasion in *Symposium* they look towards each other or exchange glances (1.12, 3.13, 8.42), which hints towards a developed sense of what the other is thinking, and a desire to respond in unison. This growing sense of connection, arising out of time spent together, is for both Callias and Araspas what turns erotic attraction into love.

When we return to Araspas' story (*Cyr.* 6.1.31: ληφθεὶς ἔρωτι), we find him pressing to sleep with Pantheia, and threatening to do so by force if she will not succumb willingly.[56] She reports this to Cyrus who subsequently speaks with Araspas, and blames himself for putting him in that irresistible (ἀμάχῳ) position (6.1.32–6). Araspas theorises that he must have two souls, one good and one bad, since otherwise he could not want to do both fine and shameful deeds. He says he has philosophised this with the unjust sophist Eros (6.1.41: νῦν τοῦτο πεφιλοσόφηκα μετὰ τοῦ ἀδίκου σοφιστοῦ τοῦ Ἔρωτος); Cyrus' helping hand has allowed his good soul to triumph. Cyrus refers to a different ambivalence in the man in love, when he asks Araspas (in their earlier encounter) why, if falling in love (ἐρασθῆναι) is a matter of free will, people cannot cease when they wish (5.1.12)? He has seen people crying with agony because of love, and enslaved to their lovers (ἑώρακα καὶ κλαίοντας ὑπὸ λύπης δι' ἔρωτα, καὶ δουλεύοντάς γε τοῖς ἐρωμένοις) – echoing Critobulus; giving them what they could not spare; and praying to be freed from love like any other disease (εὐχομένους ὥσπερ καὶ ἄλλης τινὸς νόσου ἀπαλλαγῆναι), without success. But unlike slaves, instead of themselves trying to escape, lovers keep guard on those they love to stop them running away (5.1.12). These are clearly symptoms of unrequited, or unwanted, love.

Pantheia, however, does love her husband (6.1.31: ἐφίλει γὰρ αὐτὸν ἰσχυρῶς), Adrabatas. And when Cyrus allows him to return, having sent Araspas away on a spying mission, they embrace as expected for those who had lost hope (6.1.47: ἠσπάζοντο ἀλλήλους ὡς εἰκὸς ἐκ δυσελπίστων). When he is again sent off to battle, she sheds tears down her cheeks (6.4.3: ἐλείβετο δὲ αὐτῇ τὰ δάκρυα κατὰ τῶν παρειῶν), and in exhorting him to bravery she says she would rather

---

56 As in Archil. fr. 196a W (see above).

die with him than live shamefully if he shamefully survives, because of their mutual love (6.4.6: τὴν ἐμὴν καὶ σὴν φιλίαν). When he does die in battle, she laments for him (7.3.9: ἀνωδύρατο; 7.3.14: ὀδύρομαι), then commits suicide over his body (7.3.14). The mutuality of their love is emphasised not just by 'my and your' (ἐμὴν καὶ σήν), but in the *philia* which Socrates has told us is the true end of a mutual *erôs*: an *erôs* for the soul. Critobulus was willing to go through fire for Clinias; Pantheia is willing to die with Adrabatas.[57]

Cyropaedia repeats a great many details of *erôs* episodes that appear in the Socratic works. Erotic attraction is again impelled by seeing beauty, with both the loveliness of Pantheia and vision emphasised. Spending time together and developing a connection are important, and this leads to a growing care for each other. On the lover's part, this combines with a belief his feelings are encouraged, to lead to what we would call 'falling in love'. *Erôs* is again compared to fire, and suggests illness or madness. Behavioural traits include obsessively thinking about the beloved, or trying to be with them, a willingness to be a slave to them, and to die for/with them. Time apart – whether briefly for Critobulus and Clinias, or a long time for Adrabatas and Pantheia – does not diminish true love's intensity. The best way to avoid love is, in fact, to avoid the young and beautiful in the first place.

Conclusion

The methodology that I have used, derived from emotion script theory, has helped us to 'read' a range of love experiences in *Symposium*, *Cyropaedia* and elsewhere in the Xenophontic corpus, and the picture that has built up of the pathology of love is remarkably uniform.

Erotic attraction begins when one sees a beautiful (*kalos/kalê*) person – usually the beauty of youth (*hôraios/hôraia*). This attraction is enhanced by watching them move around (especially vigorous athletic movement), and by accompanying stimulation of other senses – hearing, smell, touch. Something is reflected back from the beloved, to affect the viewer's soul. After spending a considerable time in their company, talking with them and/or doing things for their benefit, developing the feeling that one's attentions are wanted, encouraged or reciprocated, the initial erotic desire develops into 'falling in love'. Kissing the beloved

---

[57] Xen. *Hell.* 4.8.39 reports a beloved who remains to die beside his lover in battle. See further Leitao 2002: 144 with nn. 7–11. Cf. n. 41 above.

particularly stimulates the lover, and leads to an intensity of feelings that is frequently described with fire metaphors, or as madness or illness.

A range of symptoms follow. These include initially falling silent, changes in the pitch of the voice, staring at the beloved, facial expressions becoming kindlier, bodily gestures becoming freer, and feeling a strong sexual desire. On falling in love, one's thoughts also change: the beloved is on one's mind all the time, whether present or not; seeing them gladdens the heart (*euphrainein*); and their absence causes longing (*pothos*), though does not dampen love. The lover follows his beloved around, is happy to waste money on them, to give all his possessions to them, to be their slave, and to risk his life for them. If they die, he wishes to die too.

Unrequited love makes one cry with agony. The lover becomes his beloved's guard, as he jealousy keeps watch on them. His soul is divided, wanting to do both good and shameful things to the beloved – possibly resulting in violence. Requited love lasts, however (unless the beloved's bad habits are off-putting), and ends in one of two ways: either it remains a love of the beautiful, youthful body, and fades with the beloved's looks; or it engenders a love of their soul, and transforms gradually into *philia*.

Xenophon, in the extracts I have examined, provides rich illustrations of the experience of being both erotically attracted and fully 'in love'. He describes a pathology that applies to both homo- and heterosexual love, and has good claim to reflect 'real life' experience of *erôs*, at least for men – perhaps more so than any other Classical Greek author. He fully deserves to be considered alongside Plato, tragedy, and other more frequently explored authors and genres. I hope, further, to have demonstrated the value of a methodology which could, and I believe should, be used much more widely – not least in exploring the pathology of love.

Andreas N. Michalopoulos
The Pathology of Love in Ovid's *Metamorphoses*

Abstract: Love plays a leading role in the *Metamorphoses*, despite the apparent epic nature of this work, and often displays the features of a pathological emotion with dire consequences for those involved: a nymph vanishes into thin air when her love finds no response; mothers kill their children to get revenge from the men that insulted and hurt them; a daughter kills her father because she falls in love with his enemy; a sister falls in love with her brother; a daughter falls in love with her father; lovers kill or transform their rivals out of morbid jealousy, and so on. This chapter explores the pathology of love in the *Metamorphoses* by examining two love stories as case studies. The first story is about the love of a god for a nymph (Apollo and Daphne: *Met.* 1.452–567) and the second is about love between two mortals (Iphis and Anaxarete: *Met.* 14.698–761). Both stories depict *erôs* as a disease and a wound, and are discussed here in connection to Ovid's main thesis in the *Remedia amoris* that 'love is curable'. The retrospective reading of the *Remedia* sheds light upon those stories in which love takes the form of a pathological emotion.

In the fourth book of his *De Rerum Natura* Lucretius provides a thoughtful review of the Epicurean theory of erotic desire, and famously writes about the wound of love, the disease of love, and sexual desire (4.1037–1287). Lucretius elaborates on a long-established metaphor in Greek and Latin literature; however, his treatment is not at all metaphorical: he deals with love as literally a wound (4.1047–57), injurious to the mind, and as a disease that consumes one's strength and one's body from the inside. He claims that love is mixed with pain (4.1073–85) and is never satisfied (4.1086–100), and that love deludes the lover and makes him praise his mistress for her faults (4.1153–70). Lucretius uses terminology deriving from Greek lyric and Hellenistic poetry, and also from medicine:[1] *furor* (1069, 1117), *dolor* (1067), *ardor* (1077), *miser* (1076, 1096), *sanus/insanus* (1075), *ulcus* (1068), *vulnus* (1070), *lepos* (1133), and *deliciae* (1156).[2] He urges his readers to avoid love's snares (4.1058–72) and to fight against love, especially at its beginning (4.1146–52).

---
1 Betensky 1980: 292.
2 On Lucretius' terminology see Langslow 1999: 202–5.

Nearly half a century after Lucretius, Publius Ovidius Naso deservedly earned the reputation of Rome's experienced *praeceptor amoris*, 'teacher of love'. Taking over from his elegiac predecessors Cornelius Gallus, Sextus Propertius, and Albius Tibullus, Ovid embarked on an ambitious poetic oeuvre centred around love in all its manifestations. In the *Amores* he records scenes from his love affair with a beautiful but fickle woman, Corinna, while in the *Heroides* he gives pen and paper to famous women of myth to write their letters to their lovers (or husbands) who have abandoned them for various reasons. After these first two works – and, quite possibly, after a tragedy named *Medea*,[3] which unfortunately is now lost – Ovid explores, analyses, and presents love in the form of a lesson to his readers in the *Ars Amatoria* and the *Remedia Amoris*.[4] The fact that these didactic works are composed in the elegiac couplet and not the dactylic hexameter, which is the traditional metre of 'serious' didactic poetry (e.g. Hesiod's *Works and Days*, Lucretius' *De Rerum Natura*, Vergil's *Georgica*), speaks for the humorous and light-hearted way in which Ovid approaches amatory teaching. In these works the reader may learn the secrets and techniques necessary for the game of love. The foundation of Ovid's argumentation is the extensive use of mythology. Equally impressive is his intense interest in female psychology.[5] Ovid elaborates on the comic and the didactic tradition, but also apparently draws from his personal experience, already laid out in his *Amores* (*Ars* 1.29–30): *usus opus movet hoc: vati parete perito;* | *vera canam. coeptis, mater Amoris, ades* ('Experience prompts this work: listen to the expert poet: I sing true: Venus, help my venture!')[6]

---

[3] Tac. *Dial.* 12, Quint. 10.1.98. On Ovid's *Medea* see Della Corte 1970–1971; Nikolaidis 1985; Hinds 1993: 34–46; Bessone 1997: 14–19; Heinze 1997: 21–4.

[4] Before the third book of the *Ars Amatoria* (see *Ars* 3.205–6: *est mihi, quo dixi vestrae medicamina formae,* | *parvus, sed cura grande, libellus, opus* 'It is I who spoke of facial treatments for your beauty, a little book, but one whose labour took great care'), Ovid also published another didactic poem, the *Medicamina faciei femineae*, in which he offers instructions to the Roman women on the grooming of their face (cf. also Ov. *Am.* 1.14 on the same subject). Ovid parodies the serious didactic tradition and chooses, *more Hellenistico*, a theme from everyday life, with amatory ramifications. Sadly, only the first hundred lines of the work survive.

[5] Following in the footsteps of Euripides, Ovid displayed a remarkable understanding of female nature. See Haley 1924–1925; Jacobson 1974: 7; Harvey 1989; Culham 1990: 163 with nn. 21–5; Hallett 1990: 191–4; Spoth 1992: 59–62; Rimell 1999; Lindheim 2003: chs. 2 and 3; Spentzou 2003: 13–24; Fulkerson 2005: 1–18.

[6] Transl. Kline, throughout this chapter.

In the first two books of the *Ars Amatoria*,⁷ Ovid advises men on how to be winners in the game of love, how to conquer the women they love and keep them their own (*Ars* 1.35–40): *principio, quod amare velis, reperire labora, | qui nova nunc primum miles in arma venis. | proximus huic labor est placitam exorare puellam: | tertius, ut longo tempore duret amor. | hic modus, haec nostro signabitur area curru: | haec erit admissa meta terenda rota.* ('Now the first task for you who come as a raw recruit is to find out who you might wish to love. The next task is to make sure that she likes you: the third, to see to it that the love will last. That's my aim, that's the ground my chariot will cover: that's the post my thundering wheels will scrape'). In the third book of the *Ars*, published a little later, it is the turn of the women to benefit from the *praeceptor*'s wise *erotodidaxis* (*Ars* 3.1–2): *arma dedi Danais in Amazonas; arma supersunt, | quae tibi dem et turmae, Penthesilea, tuae* ('I've given the Greeks arms, against Amazons: arms remain, to give to you Penthesilea, and your Amazon troop').⁸

The *Ars Amatoria* is complemented by the *Remedia Amoris*, published between 1 BCE and 2 CE.⁹ Ovid now undertakes the task to teach the unhappy and troubled lovers specific ways to get rid of their passion (*Rem.* 43–4): *discite sanari per quem didicistis amare; | una manus vobis vulnus opemque feret* ('Learn how to be cured, from him who taught you how to love: the one hand brings the wound and the relief').¹⁰ In a way clearly reminiscent of Lucretius, Ovid now treats love as a disease and as a wound which can be healed.¹¹

---

7 The first two books were probably released together between 2 BCE and 1 BCE. A secure chronological marker is Ovid's mention of the re-enactment of the sea-battle of Salamis in 2 BCE as part of the festivities for the opening of the temple of Mars Vltor (*Ars* 1.171–2): *quid, modo cum belli navalis imagine Caesar | Persidas induxit Cecropiasque rates?* ('When, lately, Caesar, in mock naval battle, exhibited the Greek and Persian fleets').
8 Cf. Ov. *Ars* 3.811–12: *ut quondam iuvenes, ita nunc, mea turba, puellae | inscribant spoliis 'Naso magister erat'.* ('As once the boys, so now my crowd of girls inscribe on your trophies "Ovid was my master"').
9 Cf. Ovid's reference to the Parthian War of 1 BCE – 2 CE (*Rem.* 155–8): *ecce, fugax Parthus, magni nova causa triumphi, | iam videt in campis Caesaris arma suis: | vince Cupideas pariter Parthasque sagittas, | et refer ad patrios bina tropaea deos* ('Behold, the fleeing Parthian, fresh cause of a great triumph, he sees Caesar's weapons now in his own country: Conquer both the arrows of Cupid and Parthia, and bring back twin trophies to your native gods'). For the most recent discussion of the chronology of Ovid's works see Harrison 2017.
10 Cf. Ov. *Rem.* 47–8: *vulnus in Herculeo quae quondam fecerat hoste, | vulneris auxilium Pelias hasta tulit* ('Achilles' spear that once wounded Telephus, his enemy, also brought the cure for the wound'). On the theme of 'learning to love', see Fedeli on Horace (forthcoming).
11 Cf. Ov. *Rem.* 81: *opprime, dum nova sunt, subiti mala semina morbi* ('Crush the evil germs of sudden illness while they are young').

Rhetorical sophistication, humour, and the wide use of mythology are key features of the *Remedia* too.[12] Lines 55–68 are of particular interest for my discussion about the pathology of love in the *Metamorphoses*. Ovid makes a bold, metaliterary claim: some mythological characters would have been able to change their established literary history and heal themselves from their love passion, if only they had had access to his teachings (*Rem.* 55–68):[13]

>   vixisset Phyllis, si me foret usa magistro,   55
>   et per quod novies, saepius isset iter;
>   nec moriens Dido summa vidisset ab arce
>   Dardanias vento vela dedisse rates;
>   nec dolor armasset contra sua viscera matrem,
>   quae socii damno sanguinis ulta virum est.   60
>   arte mea Tereus, quamvis Philomela placeret,
>   per facinus fieri non meruisset avis.
>   da mihi Pasiphaen, iam tauri ponet amorem:
>   da Phaedram, Phaedrae turpis abibit amor.
>   crede Parim nobis, Helenen Menelaus habebit,   65
>   nec manibus Danais Pergama victa cadent.
>   impia si nostros legisset Scylla libellos,
>   haesisset capiti purpura, Nise, tuo.

Phyllis would have lived, if she'd used me as her master, and gone the way she went, nine times, more often. Dido, as she died, would not have watched the Trojan ships, from the summit of her tower, as they set sail: nor would pain have armed Medea against her children, taking vengeance on her husband by harming his offspring. By using my art, Tereus, when Philomela charmed him, would not have deserved to become a bird for his crime. Give Pasiphae to me, then, surely, she'd lose her love for the bull. Give me Phaedra: Phaedra's shameful love will vanish. Trust Paris to me, Menelaus would have Helen, and Troy not conquered to fall at the hands of Greeks. If impious Scylla could have read my books, Nisus, the purple lock would cling to your head.

Of these figures, Medea (59–60 and 261–2), Tereus (61–2 and 459–60), and Scylla (67–8) also feature in the *Metamorphoses*.[14] In this chapter, I will discuss the

---

12 Ovid takes pains to state that the cures he proposes are common for both sexes, whereas in the *Ars Amatoria* he had offered advice to men and women in separate books (*Rem.* 49–50): *sed quaecumque viris, vobis quoque dicta, puellae,* | *credite: diversis partibus arma damus* ('But believe me, girls, I tell to you whatever I tell the men: I grant weapons to either side').
13 Ovid mentions Phyllis (55–6), Dido (57–8), Medea (59–60, cf. also *Rem.* 261–2), Tereus (61–2, cf. also *Rem.* 459–60), Pasiphae (63), Phaedra (64), Paris (65–6) and Scylla (67–8). This Scylla is the daughter of Nisus, King of Megara, not the Homeric Scylla.
14 At *Rem.* 99–100 Ovid mentions Myrrha too, the daughter of Cinyras, who also features in a love story of the *Metamorphoses* (10.298–502).

Metamorphoses in the light of Ovid's teaching in the *Remedia Amoris*, i.e. that love is curable. I will attempt to show that the retrospective reading of the *Remedia Amoris* may shed light on some of the stories in the *Metamorphoses* in which love is depicted as a pathological emotion. I am using the terms 'pathology' and 'pathological' as medical terms meaning 'physical or mental illness', 'the typical behaviour of a disease', 'the manifestations of disease'. I will focus on a couple of stories of pathological love, in which love leads to destruction either both people involved, or just one of them.

The *Metamorphoses* combines elements of various genres (heroic epic, didactic poetry, comedy, tragedy, elegy, bucolic poetry, rhetoric, etc.).[15] Despite the apparent epic nature of the work, love plays a leading role in it and appears in several different forms: conjugal love, pure love, romantic love, unfulfilled love, destructive love, violent love, illicit love, unnatural love, forbidden love, love between mortals, love between gods and mortals. In the *Metamorphoses* the consequences of pathological love are impressively variegated: a nymph vanishes into thin air when her love finds no response (Echo: 3.341–510); mothers kill their children out of revenge for betrayed love (Procne: 6.424–674; Medea: 7.1–99); a daughter kills her father because she falls in love with his enemy (Scylla: 8.17–151); a sister falls in love with her brother (Byblis: 9.450–665); a daughter falls in love with her father (Myrrha: 10.298–502); lovers kill or transform their rivals out of morbid jealousy (Polyphemus and Circe respectively).

I will focus on two symptomatic love stories as case studies on the pathology of love in the *Metamorphoses*: the first is about the love of a god (Apollo) for a mortal (Daphne); the second is about the love between mortals, Iphis and Anaxarete. Where necessary, I will also refer to the story of Tereus (*Met.* 6.424–674), whom Ovid had listed among those who might have profited from his *erotodidaxis* (*Rem.* 61–2, quoted above).

---

[15] The *Metamorphoses* is a special and novel epic. Although it is composed in the dactylic hexameter – the epic metre *par excellence* – there is no unity of place, time, protagonist or plot. Ovid himself considers it a *carmen perpetuum* (ἄεισμα διηνεκές), which is *deductum* at the same time (Ov. *Met.* 1.4: *ad mea perpetuum deducite tempora carmen!*), i.e. finely woven, in accordance with the requirements of the Callimachean poetic ideal; see Hofmann 1985. *Deductum* is used by Vergil as a poetological term in his own adaptation of the prologue of Callimachus' *Aetia* in his sixth *Eclogue* (6.3–5): *cum canerem reges et proelia, Cynthius aurem | vellit et admonuit: 'pastorem, Tityre, pinguis | pascere oportet ovis, deductum dicere carmen'*. See Coleman 1977 *ad loc.* and Clausen 1994 *ad loc.* Cf. Hor. *Epist.* 2.1.225: *tenui deducta poemata filo* with Rudd 1989 *ad loc.*

Apollo and Daphne (*Met.* 1.452–567)

It is only reasonable to begin the discussion of the pathology of love in the *Metamorphoses* with the work's first love story, Apollo and Daphne. This story contains many of the features, themes, and motifs of subsequent love stories (e.g. the depiction of female beauty, the failed erotic pursuit, the equation of hunting with love). In other words, it is programmatic as far as the theme of love is concerned.[16] The story begins at line 452. Ovid introduces Daphne to his readers as the object of Apollo's love: *primus amor Phoebi Daphne Peneia* ('Phoebus' first love was Daphne, daughter of Peneus').

Immediately after Daphne's brief introduction, Ovid focuses on how Apollo ended up being in love with the nymph. This love was the result of the rage of the god Amor (*Met.* 1.451–2): *quem non | fors ignara dedit, sed saeva Cupidinis ira* ('not through chance but because of Cupid's fierce anger'). This is an ominous reference right there, at the beginning of the story. At the same time, it clearly shows that the character moving the threads of the plot is neither Daphne nor the omnipotent god Apollo; it is rather the god Amor. Ovid narrates the quarrel between Apollo and Amor over a purely manly matter: virility and valour. Apollo mocks the unwarlike Amor for handling manly weapons and proudly proclaims that the bow and the arrows are appropriate only for himself. After all, Apollo has just now wiped out the giant serpent Python, thus confirming his manhood in the most emphatic manner. Apollo is introduced in the *Metamorphoses* as the epitome of manliness. The informed reader will surely recall the confrontation between Ovid himself and the god Amor in the first elegy of the *Amores*, where Ovid, much like the epic Apollo of the *Metamorphoses*, reprimands Amor for turning his poetry from epic to elegiac,[17] just as he was about to compose an epic.[18]

---

16 See among others Davis 1983; Herter 1983; Heath 1991; Holzberg 1999; Wheeler 1999: 188.
17 For the poetological and generic aspects of the dispute between Apollo and Amor and its close relation with the prologue of Callimachus' *Aetia* as well as with the similar dispute between Ovid and Amor in *Am.* 1.1, see among others Primmer 1976; Nicoll 1980; Knox 1986: 14–18; Schmitzer 1990: 72–3; Wills 1990; Conte 1991: 149.
18 On the contrary, in the preface of the *Remedia Amoris* Ovid makes sure to placate Amor and reassure him that he does not wish to wage war against him (*Rem.* 1–4): *legerat huius Amor titulum nomenque libelli:* | '*bella mihi, video, bella parantur*' *ait.* | '*parce tuum vatem sceleris damnare, Cupido,* | *tradita qui toties te duce signa tuli.*' ('Love, having read the name and title on this book, said: "It's war, you declare against me, I see, it's war". "Cupid, don't condemn your poet for a crime, who has so often raised the standard you trusted him with, under your command"'). See also *Rem.* 11–12: *nec te, blande puer, nec nostras prodimus artes,* | *nec nova*

Back to the *Metamorphoses*, Apollo boasts of his ability in hunting and war; he is particularly aggressive towards Amor, firmly separating their jurisdiction and fields of activity (*Met.* 1.457–62): *ista decent umeros gestamina nostros, | qui dare certa ferae, dare vulnera possumus hosti, | qui modo pestifero tot iugera ventre prementem | stravimus innumeris tumidum Pythona sagittis. | tu face nescio quos esto contentus amores | inritare tua, nec laudes adsere nostras!* ('That one is suited to my shoulders, since I can hit wild beasts of a certainty, and wound my enemies, and not long ago destroyed with countless arrows the swollen Python that covered many acres with its plague-ridden belly. You should be intent on stirring the concealed fires of love with your burning brand, not laying claim to my glories!'). Responding to the insult, Amor is determined to take revenge. He announces right away that he will turn the hunter Apollo into his prey and that he is far more powerful than him (*Met.* 1.463–5): *figat tuus omnia, Phoebe, | te meus arcus' ait; 'quantoque animalia cedunt | cuncta deo, tanto minor est tua gloria nostra* ('You may hit every other thing Phoebus, but my bow will strike you: to the degree that all living creatures are less than gods, by that degree is your glory less than mine'). I will return later to this reference to hunting, Apollo's depiction as a hunter, and the conversion of hunter into prey.

The god Amor shoots Apollo with a golden arrow which causes love,[19] but he shoots Daphne with a lead arrow which drives love away (1.468–73).[20] The shooting of Amor instantly turns the epic Apollo, the mighty conqueror of the

---

praeteritum Musa retexit opus ('Sweet Boy, I've not betrayed you or my art, and this new Muse unravels no prior work'). Ovid states that his sole purpose is to save those whom their cruel erotic passion leads to death (*Rem.* 15–20): *at siquis male fert indignae regna puellae, | ne pereat, nostrae sentiat artis opem. | cur aliquis laqueo collum nodatus amator | a trabe sublimi triste pependit onus? | cur aliquis rigido fodit sua pectora ferro? | invidiam caedis, pacis amator, habes* ('But any man who suffers badly from the power of a worthless girl, shouldn't die, if he understands the help that's in my art. Why should any lover hang from a high beam, a sad weight, with a knotted rope round his neck? Why should anyone stab himself with cold steel? Lover of Peace, you earn dislike for such hateful death').

19 Ironically, Amor shoots Apollo from the top of Parnassus (467), the mountain where Apollo's famous oracle would later be established. In this oracle the priestess Pythia, who spoke the prophecies, would use laurel to inspire her divine frenzy.

20 Ov. *Met.* 1.468–73: *eque sagittifera prompsit duo tela pharetra | diversorum operum: fugat hoc, facit illud amorem; | quod facit, auratum est et cuspide fulget acuta, | quod fugat, obtusum est et habet sub harundine plumbum. | hoc deus in nympha Peneide fixit, at illo | laesit Apollineas traiecta per ossa medullas* ('And took two arrows with opposite effects from his full quiver: one kindles love, the other dispels it. The one that kindles is golden with a sharp glistening point, the one that dispels is blunt with lead beneath its shaft. With the second he transfixed Peneus' daughter, but with the first he wounded Apollo piercing him to the marrow of his bones').

Python, into an elegiac lover, infatuated with Daphne. The love-struck Apollo is stripped of his epic mantle and puts on an elegiac one, i.e. he becomes potentially and metapoetically one of those who could benefit from Ovid's *erotodidaxis*. In essence, Apollo's problem is similar to the problem that the love-stricken readers of the *Remedia Amoris* face: his love for Daphne is without response. But what is even worse for Apollo is that his passion for Daphne has been imposed on him by Amor as a harsh punishment.

It is indeed ironic that Apollo falls in love with Daphne at the peak of his intense epic activity. The irony becomes even greater in the light of Ovid's advice in the *Remedia* that lovers should start an active lifestyle in order to overcome their passion (*Rem.* 135–6): *ergo ubi visus eris nostra medicabilis arte, | fac monitis fugias otia prima meis* ('So when you're ready for my medical arts, first ban idleness, on my advice'). Likewise, Ovid advises those who want to forget about love to take up hunting or fishing (*Rem.* 199–200): *vel tu venandi studium cole: saepe recessit | turpiter a Phoebi victa sorore Venus* ('Or you can cultivate the art of hunting: often Venus retreated in shame from her conquering sister Phoebe').[21] Apollo is exactly that: he is a hunter and a fighter, but even so he falls prey to Amor.[22] There is an obvious conclusion to be drawn here: in the relentless world of the *Metamorphoses* love is inescapable; there is no safe shelter from it. Ovid's teachings in the *Remedia Amoris* against love are now cancelled.

But what does 'pathology of love' really mean in the case of Apollo? Let us now take a close look at the love symptoms that he experiences and his actions when in love, keeping in mind Ovid's advice in the *Remedia Amoris* on how to avoid love's torture. Apollo is burning with love and is being paralleled to crops on fire (*Met.* 1.492–6): *utque leves stipulae demptis adolentur aristis, | ut facibus saepes ardent, quas forte viator | vel nimis admovit vel iam sub luce reliquit, | sic deus in flammas abiit, sic pectore toto | uritur* ('As the light stubble of an empty cornfield blazes; as sparks fire a hedge when a traveller, by mischance, lets them get too close, or forgets them in the morning; so the god was altered by the flames, and all his heart burned'). He seems unable to fight against his passion and hope nourishes his love (*Met.* 1.496): *sterilem sperando nutrit amorem* ('feeding his useless desire with hope'). I believe it is worth mentioning that Tereus too is struck by Philomela's extraordinary beauty the moment he first lays eyes on her, and is paralleled to corn stubble on fire (*Met.* 6.455–7): *non secus exarsit conspecta virgine Tereus, | quam si quis canis ignem supponat aristis | aut frondem positasque cremet faenilibus herbas* ('Seeing the girl, Tereus

---

21 In the *Metamorphoses* Daphne rejects love, takes up hunting and lives in the woods (1.474–6).
22 It is also ironic that Apollo chases a devoted follower of his own sister, Diana.

took fire, just as if someone touched a flame to corn stubble, or burned the leaves, or hay stored in a loft').[23] One should also note that Tereus, too, makes no effort whatsoever to fight against his passion. He has no qualms and is ready to do anything, driven by his unbridled desire (6.465–6): *et nihil est, quod non effreno captus amore | ausit, nec capiunt inclusas pectora flammas* ('There was nothing he would not dare, possessed by unbridled desire, nor could he contain the flame in his heart').

Back to Apollo, the love-struck god does not differ at all from the elegiac lover: their symptoms and conduct are the same. Apollo's actions run contrary to Ovid's specific advice in the *Remedia* for abstinence, for withdrawal from one's beloved, and for focusing on her flaws (*Rem.* 291–356). Apollo does exactly the opposite. He rekindles his love by constantly watching and admiring Daphne's beauty. Her alluring features (hair, eyes, lips, fingers, hands) are described through Apollo's lustful gaze (497–502), a fact on which Ovid lays particular emphasis with the use of the verb *spectare* (497) and the triple repetition of the verb *videre* in lines 498, 499, 500:[24] *spectat inornatos collo pendere capillos | et 'quid, si comantur?' ait. videt igne micantes | sideribus similes oculos, videt oscula, quae non | est vidisse satis. laudat digitosque manusque | bracchiaque et nudos media plus parte lacertos; | si qua latent, meliora putat* ('He sees her disordered hair hanging about her neck and sighs "What if it were properly dressed?" He gazes at her eyes sparkling with the brightness of starlight. He gazes on her lips, where mere gazing does not satisfy. He praises her wrists and hands and fingers, and her arms bare to the shoulder: whatever is hidden, he imagines more beautiful').

Tereus too follows the footsteps of Apollo and steadily fixes his lustful gaze on Philomela (*Met.* 6.478–82): *spectat eam Tereus praecontrectatque videndo | osculaque et collo circumdata bracchia cernens | omnia pro stimulis facibusque ciboque furoris | accipit, et quotiens amplectitur illa parentem, | esse parens vellet* ('Tereus gazes at her, and imagining her as already his, watching her kisses, and her arms encircling her father's neck, it all spurs him on, food and fuel to

---

23 One more reason for Tereus' desire for Philomela is the natural inclination of the Thracians towards lust (Ov. *Met.* 6.458–60): *digna quidem facies; sed et hunc innata libido | exstimulat, pronumque genus regionibus illis | in Venerem est: flagrat vitio gentisque suoque* ('Her beauty was worthy of it, but he was driven by his natural passion, and the inclination of the people of his region is towards lust').
24 The narration is clearly phallocentric and the male glance is dominant; see Papanghelis 2009: 79.

his frenzy. Whenever she embraces her father, he wishes he were that father').[25] He keeps phantasising about her even when he is alone at night; Philomela has become an obsession for him (*Met.* 6.490–3): *at rex Odrysius, quamvis secessit, in illa | aestuat et repetens faciem motusque manusque | qualia vult fingit quae nondum vidit et ignes | ipse suos nutrit cura removente soporem* ('But though the Thracian king retired to bed, he was disturbed by thoughts of her, and remembering her features, her gestures, her hands, he imagined the rest that he had not yet seen, as he would wish, and fuelled his own fires, in sleepless restlessness').

Most pertinently for our discussion, Apollo understands his situation in medical terms, in terms of pathology. Using a well-established motif, he refers to his love as a wound '*vulnera*' (*Met.* 1.519–20): *certa quidem nostra est, nostra tamen una sagitta | certior, in vacuo quae vulnera pectore fecit!* ('My aim is certain, but an arrow truer than mine, has wounded my free heart!'). Although he is the god of medicine, Apollo declares that love cannot be cured by any herb and that he is unable to use his medical art to heal himself (*Met.* 1.521–4): *inventum medicina meum est, opiferque per orbem | dicor, et herbarum subiecta potentia nobis. | ei mihi, quod nullis amor est sanabilis herbis | nec prosunt domino, quae prosunt omnibus, artes!* ('The whole world calls me the bringer of aid; medicine is my invention; my power is in herbs. But love cannot be healed by any herb, nor can the arts that cure others cure their lord!'). In other words, on the one hand Apollo acknowledges love as a disease and, on the other, he admits that this disease is incurable. Hence, in the first, programmatic love story of the *Metamorphoses* the god of medicine himself annuls the fundamental principle of the *Remedia Amoris*, i.e. that love is curable and that it is possible for one to get rid of their passion. In hindsight, Apollo in the *Metamorphoses* ironically undermines Ovid's appeal in the *Remedia* to Apollo himself – as the patron god of both poetry and medicine – to help him teach the cures of love (75–8): *te precor incipiens, adsit tua laurea nobis, | carminis et medicae, Phoebe, repertor opis. | tu pariter vati, pariter succurre medenti: | utraque tutelae subdita cura tua est* ('Phoebus, source of the power of medicine and song, may your laurel help me, I beg of you, as I begin. Yours is the nurturing of doctor and poet alike: the protection of both falls to your care'). It is also worth noting that in this invocation Ovid has artfully inserted an allusive

---

25 Cf. Ov. *Met.* 6.515–18: *barbarus et nusquam lumen detorquet ab illa, | non aliter quam cum pedibus praedator obuncis | deposuit nido leporem Iovis ales in alto; | nulla fuga est capto, spectat sua praemia raptor* ('He never turns his eyes away from her, no differently than when Jupiter's eagle deposits a hare, caught by the curved talons, in its high eyrie: there is no escape for the captive, and the raptor gazes at its prize').

reference to Apollo's amatory side: the god's *laurea* (laurel), which Ovid calls for, unmistakably evokes Apollo's love story with Daphne, in which the god of medicine proved unable to cure himself from love.

Since not even the god of medicine is able to heal himself from love, it becomes clear that Amor will have full control in the *Metamorphoses*. The *Remedia Amoris* and Ovid's advice against love have no place in the world of the *Metamorphoses*, and this is sanctioned most authoritatively by the god of medicine himself. The Apollo of the *Metamorphoses*, as an Ovidian character, metapoetically ascertains that the teachings of the *Remedia Amoris* are utterly useless; that is why he resorts instead to the advice, practices, and stratagems of the *Ars Amatoria*. In his attempt to win over Daphne, Apollo follows – on a metaliterary level – Ovid's advice to the readers of the *Ars Amatoria* and begins with amatory persuasion (*Met.* 1.504–24).[26] His speech, however, does not bring the desired outcome and remains unanswered: Daphne gets scared and runs away. Selfishly and self-complacently Apollo attributes Daphne's flight to her ignorance about his identity (*Met.* 1.512–5). However, the god of divination is badly deceived, because Daphne rejects love altogether and does not care for *any* love partner. Amor himself has made Daphne immune to love.

Nevertheless, contrary to the characters mentioned by Ovid in the *Remedia Amoris* (55–68, quoted above) or to other characters in the *Metamorphoses*, Apollo will not be ruined by the fact that his love remains unfulfilled, simply because he is a god. In fact, he makes sure to turn his failure into a victory of sorts and joins himself eternally with Daphne by making her his emblematic plant and permanent companion (*Met.* 1.557–65):

> 'at, quoniam coniunx mea non potes esse,
> arbor eris certe' dixit 'mea! semper habebunt
> te coma, te citharae, te nostrae, laure, pharetrae;
> tu ducibus Latiis aderis, cum laeta Triumphum   560
> vox canet et visent longas Capitolia pompas;
> postibus Augustis eadem fidissima custos
> ante fores stabis mediamque tuebere quercum,
> utque meum intonsis caput est iuvenale capillis,
> tu quoque perpetuos semper gere frondis honores!'   565

---

26 In fact, he is not alone in doing so. Tereus' lust for Philomela makes him eloquent too; he zealously pleads with Pandion to allow her to travel with him to Thrace (Ov. *Met.* 6.469–70): *facundum faciebat amor, quotiensque rogabat | ulterius iusto, Procnen ita velle ferebat* ('Desire made him eloquent, and whenever he petitioned more strongly than was seemly, he would make out that Procne wished it so'). Lines 512–52 are modelled on Theocritus' *Idyll* 11, in which the uncouth Polyphemus woos the nymph Galatea.

Since you cannot be my bride, you must be my tree! Laurel, with you my hair will be wreathed, with you my lyre, with you my quiver. You will go with the Roman generals when joyful voices acclaim their triumph, and the Capitol witnesses their long processions. You will stand outside Augustus' doorposts, a faithful guardian, and keep watch over the crown of oak between them. And just as my head with its un-cropped hair is always young, so you also will wear the beauty of undying leaves.

Iphis and Anaxarete (*Met.* 14.698–761)

In the penultimate book of the *Metamorphoses* Ovid narrates the story of Iphis and Anaxarete, which takes place at Salamis of Cyprus. Iphis is a young man desperately in love with Anaxarete, who spurns him because of his lower social status. Iphis serenades Anaxarete, brings garlands to her doorstep, and approaches her nurse and servants, trying to gain access to their lady. When all his efforts fail, Iphis hangs himself from the door-posts of the cold-hearted Anaxarete. As his funeral procession is passing by her house, she throws her indifferent glance at Iphis' lifeless body and she is instantly transformed into a stone sculpture.

This story has no epic features whatsoever. The setting is distinctly elegiac: Iphis plays the part of an *exclusus amator*, 'a shut-out lover', who is kept outside the door of his beloved and sings his *paraclausithyron* song at her threshold.[27] Anaxarete is a typical *dura puella*. The elegiac tone of this story entitles us to read it through the elegiac-didactic prism of the *Remedia Amoris*. In this story, love is one-sided, as was Apollo's love for Daphne: only Iphis is in love. There is not the slightest intervention from the god Amor, as in the story of Daphne and Apollo. The only thing that Anaxarete shares with Daphne is her indifference towards the man who is in love with her.

Just like Apollo, Iphis is burning with love for Anaxarete (*Met.* 14.700): *viderat et totis perceperat ossibus aestum* ('he saw her and felt the fire of passion in every bone'). Nevertheless, unlike Apollo, Iphis tries in vain to master his passion and to fight against it with reason (*Met.* 14.701–2): *luctatusque diu, postquam ratione furorem | vincere non potuit* ('He fought it for a long time, but he could not conquer his madness by reason'). Iphis tries to cure himself using *ratio* as a *remedium* for passion. In this respect he is similar to many characters

---

[27] For Ov. *Met.* 14.698–764 as *paraclausithyron* see Copley 1956: 134–40. The *exclusus amator* character – already familiar in New and Roman comedy – got fully developed in the love elegies of Tibullus, Propertius, and Ovid himself.

of tragedy and elegy who first struggle between reason and passion but are eventually defeated by passion. Iphis would have been an ideal reader of Ovid's *Remedia Amoris*;[28] in fact, in the *prooemium* of that work Ovid designates somebody like Iphis as its ideal readership (*Rem.* 15–18):[29]

> *at siquis male fert indignae regna puellae,*
> *ne pereat, nostrae sentiat artis opem.*
> *cur aliquis laqueo collum nodatus amator*
> *a trabe sublimi triste pependit onus?*
>
> But any man who suffers badly from the power of a worthless girl, shouldn't die, if he understands the help that's in my art. Why should any lover hang from a high beam, a sad weight, with a knotted rope round his neck?

Iphis' Anaxarete may easily be considered an *indigna puella*; moreover, the mode of suicide that Ovid is talking about – suicide by hanging – clearly responds to Iphis' case, in fact with striking verbal similarities[30] (*Met.* 14.738): *atque onus infelix elisa fauce pependit* ('he hung there, a pitiful burden, his windpipe crushed').

Let us now take a close look at Iphis' actions after failing to cure himself from his passion for Anaxarete: he resorts to entreaties (702: *supplex ad limina venit*); he approaches her nurse (703–4: *et modo nutrici miserum confessus amorem, | ne sibi dura foret, per spes oravit alumnae*) and her maids (705–6: *et modo de multis blanditus cuique ministris | sollicita petiit propensum voce favorem*); he sends endearing messages to Anaxarete (707: *saepe ferenda dedit blandis sua verba tabellis*);[31] he hangs garlands on her door, drenched in tears (708–9: *interdum madidas lacrimarum rore coronas | postibus intendit*); and he lies on her threshold, mourning (709–10: *posuitque in limine duro | molle latus tristisque serae convicia fecit*).[32]

One might say that Iphis' actions follow closely Ovid's instructions in the *Ars Amatoria* (maids: 1.351–98, 2.251–8; letters: 1.437–68). On a metaliterary level, Iphis is a good reader of the *Ars Amatoria*; however, he has either not

---

28 On this see also Frings 2005: 174.
29 See Frings 2005: 173–5; Hardie 2015 on Ov. *Met.* 14.738.
30 See Frings 2005: 174.
31 Cf. Ov. *Ars* 1.439–40: *(cera tabellis) blanditias ferat illas tuas imitataque amantum | verba* ('May the wax on the tablet bring her your flattering words and play the lover').
32 Cf. Ov. *Rem.* 507–8: *nec dic blanditias nec fac convicia posti | nec latus in duro limine pone tuum* ('Don't speak fawning words, or abuse the doorpost, nor lay your body on the hard threshold'), with Frings 2005: 174.

read – or he was not willing to follow, or he did not manage to follow – Ovid's advice in the *Remedia Amoris*, except perhaps for his initial effort to fight against his love (cf. *Rem.* 79–106: 'treat it early'). Inevitably, Iphis commits a series of mistakes, which lead him straight to destruction. More specifically:

a) Iphis remains alone despite Ovid's advice to lovers in the *Remedia* to 'avoid solitude' (*Rem.* 579–608).
b) Iphis is obsessed with Anaxarete. On the contrary, Ovid teaches in the *Remedia* that 'one love is not enough' and urges his pupils to have more than one lover (*Rem.* 441–88).
c) Iphis constantly visits Anaxarete's threshold and thus constantly feeds his love. On the contrary, Ovid advises lovers in the *Remedia* to 'take long trips' (*Rem.* 213–48) and to avoid anything that could revive their love, such as being close to their beloved woman (*Rem.* 621–42).
d) Iphis complains about Anaxarete's cruelty and indifference, whereas in the *Remedia* Ovid advises lovers to remain silent and to refrain from complaints (*Rem.* 643–8).
e) Iphis is not at all cool or indifferent towards Anaxarete. Ovid advises exactly the opposite in the *Remedia*: 'be cool with her' (*Rem.* 489–522).
f) Iphis does not let Anaxarete's flaws – her cruelty and indifference[33] – alienate him. Ovid in the *Remedia* ardently enjoins his pupils to contemplate the defects of their ex-mistresses (*Rem.* 291–356).
g) Iphis does not take up other occupations and does not adopt a more active lifestyle. In the *Remedia* Ovid exhorts his pupils to 'start a life full of action' (*Rem.* 135–50) and to take up works of war or peace (*Rem.* 151–63), such as agriculture (*Rem.* 169–98), so as to forget their ex-mistresses.

In sum, Iphis does exactly the opposite from what Ovid advises in the *Remedia Amoris*. In metaliterary terms, he is a poor student of the *praeceptor* and naturally becomes the epitome of the victim of pathological love. The world of the *Metamorphoses* is totally different from that of the *Remedia Amoris*; in the *Metamorphoses* not even the god of medicine himself, Apollo, is able to heal himself from love, much less an ordinary mortal such as Iphis. Iphis' self-destructive

---

[33] Ov. *Met.* 14.711–15: *saevior illa freto surgente cadentibus Haedis, | durior et ferro, quod Noricus excoquit ignis, | et saxo, quod adhuc vivum radice tenetur, | spernit et inridet, factisque inmitibus addit | verba superba ferox et spe quoque fraudat amantem* ('But she spurned, and mocked, him, crueler than the surging sea, when the Kids set; harder than steel tempered in the fires of Noricum; or natural rock still rooted to its bed. And she added proud, insolent words to harsh actions, robbing her lover of hope, as well').

act, a result of erotic obsession, rejection, and despair, is solid proof that the rules of the love game in the *Metamorphoses* are a far cry from Ovid's teachings in the *Remedia*.

Conclusion

The retrospective reading of the *Remedia Amoris* may shed light on some of the stories of the *Metamorphoses* in which love is depicted as a pathological emotion. In the two stories used as case studies in this chapter, Apollo–Daphne and Iphis–Anaxarete, love is presented as a disease and a wound; in fact, in Apollo's case the wound is both literal and metaphorical: the god does indeed get shot by Amor's arrow. Both Apollo and Iphis suffer from love and are unable to heal themselves from their erotic disease. Ovid's teachings in the *Remedia Amoris* are not applicable in the *Metamorphoses* – nor is it even certain that they might ever be applicable at all, for that matter. On a metaliterary level, none of the characters of the *Metamorphoses* has ever read the *Remedia Amoris*. In the *Metamorphoses* love is incurable and is the driving force of the world. There is no safety net for lovers in the *Metamorphoses*. Amor is an omnipotent god, able to overcome even fellow gods, such as the mighty Apollo. If Apollo, the god of medicine, is unable to heal himself from erotic passion, then the mortals do not even stand a chance. Hence, the list of mythological characters that suffered from love and who might have benefited from Ovid's advice in the *Remedia Amoris* (*Rem.* 55–68) grows even longer.

Thea S. Thorsen
In Sickness or in Health? Love, Pathology, and Marriage in the Letters of Acontius and Cydippe (Ovid's *Heroides* 20-1)

Abstract: The elegiac epistles of Ovid's *Heroides* 20-21 recast an iconic tale of pathology and love, which is famously also found in Callimachus' *Aetia* Book 3. Here Acontius' desire for Cydippe is directly linked to her various grave illnesses: whenever she is about to marry her fiancé, she is inflicted with a serious disease as a punishment by Artemis, because she once swore (by accident) that she would marry Acontius. In Callimachus, Cydippe is cured as soon as she marries Acontius. In Ovid, they never get to this point, due to the narrative limitations of the epistolary form. This chapter argues that certain features embedded in Callimachus' episode contribute to a special kind of erotic warfare, *militia amoris*, between Acontius and Cydippe in the Heroidean letters. The most important of these features is the fact that Acontius descends from the Telchines, described by Callimachus as sorcerers and metal-workers, among other things. The arts-and-crafts element in *Heroides* 20-21 is key not only to understanding how the ancestry of Acontius relates to the disease of Cydippe, but also to the way in which both of them express their feelings, which appear surprisingly hard throughout their Heroidean letters.

This chapter offers a new interpretation of the themes of love and pathology in the epistolary pair of elegies of Acontius and Cydippe in Ovid's *Heroides* 20-1. According to this interpretation, Ovid challenges the narrative of the couple's happy marriage in Callimachus' *Aetia* by exploiting specific cues embedded in the Callimachean episode proper.[1] Pathology is key to this interpretation, as Ovid's Acontius appears not so much obsessed by love as unhealthy obsessive, and Ovid's Cydippe seems to suffer not so much from lovesickness as from actual physical disease. As will be argued, both the mental obsessiveness and the physical disease may be linked to Acontius being presented in the Callimachean

---

I would like to thank Dimitrios Kanellakis, Stephen Harrison and Stephen Heyworth for helpful comments on earlier versions of this chapter.

[1] For further examples of how Ovid exploits such cues in the Callimachean narrative, see Thorsen 2019.

episode as a descendant of the Telchines, a cue which has not been fully (if at all) discussed in scholarship so far. Moreover, this cue may be seen as related to conspicuous incompatibilities between the personalities of the hero and the heroine in their Heroidean letters, e.g. through Acontius' fixation on Cydippe's looks and disregard for what she wants in contrast to her stress on a person's inner qualities and the importance of consent. Finally, this interpretation sheds new light on a long tradition of scholarly debate over the very last couplet in the second of the two letters, *Her.* 21.247–8, whose sense has proven especially hard to grasp.

Ovid's *Heroides* 20–1 is famously one of four sources for this story in ancient literature, all of them pivoting on erotic desire, illness, and a wedding.[2] The others are Xenomedes' Cean chronicle,[3] Callimachus' *Aetia* frr. 67–75 (Pfeiffer/Harder) and Aristaenetus 1.10 (Bing/Höschele). The following are the story's main events, which are relevant to the argument in question: Acontius sees Cydippe during a religious festival on the island of Delos, and immediately falls in love with her. He then tricks her into swearing that she will marry him, by inscribing an oath on an apple, which she unwittingly reads aloud in the temple of Diana. Cydippe subsequently returns to her home island of Naxos and her father repeatedly attempts to marry her to her fiancé. Each time, she is stricken with life-threatening diseases. At last, the father consults the oracle of Apollo, which responds that the illnesses are due to Cydippe breaking her oath by trying to marry a man different from the one whose name she uttered in the temple of Diana. Finally, Cydippe is cured, she marries Acontius, and the two become the ancestors of the prosperous Acontiadae, a noble family of his native island of Ceos. Notably, this last element remains only a future possibility in *Heroides* 20–1, as the epistolary form does not allow for actual closure, unlike the other sources of the tale, which apply a third-person perspective.[4] This non-closural quality of the Heroidean[5] form facilitates the new interpretation in

---

[2] Love and/or disease are second in importance only to poetics in the treatments of the story in its ancient sources; see Barchiesi 1993 and 1999; Acosta-Hughes 2009; Lang 2009; Rynearson 2009; Kazantzidis 2014; and Cairns 2016. See Thorsen 2019 on the metapoetic qualities of Cydippe. For less romantic approaches to the tale, see Rosenmeyer 1996; Kuhlmann 2005; and Rynearson 2009: 355, referring to Rosenmeyer. The present argument corroborates the less romantic interpretations of the letters.

[3] Cf. Huxley 1965.

[4] See Thorsen 2019 for further reflections on this quality in *Heroides* 20–1, and Thorsen 2018a for the same in *Heroides* 18–19.

[5] Although the term occurs in previous scholarship as well, I borrow it from Fulkerson 2005 to refer to Ovid's generic innovation (cf. *Ars* 3.366: *ille novavit opus*), which scholarship now

question. The argument follows the lines of enquiry of the volume as a whole, focusing first on the theme of love, then on that of pathology, and finally on the marriage between Acontius and Cydippe.

nota certa furoris: Love

Without doubt, love is a major theme in *Heroides* 20–1. This element is especially conspicuous in Acontius' letter. And yet, despite being linked to issues that are generally at home in love literature, such as marriage[6] and writing, including the kind which involves descriptions of the beloved,[7] the passion of Ovid's Acontius is characterised by a surprisingly obsessive nature, centred on ideas of harm and violence, submission and superiority.

Thus, Acontius can claim (Ov. *Her.* 20.34): *si noceo quod amo, fateor sine fine nocebo* ('If I harm that which I love, I confess I shall harm endlessly').[8] To this, Cydippe responds (*Her.* 21.55–8):

> *dic age nunc, solitoque tibi ne decipe more:*
> *quid facies odio, sic ubi amore noces?*
> *si laedis quod amas, hostem sapienter amabis;*
> *me, precor, ut serves, perdere velle[9] velis!*

---

associates with both the so-called single and double *Heroides*; cf. Knox 1995 and Kenney 1996, despite the fact that the latter also includes letters from heroes.
6 Callimachus' story of Acontius and Cydippe is widely considered a model for Latin love elegy; see e.g. Hunter 2013. Yet, it should be noted that marriage is the very point at which Callimachus' model story and Latin love elegy are incompatibly distinct, as the relationships depicted by the Latin love elegists remain extra- or anti-marital; cf. e.g. Thorsen 2018b. It is not entirely clear in any of the sources whether Cydippe is already betrothed to another man before she unwittingly promises to marry Acontius; if she is, then Acontius' approach also qualifies as adultery, as he is claiming his right to marry a girl who is already promised to another man; cf. Ziogas 2016.
7 Emblematically represented in Callimachus' version, which may have circulated separately from the *Aetia* as an epyllion under the title of 'Cydippe', thus underscoring how much of a literary creation the beloved is; cf. *Rem.* 382; see Cameron 1995: 108 and Hunter 2013: 36. See also Wyke 1987; Keith 1994; Ingleheart 2012.
8 I use Kenney's text, 1996.
9 'No satisfactory parallels have been adduced for the pleonasm ... However, none of the suggested emendations is really convincing ...', Kenney 1996: 223.

> Come, tell me, and do not deceive me in your usual manner: what will you do from hatred, when you harm me so from love? If you injure the one you love, then you will be wise to love your enemy; to save me you must bring yourself to wish my doom!

Acontius, however, not only confesses that he will 'love and harm' Cydippe endlessly; he also invites her to harm him freely, in an elaboration of the elegiac *topos* of *servitium amoris*, 'slavery to love' (*Her.* 20.75–86):

> *ante tuos liceat flentem consistere vultus*
> * et liceat lacrimis addere verba suis,*
> *utque solent famuli, cum verbera saeva verentur,*
> * tendere summissas ad tua crura manus!*
> ...
> *ipsa meos scindas licet imperiosa capillos,*
> * oraque sint digitis livida nostra tuis.*
> *omnia perpetiar; tantum fortasse timebo,*
> * corpore laedatur ne manus ista meo.*
> *sed neque conpedibus nec me conpesce catenis:*
> * servabor firmo vinctus amore tui!*
>
> Let me have leave to stand weeping before your face, and leave to add words which match the tears; and let me, like slaves in fear of bitter stripes, stretch out submissive hands to touch your legs! ... With your own imperious hand you may tear my hair, and make my face black and blue with your fingers. I will endure all; my only fear perhaps will be lest that hand of yours be bruised on me. But bind me not with shackles nor with chains – I shall be kept in bonds by unyielding love for you.[10]

Acontius' embracing of *servitium amoris* may be seen as a confirmation of his role as a prototypical poet-lover.

And yet, there are certain features within his letter that call this assumption into question. An important aspect of the elegiac *servitium amoris* is that it is represented as an inescapable, unconditional, and sometimes torturous situation,[11] as may be seen in Catullus,[12] Tibullus,[13] Sulpicia[14] and Propertius,[15] and in Ovid's own works.[16] However, Acontius' *servitium amoris* appears not to be ines-

---

10 I use the Loeb translations throughout, often in slightly modified form.
11 For the *topos* in general see Copley 1947; Lyne 1979; Murgatroyd 1981; Fulkerson 2013; Thorsen (forthcoming).
12 Cf. e.g. Catull. 68.136; 85; 99.3–4, 11–12.
13 Cf. e.g. Tib. 1.1.55–6; 1.2.97–8; 1.6.37–8; 1.8.5–6; 2.3.11–30; 2.4.1–6.
14 Cf. e.g. Sulp. [Tib.] 4.5.3–4.
15 Cf. e.g. Prop. 1.12.18; 2.23.23–4; 3.17.41; for further observations, see Greene 2000.
16 Cf. e.g. Ov. *Am.* 1.2.17–18; 1.3.5; 2.17.1; *Rem.* 73; 293. Consider also *Heroides* 3, on which see below.

capable, but rather a useful means of attaining a specific goal. Tellingly, Acontius underscores the idea that those who suffer must be rewarded (*Her.* 20.67): *passo sua praemia dentur* ('Only let him who endures have his just reward'). The pretend situation of Acontius' *servitium amoris* is also underscored by the fact that he claims that he will imitate the fear, but not actually suffer lashes like a slave (cf. *Her.* 20.77–8, above). Similarly, he claims that he does not really need shackles and chains, as his love will be enough (*Her.* 20.85–6, above). The gravest breach of the *topos*, however, occurs when he commands Cydippe – in the imperative – to play her part in the game of love elegy (*Her.* 20.79–80):

> *ignoras tua iura; voca; cur arguor absens?*
> *iamdudum dominae more venire iube.*
>
> You do not know your rights: summon me! Why am I accused in my absence?
> Command me to come immediately, in the manner of a mistress of the house.

The similarity of this attitude to that of Briseis in her letter to Achilles – especially since Acontius mentions her right before his *servitium amoris* passage (*Her.* 20.69) – is striking (*Her.* 3.154): *domini iure venire iube!* ('By your right as master, bid me come'). The irony is equally striking, inasmuch as Briseis is a real slave as well as a lover.[17] By contrast, *servitium amoris* is a sheer fantasy to Acontius. For Cydippe is not really Acontius' *domina*; she may act according to the *dominae more* (cf. *Her.* 20.80, above), but only at Acontius' bidding, as he fundamentally retains the position of the master.[18]

This last point is important, for Acontius' idea of his superiority over Cydippe is soon revealed in his letter, when for a moment he addresses not Cydippe, but her fiancé, who is his rival (*Her.* 20.143–50):

> *quis tibi permisit nostras praecerpere messes?*
> *ad sepem[19] alterius quis tibi fecit iter?*
> ...
> *elige de vacuis quam non sibi vindicet alter:*
> *si nescis, dominum res habet ista suum.*

---

17 Cf. Her. 3.99–102: *nec tamen indignor nec me pro coniuge gessi | saepius in domini serva vocata torum | me quaedam, memini, dominam captiva vocabat. | 'servitio,' dixi, 'nominis addis onus'* ('And yet I am not angered, nor have I borne myself as wife because I was often summoned, a slave, to share my master's bed. Some captive woman once, I mind me, called me mistress. "To slavery," I replied, "you add a burden in that name"').
18 See Burkowski 2012: 102–7. I am grateful to the author for this reference.
19 See Hollis 1994.

> Who gave you leave to reap my harvests before me? Who laid open the road for you to trespass on another's enclosure?[20] ... Choose from among those who are free one whom another does not claim; if you do not know, that chattel has a master of its own.

The passage discloses that Acontius regards Cydippe as his property: in fact, as his 'crop', *messes*, his 'fenced land', *sepem*, and 'that chattel' of his, *res ista*. The word *dominus* is here stripped of erotic connotations and simply means 'the owner'.[21] It is hard to imagine a description more remote from the elegiac *topos* of *servitium amoris*.

The stark contrast between Acontius' address to his rival and his pretence of *servitium amoris* draws attention to his ambiguous discourse, which on the one hand appears to be in line with the elegiac 'evidence' of love, and on the other is disclosed as aggressively obsessive. The obsessiveness matches with Acontius' professed readiness to employ tricks; he uses *insidiae* (*Her.* 20.66), *fraus* (*Her.* 20.21–4, 34, and below), he is *dolosus* and *vafer* (see below), and he intends to continue in the same deceitful way (*Her.* 20.41: *mille doli restant*). In fact, Acontius even puts the blame on Love for this manipulative inclination (*Her.* 20.27–32):

> *te mihi conpositis (siquid tamen egimus) a se*[22]
>   *adstrinxit verbis ingeniosus Amor.*
> *dictatis ab eo feci sponsalia verbis*
>   *consultoque fui iuris Amore vafer.*
> *sit fraus huic facto nomen, dicarque dolosus,*
>   *si tamen est quod ames velle tenere dolus.*

> It was ingenious Love who bound you to me, with words (if I, indeed, did anything) that he drew up. In words dictated by him I made our betrothal; Love was the lawyer that taught me cunning. Let wiles be the name you give my deed, and let me be called deceitful – if only the wish to possess what one loves is deceit!

As seen from this passage, Acontius connects manipulative love with both marriage and writing. In this respect, he reflects essential qualities of Callimachus' Acontius, who is taught the art of love by the god himself (*Aet.* fr. 67.1–4). In Callimachus, this art is manifested in writing, which serves Acontius not only when he approaches his beloved through the oath inscribed on the apple, but also when he is unsure of the outcome of his approaches: he pines away with lovesickness and, in Cydippe's absence, carves verses about her beauty on the

---

20 Here the Loeb translation is particularly modified.
21 Cf. Murgatroyd 1981.
22 The text of the last metrical foot is problematic; see Casali 1997: 313–14.

bark of trees (*Aet*. fr. 73). Perhaps in Callimachus'[23] and certainly in Ovid's version, Acontius dwells on the beauty of Cydippe through the medium of writing at the same moment that this beauty wastes away as a result of the illnesses from which she suffers. More precisely, Ovid's Acontius imagines that she looks blushingly healthy and attractive (*Her*. 20.6, 53–64, 117–20), and comparable to a nymph (*Her*. 20.55–60):

> *tu facis hoc oculique tui, quibus ignea cedunt*
>   *sidera, qui flammae causa fuere meae;*
> *hoc faciunt flavi crines et eburnea cervix*
> …
> *et Thetidis qualis vix rear esse pedes.*

> This is your work, and that of your eyes, brighter than the fiery stars, and the cause of my flame; this is the work of your golden tresses and ivory throat … and feet which Thetis' own I think could scarcely equal.

Even here, where Acontius addresses Cydippe, his appraisal of her looks is reminiscent of the way in which he reifies her when he is addressing his rival, i.e. her fiancé, in the sense that she is represented as an object: this time, one made of precious materials, rather than a 'harvest', 'fenced land', or 'chattel'.

In sum, Acontius' interest in Cydippe appears harmful (cf. *sine fine nocebo*, above), self-servingly manipulative (e.g. through his professed *servitium amoris* followed by his claim to be Cydippe's *dominus*), and reifying (e.g. through the comparison between Cydippe and commodities as well as precious objects) in a way that aggressively stresses his superiority and her subordination. It therefore seems accurate when Acontius describes this interest as bearing the 'certain mark of madness' (*Her*. 20.207: *nota certa furoris*), and if this madness indeed qualifies as love, it appears to be of a distinctly pathological kind.

argenti color est: Pathology

The pathology of love is also prominent in the letter of Cydippe. In fact, disease holds much the same position in Cydippe's letter as love does in that of Acontius; like his passion, Cydippe's disease is also aggressive in nature (*Her*. 21.37–8, 54) and she links it both to wedlock (*Her*. 21.157–72) and writing (*Her*. 21.17–28; 207; 248). In fact, even the deity of wedlock himself, Hymenaeus, equates

---

[23] The fragmentary state of the text simply does not let us know for sure.

her (planned) wedding with disease on the verge of death (*Her.* 21.155–72 (cf. 21.45)):

> nam quare, quotiens socialia sacra parantur,   155
>   nupturae totiens languida membra cadunt?
> ter mihi iam veniens positas Hymenaeus ad aras
>   fugit et a thalami limine terga dedit,
> vixque manu pigra totiens infusa resurgunt
>   lumina, vix moto corripit igne faces.   160
> saepe coronatis stillant unguenta capillis
>   et trahitur multo splendida palla croco.
> cum tetigit limen, lacrimas mortisque timorem
>   cernit et a cultu multa remota suo,
> et pudet in tristi laetum consurgere turba,   165
>   quique erat in palla, transit in ora rubor;
> proicit ipse sua deductas fronte coronas,
>   spissaque de nitidis tergit amoma comis.
> at mihi, vae miserae, torrentur febribus artus
>   et gravius iusto pallia pondus habent,   170
> nostraque plorantes video super ora parentes,
>   et face pro thalami fax mihi mortis adest.

For why is it that, as oft as the sacraments for marriage are made ready, so oft the limbs of the bride-to-be sink down in languor? Thrice now has Hymenaeus come to the altars reared for me and fled, turning his back upon the threshold of my wedding-chamber; the lights so oft replenished by his lazy hand scarce rise again, scarce does he keep the torch alight by waving it. Oft does the perfume distil from his wreathed locks, and the mantle he sweeps along is splendid with much saffron. When he has touched the threshold, and sees tears and dread of death, and much that is far removed from the ways he keeps; he shames to stand forth glad in a gloomy throng, and the blush that was in his mantle passes to his cheeks; with his own hand he tears the garlands from his brow and casts them forth, and dries the dense balsam from his glistening locks. But for me – ah, wretched! – my limbs are parched with fever, and the stuffs that cover me are heavier than their wont; I see my parents weeping over me, and instead of the wedding-torch the torch of death is at hand.

When Cydippe includes less sinister representations of marriage in her letter, the prospect of wedlock is predominantly associated not with Acontius, but her fiancé (*cui destinor uxor*, below), whom she portrays as Acontius' opposite in the sense that he is respectful, gentle and caringly worried (*Her.* 21.189–202):

> nec tu credideris illum, cui destinor uxor,
>   aegra superposita membra fovere manu.   190
> assidet ille quidem, quantum permittitur, ipse
>   sed meminit nostrum virginis esse torum.
> et iam nescioquid de me sensisse videtur,

> *nam lacrimae causa saepe latente cadunt,*
> *et minus audacter blanditur et oscula rara*   195
>   *appetit et timido me vocat ore suam.*
> *nec miror sensisse, notis cum prodar apertis;*
>   *in dextrum vertor, cum venit ille, latus,*
> *nec loquor, et tecto simulatur lumine somnus,*
>   *captantem tactus reicioque manum.*   200
> *ingemit et tacito suspirat pectore meque*
>   *offensam, quamvis non mereatur, habet.*

Do not believe that he whose destined wife I am lays his hand on me to fondle my sick limbs. He sits by me, indeed, as much as he may, but does not forget that mine is a virgin bed. He seems already, too, to feel in some way suspicion of me; for his tears oft fall for some hidden cause, his flatteries are less bold, he seeks few kisses, and calls me his own in tones that are but timid. Nor do I wonder he suspects, for I betray myself by open signs; I turn upon my right side when he comes, and do not speak, and close my eyes in simulated sleep, and when he tries to touch me I throw off his hand. He groans and sighs in his silent breast, and he suffers my displeasure without deserving it.

Moreover, while Cydippe, like Acontius, writes about her body, her self-portrayal is nothing like the objectifying image Acontius draws of her in his letter – a fact that she explicitly comments upon (*Her.* 21.221–2): *si me nunc videas, visam prius esse negabis* | *'arte nec est' dices 'ista petita mea'* ('Should you see me now, you will declare you have never seen me before, and say "No art of mine ever sought to win that girl"').[24]

Paradoxically, the connection between Acontius' art/trick and the deterioration of Cydippe's body actualises the relevance of his Telchinian ancestry. Certainly, the idea that Acontius is a Telchinian is contentious and has yet to be discussed in scholarship – naturally so, one might add, as it seems entirely incompatible with the well-established understanding of Acontius as the prototypical Callimachean poet-lover.[25] In the prologue of Callimachus' *Aetia*, the Telchines are 'ignorant men who are no friends of the Muse' (*Aet.* fr. 1.2: νήιδες οἳ Μούσης οὐκ ἐγένοντο φίλοι), and famously represent the artistic adversaries of the poet. Furthermore, the Telchines occur twice more in the Callimachean corpus in a less metaphorical capacity, which nevertheless serves to stress how they negatively mirror the ideal artist, as represented by the Callimachean poet.

---

24 Stephen Heyworth kindly suggests, in private communication, that *arte* here also encompasses the meaning 'trick'. I have chosen to retain the word 'art', as it reveals the metapoetic aspects of Acontius and Cydippe's discourse.
25 See Thorsen 2019 with references.

One of these instances is in the story of how Zeus punished the Telchines' hubris through their extinction, sparing but a few (*Aet.* fr. 75.64–9):

> ἐν δ' ὕβριν θάνατόν τε κεραύνιον, ἐν δὲ γόητας
>   Τελχῖνας μακάρων τ' οὐκ ἀλέγοντα θεῶν   65
> ἠλεὰ Δημώνακτα γέρων ἐνεθήκατο δέλτοις
>   καὶ γρηῢν Μακελώ, μητέρα Δεξιθέης,
> ἃς μούνας, ὅτε νῆσον ἀνέτρεπον εἵνεκ' ἀλ[ι]τρῆς
>   ὕβριος, ἀσκηθεῖς ἔλλιπον ἀθάνατοι·

> The insolence and the lightning death and therewith the wizards Telchines and Demonax who foolishly disregarded the blessed gods, the old man [Xenomedes] put in his tablets, and aged Macelo, mother of Dexithea, the two of whom the deathless gods alone left unscathed, when for sinful insolence they overthrew the island.

Next, the Telchines occur in an episode which highlights their metallurgical skills (Callim. *Hymn* 4.31): ἄορι τριγλώχινι, τό οἱ Τελχῖνες ἔτευξαν ('... the three-forked sword which the Telchines fashioned').[26] Thus, while the Telchines may be readily identified as 'famous artists' (Stat. *Theb.* 2.247: *notique operum Telchines*) and excellent, hence envied, metallurgists,[27] they are also wizards and sorcerers,[28] that is, possessors of 'the evil eye',[29] as well as poisoners of food.[30] The ambiguity is also seen in the fact that the Telchines are frequently represented in the service of gods,[31] as well as being guilty of hubris and punished accordingly, as referred to above. Surely, from this survey, the Telchines appear to have nothing in common with, let alone any connection with, Acontius.

And yet, Acontius is indeed related to the Telchines; in fact, Acontius' Telchinian descent is a mark of ring-composition in the episode in Callimachus' *Aetia*: at the outset of the episode, Acontius is referred to as a descendant of Euxantius, son of Dexithea (fr. 67.7), who in turn is reported as one of the survivors of Zeus' punishment towards the end of the episode (fr. 75.67). Now, this

---

[26] The passage occurs in Callimachus' *Hymn to Delos* – a text of which Cydippe's letter shows especially intimate knowledge (*Her.* 21.65–114).
[27] And jewellers, making *inter alia* the necklace of Harmonia (see Stat. *Theb.* 2.265–7), and even images of the gods (Diod. Sic. 5.55.2).
[28] Callim. *Aet.* fr. 75.64 (see above), and *Suda* T 293.
[29] Ov. *Met.* 7.365.
[30] Cf. Strabo 14.2.7; Tzetzes, *Chil.* 7.15.
[31] They are in charge of the upbringing of Poseidon (Diod. Sic. 5.55.1) or of Zeus (Strabo 10.3.19). They were also recorded as worshippers of gods, such as Hera (Diod. Sic. 5.55.2) and Athena (Paus. 9.19.1).

link between the Telchines and Acontius may be regarded as broken, or at least significantly weakened, by the gods' salvage of Dexithea and her mother Macelo, which indeed may have offered the survivors a fresh start.[32] But while the gods have set an example of what may happen to those who are guilty of hubris for the descendants of those who survived, the possibility of committing such offences is still a reality for these persons,[33] as Pindar's depiction of Dexithea's son Euxantius makes clear (*Isthm.* 2.35–45):

> ... λόγο[ν ἄν]ακτος Εὐξαν[τίου
> ἐπαίνεσα [Κρητ]ῶν μαιομένων ὃς ἀνα[ίνετο
> αὐταρχεῖν, πολίων δ' ἑκατὸν πεδέχει[ν
> μέρος ἕβδομον Πασιφ[ά]ας <σὺν> υἱ-
>   οῖ]σι· τέρας δ' ἐὸν εἶ-
>   πέν σφι· "τρέω τοι πόλεμον
>   Διὸς Ἐννοσίδαν τε βαρ[ύ]κτυπον.
> χθόνα τοί ποτε καὶ στρατὸν ἀθρόον
> πέμψαν κεραυνῷ τριόδοντί τε
> ἐς τὸν βαθὺν Τάρταρον ἐμὰν μα-
> τέρα λιπόντες καὶ ὅλον οἶκον εὐερκέα·

> I approve the words of lord Euxantius, who refused to rule over the Cretans, although they were eager, and to share a seventh part of one hundred cities with the sons of Pasiphaë. But he told them his own omen: 'Truly I fear war with Zeus and I fear the loud-rumbling Earthshaker. With their thunderbolt and trident they once sent the land and all the people into deep Tartarus, sparing my mother and the entire well-fenced house.'

Thus, there is still the possibility that the descendants of the Telchines, such as Euxantius and his future relative Acontius, may perpetuate the vices of their breed and offend the gods.

In what follows, I argue that there are three elements in Cydippe's letter which, taken together, exploit this possibility and conjure up the shadow of 'Acontius the Telchine'. These elements are (1) poison/sorcery, which the Telchines reportedly employed, (2) metal, which is the material of Telchinian art, and (3) hubris in the form of lack of fear of the gods, which was precisely the vice for which the gods punished the Telchines with (near-)extinction.

First, Cydippe refers to the notion that she may have been poisoned or that she is the victim of sorcery (*Her.* 21.52): *facta veneficiis pars putat ista tuis* ('Some think that this is the working of your [sc. Acontius'] sorcery/ poison'). The term

---

32 In the manner of Deucalion and Pyrrha, and Philemon and Baucis, who were also spared.
33 It is not even certain who survived; for example, in Ovid's *Ibis*, Macelo too is struck down by the punishment of Zeus (*Ib.* 475), though Dexithea still survives (*Ib.* 469–70).

veneficium neatly refers to both sorcery and poison, which the Telchines are known to employ.[34] And the way in which Cydippe describes her body may certainly be consistent with having been poisoned, or even exposed to the evil eye.[35] Moreover, given that in some accounts the Telchines actually poisoned plants,[36] the role of the apple becomes conspicuous and suspicious. Could the apple have been poisoned? Was that how Acontius administered his *veneficium* to Cydippe? And even if Acontius did not poison the apple Cydippe picked up in the temple of Artemis (after all, there is no indication that the nurse who picked the apple up first got ill, nor that Cydippe took a bite of it),[37] then Ovid's Acontius[38] is physically close enough as they write their letters to be able to continue to administer poison to Cydippe in other ways, since he is actually outside her house (*Her.* 20.129–30): *ne tamen ignorem quid agas, ad limina crebro | anxius huc illuc dissimulanter eo* ('Yet, so that I am not unaware of what you do, I often go to and fro at your doorstep, anxious and in secret'). Who knows for how long he has been around? It is worth noting that, although *dissimulanter* may be rendered as 'in secret', it may also suggest 'in the concealment of one's real purpose',[39] which, as already suggested, may be to continue to cast spells on or poison Cydippe and thus scare her off of marrying Acontius' rival and induce her to accept marrying Acontius himself.

Secondly, Cydippe associates her body with various kinds of metalwork, most notably by using arresting and unique imagery,[40] as she describes her complexion thus (*Her.* 21.219–20) *argenti color est inter convivia talis, | quod tactum gelidae frigore pallet aquae* ('Such is the colour of silver at the banquet table, pale with the chill touch of icy water'). While the image is evoking the festive setting of *convivium*, the point is the particular colour that emerges from water condensing on silverware, which, when it is the colour of someone's complexion, is singularly unhealthy. Since a crucial element in this image is silver, it may be regarded as a sinister counterpart to Acontius' comparison of Cydippe's feet to

---

34 *OLD*, s.v. 1 'The use of magical arts, sorcery', 2 'The act of poisoning', 2b 'a poisonous substance, poison'.
35 Cf. *languor* (21.13), *fessa* (21.14), *pallida* (21.16), *gemo* (21.36), *torrentur febribus artus* (21.169), *quam* (sc. Cydippe) *ferus indigna tabe perire sinis* (21.60), *languida membra* (21.156), *miserabile corpus* (21.213), *macie* (21.215), *color est sine sanguine* (21.215).
36 E.g. Strabo 14.2.7.
37 Although one might speculate.
38 This is an element not found in the other sources and may be considered as Ovid's invention.
39 OLD, s.v.
40 'No parallel for this extra-ordinary image is forthcoming', Kenney 1996: 243.

those of Thetis (*Her.* 20.60), which were proverbially like silver. Certainly, the goddess is not unhealthy, but it is arguably the implicit and positive comparison that Acontius makes between Cydippe and silver through the evocation of Thetis that Cydippe appears to counter through her own explicit and negative comparison between her own hue and the colour of silverware. Moreover, such silverware may be said to evoke the kind of artisan's objects that are useful, made of metal and not as precious as finer art – that is, of the kind that the Telchines produced. Also relevant is Cydippe's ironic self-characterisation as 'the great trophies of your [sc. Acontius'] artistic talent' (*Her.* 21.214: *ingenii magna tropaea tui*). Clearly, in this context *tropaea* has a metaphorical significance, like that of 'trophy' in modern English. Yet, as *tropaea* originally means 'armour taken from an enemy and hung on a stake',[41] it may also, alongside *ingenium*, which may translate as 'artistic talent', evoke metallurgic craftsmanship. Therefore, one common denominator of these arresting and allusive images is metal, which is the material of the metallurgic artists, the Telchines, forefathers of Acontius.

Finally, fear, especially of the gods, is an element not only of Cydippe's, but also of Acontius' letter, which becomes particularly conspicuous when one considers the gravest of the Telchines' vices, namely hubris, the single offence that Callimachus stresses in relation to the Telchines in the Acontius and Cydippe episode (*Aet.* fr. 75.64–9). Hubris in this context is explicitly understood as a lack of fear of the gods (cf. esp. fr. 75.65–6: μακάρων τ' οὐκ ἀλέγοντα θεῶν | ἠλεὰ Δημώνακτα). Upon closer inspection, not only does Ovid's Acontius clearly lack fear of the gods, he also appears to try to entangle Cydippe in the same offence, telling her to stop fearing even when he claims that she is already deceiving the gods (see below). However, Cydippe resists Acontius' admonition that she should be fearless and his claim that she disregards the gods till the end: a resistance which, paradoxically, may be her motive in accepting marriage to Acontius.

While the gods, particularly Diana, are prominent in the letter of Acontius, his irreverence of the divinities also seeps out of his text. Thus, in what almost amounts to a paradox, Acontius claims that 'the issue rests with the gods, but you will be taken nonetheless' (20.44: *exitus in dis est, sed capiere tamen*). While Acontius thus reveals his own lack of respect for the gods, his hubris, one might say, he also bids Cydippe to lay aside her fear from the very start of his letter: 'Lay aside your fears!' (20.1: *pone metum*), and then again, 'Stay your fears, maiden!' (20.181: *siste metum, virgo!*). At the same time, Acontius suggests that

---

41 OLD s.v. 1.

Cydippe's own actions do not comply with fear of the gods and therefore merit punishment, thus implying that she too is guilty of hubris (*Her.* 20.189–96):

> *admonita es modo voce mea cum casibus istis,*
> *quos, quotiens temptas fallere, ferre soles.* 190
> *his quoque vitatis in partu nempe rogabis,*
> *ut tibi luciferas adferat illa manus.*
> *audiet et repetens quae sunt audita requiret*
> *iste tibi de quo coniuge partus eat.*
> *promittes votum: scit te promittere falso;* 195
> *iurabis: scit te fallere posse deos!*

> You have but now been admonished not only by word of mine, but as well by those mishaps of health you are wont to suffer as oft as you try to evade your promise. Even if you escape these ills, in childbirth will you dare pray for aid from her light-bringing hands [of Diana/Lucina]. She will hear these words – and then, recalling what she has heard, will ask of you from what husband come those pangs. You will promise a votive gift – she knows your promises are false; you will make oath – she knows you can deceive the gods!

Acontius' threat is particularly grave for two reasons, the first being the non-closural quality of the Heroidean form, which infuses the prospect with realism, as Cydippe cannot possibly know what will eventually happen from her present point of view; second, the threat recalls the actual outcome of Nicander's story of Hermochares and Ctesylla,[42] which Ovid knew (cf. *Met.* 7.369–70) and which ancient sources explicitly compare with that of Acontius and Cydippe (Ant. Lib. *Met.* 1.1–2): here the female protagonist actually dies in childbirth at the will of the gods.[43] While thus insinuating that Cydippe lacks fear of the gods, i.e. Diana, Acontius' threat is also a reminder of how stories similar to that of Acontius and Cydippe may end unhappily.

Cydippe, by contrast, stresses both her fear and obedience in the face of divine will throughout her letter. Thus, she starts by informing Acontius that she is terrified: *pertimui* (21.1), and continues in the same vein: *vereor* (21.12), *timor*

---

[42] Nicander frr. 49–50; Gow/Scholfield 1997: 207.
[43] 'This tragedy is arguably aggravated by the divine intervention that is reported at two important junctures in Antoninus Liberalis' Nicandrian paraphrase. For while there is initially no mention of any god in Antoninus Liberalis' summary, as Hermochares conceives of and executes his plan involving the apple, Ctesylla reads the oath aloud and throws the apple away, blushes ... and is "badly upset" (χαλεπῶς ἤνεγκεν, "se mit en colère"), ... in the later phase of the story, Ctesylla falls in love κατὰ θεῖον "according to a divine decree" and dies in childbirth κατὰ δαίμονα "in accordance with the god's wishes" (*Met.* 1.4). Ctesylla thus appears to love and die at the whims of an unpredictable, superior and merciless power ...', Thorsen 2019: 139.

(21.17), *incerta* (21.31), *timeo* (21.47; 153), *vae miserae* (21.169). However, once it becomes clear that the divine will, as expressed by Apollo, is that she must marry Acontius, she immediately accepts it (21.239): *numen ipsa sequor deorum* ('I myself follow the will of the gods') and then chastises herself for having had the nerve to write back to Acontius, despite being a god-fearing virgin (21.143–4): *plus hoc quoque virgine factum,* | *non timuit tecum quod mea charta loqui* ('Even this, that my letter has not feared to speak with you, is more than a virgin should do'). And while this acceptance may on the surface seem to coincide with a conventionally happy ending, the final couplet of Cydippe's letter also allows for a different interpretation of its conclusion.

cupio ... tecum: Marriage

The tale of Acontius and Cydippe is supposed to end in marriage. Any reader familiar with the story as told by Callimachus expects to find signs of this outcome in the Heroidean letters. To such readers it may be hard to grasp what Cydippe actually says in the final couplet, which *prima facie* signals her voluntary and positively motivated consent to marry Acontius, thus offering 'narrative relief' by fulfilling the reader's expectations.

However, an important prerequisite for such relief on the part of any reader is to neglect all the elements in the letters that have been scrutinised in this chapter and which make it highly unlikely that Cydippe should suddenly desire to be with Acontius. The most obvious of these elements are the differently construed elements between the personalities of the two. In addition to the way in which love and pathology are treated differently in the two letters, as discussed above, the differences are particularly conspicuous in the correspondents' approach to physical appearances *vs* inner qualities and the idea of compulsion as contrasted with consent.

To begin with appearances: Acontius is obsessed with them; Cydippe's beauty is the cause of his passion (*Her.* 21.53–64); Acontius thinks of Cydippe in terms of beauty even when she is almost dead from disease and chastises her for ruining her good looks by stubbornly rejecting him – and, as a consequence, remaining ill (20.117–18): *parce, precor, teneros corrumpere febribus artus:* | *servetur facies ista fruenda mihi* ('Cease, I entreat, to spoil your tender limbs with fever; preserve that face of yours for me to enjoy'). She, on the other hand, laments her good looks and wishes that she were less appealing, so that she might never have been desired by Acontius (21.31–8):

> *ergo te propter totiens incerta salutis*
> *commentis poenas doque dedique tuis;*
> *haec nobis formae te laudatore superbae*
> *contingit merces, et placuisse nocet.*
> *si tibi deformis, quod mallem, visa fuissem,* 35
> *culpatum nulla corpus egeret ope;*
> *nunc laudata gemo, nunc me certamine vestro*
> *perditis, et proprio vulneror ipsa bono.*

> So, then, it is on your account that I am so many times uncertain of health, and it is for your lying tricks that I am and have been punished; this is the reward that falls to my beauty, proud in your praise; I suffer for having pleased. If I had seemed ugly to you – and would I had! – you would have thought ill of my body, and it would need no medical care;[44] but I met with praise, and now I groan; now you two [the fiancé and Acontius] with your strife destroy me, and I am wounded by my own excellence/property.

Cydippe is beautiful, and although this beauty may take haughty pride in praise (a notion conveyed by the negative description of her *formae superbae* and the ironic *merces*), this really holds no value for her now, as is expressed through the paradoxical *proprio vulneror ipsa bono* (see above); in fact, she wishes that Acontius could see how her beauty has deteriorated in her state of illness, so that he would cease to desire her and regret that he made her promise to marry him (21.213–22).

Moreover, Acontius openly boasts of his plot, deceit, and ambush – and contradicts himself on the subject of how blameworthy he is for tricking her into swearing to marry him. A key word in relation to this inconsistency on Acontius' part is *crimen*. Thus, Acontius first claims that asking her to wed him is not a crime (20.8: *non crimina*) and wonders how writing a letter can be a criminal offence compared to employing weapons in order to capture a girl (20.38). However, when he insists on being awarded his desired prize, he calls his way of proceeding precisely *tanto crimine* (20.68: 'such a great crime/charge/reproach'). This claim appears to be a slip of the tongue, which undercuts Acontius' final self-characterisation as someone distinguished by *sine crimine mores* (20.225: 'irreproachable behaviour'). Cydippe's response to Acontius' boasting of his manipulative strategies is twofold. Firstly, she scorns him for having chosen such an easy target by tricking an innocent virgin (21.115–16): *improbe, quid gaudes aut quae tibi gloria parta est | quidve vir elusa virgine laudis habet* ('Shameless man, why do you rejoice? Or what glory have you gained? Or what praise have you won, being a man, from tricking a girl?'). Her second strategy is to lecture Acontius on the

---

44 Here the Loeb translation is modified.

difference between the spirit and the letter of the law (21.129–44), especially through the axiom *quod iurat, mens est* (21.135: 'that which swears is the mind').[45] This is a striking allusion to Euripides' *Hippolytus* (612), aligning Cydippe with the eponymous hero of the tragedy. The association is further sustained through Cydippe's repeated appeals to the favourite goddess of Hippolytus, Diana, to protect another virgin, i.e. herself (*Her.* 21.7–12; 173–82), and through Acontius' association with Phaedra, with his ominous imperative *perlege* (20.3) echoing that of Hippolytus' stepmother in her letter (4.3).[46]

Despite Cydippe's learned allusions to Euripides' *Hippolytus* and her legalistic reasoning, Ovid's Acontius implies that she is ignorant. Thus, he inserts colloquial elements like *si sapias* (20.174: 'if you were smart') and *ignoras tua iura* (20.79: 'you do not comprehend your rights'), a claim which seems particularly outrageous considering Cydippe's subsequent learned lecture on the difference between the letter and the spirit of the law. While Acontius assumes Cydippe is uneducated, she laments her learnedness, because her literacy allowed her to read the oath aloud to the illiterate nurse who initially picked up Acontius' apple (21.181–2): *nil ego peccavi, nisi quod periuria legi | inque parum fausto carmine docta fui* ('I did nothing wrong, except that I read a false oath and showed myself to be literate with an unlucky verse'). What Acontius sees little of in Cydippe, namely her education, she finds excessive.

Acontius further reveals his systematic manipulation of Cydippe through another contradiction, in addition to that relating to the blameworthiness of his deceitful approach: his willingness to use violence if Cydippe continues to resist. Initially, Acontius brags about his bloodless conquest, when, by contrast, 'with swords other men have captured/raped pleasing girls' (20.37: *per gladios alii placitas rapuere*[47] *puellas*). Yet, a little later in his letter, Acontius proves to be not so different from *alii* after all, as he menacingly claims that 'if trickery does not succeed, I shall resort to arms, and you, captured/raped, will be borne away in an embrace that lusts for you' (20.47–8: *si non proficient artes, veniemus ad arma, | inque tui cupido rapta ferere sinu*). The use of the simple future, as if Acontius were stating a future fact, the application of *rapta* and *ferere* to Cydippe in combination with the carnally lustful embrace of Acontius, and the *arma*, which can be moti-

---

45 See Kenney 1969, 1970b, and 1979; Ziogas 2016.
46 By associating Cydippe with Hippolytus, Ovid anticipates a similar connection to the one made by Rynearson 2009: 346–7 between Euripides' play and Callimachus' episode of Acontius and Cydippe.
47 *OLD*, s.v. 4 'to carry off (and violate), ravish'. As argued below, the parentheses are hardly necessary in the case of *Her.* 20.

vated only by Cydippe's resistance, explicitly proposes sexual violence and rape. In response to such threats, Cydippe points out the inappropriateness of Acontius' sense of triumph, as she does not carry weapons herself, unlike many heroines, such as Penthesilea and Hippolyte (21.117–20). Moreover, Cydippe lectures Acontius on how to approach someone according to the art of love, simultaneously and subtly undercutting Acontius' claim to have a special bond with the god of love (21.125–32):

> at fuerat melius, si te puer iste tenebat,　　　　　　　　　125
> 　　quem tu nescioquas dicis habere faces,
> more bonis solito spem non corrumpere fraude:
> 　　exoranda tibi, non capienda fui!
> cur, me cum peteres, ea non profitenda putabas
> 　　propter quae nobis ipse petendus eras?　　　　　　　130
> cogere cur potius quam persuadere volebas,
> 　　si poteram audita condicione capi?

> Yet it would have been better for you – if that boy really held you captive who you say has torches of some sort – to do as good men usually do, and not cheat your hope by dealing falsely; you should have won me by persuasion, not by stealing me! Why, when you sought my hand, did you not think it worthwhile declaring those things that made your own hand worthy of my seeking? Why did you wish to compel me rather than persuade, if I could be won by listening to your suit?

The passage amounts to a miniature *Ars Amatoria* from Cydippe's point of view, echoing precepts of Ovid's love manual, such as 'your next task is to win the girl you fancy' (*Ars* 1.37: *proximus huic labor est placitam exorare puellam*).[48]

Finally, Cydippe proceeds to connect the illegitimacy of Acontius' alleged right to marry her with the lack of legal consent, as she states (*Her.* 21.135–44):

> quae iurat, mens est; sed nil iuravimus illa;　　　　　　　135
> 　　illa fidem dictis addere sola potest.
> consilium prudensque animi sententia iurat,
> 　　et nisi iudicii vincula nulla valent.
> si tibi coniugium volui promittere nostrum,
> 　　exige polliciti debita iura tori;　　　　　　　　　　　140
> sed si nil dedimus praeter sine pectore vocem,
> 　　verba suis frustra viribus orba tenes.
> non ego iuravi: legi iurantia verba;
> 　　vir mihi non isto more legendus eras.

---

48 Cydippe's mini-*Ars Amatoria* is only one among several elements that associate her with the poet Ovid. See Thorsen 2019, *passim*.

> It is the mind that swears, and I have taken no oath with that; it alone can lend good faith to words. It is counsel and the prudent reasoning of the soul that swear, and, except the bonds of the judgment, none avail. If I have willed to pledge my hand to you, exact the due rights of the promised marriage-bed; but if I have given you naught but my voice, without my heart, you possess in vain but words without a force of their own. I took no oath – I read words that formed an oath; that was no way for you to be chosen to husband by me.

Thus, while Acontius stresses appearances, Cydippe focuses on inner qualities, and while Acontius shows his disdain for consent through his attitude to tricks and rape, Cydippe champions the importance of consent throughout her letter.

Given the differences in attitudes and thoughts between Acontius and Cydippe, there is one question that remains more pressing than any other: how can someone like Cydippe, as far as we may know her from her letter, address the positively consensual words *cupio ... tecum*[49] to someone like Acontius, as far as we may know him from his letter? For the conclusion of Cydippe's letter, as it has been handed down to us, does indeed include the words *cupio* ('I wish/desire') and *tecum* ('with you'). This is puzzling not only considering how Cydippe emerges as a god-fearing virgin not too interested in men, but also, and more importantly, considering their incompatible construed *personae*. However, the closing couplet also includes several other problems, whose disentanglement may help us find an answer.

The couplet belongs to a chunk of *Heroides* 21 that has been transmitted in incunabula printed in the 1470s and 1480s, and the major *variae lectiones* are: *cupio mihi iam contingere* (π), *cupio me iam contingere* (L) and *cupio me iam coniungere* (*editio veneta*). π is the so-called Parma edition by Corallus from 1477; L has the final part of *Heroides* 21.9–248 added in handwriting dated to the 15th century;[50] and the 'Venetian edition', according to Dörrie, is from 1480.[51] Since Dörrie's *Heroides* edition (1971), π has usually been assumed to be the basis for the later variations.[52]

Yet the possibility that the *lectiones* of L or even the 'Venetian edition' may represent an earlier stage of the transmission cannot be completely ruled out.[53]

---

49 '*tecum* also seems to have the slight suggestion that Cydippe wants to be with Acontius', Thompson 1989: 331.
50 Cf. Dilthey 1863: 133–6; Palmer 1898 = Palmer/Kennedy 2005 *ad loc.*
51 Dörrie 1971 *ad loc.*
52 Cf. Dörrie 1971: 4, 12; Kenney 1996; Heyworth 2016.
53 As White (2006: 198 n. 19) observes concerning precisely this couplet: 'The text *quid nisi quod cupio me iam coniungere tecum* is "handschriftlich bezeugt" (to use Dörrie's words. cf. *Nachr. Akad. Wiss. Gött. Philol.-Hist. Kl.* [1960], 3789, as is evident from the negative *apparatus*

This caveat is all the more relevant considering the fact that the pre-Dörrie editions of Palmer (originally published in 1898 and reprinted in 2005) and that of Showerman (originally published in 1913 in the Loeb series and continuously reprinted since)[54] are widely used today. Consequently, it is also important to look into the reasons why Palmer rejected L's *me iam contingere tecum*:

> 247. *nisi quod cupio me iam contingere* L, quod paullo fortius est quam Cydippam deceat. Innuere non aperte dicere, se iam matrimonium Acontii optare personae virginis magis conveniebat.

> 247. *nisi quod cupio me iam contingere* L: *contingere* is somewhat stronger than what would befit Cydippe ... To suggest, rather than openly say, that she desires to immediately get married to Acontius would be more appropriate for a virgin's character. [Palmer/Kennedy 2005, vol. 1: 157.]

Clearly, Palmer regarded *contingere*, in the concrete sense 'to physically touch', as too erotically invested for a virgin like Cydippe. Instead, Palmer prefers the variant *coniungere* of the 'Venetian edition', which is a physically less intense and, according to Palmer, more acceptable way of expressing the same prospect of union with Acontius. It should be noted that such a sentence construction leaves *tecum* highly problematic, not to say impossible, but Palmer refrains from discussing that issue.[55]

'I find [Palmer's] note not altogether easy to interpret [...]', Kenney observes in an article published prior to his 1996 edition of the double *Heroides*, and explains: '*contingere* is said to be *paullo fortius ... quam Cydippam deceat*, which makes it quite evident that Palmer did not understand it'.[56] Kenney, who in his reading of the couplet retains *mihi* alongside *contingere*,[57] as he clearly regards π as the authoritative edition of the incunabula mentioned above, seems to disregard Palmer's point about the accusative-with-infinitive construction, which

---

criticus of Sedlemayer's edition (Wien 1886). Since the manuscript tradition of the *Heroides* is "completely contaminated" (so Kenney, *Gnomon* [1961], p. 480), owing to the "transmissione orizzontale" which is not taken into consideration by Dörrie (he is a follower of the Lachmannian theory of "transmissione verticale"). The upshot of all this is that the wording indicated above is more likely to belong to the tradition and to be therefore genuine, instead of being an invention by one "Drucker" (to use Dörrie's words) which miraculously spread into all the *recentiores*'.

54 Showerman's edition was revised by G. P. Goold and reissued in 1977, but the original dates as far back as to 1913.
55 Solutions seem hard to find.
56 Kenney 1970a: 184.
57 Kenney 1970a.

would render *contingere* in its most basic meaning, i.e. 'to touch physically' (notwithstanding the problem of *tecum*, which neither Palmer nor Kenney discusses). More importantly, Kenney acknowledges quite correctly that any desire on Cydippe's part to touch or marry Acontius would be quite incompatible with her personality as portrayed in her letter:

> ... [Cydippe's] eagerness to be married to Acontius, [is] an emotion which, however plausible in isolation, is totally out of keeping with the picture of his heroine that Ovid has been at some pains to build up throughout the poem.[58]

Instead, Kenney assumes that Cydippe accepts marriage to Acontius not out of love, but out of her wish to get well: that is, for the prospect of health, rather than sickness. The word *contingere* is then to be understood as a part of an idiomatic expression, which denotes 'to fall to someone's lot' (*Her.* 21.247–8):[59]

> *quid, nisi, quod cupio mihi iam contingere tecum,*
> *restat, ut ascribat littera nostra vale?*

> Nothing is left except for my letter to add [the usual wish for] good health, which I desire will now be mine[60] along with [my marriage to] you.[61]

Kenney also points out that the *contingere* of Cydippe's closing couplet is echoed in Acontius' letter, where he writes (20.233–5): *iuncta salus nostra est: miserere meique tuique;| quid dubitas unam ferre duobus opem? | quod si contigerit ...* ('Your health is joined with mine – have compassion on me and on yourself; why hesitate to aid us both at once? If this happens ...') However, considering how ill-disposed Cydippe generally is towards all of Acontius' lines of reasoning, she is much more likely to regard this claim that Acontius, who in fact is in good health as they exchange letters, shares the same *salus* as she, who is on the verge of death from disease, as a provocation rather than a genuine prospect of salvation.

Indeed, the only other occurrence in the two Heroidean letters of the verb *contingo* may be of better help in making sense of Cydippe's closing remarks. In a passage quoted above (21.31–4), which Kenney suggests is best understood as

---

58 Kenney 1970a: 184.
59 OLD s.v. 8.
60 Or, more literally here, 'fall to my lot'.
61 Kenney's translation 1970: 185. The brackets are the author's and reveal how difficult the lines are. In private communication Stephen Heyworth points out that 'Kenney misunderstands; I think "which I want to come to me as well as to you" is the sense'.

'a single heavily ironical statement',[62] we find the verb in *haec nobis formae ... contingit merces*. Moreover, concerning this phrase, Thompson observes 'Cydippe's use of a positive word [i.e. *contingit*] to describe her illness is ironic – the verb is normally used of good things happening (cf. 20.237, see above)'.[63] Thus, the transmitted text of π, which is fairly well established as the authoritative source, makes it clear that Cydippe does not want Acontius as much as she wants her good health. Moreover, the use of irony in Cydippe's letter, not least in the case of the only other occurrence of the verb *contingo*, makes it possible to catch a glimpse not of Cydippe's desire for good health, but for vengeance; for if she is deadly ill and Acontius and she get together, then maybe she will infect him, so that he suffers too.[64] Notably, in both Callimachus and Aristaenetus, Cydippe is cured *before* she marries Acontius and *after* she has revealed to her parents what has happened (*Aet.* fr. 75.40). However, in *Heroides* 21, which necessarily must be written *before* her wedding to Acontius, Cydippe still has *invalidos artus* (21.245) and *manus aegra* (21.246) even *after* she has told her mother about the oath (21.241–2); thus, the possibility of her affecting others with her disease becomes more pressing. From this perspective, Cydippe's closing *vale* would not only be ironic, but downright threatening.

Conclusion

The pathology of love is a major theme in Ovid's *Heroides* 20–1. This chapter has argued that Ovid's Acontius is not so much obsessed by love as simply obsessive, and that Cydippe suffers not so much from lovesickness as from bodily sickness. Furthermore, their different personalities, as these are construed in their Heroidean letters, strongly suggest that a union between the two is bound to be unhealthy. Indeed, from an external perspective, Ovid's Acontius and Cydippe may very well end up as founders of a noble family and, as such, qualify as 'happy'. Yet, on a personal level, their union seems likely to become an unhappy rape-marriage in which the husband-*dominus* regards his wife as his property, as Acontius does in the Heroidean letters. There are two features in particular that Ovid exploits in order to activate these two parallel layers of happiness and unhappiness in the Acontius and Cydippe story: the evocation of

---

62 Kenney 1996: 220.
63 Thompson 1989: 201.
64 To this one may add that the verb *contingo* can mean not simply 'to touch', but also 'to affect with disease'; cf. *OLD*, s.v. 6.

Acontius' Telchinian descent, which is already embedded in Callimachus, and, most importantly, Cydippe's perspective, which may too be regarded as embedded *in nuce* in Callimachus,[65] but is only brought to full flower in the *Heroides*, where she pens an entire letter that is even a couple of lines longer than that of Acontius. It may feel counterintuitive to follow the interpretation presented in this chapter, as it means simultaneously setting aside the narrative of Acontius and Cydippe as we know it from Callimachus. Nevertheless, if the ideals of Callimacheanism are marked by surprise, subtleties, innovation, and sophistication, then the turning of a well-known story upside down in this fashion is entirely in keeping with such ideals. From this perspective, it also appears fair to conclude that what Cydippe wants (*cupio*) is not to be with Acontius for love of him, but to get her good health back – or perhaps, on a more speculative note, to get together (*tecum*) only in order to get even.

---

[65] 'In the very last lines of the episode, Callimachus refers to the prose historiographer Xenomedes, and explains that this is the source "from which the child's story moved swiftly on to our Calliope" (ἔνθεν ὁ παιδὸς | μῦθος ἐς ἡμετέρην ἔδραμε Καλλιόπην, fr. 75.76–7). The precise sense is ambiguous, as ὁ παιδὸς μῦθος may be rendered as "the child's story," "the girl's story" or "the boy's story." What is more, ὁ παιδὸς μῦθος neatly translates as either a genitive of the subject or of the object. Thus, it may just as well be "a story about her" as "about him." Tellingly, translations differ ... Despite the fact that Cydippe's perspective remains eclipsed by that of Acontius in the *Aetia*, the striking inclusiveness of the enigmatic summary that Callimachus gives us in the words ὁ παιδὸς μῦθος provides a final opportunity to consider Cydippe just as important as Acontius, which is precisely the opportunity that is realized in Ovid's *Heroides* 20–1.' Thorsen 2019: 136–7.

Fig. 5: Robinet Testard, *Cydippe writes a letter to Acontius*. Illustration from Octavien de Saint-Gelais' translation of Ovid's *Heroides*, Paris 1497. Bibliotèque Nationale de France, MS Fr.875 fol.124v.

Ioannis M. Konstantakos
Pathological Love in the 'Open' or 'Fringe' Novels

Abstract: The 'canonical' or 'erotic' Greek novels place at the centre of the plot an orthodox, heterosexual, monogamous and lifelong love affair between a young man and a maiden. By contrast, the so-called 'open' or 'fringe' novels treat *erôs* in a starkly different manner: love stories are pushed to the margins of the narrative, in peripheral episodes, and instead of idealised love, there is a variety of deviant passions, forbidden liaisons or sexual aberrations. The creators of the 'open' texts consciously adopted the exact opposite practice to the erotic novels, to clearly demarcate their genre as a different mode of fictional storytelling. The pathology of love thus became a marker of generic identity. In this chapter, four examples are adduced from the corpus of the 'open' novels to illustrate this proposition. In the *Alexander Romance* the only love affair, placed in the preliminaries of the story, is the adulterous liaison between Nectanebo and Queen Olympias. Similarly, the *Life of the Philosopher Secundus* begins with a scene of near-incest, which motivates the rest of the narrative. In the *History of Apollonius King of Tyre* the traditional love plot is fragmented, rearranged in a peculiar manner and prefaced by a horrendous episode of father-daughter incest. Finally, the *Life of Aesop* offers an assortment of tales about various aspects of perverse eroticism: exhibitionism, nymphomania, adultery, necrophilia, bestiality, incest and rape.

The literary landscape of ancient fiction is as rich and variegated as that of, for example, Greek drama, medieval storytelling and modern television serials. The Greek and Latin works that are usually classified under the category of prose fiction comprise several different forms of writing, types of plot, thematic tendencies and narrative materials.[1] Nevertheless, amidst this multiform panorama of narrative production there is one small group of texts which stand out today as the most celebrated and well-studied fictional creations of antiquity. These texts are considered by many modern scholars to represent the ancient novel *par excellence*, the mainstream and canonical form of this type of literary

---

[1] For a comprehensive overview of the diverse works, forms and genres included in the category of ancient fiction see the contributions of many scholars in Morgan/Stoneman 1994; Schmeling 2003a; Cueva/Byrne 2014.

expression; the very terms 'ancient novel' or 'ancient Greek novel' are often used in a specialised sense, so as to apply in particular to this restricted group of kindred works.[2] The texts in question are the so-called 'erotic' or 'ideal' Greek novels, popularly also known as 'the big five': that is, the romances of love and adventure by Chariton, Xenophon of Ephesus, Achilles Tatius and Heliodorus, together with the more idiosyncratic bucolic fantasy of Longus. The same typical features and themes are also found in the testimonia and the papyrus fragments of some lost Greek novels, such as *Metiochus and Parthenope*. It seems likely that this literary form was widespread in the postclassical Greek world and included more specimens than the five fully extant ones.[3]

There is, of course, some variety of styles, narrative techniques and episodic inventions within this small novelistic cycle. Nevertheless, all the texts of this group display a fundamental similarity in themes and plot patterns, a basic common denominator in terms of the *materia narrandi*, which unifies the individual compositions and warrants their classification as specimens of the same genre. At the centre of the plot there is always a love story, an affair between a young man and a maiden. Both of them are portrayed as paragons of almost every laudable quality; they are stunningly beautiful, well-bred and virtuous, pure and faithful to each other, dedicated to the highest moral ideals, steadfast and persevering through adversity.[4]

Like the characters of the main hero and heroine, the love between them is also idealised, admirable and morally uplifting. If there is anything in the sphere of *erôs* that can be called 'orthodox', 'canonical' or 'exemplary', at least by the standards of traditional western societies, this is it. The two young heroes fall in love at first sight and the passion kindled at their first encounter endures for the rest of their lives. Their love is so strong that it sustains both of them and supports their loyalty to each other through innumerable ordeals, hardships and misfortunes. The two lovers repeatedly separate and reunite, as they travel

---

[2] See e.g. Hägg 1983: 1–73; Reardon 1991: 4–7; Billault 1991: 7–17; Scarcella 1993: 47–8; Stephens/Winkler 1995: 4–5; MacAlister 1996: 1–4; Holzberg 2003: 12–6; Graverini 2006: 15–7; Müller 2006: 391–444; Tilg 2010: 1–4; cf. Bowie 1985; Whitmarsh 2008: 1–14; Morales 2009: 2–4; Futre Pinheiro 2014; Whitmarsh 2018: 9–13.
[3] Cf. Bowie 1985: 684–5; Stephens/Winkler 1995: 72–100, 277–313, 391–9; Stephens 2003: 657–62; Tilg 2010: 2–3, 92–126; Stephens 2014.
[4] This should not be taken to mean that the young hero and heroine are faultless and superhumanly perfect. The term 'idealised', which is often used in scholarship (including the present chapter), should always be taken *cum grano salis*. See now the nuanced discussion of De Temmerman 2014: 15–26, 46–61, 248–50, 310-7; see also Anderson 1984: 62–5; Billault 1991: 151–3; Billault 2003: 115–9, 126–8; Johne 2003: 169–81, 185–207.

away from their home town and all through the Eastern Mediterranean. Each one of them may be seized by pirates or bandits, sold to slavery, thrown to prison, condemned to death, subjected to mock execution or very nearly sacrificed to barbarian gods. Both the young man and the maiden attract the amorous attention of other powerful characters (masters and slave-owners, officials and even kings), who try to seduce them, rape them or marry them by force. However, the two young protagonists remain firm in their devotion to each other; as a rule, they refuse to succumb to temptation and erotic pressure (or at least they do so only under extreme adversity) and preserve their fidelity to the end. Finally, after many adventures, the young man and his beloved girl come together again and enjoy a happy union in marriage, which is bound to last until the end of their days.

This is, in very broad outline, the story pattern of the ancient erotic novels, the standard scenario which defines this form of fiction.[5] The love between the protagonists is heterosexual, monogamous, lifelong, faithful, consummated only in marriage, destined to family life and central to the plot. The narrative may of course include different kinds of *erôs*, deviant or illicit forms of passion such as adultery, pederasty or affairs of the type of 'Potiphar's wife'.[6] As a rule, these are peripheral to the main action, connected with secondary characters or relegated to incidental episodes, minor subplots or inserted digressions. The main storyline, from beginning to end, is taken up by the pivotal sentimental love between the virtuous youth and the pure maiden. And yet the reader may wonder: is this all that ancient fiction has to offer in the theme of love?

'Open' or 'Fringe' Narratives

Opposite the largely uniform cycle of the erotic novels, modern scholars have set up another group of ancient narrative compositions. These other works are also extensive texts of prose fiction, characterised by narrative ampleness and a mythopoeic storyline, like the erotic novels. In other respects, however, they substantially differ from the ideal novels; they exhibit a wholly different kind of

---

[5] Good discussions of the story pattern of the erotic novels are provided by Stark 1989; Reardon 1991: 15–42, 102–26; Billault 1991: 191–243; Konstan 1994: 7–26, 30–59; Fusillo 1994: 239–43; Holzberg 1995: 1–11; MacAlister 1996: 19–33; Müller 2006: 399–406; Redondo Moyano 2012.
[6] See for example Xen. Ephes. 3.2, 3.12, 5.9.3, 5.13.5; Ach. Tat. 1.7–8, 2.34–8; Long. 4.11–2, 4.16–9; Heliod. 1.9–17, 2.25, 7.3; Konstan 1994: 26–30, 52–3; Morales 2008; Whitmarsh 2011: 156–67; Makowski 2014; Lefteratou 2018: 129–75.

poetics and operate with different rules and practices in terms of literary structure, morphology, compositional techniques and thematic concerns. Modern scholarship has not yet settled on a standard, comprehensive and universally recognised name for this category of texts, which were of course entirely neglected by ancient theorists and grammarians. Niklas Holzberg has christened them 'fringe novels', a term which was taken up in important subsequent studies.[7] The designation of 'fringe' inevitably presupposes that the erotic novels are regarded as the 'core' form of ancient fiction, although it need not imply an evaluative judgement on the quality or the aesthetics of the texts involved in the former or the latter category. Nevertheless, the concept of the literary 'fringe' has drawn some criticism from theoretically orientated experts, who call attention to the problematic character of the dichotomy between 'central' and 'marginal' texts or genres within the ancient literary canon and argue for the advantages of a more fluid and flexible approach, beyond such categorisations.[8]

In an equally influential article, David Konstan introduced the term 'open text' for some of these works.[9] The quality of 'openness', in the context of this approach, refers primarily to the peculiar manner of the production and transmission of these texts, which circulated in multiple variant versions in the course of their long history. The coexistence of different parallel versions, in turn, is inextricably connected with the lax, open structure of the narrative, which may accommodate or exclude various additional episodes or textual chunks and may thus substantially differ from one version to another in terms of length and layout. Unfortunately, the term 'open text' does not cover other important common traits of the works under discussion, such as their biographical orientation or the construction of the main characters – traits that are equally vital for the definition of the nature of these works and for the appreciation of the literary affinity among them.

This category of texts is characterised by much greater fluidity and diversity than the close-knit cycle of the erotic novels. It accommodates works of different narrative substance, thematic tendencies and compositional materials. Konstan's 'open texts' comprise various novelistic biographies, which revolve around historical figures or legendary cultural heroes and recount their career in a heavily fictionalised manner, with many invented episodes and mythopoeic motifs. Here belong the *Life of Aesop*, the *Alexander Romance* and the novelistic

---

7 See Holzberg 1995: 11–26; Holzberg 2003; Keulen 2006; Karla 2009a; Nawotka 2017: 17–8.
8 See Morales 2009; Hunter 2009.
9 Konstan 1998; cf. also Thomas 1998; Panayotakis 2007: 299–302; Karla 2009b: 24–7; Hägg 2012: 99–101, 146–7.

Lives of Homer, together with shorter narratives, such as the *Life of the Philosopher Secundus*.[10] Apart from these, the group also includes the *History of Apollonius King of Tyre*, an idiosyncratic romance of adventure about fictional heroes, which presents unmistakable affinities with the ordinary erotic novels but also shares many of the characteristics of the aforementioned fictionalised *Lives*. Holzberg's 'fringe novels' also include other types of fictional narrative, such as fantastic travel tales, epistolary romances and early Christian apocryphal Acts. These works, however, do not treat erotic love as a theme and will not be discussed in the present chapter. Furthermore, these compositions do not share the fluid textual transmission and the variable narrative structure which are emblematic of the 'open texts' listed above. Outside the well-defined and homogeneous group of the ideal novels, the landscape of ancient fictional writing is truly polymorphous, disparate and not reducible to uniformity.

Nevertheless, at least the works gathered by Konstan under the heading of 'open text' do exhibit a number of important common features in form and content. These common characteristics bind the so-called 'open texts' together and legitimise their study as a distinct group with its own identifiable literary physiognomy. Even if the works of this group cannot be collectively considered as a special genre or sub-genre of fiction, they represent a peculiar and recognisable manner of fictional storytelling.[11] Firstly, all the 'open' novels, regardless of whether their heroes are historical, legendary or fictional characters, follow a biographical pattern. They offer a linear narrative of the main protagonist's lifespan, from his birth or youth to his death or at least to the completion of his life's purpose. The structure of their plot is conglomerate and non-organic. Unlike what happens in the erotic novels, in which the adventures of the hero and the heroine build up an enthralling, suspenseful and consequentially evolving plot, the storyline of the 'open texts' is a string of loosely connected episodes, which give the impression of independent tales rather haphazardly assembled together. These tales follow the protagonist's career and accumulatively set out his various exploits or mishaps.

---

10 On these biographical novels and their peculiar features cf. Adrados 1979; Gallo 1996; Pervo 1998: 77–85; Karla 2009b; Jouanno 2009; Hägg 2009; Hägg 2012: 99–147; Ruiz Montero 2014: 257–8.

11 On the identifying characteristics of this category of narrative texts, apart from the analyses of Konstan 1998 and Thomas 1998, see the remarks of Gallo 1996: 237–40 and Hansen 1998: xvii–xxvi concerning the products of the so-called 'popular literature' or 'letteratura di consumo'.

In fact, the arrangement of the episodes in the 'open' novels may well follow an underlying and carefully constructed plan.[12] This plan, however, is based on strategies that are typical of the folk narrative tradition, such as the repetition and parallelism of patterns and leitmotifs, the symmetrical contrast of individual scenes and the organisation of the material in triads. The overall design is thus very different from the well-crafted artistic plot, in which events evolve out of each other according to plausibility or necessity, in the Aristotelian sense (*Poet.* 1451a38). As for the main hero, in contrast to the idealised protagonists of the erotic novels, he is depicted as a rogue, a trickster full of cunning, who advances in life by means of his cleverness and expert manipulation of language.[13] Much of the narrative consists of episodes of a competitive or 'agonistic' type, in which the clever hero deceives an adversary, turns the tables on him or gains advantage through ready wit and glib tongue.

In terms of narrative material, the 'open' novels are agglomerations of miscellaneous content. They gather together many different forms of tale, drawn especially from the repository of folk storytelling: fables, anecdotes and jokes, piquant or sensational novellas, picaresque and adventurous stories, travelogues, magical *Märchen*, and also various types of wisdom literature, such as clever apophthegms, moral maxims, proverbs and riddles. In this respect, the 'open texts' are the closest ancient analogues to the all-embracing medieval and Renaissance compilations, such as the *Canterbury Tales* or the oeuvre of Rabelais, which aimed at epitomising the total of the genres of storytelling current at their time.[14] In the course of an 'open' novel, the identity of the main hero may absorb many traditional roles of the popular narrative repertoire; apart from the cunning trickster who outwits his adversaries, the protagonist may appear as a picaresque adventurer, as a traveller who roams around the world and undergoes extraordinary experiences, as the wise advisor of kings and rulers or as the central figure of a 'hero myth' who works his way from illegitimate birth and irregular circumstances to success and glory. The story of this character's life functions as a kind of framework that attracts the multifarious types of popular material mentioned above. The loose structure of the plot, combined with the medley of disparate materials, make the 'open' novel look like a composite and

---

12 See e.g. Holzberg 1992, Holzberg 2002: 75–93, and Ruiz Montero 2014 on the *Life of Aesop*; Cizek 1978 and Karla 2012 on the *Alexander Romance*; Archibald 1991: 12–26, Schmeling 1999 and 2003b: 544–50 on the *History of Apollonius*.
13 See Konstan 1998: 129–36; cf. Adrados 1979: 93–103, 109–12; Jedrkiewicz 1989: 165–6; Pervo 1998: 81–2; Jouanno 2009: 40–7.
14 Cf. Aune 1988: 123–4; Merkle 1996; Konstan 1998: 124–6; Karla 2009b: 24–7; Hägg 2012: 99–100, 303–4; and on the medieval examples Cooper 1983: 52–3, 72–90.

heterogeneous creation that has been pieced together from earlier autonomous traditions.

Because of their heterogeneous composition, the 'open texts' are prone to a fluid and complicated textual transmission. Unlike the ideal novels and the other works of the ancient Greek literary canon, the 'open' novels do not consist of a fixed text which is more or less faithfully reproduced in all the extant sources. Rather, these works circulate in many variant versions or redactions, which share the same rudimentary storyline but widely vary in terms of diction, style and particular episodes. Since the 'open texts' were made up of so multifarious ingredients, copyists and editors down the ages felt free to make their own contributions to them; they liberally altered the style, expanded or abridged the plot, removed individual incidents or interpolated new materials. Individual versions of these works may have been composed over successive periods; but there are also indications that different redactions of an 'open' text were in parallel circulation at the same time.

This set of common features, apart from binding the 'open texts' together, also serves to distinguish them from the ideal erotic novels, which adopt an entirely separate system of compositional methods and rules of poetics. Hence it seems legitimate to confront the 'open texts' as a group with the cycle of the erotic novels comparing them with the latter in terms of literary practices, narrative strategies and the presentation of particular themes – in the same way that one might compare e.g. epic with lyric poetry or tragedy with comedy with regard to opposed aesthetic effects, artistic techniques and elements of subject-matter. The main part of the present chapter is dedicated to one facet of this far-reaching antithesis between the 'open' and the ideal novels, namely, the narrative treatment and function of the theme of love.[15] The opposition between these two distinct forms of fiction is evident also in the field of *erôs*.

The idealised image and central narrative role of love in the erotic novels has been delineated above. The 'open texts' also exploit love as material of their mythopoeia; they include stories about amorous affairs and erotic liaisons but handle them in a manner that starkly contrasts with the practice of the 'big five'

---

15 Due to the limitations of space and the special focus of this chapter on the 'open texts', it is impossible to consider here another group of ancient fictional works: the so-called 'comic' novels, such as Petronius' *Satyricon*, Apuleius' *Metamorphoses* and the Greek *Lucius or The Ass*, which need to be treated at some length and should properly form the subject of a separate study. These works also treat erotic themes in a lively and fascinating way, much different than the romantic *manière* of the ideal novels. Also, by comparison to the 'open texts', they award a more prominent narrative role to the various manifestations of pathological love and weave them into more complex and variegated patterns.

romantic novels. Two broad differences stand out. Firstly, in the 'open' novels the love stories are not placed at the centre of the plot but are pushed to the margins of the narrative. *Erôs* is not the permanent driving force of the main action but is only treated in peripheral scenes, in secondary incidents with restricted impact on the overall development of the storyline, or in brief inserted tales which are unconnected with the principal character's adventures and function only as paradigmatic *exempla*.[16] Secondly, the love affairs of the 'open texts' do not belong to the normative, model type of the erotic novels. They are of course exclusively heterosexual,[17] just like the central love plots of the ideal romances, and never include cases of homosexuality of pederasty (unlike some of the secondary subplots and digressions of the ideal novels). Otherwise, however, the love episodes of these peculiar narrative works exemplify a variety of alternative forms of eroticism, deviant passions, forbidden liaisons or sexual aberrations. Instead of the uniform, prescriptive and ideal love of the canonical Greek romances, the 'open' novels collectively offer a panorama of pathological *erôs* in its multiple and chameleonic manifestations.

Pathological Love in the 'Open' Novels

The cases of pathological love in the 'open' novels may be arranged in various patterns and perform a range of functions in the overall design of the plot, depending on the particular work. The simplest kind of structure is presented by the so-called *Alexander Romance* by Pseudo-Callisthenes, an extensive biographical fiction about the life and exploits of Alexander the Great. The date of composition of this work is a matter of debate. According to most scholars, the *Alexander Romance*, in the form now known to us, must have been compiled around the third century CE; however, Richard Stoneman has been making for over two decades an ever more convincing case for a prototype dated in the Hellenistic period.[18] In any case, the novel of Pseudo-Callisthenes was based on earlier narrative materials; it incorporates large portions of previous historical

---

16 Cf. Karla 2009b: 15, 18–9; Jouanno 2009: 35; Papademetriou 2009: 49–51; Hägg 2009: 81–5.

17 Even the tale of bestiality in the *Life of Aesop* 131 (see below, p. 176), the only case in the corpus of texts under discussion which does not involve an erotic couple of man and woman, concerns nevertheless a sexual act between a man and a female animal.

18 On the late dating see, for example, Fraser 1996: 221–3; Jouanno 2002: 13–6, 26–8, 34; Nawotka 2017: 3–5; cf. Callu 2010: 23–31. On the Hellenistic origins see Stoneman 1991: 8–17, and 2007: xxviii–xxxiii, liii–lvi; Whitmarsh 2018: 132–3.

and fictional works, many of which circulated already since Hellenistic times, as shown by papyrus finds.[19]

The earlier half of the romance focuses on Alexander's youth and his wars, first against the resistant cities of mainland Greece and then in the context of his military expedition to Asia, which leads to Alexander's confrontation with King Darius and the conquest of the Persian Empire. The basic material of this part is apparently drawn from one or more historical sources; the narrative includes some familiar historical battles and episodes, but all of them are fictionalised, filtered through legendary patterns and adorned with novelistic, adventurous or didactic motifs. In the second part of the novel the main theme changes. The narrative now focuses on Alexander's subsequent voyages and explorations in the furthest regions of the East. The Macedonian hero becomes a kind of Odysseus or Sinbad, a traveller who wanders in extraordinary lands at the edges of the world and encounters marvels and monsters. The finale consists in a kind of conspiracy thriller, which relates how Alexander was murdered by poison, as a result of an insidious plot hatched by officials of his entourage.

The element of love is notably absent from all these parts of the narrative. Alexander is never shown falling in love or pursuing an amorous affair. In the second book, after his conquest of Iran, he marries Roxane, who is introduced as King Darius' daughter (2.22.6–18); but their marriage is presented more or less as a case of moral duty, undertaken by Alexander in order to fulfil the last wish of the dying Persian king (2.20.11–12). Roxane takes care of her sick husband at the end of the work, when Alexander is poisoned (3.32.6–7); the Macedonian hero is also mindful of her welfare and provisions for her in his will (3.33.11). However, there is no romantic attachment between them, no kind of flirtation, courtship or any other ingredients of a love story.[20]

Significantly, even episodes which could have developed in an amorous direction are kept clear of any tinge of eroticism. Alexander's encounter with Candace Queen of Ethiopia was turned into a proper love romance in the medieval offshoots of Alexander's legend, in Byzantium, in Western Europe and in the

---

19 On the sources of the *Alexander Romance* see Fraser 1972: I 677–80, II 946–50; Merkelbach 1977; Fraser 1996: 210–20; Gallo 1996: 240–44; Jouanno 2002: 17–26; Stoneman 2007: xxv–xxviii, xliii–l; Nawotka 2017: 18–25.
20 Cf. Liviabella Furiani 2001: 250–2; Jouanno 2002: 152–3, 393–4; Stoneman 2008: 129; Karla 2009b: 18; Hägg 2009: 82–3; Müller 2012: 301–3. The only exception, within the Greek tradition of Pseudo-Callisthenes, is the heavily reworked and idiosyncratic Middle Byzantine recension ε (8th century CE), which abundantly introduces the element of sentimentalism and romantic love into the narrative.

East.²¹ In the Greek novel, however, the narrative is entirely free of such overtones (3.18–23). There is no sexual union, amorous dalliance or erotic tension between the Macedonian hero and the Ethiopian matron. Candace is described as an impressive but middle-aged woman (3.18.2). Alexander views her as a mother figure, comparable to his own mother Olympias (3.22.1); Candace herself wishes that Alexander were her son (3.23.8).²² Another famous tradition, which had already been introduced by some fanciful Hellenistic historians, was Alexander's sexual encounter with the queen of the Amazons in Central Asia.²³ In the *Alexander Romance* the Macedonian king also approaches the realm of the Amazons and exchanges a few letters of negotiation with them; the warrior women submit to his power and offer him tribute and reinforcements for his army (3.25–6). However, no mention is made of an erotic union between Alexander and an Amazon leader. The Alexander of Pseudo-Callisthenes has been consistently de-eroticised; he is barred from every possibility of love interest, as though the creator of the text wished to emphasise that this hero is not the protagonist of a romantic novel.²⁴

There is only one love affair in the *Alexander Romance*: the tale of Nectanebo and his seduction of Queen Olympias at the beginning of the first book (1.3–12). Nectanebo, the last pharaoh of Egypt, flees his country before the Persian invaders and takes refuge to the Macedonian court, disguised as an itinerant magician. There he meets Olympias, while her husband, King Philip, is away on an expedition, and is filled with desire for her. To seduce the beautiful queen, Nectanebo practises a cunning plan. He draws up Olympias' horoscope and prophesies that she is fated to have intercourse with the god Ammon and give birth to his child. The queen is tempted by this prospect and asks Nectanebo to contrive a meeting between her and the god. For this purpose, the Egyptian magician asks to be given a room close to the queen's own bedroom, supposedly in order to perform the magic rituals required. In the night, the wily Nectanebo disguises himself as the ram-headed Ammon, enters Olympias' bedroom and has sex with her in the guise of the god. The queen becomes pregnant and in

---

21 See Wilmanns 1901; Cary 1956: 219–20, 231–2, 329–31; Gaullier-Bougassas 1991; Boitani *et al.* 1997: lv–lvii, 174–195, 557–9; Jouanno 2002: 435; Stoneman 2008: 134–40; Müller 2008: 274; Doufikar-Aerts 2010: 249, 259–60.
22 On the story and figure of Candace in the Greek novel see Cracco Ruggini 1974: 142–51; Jouanno 2002: 88–90, 207–17, 317–24; Stoneman 2008: 134–8; Szalc 2014; Nawotka 2017: 211–8.
23 On this tradition see Mederer 1936: 84–93; Daumas 1992; Baynham 2001; Stoneman 2008: 129–34; Munding 2011; Mayor 2014: 320–38, 474–5.
24 Cf. Cary 1956: 218–20; Liviabella Furiani 2001; Jouanno 2002: 152–3, 166, 393–4, and 2009: 35; Stoneman 2008: 128–9, 134–5; Hägg 2009: 83–4, and 2012: 130; Nawotka 2017: 17–8, 28, 211, 221.

due course gives birth to Alexander. Nectanebo thus establishes his position in the palace and continues to disguise himself and sleep with the queen, who still unsuspectingly mistakes him for Ammon. King Philip, upon returning from the war, is at first doubtful about the paternity of the baby. Nectanebo therefore magically engineers and sends him a series of deceptive visions, which finally convince the Macedonian monarch that Olympias is truly expecting the god's child.

This story, probably based on an original Egyptian narrative,[25] is a fully-fledged novella of adultery and includes all the main ingredients of this kind of tale; there is the love triangle, the cunning adulterer and his intrigues, the naive wife and her duped cuckolded husband, as in all the famous specimens of the genre from Apuleius to Boccaccio. The same storyline, in which the clever lover disguises himself as a divine being in order to seduce the woman, is widely attested in the world narrative tradition, from Classical antiquity to the Italian *novellistica* of the Renaissance and the vast compilations of Indian fantastic tales.[26] The affair illustrated in this episode is a far cry from the idealised and pure love of the erotic novels.[27] It is an unlawful liaison between a married woman and an unscrupulous seducer, a deceitful union out of wedlock, contrary to all moral commandments and social conventions; it is inspired by unruly lust, produces a bastard child and dissolves the family bonds.

In the *Alexander Romance* this coup of pathological love is characteristically placed outside the main narrative, in the preliminaries of the story, before the central hero's birth. It sets the action of the novel in motion and provides the starting point for all the subsequent adventures, since it is this adulterous union that brings Alexander into the world. Alexander's illegitimate origins are also echoed in a few other early scenes in the first book. Philip feels occasionally disturbed because his supposed child does not physically look like him, and this places some strain on his relationship with Alexander (1.14.1–2, 1.16.5, 1.21–2); in other episodes, however, Philip treats Alexander as his lawful and beloved son and heir, as though the issue of the young man's doubtful parentage had never arisen (1.18.1–4, 1.23.4, 1.24.4–11). Significantly, Alexander's claim to the Macedonian throne and the legitimacy of his rule are never questioned in the

---

[25] For analysis of this story, its formation and provenance, see Braun 1938: 19–43; Perry 1966; Merkelbach 1977: 77–83; Jasnow 1997; Aufrère 2000; Jouanno 2002: 57–65, 83–8; Stoneman 2007: 476–90, and 2008: 6–24; Konstantakos 2009; Matthey 2011, 2016, and 2017; Nawotka 2017: 25–6, 37–70; Whitmarsh 2018: 137–44.
[26] See Weinreich 1911; Stoneman 2007: 476–8, and 2008: 15–7.
[27] Cf. Liviabella Furiani 2001: 247–9.

narrative (see e.g. the episode of Alexander's succession to kingship, 1.24–6). Conversely, when Alexander conquers Egypt, he openly reveals his kinship with Nectanebo to the Egyptians; he is thus recognised as the rightful heir to the Egyptian throne and establishes more firmly his dominion over the land of the Nile (1.34).[28]

Apart from these sporadic echoes, and beyond its initial igniting and way-paving function, the episode of Nectanebo's adultery has no further essential reverberations on the storyline of the novel. Alexander's campaigns in Greece and his war against the Persians, his confrontation with Darius and his conquest of the eastern empire, his marvellous travels to the edges of the earth and his insidious death – all these elements, which form the main fabric of the plot, are not affected or overshadowed by the introductory tale of the exiled pharaoh's amours. Instead of a central idealised love romance, Pseudo-Callisthenes offers an erotic anomaly in the margin of the narrative.

A similar pattern, although in miniature scale, underlies the *Life of the Philosopher Secundus*, a kind of short story or didactic novella composed in the late second century CE.[29] This narrative consists of only two main episodes. The first one reworks a sensational folktale which is widespread in international tradition, from Europe to the Far East.[30] Secundus, the protagonist, is sent away from home while he is still a small boy, in order to be educated. When he grows up, he hears the popular saw that every woman is a whore, and decides to test it. He therefore disguises himself as a Cynic philosopher, returns home unrecognised and makes amorous advances on his own mother, offering her money in return for sex. The woman accepts and receives the young man in her bedroom. Secundus, however, spends the night chastely by her side and reveals his true identity to her in the morning. The mother hangs herself from shame. Secundus blames his tongue for this misfortune and vows never to speak again. He thus becomes famous as the silent philosopher.

In the second part of the story Secundus comes to the attention of the Emperor Hadrian. The emperor wishes to test the silent philosopher's resolve and makes repeated attempts to engage in conversation with him, but to no avail. In the end, Hadrian threatens Secundus with execution if he does not break his silence; but the philosopher is not frightened and courageously prepares to die.

---

28 Cf. Jouanno 2002: 62–5; Stoneman 2007: 546–9; Matthey 2011: 326–7, and 2016: 160–2.
29 Cf. Hägg 2012: 300–4. For text, translation and discussion of this work see Perry 1964; see also Perry 1960: 83–9; Adrados 1978; Gallo 1980: 393–429; Aune 1988; Gallo 1996; Hansen 1998: 64–75.
30 See Krappe 1927: 181–90; Aune 1988: 111–2; Hansen 1998: 65–6.

Finally, Hadrian admires Secundus' constancy and spares his life at the last moment. Afterwards the emperor asks Secundus to write down his answers to a series of theoretical questions. The text ends with the transcript of the silent philosopher's sententious replies.

This narrative also begins with a scene of perverse and unlawful eroticism: a case of near-incest between mother and son, which is averted at the last moment, because the rash hero intended it only as a cruel and shameful ruse. As in the *Alexander Romance*, this initial scene of pathological *erôs* motivates the rest of the story and determines the evolution of the plot. Because of the tragic outcome of the near-incest, the protagonist becomes a philosopher sworn to silence; the rest of his life, up to and including his confrontation with the emperor, is sealed by this attitude. The central focus of the brief didactic narrative is Secundus' philosophical courage and power of will. The anomalous love affair is a preliminary incident which affords the hero the opportunity to develop these extraordinary ethical qualities.

A more developed and complex pattern is displayed by the idiosyncratic *History of Apollonius King of Tyre*, which survives in late Latin redactions of the fifth of sixth century CE. These are often considered to have stemmed from an earlier original of the third century CE, but it is still a disputed question whether this prototype version was composed in Latin or in Greek.[31] The *History of Apollonius* holds a constant, creative and sophisticated conversation with the ordinary Greek erotic novels. Many of the standard motifs and plot devices of these latter texts are borrowed in the Latin narrative, but they are reworked in an unusual and innovative way, arranged in new combinations or given a different orientation than in the Greek romantic fictions. These features make the *History of Apollonius* a unique specimen in the ancient novelistic corpus.

The canonical theme of the idealised monogamous love between the young hero and a noble maiden is retained, but it does not constitute the pivotal concern of the plot. Apollonius, the protagonist, is shipwrecked near Cyrene in the course of his travels, and the local king's daughter falls in love with him (12–7). After some courtship and amorous intrigues, Apollonius marries the princess (18–23). However, their love story occupies hardly one fifth of the total extent of the book; it is not the main design but only one of many intertwined threads within a multiform narrative web. The separation and the adversities follow after the couple's marriage; the princess suffers *Scheintod* at childbirth, during a

---

[31] For opposite answers to this question see Puche López 1997: 21–33; Wolff 2001; Kuhlmann 2002; Schmeling 2003b: 526–8; Kortekaas 2004: 10–96; Garbugino 2014; cf. the surveys of scholarship in Archibald 1991: 6–9 and Panayotakis 2012: 1–8.

stormy sea voyage, and is abandoned for dead in the waves, enclosed in a coffin. Eventually, she is washed up at Ephesus, where she is revived by a physician and assigned to serve in the temple of Diana (25–7). There she will wonderfully reunite with her husband after fourteen years, when Apollonius visits Ephesus and discovers again his long-lost wife in the finale (48–9). In the meantime, the largest part of the novel is taken up by other episodes.

The maiden who struggles to preserve her virginity from unwanted lovers is also present. However, in the *History of Apollonius* this motif is not applied to the main hero's ladylove but is transferred to the daughter of the couple, Tarsia. After her mother's apparent death, Tarsia is unwittingly entrusted by her grieving father to the foster care of an envious and hypocritical woman, who eventually plans to murder her; but before this evil scheme is carried out, Tarsia is abducted by pirates and sold to a brothel in Mytilene (28–33). There the young maiden uses her talent in music and storytelling in order to avoid prostitution. Her sad story moves to tears all the clients of the brothel, who forget about having sex with her; her sweet songs earn her enough money to satisfy the pimp and put off his pressure (34–6), until Apollonius arrives by chance at Mytilene and finally recognises and reclaims his daughter (39–45). In essence, the *History of Apollonius* breaks to pieces the central romantic plot of the Greek novels and then rejoins some of the splinters in a most peculiar manner, producing a distorted image of the idealised love story – somewhat like a human figure cubistically segmented and reconstructed by Picasso.[32]

This highly eccentric narrative is prefaced by a horrendous case of pathological *erôs*, which opens the novel and sets the action in motion, like the adulterous affair in the *Alexander Romance*. King Antiochus of Syria conceives a perverse lust for his own beautiful daughter; he rapes the maiden and secretly maintains an incestuous relationship with her. To ward off potential suitors of his daughter, Antiochus poses them a difficult riddle as an ordeal and has them executed when they fail to find the solution (1–3). Apollonius also comes to claim the princess' hand and hears the riddle propounded by Antiochus: *Scelere vehor, maternam carnem vescor, quaero fratrem meum, meae matris virum, uxoris meae filium: non invenio* ('I am borne by crime, I eat my mother's flesh, I seek

---

[32] On the similarities and differences between the *History of Apollonius* and the Greek erotic novels see Garin 1914; Chiarini 1983: 285–92; Szepessy 1985–8; Müller 2006: 486–91; Archibald 1991: 31–6, 82–92; Konstan 1994: 100–13; Puche López 1997: 34–45; Schmeling 1999: 124–7, and 2003b: 536, 540–50; Wolff 2001; Kuhlmann 2002; Panayotakis 2007: 302–3, and 2012: 7, 299; Garbugino 2014: 140–2.

my brother, my mother's husband, my wife's son, but I do not find him', 4).³³ The hero immediately understands that the answer to this conundrum is the king's incest with his own child.³⁴ Seized by panic before this monstrous discovery, Apollonius flees, while Antiochus orders his agents to chase and murder him (5–8). Thus begin Apollonius' travels and adventures around the Mediterranean, which take up the bulk of the narrative, including his shipwreck at Cyrene, his marriage, his separation from his wife and his daughter and their final reunion.

Once again, as in the *Alexander Romance*, a case of anomalous love inaugurates the storyline, provides the driving force for the entire sequence of incidents that make up the plot, but otherwise remains peripheral to the main narrative. In Pseudo-Callisthenes the preliminary episode of pathological eroticism gives way to a narrative totally deprived of the element of love. In the *History of Apollonius* an analogous prologue of erotic anomaly leads to a tortuous fragmentation of the usual novelistic pattern of idealised love, which struggles here with the other themes of the narrative but does not manage to regain the integrity and centrality it enjoyed in the ideal Greek novels. Although the episode of Antiochus, as a whole, introduces important themes which permeate the rest of the story, such as riddles or the relationship of father and daughter, the incest of the Syrian king and his child *per se* does not belong to the core of the novel. On the contrary, this perverse passion is antithetically evoked towards the end of the narrative, when Apollonius recognises his own daughter Tarsia and avoids an incestuous union with her (40–5). In essence, the plot of the *History of Apollonius* moves towards a negation and annulment of incest.³⁵

---

33 This is the text of the redaction A of the novel; see the editions of Schmeling 1988: 3 and Kortekaas 2004: 110.

34 This is Apollonius' answer, again from the redaction A (ch. 4): *Quod dixisti: scelere vehor, non es mentitus: te respice. Et quod dixisti: maternam carnem vescor, nec et hoc mentitus es: filiam tuam intuere* ('When you said: "I am borne by crime", you did not lie; look at yourself. And when you said: "I eat my mother's flesh", you did not lie either; look at your daughter'). Of course, this solution only elucidates the first half of the riddle, while it makes no reference to the second half. Nevertheless, it is clear that within the fictional world of the novel, Apollonius' explanation is regarded as the correct one (see Antiochus' own remarks, chs. 5–6). On the interpretation of this much-debated riddle see most recently Panayotakis 2012: 95–103 (with an excellent survey of earlier scholarship) and Beta 2016: 74–6, 79–80.

35 On this horrendous episode in general and its function in the narrative see Perry 1967: 295–302; Chiarini 1983; Müller 2006: 476–91; Archibald 1991: 12–24, 37–44, 64–5, 98–100; Puche López 1997: 43–8; Kortekaas 2004: 53–6, and 2007: 1, 38–9, 73; Laird 2005: 225–33; Panayotakis 2006 and 2012: 46–150; Konstantakos 2010: 271–4.

Among all the 'open' novels the richest one in terms of pathological *erôs* is the *Life of Aesop*, a fictional biography of the legendary fabulist, written in a raunchy comic tone which approximates the picaresque storytelling of the *Satyricon* and of *Lucius or The Ass*. The text, composed around the first or second century CE,[36] follows Aesop's spectacular rising career as he moves around the Greek and Near-Eastern world. Initially a mute and much-suffering slave, Aesop is nonetheless pious and very intelligent. As a reward for his piety, he is blessed by Isis and the Muses with the gift of eloquent speech and the talent of composing fables. Eventually he is sold to Xanthos, a pedantic professor of philosophy in the island of Samos, and remains in Xanthos' service throughout the central part of the novel. The cunning slave plays many jokes on his conceited master and mocks his inanity; but he also saves Xanthos from embarrassing situations and solves many hard problems for his sake. In the end Aesop wins his freedom by offering valuable political advice to the Samians in the matter of their conflict with King Croesus of Lydia. Afterwards, the liberated Aesop turns into an itinerant sophist and eventually arrives at Babylon, where he becomes the counsellor of King Lycorus. He helps the Babylonian king win many contests of wisdom against other monarchs – in particular, a long and crucial competition against the pharaoh of Egypt. Finally, Aesop visits Delphi and angers the stingy local inhabitants with his mockery. The Delphians frame him with false accusations of sacrilege, sentence him to death and throw him into the precipice. As a result, they are punished by the gods with a plague and are obliged to expiate Aesop's murder.

As in the *Alexander Romance*, there is no place for love affairs in the main hero's biographical curriculum. Aesop is hardly the type of the idealised lover familiar from the erotic novels. He is extremely ugly, intensely misogynous, cynical and coarse in his behaviour – a character entirely unfit for the games of amorous dalliance and romantic passion.[37] *Erôs* comes into his story only in peripheral scenes and in bawdy or deviant forms.[38] Upon being introduced into

---

36 On the date, textual tradition and versions of the *Life of Aesop* see the useful overviews provided by Perry 1933; 1936: 1–70; 1952: 1–5, 10–32; La Penna 1962: 264–73; Ferrari 1997: 41–5; Karla 2001: 8–15.
37 Cf. Anderson 1984: 101–2; Jedrkiewicz 1989: 169–71; Karla 2009b: 19; Papademetriou 2009: 62–4, 71–4; Zafiropoulos 2015: 136–43. On Aesop's ugliness in particular see Papademetriou 1997: 7–42; Ruiz Montero and Sánchez Alacid 2003. On his misogynism cf. La Penna 1962: 309–11; Jedrkiewicz 1989: 124–5; Adrados 1999: 680–1.
38 On these episodes of bawdy *erôs* in the *Life of Aesop* cf. Adrados 1979: 95–6, and 1999: 279–80, 680–1; Winkler 1985: 280–5; Holzberg 1992: 52–3; Pervo 1998: 87–90; Jouanno 2005: 402–5, 416; Papademetriou 2009; Zafiropoulos 2015: 140–1.

Xanthos' household, Aesop is mocked by the pert slave-girls of the house for his ugliness; he responds with an obscene joke which is probably accompanied by an exhibitionistic demonstration of his virile member (30). Shortly afterwards, he openly accuses Xanthos' wife of adulterous lust. According to Aesop, the lady is a nymphomaniac and wishes to be surrounded by young and handsome male slaves in order to enjoy their sexual favours (32).

After some time, the lady's debauchery is indeed revealed, although it is directed towards an unexpected target. One day, as Aesop is exercising naked, Xanthos' wife ogles him and is seized by desire for his sizeable *membrum*. She therefore asks him to copulate with her for ten consecutive times, in return for a suit of new clothes. Aesop does manage well for nine times but botches his tenth attempt, and the lady refuses to give him his reward. Aesop therefore appeals to the master, Xanthos himself, and presents him the case in the form of an allegorical riddle, so that the cuckolded husband may grasp the substance of the dispute without suspecting the adultery. The duped philosopher rules indeed in favour of the wily Aesop (75–6). This saucy tale of adultery, placed at the middle of the story arc of the novel, constitutes Aesop's single sexual experience in the entire narrative.[39]

More examples of pathological love follow in the final part of the work, which relates Aesop's inglorious end at Delphi. These are not integrated in the plotline but are introduced as digressive exemplary stories, which are recounted by Aesop himself in the course of his final adventures.[40] Two of them are addressed to a friend who visits Aesop at gaol, while the condemned fabulist is awaiting execution; these stories function as parables that illustrate Aesop's imprudence and his dire fate. The first one is a variant of the famous tale-type of the 'Widow of Ephesus' (129).[41] A matron is lamenting over the grave of her husband, who has recently died; a farmer, who is ploughing his field nearby, sees and desires her. He therefore approaches the woman and pretends to be a bereaved man, who is mourning for his own deceased wife. Gradually the farmer seduces the matron and they end up making love on the spot, in front of the grave, until the farmer's oxen, which had been left unattended, are stolen by a thief. Now the farmer has a true reason to mourn. This wry tale combines two

---

39 Cf. Hägg 2012: 108. For detailed studies of this episode see Konstantakos 2006 and Papademetriou 2009: 54–64.
40 On these inserted ribald tales see Jedrkiewicz 1989: 187–8; van Dijk 1995: 141–4, 148–50; Merkle 1996: 216, 226–8; Jouanno 2005: 404–5; Papademetriou 2009: 64–70; Kurke 2011: 87–90, 186–8, 213–7.
41 On this Greek version of the famous tale see Weinreich 1931: 53–8; Perry 1962: 329–30; Anderson 1984: 161–4; van Dijk 1995: 141–3.

aspects of erotic abnormality: seduction of a faithful widow, virtually a kind of 'metaphysical adultery', and sex in the graveyard, which carries an unmistakable tinge of morbidity and necrophilia.

Aesop's second tale concerns a stupid girl who knew nothing about the sexual act. Every day she heard her mother praying and asking the gods to put some sense into her daughter. One day, during an excursion to the countryside, the girl saw a herdsman who was mating with a she-ass. Puzzled before the unfamiliar spectacle, she asked the man what he was doing, and he gave a euphemistic answer: 'I am putting some sense into her'. The silly maiden took this statement literally and asked the man to perform the exact same service for her; the herdsman willingly obliged (131). This story also displays a mixed repertoire of sexual deviances; bestiality is followed by the statutory rape of a mentally retarded person.

The third sexual tale is told by Aesop as a warning to his Delphian persecutors, when they are leading him to the precipice for execution. This story concerns the paragon of sexual crimes, father-daughter incest. A man once conceived an abominable lust for his own daughter. He therefore sent his wife away to the fields on a pretext and raped the girl, ignoring the poor maiden's cries: 'Father, I would rather give myself to a hundred other men than to you!' By analogy, Aesop claims that he would have preferred to travel around Syria, Phoenicia and Judaea, rather than die in Delphi at the hands of these wretched rascals (141).

In the *Life of Aesop* the divergence from the model of the erotic novels is more pronounced, as though the author took care to emphasise and draw attention to the difference. The narrative includes an entire series of tales of illicit or perverted eroticism. Every one of these tales introduces one or more different manifestations of deviant sex: exhibitionism, nymphomania, adultery, necrophilia, bestiality, rape, incest. This novel offers almost an anthology of cases of pathological *erôs*, which are dispersed throughout the narrative; sexual pathology runs through the text as a leitmotif. However, none of these episodes plays a central role in the plot. They are either inserted paradigmatic novellas or secondary incidents without substantial reverberations on the development of the action, the main hero's fate or the evolution of his character. It might be argued that the creator of the *Life of Aesop* consciously strove to overturn the standard pattern of the erotic novels. Instead of a single, orthodox and idealised love affair placed at the focal point of the story and determining the plot, this novelistic *Life* uses many and multifarious cases of anomalous *erôs*, all of them consigned to marginal or interlude positions.

The Generic Function of Love Themes

What conclusion can be drawn from this survey of pathological eroticism in the 'open' novels? Perhaps the divergence of these works from the model use of romantic love in the erotic novels was a deliberate creative choice and aimed at a clear demarcation between these two different forms of fiction. With regard to the narrative depiction of love, as also in many other thematic and structural aspects, the 'open texts' adopted the exact opposite practice than the erotic novels, in order to be distinguished from this latter genre and establish their own independence as a different mode of fictional storytelling.

An analogous phenomenon may be observed in the case of the two main forms of classical Attic drama, tragedy and comedy. These were established as opposed and rival poetic genres and followed entirely different conventions and tactics with regard to many aspects of content and morphology. Aristotle already notes the different practices of tragedy and comedy in connection with various matters, such as the ending of the play, the construction of dramatic characters, the material of the plot and the emotions aroused in the audience (*Poet.* 1448a16–8, 1448b24–1449a6, 1451b11–23, 1453a30–8). Modern researchers have drawn attention to an even greater number of divergences, which extend to subtle thematic choices and technical devices, for example, the handling of dramatic space and time, the interaction between the characters and the chorus, the fabrication of dramatic illusion and the reference to contemporary reality.[42] Tragic and comic poets were doubtless aware of these different sets of rules, which distinguished their respective genres in a strict manner.

A similar dichotomy may have applied to the authors of the erotic and the 'open' novels during the late Hellenistic and the Imperial age. There are no writings of ancient theory about the artistic rules of these two types of fiction, because ancient scholars did not deign to treat in detail such works that fell outside the established grammatological canon. However, the forms and traits of the texts themselves indicate that the erotic and the 'open' novels operate *de facto* with entirely separate and often opposed sets of rules and conventions; they employ different strategies with regard to the structure of the plot, the construction of characters, the assimilation of narrative material and the use of the narrator's voice.[43] It is plausible to suppose that the authors who cultivated the one or the other type of novel were aware of the conventions, literary prac-

---

42 See e.g. Taplin 1986.
43 See Karla 2009b for a detailed list of differences; cf. Hägg 2009.

tices and features which pertained to their own form of composition and determined its peculiar identity. The treatment of the love theme may have been one of the parameters which distinguished these two forms of fictional writing from each other. The erotic novels typically placed at the centre of the plot an orthodox and idealised love affair. By contrast, and as a means of self-definition and dissociation from the other genre, the 'open' novels opted for anomalous forms of eroticism and located them in the margins of the narrative.

The pathology of love thus became a marker of generic identity for one of the most fascinating categories of fictional writing in the early literature of the West. It was bound to exercise an analogous function also in later instances of the European literary history. In the same way, for example, the variety of illicit or deviant forms of love distinguishes the medieval collections of piquant novellas from the idealised romances of chivalry; and it strongly demarcates the libertine fictions of Sade, such as the audacious *A Hundred and Twenty Days of Sodom*, from the sentimental novels of Samuel Richardson or Jean-Jacques Rousseau. This, however, is a different and much longer tale.

Dimitrios Kanellakis
Appendix: An Anthology of the Pathologies of Love

As a complement to the analytic case studies of the volume, and in accordance with the introduction, this anthology offers a representation of all major genres and authors of classical antiquity who dealt with the subject matter. The reader is guided through the variety of pathologies (physical, emotional, mental, social, political etc.) which are associated with different kinds of love (sexual, romantic, familial, self-love etc.) in ancient Greek and Latin literature. The passages compiled are listed in chronological order, by language, and unless otherwise specified, the translations are from the Loeb editions. The anthology does not aspire to be exhaustive, as the word itself signifies, but a useful tool for teaching and further research.

Hom. *Il.* 14.294–5

Ὣς δ' ἴδεν, ὥς μιν ἔρως πυκινὰς φρένας ἀμφεκάλυψεν,
οἷον ὅτε πρῶτόν περ ἐμισγέσθην φιλότητι

And when he saw her, then love engulfed his shrewd mind, just as when they first had joined in love.

Hom. *Il.* 14.214–7

Ἦ καὶ ἀπὸ στήθεσφιν ἐλύσατο κεστὸν ἱμάντα
ποικίλον, ἔνθα δέ οἱ θελκτήρια πάντα τέτυκτο·
ἔνθ' ἔνι μὲν φιλότης, ἐν δ' ἵμερος, ἐν δ' ὀαριστὺς
πάρφασις, ἥ τ' ἔκλεψε νόον πύκα περ φρονεόντων.

She spoke, and loosed from her bosom the embroidered strap, inlaid, in which are fashioned all manner of allurements; in it is love, in it desire, in it dalliance – persuasion that steals the senses even of the wise.

Hom. *Od.* 15.420–2

πλυνούσῃ τις πρῶτα μίγη κοίλῃ παρὰ νηῒ
εὐνῇ καὶ φιλότητι, τά τε φρένας ἠπεροπεύει
θηλυτέρῃσι γυναιξί, καὶ ἥ κ' εὐεργὸς ἔῃσιν.

First, as she was washing clothes, one of them lay with her in love by the hollow ship; for this beguiles the minds of women, even though one be upright.

Hes. *Theog.* 120–2

ἠδ' Ἔρος, ὃς κάλλιστος ἐν ἀθανάτοισι θεοῖσι,
λυσιμελής, πάντων τὲ θεῶν πάντων τ' ἀνθρώπων
δάμναται ἐν στήθεσσι νόον καὶ ἐπίφρονα βουλήν.

And Eros, who is the most beautiful among the immortal gods, The limb-melter – he overpowers the mind and the thoughtful counsel of all the gods and of all human beings in their breasts.

Archil. 196 W

Ἀλλά μ' ὁ λυσιμελὴς ὦταῖρε δάμναται πόθος.

But, my friend, limb-loosening desire overwhelms me.

Archil. 193 W

δύστηνος ἔγκειμαι πόθῳ,
ἄψυχος, χαλεπῇσι θεῶν ὀδύνῃσιν ἕκητι
πεπαρμένος δι' ὀστέων.

I am in the throes of desire, miserable and lifeless, pierced through my bones with grievous pangs thanks to the gods.

Alcm. 59a *PMG*

Ἔρως με δηὖτε Κύπριδος ϝέκατι
γλυκὺς κατείβων καρδίαν ἰαίνει.

At the command of the Cyprian, Eros once again pours sweetly down and warms my heart.

Sappho 130 L-P

Ἔρος δηὖτέ μ' ὁ λυσιμέλης δόνει,
γλυκύπικρον ἀμάχανον ὄρπετον

Once again limb-loosening Love makes me tremble, the bitter-sweet, irresistible creature.

Sappho 47 L-P

Ἔρος δ' ἐτίναξέ μοι φρένας, ὡς ἄνεμος κὰτ ὄρος δρύσιν ἐμπέτων.

Love shook my heart like a wind falling on oaks on a mountain.

Alc. 283 L-P (ed. Campbell)

κἀλένας ἐν στήθ[ε]σιν [ἐ]πτ[όαισε
θῦμον Ἀργείας, Τροΐω δ' [ὐ]π' ἄν[δρος
ἐκμάνεισα ξ[εν]ναπάτα 'πὶ π[όντον
ἔσπετο νᾶϊ,

And [Love?] excited the heart of Argive Helen in her breast; and crazed by the Trojan man, the deceiver of his host, she accompanied him over the sea in his ship.

Ibyc. 6 *PMG*

Ἔρος αὖτέ με κυανέοισιν ὑπὸ
   βλεφάροις τακέρ' ὄμμασι δερκόμενος
κηλήμασι παντοδαποῖς ἐς ἄπει-
   ρα δίκτυα Κύπριδος ἐσβάλλει·

Again Love, looking at me meltingly from under his dark eyelids, hurls me with his manifold enchantments into the boundless nets of the Cyprian.

Anacr. 68 *PMG*

Μεγάλῳ δηὖτέ μ' Ἔρως ἔκοψεν ὥστε χαλκεὺς
πελέκει, χειμερίῃ δ' ἔλουσεν ἐν χαράδρῃ.

Once again Love has struck me like a smith with a great hammer and dipped me in the wintry torrent.

Aesch. *Sept.* 686–8

τί μέμονας, τέκνον; μή τί σε θυμοπλη-
θὴς δορίμαργος ἄτα φερέτω· κακοῦ δ'
ἔκβαλ' ἔρωτος ἀρχάν.

Why this mad passion, child? You must not let yourself be carried away by this spear-mad delusion that fills your heart.

Pind. *Nem.* 11.47–8

κερδέων δὲ χρὴ μέτρον θηρευέμεν·
ἀπροσίκτων δ' ἐρώτων ὀξύτεραι μανίαι.

One must seek due measure of gains; too painful is the madness of unattainable desires.

Pind. fr. 123.10–12 (ed. Snell-Maehler)

ἀλλ' ἐγὼ τᾶς ἕκατι κηρὸς ὣς δαχθεὶς ἕλᾳ
ἱρᾶν μελισσᾶν τάκομαι, εὖτ' ἂν ἴδω
παίδων νεόγυιον ἐς ἥβαν·

But I, because of her [=Aphrodite], melt like the wax of holy bees bitten by the sun's heat, whenever I look upon the new-limbed youth of boys.

Soph. *Ant.* 781–90

Ἔρως ἀνίκατε μάχαν,
Ἔρως, ὃς ἐν κτήμασι πίπτεις, [...]
καί σ' οὔτ' ἀθανάτων φύξιμος οὐδεὶς
οὔθ' ἀμερίων σέ γ' ἀν-
θρώπων, ὁ δ' ἔχων μέμηνεν.

Love invincible in battle, Love who falls upon men's property ... None among the immortals can escape you, nor any among mortal men, and he who has you is mad.

Hdt. 1.8.1–2

Οὗτος δὴ ὦν ὁ Κανδαύλης ἠράσθη τῆς ἑωυτοῦ γυναικός, ἐρασθεὶς δὲ ἐνόμιζέ οἱ εἶναι γυναῖκα πολλὸν πασέων καλλίστην. Ὥστε δὲ ταῦτα νομίζων, [...] τὸ εἶδος τῆς γυναικὸς ὑπερεπαίνεε. [...] χρῆν γὰρ Κανδαύλῃ γενέσθαι κακῶς

This Candaules, then, fell in love with his own wife, so much that he supposed her to be by far the fairest woman in the world; and being persuaded of this, he raved of her beauty ... and he was doomed to ill-fortune ...

Eur. *Hipp.* 392–4

Ἐπεί μ' ἔρως ἔτρωσεν, ἐσκόπουν ὅπως
κάλλιστ' ἐνέγκαιμ' αὐτόν. Ἠρξάμην μὲν οὖν
ἐκ τοῦδε, σιγᾶν τήνδε καὶ κρύπτειν νόσον·

When love wounded me, I considered how I might best bear it. My starting point was this, to conceal my malady in silence.

Thuc. 3.45.5

ἥ τε ἐλπὶς καὶ ὁ ἔρως ἐπὶ παντί, ὁ μὲν ἡγούμενος, ἡ δ' ἐφεπομένη, καὶ ὁ μὲν τὴν ἐπιβουλὴν ἐκφροντίζων, ἡ δὲ τὴν εὐπορίαν τῆς τύχης ὑποτιθεῖσα πλεῖστα βλάπτουσι ...

Then, too, Hope and Desire are everywhere; Desire leads, Hope attends; Desire contrives the plan, Hope suggests the facility of fortune; the two passions are most baneful ...

Ar. *Eccl.* 954–7

Πάνυ γὰρ δεινός τις ἔρως με δονεῖ
τῶνδε τῶν σῶν βοστρύχων.
ἄτοπος δ' ἔγκειταί μοί τις πόθος,
ὅς με διακναίσας ἔχει.

A powerful passion sets me awhirl for those curly locks of yours. A strange longing besets me and grinds me in its grip.

Lys. 3.39

καὶ οἱ μὲν ἄλλοι, ὅταν ἐρῶσι καὶ ἀποστερῶνται ὧν ἐπιθυμοῦσι καὶ συγκοπῶσιν, ὀργιζόμενοι παραχρῆμα τιμωρεῖσθαι ζητοῦσιν ...

Everyone else, when in love, and deprived of the object of desire, and battered with blows, immediately in his anger seeks redress ...

Isoc. 8.113

Ὅπου δ' οἱ πρωτεύοντες καὶ δόξας μεγίστας ἔχοντες τοσούτων κακῶν ἐρῶσιν, τί δεῖ θαυμάζειν τοὺς ἄλλους εἰ τοιούτων ἑτέρων ἐπιθυμοῦσιν;

And when men who are of the foremost rank and of the greatest reputation are enamoured of so many evils, is it any wonder that the rest of the world covets other evils of the same kind?

Xen. *Mem.* 1.2.22

πολλοὶ γὰρ καὶ χρημάτων δυνάμενοι φείδεσθαι, πρὶν ἐρᾶν, ἐρασθέντες οὐκέτι δύνανται·

For many who are careful with their money no sooner fall in love than they begin to waste it.

Xen. *Symp.* 4.14,16

ἐγὼ γοῦν καίπερ εἰδὼς ὅτι χρήματα ἡδὺ κτῆμα ἥδιον μὲν ἂν Κλεινίᾳ τὰ ὄντα διδοίην ἢ ἕτερα παρ' ἄλλου λαμβάνοιμι, ἥδιον δ' ἂν δουλεύοιμι ἢ ἐλεύθερος εἴην, εἴ μου Κλεινίας ἄρχειν ἐθέλοι. καὶ γὰρ πονοίην ἂν ῥᾷον ἐκείνῳ ἢ ἀναπαυοίμην, καὶ κινδυνεύοιμ' ἂν πρὸ ἐκείνου ἥδιον ἢ ἀκίνδυνος ζῴην. [...] ἐγὼ γοῦν μετὰ Κλεινίου κἂν διὰ πυρὸς ἰοίην·

I do realize that money is good to have, but I'd be happier giving what I have to Cleinias than getting more from someone else; and I'd be happier being a slave than being a free man, if Cleinias were willing to be my master. For I should find it easier to work for him than to rest, and I'd be happier to risk my life for him than to live in safety ... I'd even go through fire with Cleinias.

Pl. *Symp.* 186b

Ἡ γὰρ φύσις τῶν σωμάτων τὸν διπλοῦν Ἔρωτα τοῦτον ἔχει. τὸ γὰρ ὑγιὲς τοῦ σώματος καὶ τὸ νοσοῦν ὁμολογουμένως ἕτερόν τε καὶ ἀνόμοιόν ἐστι, τὸ δὲ ἀνόμοιον ἀνομοίων ἐπιθυμεῖ καὶ ἐρᾷ. ἄλλος μὲν οὖν ὁ ἐπὶ τῷ ὑγιεινῷ ἔρως, ἄλλος δὲ ὁ ἐπὶ τῷ νοσώδει.

This double Love belongs to the nature of all bodies: for between bodily health and sickness there is an admitted difference or dissimilarity, and what is dissimilar craves and loves dissimilar things. And so the desire felt by a sound body is quite other than that of a sickly one.

Pl. *Resp.* 573d

Ἔρως τύραννος ἔνδον οἰκῶν διακυβερνᾷ τὰ τῆς ψυχῆς ἅπαντα.

Souls are entirely swayed by the indwelling tyrant Eros.

Hippoc. *Epid.* 3.3.17(16)

νεηνίσκος ἐκ ποτῶν καὶ ἀφροδισίων πολλῶν πουλὺν χρόνον θερμανθεὶς κατεκλίθη· φρικώδης δὲ καὶ ἀσώδης ἦν, καὶ ἄγρυπνος, καὶ ἄδιψος. [...] Δεκάτῃ, παρέκρουσεν ἀτρεμέως, ἦν δὲ κόσμιός τε καὶ ἥσυχος· δέρμα καρφαλέον καὶ περιτεταμένον· διαχωρήματα ἢ πολλὰ, λεπτὰ, ἢ χολώδεα, λιπαρά. Τεσσαρεσκαιδεκάτῃ, πάντα παρωξύνθη· παρεκρούσθη, πολλὰ παρέλεγεν. Εἰκοστῇ, ἐξεμάνη· βλῆστρισμός· οὐδὲν οὔρει· σμικρὰ ποτὰ κατείχετο. Τῇ εἰκοστῇ τετάρτῃ, ἀπέθανεν.

A youth took to his bed after being for a long time heated by drunkenness and sexual indulgence. He had shivering fits, nausea, sleeplessness, but no thirst ... Tenth day: delirious but quiet, for he was orderly and silent; skin dry and tense; stools either copious and thin or bilious and greasy. Fourteenth day: general exacerbation; delirious with much wandering talk. Twentieth day: wildly out of his mind; much tossing; urine suppressed; slight quantities of drink were retained. Twenty-fourth day: death.

[Arist.] *Physiognom.* 805a, 6–8

Τῆς ψυχῆς παθήμασι τὸ σῶμα συμπάσχον φανερὸν γίνεται περί τε τοὺς ἔρωτας καὶ τοὺς φόβους τε καὶ τὰς λύπας καὶ τὰς ἡδονάς.

The body suffers sympathetically with affections of the soul is evident in love, fear, grief and pleasure.

[Dem.] 40.27

ὥστε πολὺ μᾶλλον εἰκὸς ἦν αὐτὸν διὰ τὴν ζῶσαν γυναῖκα, ἧς ἐρῶν ἐτύγχανε, τὸν τῆς τεθνεώσης υἱὸν ἀτιμάζειν, ἢ [... τοὺς] παῖδας μὴ ποιεῖσθαι.

So that it was much more likely that for the sake of the living woman, with whom he was in love all this time, he would dishonour the son of her who was dead, than ... he would refuse to acknowledge the children of her.

Callim. *Epigr.* 46.3–7 (ed. Pfeiffer)

αἱ Μοῖσαι τὸν ἔρωτα κατισχναίνοντι, Φίλιππε·
 ἦ πανακὲς πάντων φάρμακον ἁ σοφία.
τοῦτο, δοκέω, χἀ λιμὸς ἔχει μόνον ἐς τὰ πονηρὰ
 τὠγαθόν· ἐκκόπτει τὰν φιλόπαιδα νόσον.
ἔσθ' ἁμὶν †χ'ακαστας ἀφειδέα ποττὸν Ἔρωτα·

The Muses, O Philippus, reduce the swollen wound of love. Surely the poet's skill is sovereign remedy for all ill. I think that hunger, too, has this good – and this alone – in regard to evil: it drives away the disease of love. We have both remedies against you, remorseless Love!

Theoc. *Id.* 2.82–90 (ed. Hopkinson)

χὠς ἴδον, ὣς ἐμάνην, ὥς μοι πυρὶ θυμὸς ἰάφθη
δειλαίας, τὸ δὲ κάλλος ἐτάκετο. οὐκέτι πομπᾶς
τήνας ἐφρασάμαν, οὐδ' ὡς πάλιν οἴκαδ' ἀπῆνθον
ἔγνων, ἀλλά μέ τις καπυρὰ νόσος ἐξεσάλαξεν,
κείμαν δ' ἐν κλιντῆρι δέκ' ἄματα καὶ δέκα νύκτας [...]
καί μευ χρὼς μὲν ὁμοῖος ἐγίνετο πολλάκι θάψῳ,
ἔρρευν δ' ἐκ κεφαλᾶς πᾶσαι τρίχες, αὐτὰ δὲ λοιπὰ
ὀστί' ἔτ' ἦς καὶ δέρμα.

And when I saw them I was seized with madness, and my wretched heart was caught with fire, and my beauty wasted away. I no longer took notice of that procession, and I had no idea how I got home again, but a burning fever shook me, and I lay on my bed ten days and ten nights ... Often my skin would become as pale as fustic, and all the hair began to fall from my head, and only my skin and bones were left.

Phld. *AP* 5.306 (ed. Tueller)

Δακρύεις, ἐλεεινὰ λαλεῖς, περίεργα θεωρεῖς,
ζηλοτυπεῖς, ἅπτῃ πολλάκι, πυκνὰ φιλεῖς·
ταῦτα μέν ἐστιν ἐρῶντος. ὅταν δ' εἴπω "παράκειμαι"
καὶ σὺ μένῃς, ἁπλῶς οὐδὲν ἐρῶντος ἔχεις.

You weep, you talk piteously, you watch me excessively, you show your jealousy, you touch me often, you kiss me hard; these are the deeds of a lover. But when I say, 'Here I am next to you,' and you wait, you simply have nothing of the lover in you.

Plut. *Per.* 20.4

πολλοὺς δὲ καὶ Σικελίας ὁ δύσερως ἐκεῖνος ἤδη καὶ δύσποτμος ἔρως εἶχεν, ὃν ὕστερον ἐξέκαυσαν οἱ περὶ τὸν Ἀλκιβιάδην ῥήτορες.

Many also were possessed already with that inordinate and inauspicious passion for Sicily which was afterwards kindled into flame by such orators as Alcibiades.

Gal. *Praecog.* 14.630 K.

τῶν σοφιστῶν ἰατρῶν ἔνιοι, ἀγνοούμενοι τίνι λόγῳ τὸν ἔρωτα τῆς παλλακῆς τοῦ πατρὸς Ἐρασίστρατος ἐγνώρισεν, ἔγραψαν τῶν ἀρτηριῶν τοὺς σφυγμοὺς τοῦ νεανίσκου, σφυζουσῶν ἐρωτικῶς ἐξευρεῖν αὐτόν, οὐκέθ' ὑπομείναντες εἰπεῖν ἐκ τῶν σφυγμῶν εὑρεθῆναι.

Some of the sophistic doctors, not knowing on what grounds Erasistratus discovered the young man's love for his father's concubine, have suggested that he found the arteries pulsating madly with love, although they cannot yet bear to say that this was discovered through his pulse beats. [Transl. Nutton]

Charit. 1.1.8–10

Χαιρέας δὲ νεανίας εὐφυὴς καὶ μεγαλόφρων, ἤδη τοῦ σώματος αὐτῷ φθίνοντος, ἀπετόλμησεν εἰπεῖν πρὸς τοὺς γονεῖς ὅτι ἐρᾷ καὶ οὐ βιώσεται τοῦ Καλλιρρόης γάμου μὴ τυχών. [...] Εἶθ' ὁ μὲν πατὴρ παρεμυθεῖτο τὸν παῖδα, τῷ δ' ηὔξετο τὸ κακόν, ὥστε μηδ' ἐπὶ τὰς συνήθεις προϊέναι διατριβάς. Ἐπόθει δὲ τὸ γυμνάσιον Χαιρέαν καὶ ὥσπερ ἔρημον ἦν· ἐφίλει γὰρ αὐτὸν ἡ νεολαία. Πολυπραγμονοῦντες δὲ τὴν αἰτίαν ἔμαθον τῆς νόσου, καὶ ἔλεος πάντας εἰσῄει μειρακίου καλοῦ κινδυνεύοντος ἀπολέσθαι διὰ πάθος ψυχῆς εὐφυοῦς.

But when Chaereas, a well-bred and spirited youth, began to waste away, he had the courage to tell his parents that he was in love and could not live without Callirhoë as his wife. [...] the boy's malady grew worse, and he no longer went out even to his usual pastimes. The gymnasium missed Chaereas and was virtually deserted, for the young people loved him. The curiosity (of his friends) found out the cause of his sickness, and all felt pity for a handsome youth who seemed likely to die from the passion of an honest heart.

Plaut. *Asin.* 883

> *me ex amore huius corruptum oppido;*

I'm utterly corrupted because of my love for this girl.

Plaut. *Aul.* 592–4

> *nam qui amanti ero seruitutem seruit, quasi ego seruio,*
> *si erum uidet superare amorem, hoc serui esse officium reor,*
> *retinere ad salutem, non enim quo incumbat eo impellere*

Someone who serves a lovesick master, just as I do now, if he can see that love is gaining the upper hand over his master, well then, I think it's the servant's duty to restrain him for his own good, and not to push him further in the direction he inclines to.

Ter. *And.* 307–10

> BYR *ah! quanto satiust te id dare operam qui istum amorem ex animo amoveas,*
>   *quam id loqui quo magis lubido frustra incendatur tua!*
> CHA *facile omnes quom valemus recta consilia aegrotis damus.*
>   *tu si hic sis aliter sentias.*

> BYR Oh! How much better to set about banishing that love from your heart than to say things which only inflame your desire to no purpose!
> CHA We can all readily give good advice to the sick when we're well. If you were in my place, you would feel differently.

Cic. *Tusc.* 4.26, 68

> *Aegrotationi autem talia quaedam subiecta sunt: avaritia, ambitio, mulierositas, pervicacia, ligurritio, vinolentia, cuppedia et si qua similla. [...] Totus vero iste, qui vulgo appellatur amor – nec hercule invenio quo nomine alio possit appellari – tantae levitatis est, ut nihil videam quod putem conferendum.*

There are moreover certain subdivisions of sickness of the following kind: avarice, ambition, love of women, stubbornness, love of good living, intoxication, daintiness and anything similar ... In fact, the whole passion ordinarily termed 'love' (and heaven help me if I can think of any other term to apply to it) is of such exceeding triviality that I see nothing that I think comparable with it.

Lucr. *DRN* 4.1076–83

> *... etenim potiundi tempore in ipso*
> *fluctuat incertis erroribus ardor amantum,*
> *nec constat quid primum oculis manibusque fruantur.*

> *quod petiere, premunt arte faciuntque dolorem*
> *corporis, et dentes inlidunt saepe labellis*
> *osculaque adfligunt, quia non est pura voluptas*
> *et stimuli subsunt qui instigant laedere id ipsum,*
> *quodcumque est, rabies unde illaec germina surgunt.*

Indeed, in the very time of possession, lovers' ardour is storm-tossed, uncertain in its course, hesitating what first to enjoy with eye or hand. They press closely the desired object, hurting the body, often they set their teeth in the lips and crush mouth on mouth, because the pleasure is not unmixed and there are secret stings which urge them to hurt that very thing, whatever it may be, from which those germs of frenzy grow.

Lucr. *DRN* 4.1153–4

> *nam faciunt homines plerumque cupidine caeci*
> *et tribuunt ea quae non sunt his commoda vere.*

For this is what men usually do when blinded with desire, and they attribute to women advantages which they really have not.

Catull. 76.21–6

> *heu, mihi surrepens imos ut torpor in artus*
>   *expulit ex omni pectore laetitias!*
> *non iam illud quaero, contra me ut diligat illa,*
>   *aut, quod non potis est, esse pudica velit:*
> *ipse valere opto et taetrum hunc deponere morbum.*

Ah me! what a lethargy creeps into my inmost joints, and has cast out all joys from my heart! No longer is this my prayer, that she should love me in return, or, for that is impossible, that she should consent to be chaste. I would myself be well again and put away this baleful sickness.

Verg. *Ecl.* 2.68–9

> *me tamen urit amor; quis enim modus adsit amori?*
> *a, Corydon, Corydon, quae te dementia cepit!*

Yet love still burns in me; for what bound can be set to love? Ah, Corydon, Corydon, what madness has gripped you?

Verg. *Ecl.* 8.47–9

> *saevus Amor docuit natorum sanguine matrem*
> *commaculare manus; crudelis tu quoque, mater.*
> *crudelis mater magis an puer improbus ille?*

Ruthless Love taught a mother [= Medea] to stain her hands in her children's blood; cruel, too, were you, O mother. Who was more cruel, the mother or that wicked boy?

Hor. *Sat.* 1.4.25–7

hic nuptarum insanit amoribus, hic puerorum;

One is mad with love for somebody's wife, another for boys.

Hor. *Carm.* 4.1.1–7

> *Intermissa, Venus, diu*
> *rursus bella moves? parce precor, precor.*
> *non sum qualis eram bonae*
> *sub regno Cinarae. desine, dulcium*
> *mater saeva Cupidinum,*
> *circa lustra decem flectere mollibus*
> *iam durum imperiis: abi*

Are you making war again, Venus, after so long a truce? Have mercy, I beg you, I beg you! I am not the man I was in the reign of Cinara the Good. Stop, o cruel mother of sweet Desires, stop driving one who after nearly fifty years is now too hardened to answer your soft commands. Away!

Livy, *AUC* 1.9.15–16

Saepe ex iniuria postmodum gratiam ortam, eoque melioribus usuras viris, quod adnisurus pro se quisque sit ut, cum suam vicem functus officio sit, parentium etiam patriaeque expleat desiderium. Accedebant blanditiae virorum factum purgantium cupiditate atque amore, quae maxime ad muliebre ingenium efficaces preces sunt.

A sense of injury had often given place to affection, and they [= the Sabine Women] would find their husbands the kinder for this reason, that every man would earnestly endeavour not only to be a good husband, but also to console his wife for the home and parents she had lost. His [=Romulus'] arguments were seconded by the wooing of the men, who excused their act [=abduction] on the score of passion and love, the most moving of all pleas to a woman's heart.

Tib. 2.5.109–12

> *... iaceo dum saucius annum*
> *et faveo morbo, nam iuvat ipse dolor,*
> *usque cano Nemesim, sine qua versus mihi nullus*
> *verba potest iustos aut reperire pedes.*

For a year now, afflicted from his stroke and siding with my malady (for the pain itself is pleasure), I sing unceasingly of Nemesis, apart from whom no verse of mine can find its words or proper feet.

Tib. 2.6.15–18

acer Amor, fractas utinam tua tela sagittas,
  si licet, extinctas aspiciamque faces!
tu miserum torques, tu me mihi dira precari
  cogis et insana mente nefanda loqui.

Fierce Love, oh, if this could be, I would see your arms destroyed, the arrows broken, and the torches quenched. You rack me with anguish: you force me to curse myself and in impious speech to vent the frenzy of my soul.

Prop. 1.1.3–4, 25–6

tum mihi constantis deiecit lumina fastus
  et caput impositis pressit Amor pedibus, [...]
aut vos, qui sero lapsum revocatis, amici,
  quaerite non sani pectoris auxilia.

It was then that Love made me lower my looks of stubborn pride and trod my head beneath his feet ... You my friends, who too late call back the fallen, seek medicines for a heart that is sick.

Prop. 1.5.27–30

non ego tum potero solacia ferre roganti,
  cum mihi nulla mei sit medicina mali;
sed pariter miseri socio cogemur amore
  alter in alterius mutua flere sinu.

Then when you ask me, I will be unable to bring you any comfort, since I have no medicine for my own malady; but, comrades in love and woe, we shall be equally compelled to weep each in turn on the other's bosom.

Prop. 3.24.13–14

correptus saevo Veneris torrebar aëno;
  vinctus eram versas in mea terga manus.

Venus seized me and roasted me in her cruel cauldron: I was a prisoner with hands bound behind my back.

Ov. Rem. (sel.)

15–6	At siquis male fert indignae regna puellae,
	Ne pereat, nostrae sentiat artis opem. [...]
43–4	Discite sanari, per quem didicistis amare:
	Una manus vobis vulnus opemque feret. [...]
53–4	Utile propositum est saevas extinguere flammas,
	Nec servum vitii pectus habere sui. [...]
81	Opprime, dum nova sunt, subiti mala semina morbi, [...]
101–2	Vidi ego, quod fuerat primo sanabile, vulnus
	Dilatum longae damna tulisse morae. [...]
135–6	Ergo ubi visus eris nostra medicabilis arte,
	Fac monitis fugias otia prima meis. [...]
225–6	Dura aliquis praecepta vocet mea; dura fatemur
	Esse; sed ut valeas, multa dolenda feres. [...]
491–4	Quamvis infelix media torreberis Aetna,
	Frigidior glacie fac videare tuae:
	Et sanum simula, ne, siquid forte dolebis,
	Sentiat; et ride, cum tibi flendus eris

But if any endures the tyranny of an unworthy mistress, lest he perish, let him learn the help my art can give ... Learn healing from him through whom you learnt to love: one hand alike will wound and succour ... A profitable aim it is to extinguish savage flames, and have a heart not enslaved to its own frailty ... Crush, while yet they are new, the baneful seeds of sudden disease ... I have seen a wound, that at first was healable, by tarrying suffer the penalty of long delay ... When therefore I shall find you amenable to my skill, obey my counsels and first of all shun leisure ... Some may call my counsels cruel: cruel I confess they are; but, to recover health, you are willing to bear much pain ... Though you are miserably scorched in Aetna's midst, yet make yourself seem colder than ice to your mistress; and feign to be heart-whole, lest, if perchance you show your anguish, she notice it; and laugh, when you would mourn your plight.

Sen. Tranq. 2.7

Hoc oritur ab intemperie animi et cupiditatibus timidis aut parum prosperis, ubi aut non audent quantum concupiscunt, aut non consequuntur ...

This [=dissatisfaction] springs from a lack of mental poise and from timid or unfulfilled desires, when men either do not dare, or do not attain, as much as they desire ...

Sen. Tranq. 2.12

Ut ulcera quaedam nocituras manus adpetunt et tactu gaudent, et foedam corporum scabiem delectat quicquid exasperat, non aliter dixerim his mentibus, in quas cupiditates velut mala ulcera eruperunt, voluptati esse laborem vexationemque.

Just as there are some sores which crave the hands that will hurt them and rejoice to be touched, and as a foul itch of the body delights in whatever scratches, exactly so, I would say, do these minds upon which, so to speak, desires have broken out like wicked sores find pleasure in toil and vexation.

Mart. 9.56.9–10

quisquis ab hoc fuerit fixus, morietur amore.
  o felix, si quem tam bona fata manent!

Whoever is pierced by this boy, will die of love. Happy he, whomsoever so good a death awaits!

Mart. 9.79.3–4

at nunc tantus amor cunctis, Auguste, tuorum est
  ut sit cuique suae cura secunda domus.

But now, Augustus, your following is so loved of all men that each of us puts his own household in second place;

Mart. 11.78.9–12

heu quantos aestus, quantos patiere labores,
  si fuerit cunnus res peregrina tibi!
ergo Suburanae tironem trade magistrae.
  illa virum faciet; non bene virgo docet.

Ah what embarrassments, what ordeals you will suffer if a cunt is something foreign to you! Therefore, hand yourself over as a novice to an instructress in Subura. She will make a man of you. A virgin is a poor teacher.

Juv. 6.28–32

certe sanus eras. uxorem, Postume, ducis?
dic qua Tisiphone, quibus exagitere colubris.
ferre potes dominam salvis tot restibus ullam,
cum pateant altae caligantesque fenestrae,
cum tibi vicinum se praebeat Aemilius pons?

Well, you used to be sane, all right. Postumus, are you really getting married? Tell me what Tisiphone and what snakes are driving you mad. Can you put up with any woman as your boss with so many ropes available, when those dizzily high windows are wide open, when the Aemilian bridge offers itself to you so conveniently?

Juv. 14.138–9

interea, pleno cum turget sacculus ore,
crescit amor nummi quantum ipsa pecunia crevit,

In the meantime, when your little purse is bulging with its mouth full, your love of cash grows as much as the money itself has grown.

Cael. Aur. *TP* 4.9

Molles sive subactos Graeci malthacos vocaverunt, quos quidem esse nullus facile virorum credit. [...] quae sint a passionibus corporis aliena sed potius corruptae mentis vitia. [...] est enim, ut Soranus ait, malignae ac foedissimae mentis passio. [...] Nam neque ulla curatio corporis depellendae passionis causa recte putatur adhibenda, sed potius animus coërcendus, qui tanta peccatorum labe vexatur.

People find it hard to believe that effeminate men or pathics really exist ... Now this condition is different from a bodily disease; it is rather an affliction of a diseased mind ... For, as Soranus says, this affliction comes from a corrupt and debased mind ... There exists no bodily treatment which can be applied to overcome the disease; it is rather the mind that is affected in these disgraceful vices, and it is consequently the mind that must be controlled. [transl. Drabkin].

List of Contributors

Claude Calame is Director of Studies at the École des Hautes Études en Sciences Sociales (Centre AnHiMA: Anthropologie et Histoire des Mondes Antiques) in Paris. He has also taught at the Universities of Urbino and of Lausanne and at Yale University. In English he has published *The Craft of Poetic Speech in Ancient Greece* (1995), *The Poetics of Eros in Ancient Greece* (1999), *Choruses of Young Women in Ancient Greece* (2001), *Masks of Authority: Fiction and Pragmatics in Ancient Greek Poetics* (2005), *Poetic and Performative Memory in Ancient Greece* (2009) and *Greek Mythology: Poetics, Pragmatics and Function* (2009).

Thomas K. Hubbard is the James R. Dougherty, Jr. Centennial Professor of Classics at the University of Texas, Austin, which he joined in 1988. His monographs are *Pipes of Pan: Intertextuality and Literary Filiation in the Pastoral Tradition from Theocritus to Milton* (1998), *The Mask of Comedy: Aristophanes and the Intertextual Parabasis* (1991), and *The Pindaric Mind: A Study of Logical Structure in Early Greek Poetry* (1985). He has edited a *Companion to Greek and Roman Sexualities* (2014), *Homosexuality in Greece and Rome* (2003), *Greek Love Reconsidered* (2000), and co-edited *Censoring Sex Research: The Debate Over Male Intergenerational Relations* (2013).

Dimitrios Kanellakis is a Research Associate in Classics at the University of Oxford, where he recently completed his doctoral studies, funded by the A.S. Onassis, A.G. Leventis, and L. Voudouri Foundations. His research interests include Greek drama, archaic lyric, Modern Greek poetry, and classical reception. He is the author of *Aristophanes and the Poetics of Surprise* (De Gruyter 2020) and co-editor of *Ancient Greek Comedy: Genre – Texts – Reception* (De Gruyter 2020). He has taught Greek literature at the Universities of Oxford and of Cyprus and is currently preparing a commentary on Mimnermus.

Ioannis M. Konstantakos is Professor of Ancient Greek Literature at the National and Kapodistrian University of Athens, where he has been teaching since 2003. His scholarly interests include Greek and Roman comedy, the history of European comic theatre, Herodotus, ancient fiction, folktales and popular lore, and the literatures and cultures of the ancient Near East. His study *Akicharos: The Tale of Ahiqar in Ancient Greece* (2008) has been awarded the prize of the Academy of Athens for the best classical monograph published between 2004–2009. He recently co-edited a volume on *Suspense in Ancient Greek Literature* (De Gruyter 2021).

Andreas N. Michalopoulos is Professor of Latin at the National and Kapodistrian University of Athens. He has published extensively on Latin literature of the 1st centuries BCE and CE, his research interests including Augustan poetry, Ancient Etymology, the Roman drama, the Roman novel, and classical reception. He is the author of *Ancient Etymologies in Ovid's Metamorphoses: A Commented Lexicon* (2001), *Ovid, Heroides 16 and 17: Introduction, Text, and Commentary* (2006), and *Ovid, Heroides 20 and 21: Introduction, Text, and Commentary* (2014). He has co-edited numerous volumes, the most recent being *The Rhetoric of Unity and Division in Ancient Literature* (De Gruyter 2021).

Ed Sanders is an Honorary Research Associate at Royal Holloway, University of London. His research revolves around emotions in Classical Greek literature, and currently primarily focuses on oratorical strategies that involve arousing the emotions of an audience, especially in Attic oratory and the speeches in Thucydides and Xenophon. He is the author of *Envy and Jealousy in Classical Athens: A Socio-Psychological Approach* (2014), has edited a volume on *Eros and the Polis: Love in Context* (2013), and co-edited *Erôs in Ancient Greece* (2013) and *Emotion and Persuasion in Classical Antiquity* (2016).

Thea S. Thorsen is Professor of Classical Studies at The Norwegian University of Science and Technology, Trondheim. She is the author of *Ovid's Early Poetry* (2014), editor of *The Cambridge Companion to Latin Love Elegy* (2013) and *Greek and Roman Games in the Computer Age* (2012), and co-editor of the volumes *Greek and Latin Love: The Poetic Connection* (2021), *Roman Receptions of Sappho* (2019) and *Dynamics of Ancient Prose* (De Gruyter 2018). She is the principal investigator of a research project funded through the Research Council of Norway's Young Research Talents' scheme, *The Heterosexual Tradition of Homoerotic Poetics*.

Chiara Thumiger is a Research Fellow at the Cluster of Excellence Roots at Kiel University. She is the author of *A History of Mind and Mental Health in Classical Greek Medical Thought* (2017) and *Hidden Paths: Notions of the Self, Tragic Characterisation and Euripides' Bacchae* (2007); her monograph on the ancient disease Phrenitis is forthcoming. She has also edited the volume *Holism in Ancient Medicine and Its Reception* (2020), and co-edited *Mental Illness in Ancient Medicine* (2018), *Homo patiens: Approaches to the Patient in the Ancient World* (2015), and *Erôs in Ancient Greece* (2013). Her current project, 'Ancient Guts', focuses on medical and cultural representations of human nutrition and on the 'belly' as a body part and a metaphor.

Anastasia-Stavroula Valtadorou has recently completed her doctoral degree at the University of Edinburgh, with a thesis on *Eros, Euripides, and a Re-Evaluation of Greek Sexuality*, funded by the AHRC, the University of Edinburgh and the A.G. Leventis Foundation. She is currently preparing a monograph on the positive representation of *erôs* in tragedy. She has published articles and chapters on Greek tragedy and its reception – her contribution to the volume *Greek Drama V* (2020) was awarded the Constantinidis Award for best essay on Greek drama – and her latest piece on slavery, bastardy, and legitimation in *Andromache* will appear in *The Classical Journal*.

Bibliography

Acosta-Hughes, B. (2009) 'Ovid and Callimachus: re-writing the master', in *A Companion to Ovid*, ed. P. E. Knox. Chichester: 236–52.
Acosta-Hughes, B. (2010) *Arion's Lyre: Archaic Lyric into Hellenistic Poetry*. Princeton.
Adrados, F. R. (1978) 'Elementos cínicos en las "Vidas" de Esopo y Secundo y en el "Diálogo de Alejandro y los gimnosofistas"', in *Homenaje a Eleuterio Elorduy, S.J.*, eds. F. Rodríguez and J. Iturriaga. Bilbao: 309–28.
Adrados, F. R. (1979) 'The "Life of Aesop" and the origins of novel in antiquity', *QUCC* 1: 93–112.
Adrados, F. R. (1999) *History of the Graeco-Latin Fable*, vol. 1: *Introduction and from the Origins to the Hellenistic Age*. Leiden.
Agamben, G. (1993) *Stanzas: Word and Phantasm in Western Culture*. Minneapolis.
Allan, W. (2014) 'The body in mind: medical imagery in Sophocles', *Hermes* 142: 259–78.
Allan, W. (2021) 'The virtuous emotions of Euripides' *Medea*', *G&R* 68: 27–44.
Amundsen, D. W. (1974) 'Romanticising the ancient medical profession: the characterisation of the physician in the Graeco-Roman world', *BHM* 48: 328–37.
Anagnostou-Laoutides, E. (2015) 'An instance of pathological love in the *Greek Anthology* and Elizabethan poetry', *GRBS* 55: 558–82.
Ancona, R. and Greene, E. (eds.) (2005) *Gendered Dynamics in Latin Love Poetry*. Baltimore.
Anderson, G. (1984) *Ancient Fiction: The Novel in the Graeco-Roman World*. London/Sydney.
Archibald, E. (1991) *Apollonius of Tyre: Medieval and Renaissance Themes and Variations*. Cambridge.
Armstrong, D. and Ratchford, E. A. (1985) 'Iphigenia's veil: Aeschylus, *Agamemnon* 228–48', *BICS* 32: 1–12.
Arruzza, C. (2018) *A Wolf in the City: Tyranny and the Tyrant in Plato's Republic*. Oxford.
Aufrère, S. H. (2000) 'Quelques aspects du dernier Nectanébo et les échos de la magie égyptienne dans *Le Roman d'Alexandre*', in *La magie. Actes du colloque international de Montpellier*, vol. 1, eds. A. M. Moreau and J.-C. Turpin. Montpellier: 95–118.
Aune, D. E. (1988) 'Greco-Roman biography', in *Greco-Roman Literature and the New Testament: Selected Forms and Genres*, ed. D. E. Aune. Atlanta: 107–26.
Austin, J. N. H. (1994) *Helen of Troy and her Shameless Phantom*. London.
Bain, D. (1991) 'Six Greek verbs of sexual congress', *CQ* 41: 51–77.
Barchiesi, A. (1993) 'Future reflexive: two modes of allusion in Ovid's *Heroides*', *HSCPh* 95: 333–65.
Barchiesi, A. (1999) 'Vers une histoire à rebours de l'élégie latine: Les *Héroïdes* "doubles" (16–21)' in *Élégie et épopée: Mélanges offerts à S. Viarre*, eds. A. Deremetz and J. Fabre-Serris. Lille: 53–67.
Barrett, W. (ed.) (1964) *Euripides: Hippolytos*. Oxford.
Barthes, R. (1978) *A Lover's Discourse: Fragments*. New York.
Bartsch, S. (2006) *The Mirror of the Self: Sexuality, Self-Knowledge, and the Gaze in the Early Roman Empire*. Chicago.
Bathrellou, E. (2012) 'Menander's *Epitrepontes* and the festival of the Tauropolia', *ClAnt* 31: 151–92.
Baynham, E. (2001) 'Alexander and the Amazons', *CQ* 51: 115–26.
Beauchamp, Z. (2018) 'Incel, the misogynist ideology that inspired the deadly Toronto attack, explained', *Vox*: 25 April 2018.

Bendz, G. (ed.) (1993) *Caelius Aurelianus: Celerum Passionum Libri III. Tardarum Passionum Libri V. Pars II: Tard. Pass. Lib. III–V*. Berlin.
Béres Rogers, K. (2019) *Creating Romantic Obsession: Scorpions in the Mind*. Cham.
Bernabé Pajares, A. (2016) 'Two orphic images in Euripides: *Hippolytus* 952–957 and *Cretans* 472 Kannicht', *Trends in Classics* 8: 183–204.
Bessone, F. (ed.) (1997) *P. Ovidii Nasonis Heroidum epistula XII: Medea Iasoni*. Florence.
Beta, S. (2016) *Il labirinto della parola: Enigmi, oracoli e sogni nella cultura antica*. Turin.
Betensky, A. (1980) 'Lucretius and love', *CW* 73: 291–9.
Bierl, A. and Lardinois, A. (eds.) (2016) *The Newest Sappho. P. Sapph. Obbink and P. GC inv. 105, frs 1-4*. Leiden/Boston.
Biesterfeldt, H. H. and Gutas, D. (1984) 'The malady of love', *JAOS* 104: 21–55.
Billault, A. (1991) *La création romanesque dans la littérature grecque à l'époque impériale*. Paris.
Billault, A. (2003) 'Characterization in the ancient novel', in Schmeling 2003a: 115–29.
Bing, P. and Höschele, R. (eds.) (2014) *Aristaenetus: Erotic Letters*. Atlanta.
Blondell, R. (2013) *Helen of Troy: Beauty, Myth, Devastation*. Oxford.
Blum, H. (2007) 'A psychoanalytic inquiry into Pandora's box', in *Language, Symbolization and Psychosis*, eds. G. Ambrosio, S. Argentieri and J. Canestri. London: 3–20.
Boehringer, S. (2013) '"Je suis Tithon, je suis Aurore": performance et érotisme dans le "nouveau" fr. 58 de Sappho', *QUCC* 133 : 23–44.
Boehringer, S. (2019) 'After before: trente ans de sexualité antique et autant de voyages transatlantiques', in *Bien avant la sexualité. L'expérience érotique en Grèce ancienne*, eds. D. M. Halperin, J. J. Winkler and F. I. Zeitlin. Paris: 7–29.
Boitani, P., Bologna, C., Cipolla, A. and Liborio, M. (1997) *Alessandro nel medioevo occidentale*. Milan.
Bonanno, M. (1990) *L'allusione necessaria: Ricerche intertestuali sulla poesia greca e latina*. Rome.
Bonanno, M. (2002) 'Per una grammatica del *coup de foudre* (da Saffo a Virgilio, e oltre)', in *Arma Virumque ... Studi di poesia e storiografia in onore di Luca Canali*, ed. E. Lelli. Pisa: 5–18.
Bowie, E. L. (1985) 'The Greek novel', in *The Cambridge History of Classical Literature*, vol. 1: *Greek Literature*, eds. P. E. Easterling and B. M. W. Knox. Cambridge: 683–99.
Braun, M. (1938) *History and Romance in Graeco-Oriental Literature*. Oxford.
Braund, S. H. (1992) 'Juvenal: misogynist or misogamist?', *JRS* 82: 71–86.
Brendel, O. J. (1970) 'The scope and temperament of erotic art in the Greco-Roman world', in *Studies in Erotic Art*, eds. T. Bowie and C. V. Christenson. New York: 3–108.
Briand, M. (2021), 'Mouvement, regard et son dans la *Newest Sappho*. Poésie chantée-dansée, kinesthésie et synesthésie érotiques et musicales', *Greek and Roman Musical Studies* 9: 13–48.
Brown, M. P. (ed. and transl.) (1997) *Lucretius: De Rerum Natura III*. Warminster.
Brown, P. G. McC. (1993) 'Love and marriage in Greek New Comedy', *CQ* 43: 184–205.
Brunelle, C. (2005) 'Ovid's satirical remedies', in Ancona/Greene 2005: 141–58.
Budelmann, F. (ed.) (2018) *Greek Lyric: A Selection*. Cambridge.
Burkert, W. (1983) *Homo necans: The Anthropology of Ancient Greek Sacrificial Ritual and Myth*. Berkeley/London.
Burkowski, J. M. C. (2012) *The Symbolism and Rhetoric of Hair in Latin Elegy*. Diss. Oxford.
Burnett, A. P. (1983) *Three Archaic Poets: Archilochus, Alcaeus, Sappho*. London.

Burris, S. P. (2017) 'A new join for Sappho's "Kypris poem": P. GC. inv. 105 fr. 4 and P. Sapph. Obbink', *ZPE* 201: 12–14.
Butler, S. and Purves, A. (eds.) (2013) *Synaesthesia and the Ancient Senses*. Oxford/New York.
Byl, S. (2006) 'Autour du vocabulaire médical d'Aristophane: le mot sans son contexte', *AC* 75: 195–204.
Cairns, D. L. (2004) 'Ethics, ethology, terminology: Iliadic anger and the cross-cultural study of emotion', *YClS* 32: 11–49.
Cairns, D. L. (2005) 'Bullish looks and sidelong glances: social interaction and the eyes in ancient Greek culture', in *Body Language in the Greek and Roman Worlds*, ed. D. L. Cairns. Swansea: 123–55.
Cairns, D. L. (2008) 'Look both ways: studying emotion in ancient Greek', *Critical Quarterly* 50: 43–63.
Cairns, D. L. (2011) 'Looks of love and loathing: cultural models of vision and emotion in ancient Greek culture', *Mètis* 9: 37–50.
Cairns, D. L. (2013) 'The imagery of *erôs* in Plato's *Phaedrus*', in Sanders *et al.* 2013: 233–50.
Cairns, D. L. (2016) *Sophocles: Antigone*. London/New York.
Cairns, D. L. (2017) 'Mind, metaphor, and emotion in Euripides (*Hippolytus*) and Seneca (*Phaedra*)', *Maia* 69: 247–67.
Cairns, D. L. (2021) 'The dynamics of emotion in Euripides' *Medea*', *G&R* 68: 8–26.
Cairns, F. (2002) 'Acontius and his οὔνομα κουρίδιον: Callimachus *Aetia* 67.1–4', *CQ* 52: 471–7.
Cairns, F. (2016) *Hellenistic Epigrams: Contexts and Explorations*. Cambridge.
Calame, C. (1983) *Alcman: Introduction, texte critique, témoignages, traduction et commentaire*. Rome.
Calame, C. (1997) 'Diction formulaire et fonction pratique dans la poésie mélique archaïque', in *Hommage à Milman Parry: Le style formulaire de l'épopée homérique et la théorie de l'oralité poétique*, ed. F. Létoublon. Amsterdam: 215–22.
Calame, C. (1999) *The Poetics of Eros in Ancient Greece*. Princeton [= (2009) *L'Eros dans la Grèce antique*, 3rd edn. Paris].
Calame, C. (2004) 'Deictic ambiguity and auto-referentiality: some examples from Greek poetics', *Arethusa* 37: 415–43.
Calame, C. (2005) *Masks of Authority: Fiction and Pragmatics in Ancient Greek Poetics*. Ithaca, NY/London.
Calame, C. (2009) 'Émotions et performance poétique: la "katharsis" érotique dans la poésie mélique des cités grecques', in *Violentes émotions: Approches comparatistes*, eds. Ph. Borgeaud and A.-C. Rendu Loisel. Geneva: 29–56.
Calame, C. (2013) 'La poésie de Sappho aux prises avec le genre: polyphonie, pragmatique et rituel (à propos du fr. 58b)', *QUCC* 133: 45–67.
Calame, C. (2014) 'Compétences et performances poétiques en Grèce classique: Hélène et le chant rituel', in *Compétence et performance: Perspectives interdisciplinaires sur une dichotomie classique*, eds. S. Bornand and C. Leguy. Paris: 27–39.
Calame, C. (2016a) 'The amorous gaze: a poetic and pragmatic *koinê* for erotic melos', in Cazzato/Lardinois 2016: 288–306.
Calame, C. (2016b) '"Eros à nouveau maintenant" et la pragmatique mélique: note à G. Nagy, "Once again *this* time in Song 1 of Sappho"', *Classical Enquiries:* 18 Jan. 2016.
Calame, C. (2019a) 'Greek lyric poetry, a non-existent genre?', in *Oxford Readings in Greek Lyric Poetry*, ed. I. Rutherford. Oxford: 33–60 [= (1998) 'La poésie lyrique grecque, un genre inexistant?', *Littérature* 111: 87–110].

Calame, C. (2019b) *Les chœurs de jeunes filles en Grèce ancienne: Morphologie, fonction religieuse et sociale (Les parthénées d'Alcman)*. Paris [= (2001) *Choruses of Young Women in Ancient Greece: Their Morphology, Religious Role, and Social Functions*. Lanham].
Callu, J.-P. (2010) *Julius Valère: Roman d'Alexandre*. Turnhout.
Cameron, A. (1995) *Callimachus and his Critics*. Princeton.
Cantarella, R. (ed.) (1964) *Euripide: I Cretesi, Testi e commento*. Milan.
Carey, C. (1995) 'Rape and adultery in Athenian law', *CQ* 45: 407–17.
Carson, A. (1986) *Eros the Bittersweet*. Princeton.
Cary, G. (1956) *The Medieval Alexander*. Cambridge.
Casali, S. (1997) 'The Cambridge *Heroides*', *CJ* 92: 305–14.
Casali, S. (1998) 'Ovid's Canace and Euripides' *Aeolus*: two notes on *Heroides* 11', *Mnemosyne* 51: 700–10.
Caston, R. R. (2006) 'Love as illness: poets and philosophers on romantic love', *CJ* 3: 271–98.
Cazzato, V. (2013) 'Worlds of *erôs* in Ibycus fragment 286 (*PMGF*)', in Sanders *et al.* 2013: 267–76.
Cazzato, V. and Lardinois, A. (eds.) (2016) *The Look of Lyric: Greek Song and the Visual. Studies in Archaic and Classical Greek Song*. Leiden/Boston.
Chiarini, G. (1983) 'Esogamia e incesto nella "Historia Apollonii regis Tyri"', *MD* 10–11: 267–92.
Cizek, A. (1978) 'Historical distortions and saga patterns in the Pseudo-Callisthenes romance', *Hermes* 106: 593–607.
Clarke, J. (1998) *Looking at Lovemaking: Constructions of Sexuality in Roman Art (100 BC-AD 250)*. Berkeley.
Clausen, W. (ed.) (1994) *Vergil: Eclogues*. Oxford.
Cohen, D. (1985) 'A note on Aristophanes and the punishment of adultery in Athenian law', *ZRG* 102: 285–7.
Cohen, D. (1991) *Law, Sexuality, and Society: The Enforcement of Morals in Classical Athens*. Cambridge.
Cohen, E. E. (2015) *Athenian Prostitution: The Business of Sex*. Oxford.
Cole, S. G. (1984) 'Greek sanctions against sexual assault', *CPh* 79: 97–113.
Coleman, R. (ed.) (1977) *Vergil: Eclogues*. Cambridge.
Collard, C. (2005) 'Euripidean fragmentary plays: the nature of sources and their effect on reconstruction', in *Lost Dramas of Classical Athens*, eds. F. McHardy, J. Robson and D. Harvey. Exeter: 49–62.
Collard, C. (2017) 'Fragments and fragmentary plays', in *A Companion to Euripides*, ed. L. McClure. New Jersey: 347–64.
Collard, C., Cropp, M. J. and Lee, K. (eds.) (1995) *Euripides: Selected Fragmentary Plays*, vol. 1. Warminster.
Collard, C., Cropp, M. J. and Gibert, J. (eds.) (2004) *Euripides: Selected Fragmentary Plays*, vol. 2. Oxford.
Collard, C. and Cropp, M. J. (eds. and transl.) (2008a) *Euripides: Fragments. Aegeus–Meleager*. Cambridge, MA/London.
Collard, C. and Cropp, M. J. (eds. and transl.) (2008b) *Euripides: Fragments. Oedipus–Chrysippus, Other Fragments*. Cambridge, MA/London.
Conte, G. B. (1991) *Generi e lettori: Lucrezio, l'elegia d'amore, l'enciclopedia di Plinio*. Milan.
Cooper, H. (1983) *The Structure of the Canterbury Tales*. London.
Copley, F. O. (1947) 'Servitium amoris in the Roman Elegists', *TAPhA* 78: 285–300.
Copley, F. O. (1956) *Exclusus Amator: A Study in Latin Love Poetry*. New York.

Cozzoli, A.-T. (2001) *Euripide: Cretesi*. Pisa/Rome.
Cracco Ruggini, L. (1974) 'Leggenda e realtà degli Etiopi nella cultura tardoimperiale', in *IV Congresso Internazionale di Studi Etiopici*, vol. 1. Rome: 141–93.
Craik, E. (2001) 'Medical references in Euripides', *BICS* 45: 81–95.
Craik, E. (2003) 'Medical language in the Sophoklean fragments', in *Shards from Kolonos: Studies in Sophoclean Fragments*, ed. A. H. Sommerstein. Bari. 45–56.
Croiset, M. (1915) 'Les *Crétois* d'Euripide', *REG* 28: 217–33.
Cropp, M. and Fick, G. (1985) *Resolutions and Chronology in Euripides: The Fragmentary Tragedies*. London.
Cueva, E. P. and Byrne, S. N. (eds.) (2014) *A Companion to the Ancient Novel*. Chichester.
Culham, P. (1990) 'Decentering the text: the case of Ovid', *Helios* 17: 161–70.
Cummings, C. (2009) *Metaphor and Emotion: Eros in the Greek Novel*. Diss. Edinburgh.
Cusset, C. (2014) 'Melancholic lovers in Menander', in *Menander in Contexts*, ed. A. H. Sommerstein. New York: 167–79.
Cyrino, M. S. (1995) *In Pandora's Jar: Lovesickness in Early Greek Poetry*. Lanham.
D'Alessio, G. B. (2017) 'Aphrodite's torture: Sappho, "Kypris poem" v. 5', *ZPE* 203: 25–6.
D'Angour, A. (2013) 'Love's battlefield: rethinking Sappho fragment 31', in Sanders *et al.* 2013: 59–72.
Danzig, G. (2005) 'Intra-Socratic polemics: the *Symposia* of Plato and Xenophon', *GRBS* 45: 331–57.
Das, A. (2015) *Medical Language in the Speeches of Demosthenes*. Diss. Washington.
Daumas, M. (1992) 'Alexandre et la reine des Amazones', *REA* 94: 347–54.
Davidson, J. (1998) *Courtesans and Fishcakes: The Consuming Passions of Classical Athens*. New York.
Davis, G. (1983) *The Death of Procris: Amor and the Hunt in Ovid's* Metamorphoses. Rome.
Dawson, L. (2008) *Lovesickness and Gender in Early Modern English Literature*. Oxford.
de Jong, I. (2018) 'Homer', in *Characterization in Ancient Greek Literature*, eds. K. De Temmerman and E. van Emde Boas. Leiden: 27–45.
de Pina-Cabral, J. (1989) 'The Mediterranean as a category of regional comparison: a critical view', *Current Anthropology* 30: 399–406.
De Temmerman, K. (2014) *Crafting Characters: Heroes and Heroines in the Ancient Greek Novel*. Oxford.
Deacy, S. and Pierce, K. F. (eds.) (1997) *Rape in Antiquity*. London.
Della Corte, F. (1970–1971) 'La *Medea* di Ovidio', *SCO* 19/20: 85–9.
Devereux, G. (1970) 'The nature of Sappho's seizure in fr. 31 as evidence of her inversion', *CQ* 20: 17–31.
Di Benedetto, V. (1985) 'Intorno al linguaggio erotico di Saffo', *Hermes* 113: 145–56.
Diamond, L. M. (2014) 'Romantic love', in *Handbook of Positive Emotions*, eds. M. M. Tugade, M. N. Shiota and L. D. Kirby. New York: 311–28.
Dixon, T. (2003) *From Passions to Emotions: The Creation of a Secular Psychological Category*. Cambridge.
Doblhofer, G. (1994) *Vergewaltigung in der Antike*. Stuttgart.
Dolfi, E. (1984) 'Su i *Cretesi* di Euripide: passione e responsabilità', *Prometheus* 10: 121–38.
Dols, M. W. (1992) *Majnūn: The Madman in Medieval Islamic Society*. Oxford.
Dörrie, H. (ed.) (1971) *P. Ovidii Nasonis Heroidum Epistulae*. Berlin.
Doufikar-Aerts, F. (2010) *Alexander Magnus Arabicus. A Survey of the Alexander Tradition Through Seven Centuries: From Pseudo-Callisthenes to Șūrī*. Leuven.

Dover, K. J. (1968) *Aristophanes: Clouds*. Oxford.
Drinkwater, M. O. (2013) '*Militia amoris*: fighting in love's army', in Thorsen 2013: 194–206.
Duckworth, G. (1971) *The Nature of Roman Comedy*. Princeton.
Duffin, J. (2005) *Lovers and Livers: Disease Concepts in History*. Toronto.
Dye, R. E. (2004) *Love and Death in Goethe: One and Double*. Rochester, NY.
Ebbott, M. (1999) 'The wrath of Helen: self-blame and nemesis in the *Iliad*', in *Nine Essays on Homer*, eds. M. Carlisle and O. Levaniouk. Lanham, MD: 3–20.
Evzonas, N. (2017) 'Achilles: a Homeric hero enamoured with the absolute', *International Journal of Psychoanalysis* 99: 1165–85.
Fairclough, H. (ed. and transl.) (1999) *Virgil: Eclogues. Georgics. Aeneid, Books 1–6*. Cambridge.
Fantham, E. (1972) *Comparative Studies in Republican Latin Imagery*. Toronto.
Fantham, E. (1975) 'Sex, status, and survival in Hellenistic Athens: a study of women in New Comedy', *Phoenix* 29: 44–74.
Fantuzzi, M. (2012) *Achilles in Love: Intertextual Studies*. Oxford.
Fantuzzi, M. and Hunter, R. (2004) *Tradition and Innovation in Hellenistic Poetry*. Cambridge.
Faraone, C. (1999) *Ancient Greek Love Magic*. Cambridge, MA.
Faulkner, A. (2011) 'Callimachus' *Epigram* 46 and Plato: the literary persona of the doctor', *CQ* 61: 178–85.
Fearn, D. (2017) *Pindar's Eyes: Visual and Material Culture in Epinician Poetry*. Oxford.
Fedeli, G. (forthcoming) 'The sorrows of young Horace, or: the story of a person(a) who learnt to love, through love', *CQ*.
Fehr, B. and Russell, J. A. (1984) 'Concept of emotion viewed from a prototype perspective', *Journal of Experimental Psychology: General* 113: 464–86.
Ferrari, F. (1997) *Romanzo di Esopo*. Milan.
Ferrari, F. (2001) 'Saffo: nevrosi e poesia', *SIFC* 19: 3–31.
Ferrari, F. (2007) 'Ad Afrodite' and 'Patografie 1: panico', in *Una Mitra per Kleis: Saffo e il suo pubblico*. Pisa: 151–8 and 159–78.
Ferrari, F. (2010) *Sappho's Gift: The Poet and Her Community*. Ann Arbor.
Ferrini, F. (1978) 'Tragedia e patologia: lessico ippocratico in Euripide', *QUCC* 29: 49–62.
Fisher, N. R. E. (2001) *Aeschines: Against Timarchos*. Oxford.
Fisher, N. R. E. (2013) 'Erotic *charis*: what sorts of reciprocity?' in *Erôs and the Polis: Love in Context (BICS Supplement 119)*, ed. E. Sanders. London: 39–66.
Flacelière, R. (1965) *Daily Life in Greece at the Time of Pericles*. London.
Foerster, R. (ed.) (1893) *Pseudo-Polemon: Physiognomonica. Scriptores physiognomonici Graeci et Latini*, vol. 1. Leipzig.
Foley, H. P. (1982) 'Marriage and sacrifice in Euripides' *Iphigeneia in Aulis*', *Arethusa* 15: 159–80.
Foley, H. P. (2013) 'Performing gender in Greek Old and New Comedy', in *The Cambridge Companion to Greek Comedy*, ed. M. Revermann. Cambridge: 259–74.
Foley, H. P. (2020) 'Heterosexual bonding in the fragments of Euripides', in *Female Characters in Fragmentary Greek Tragedy*, eds. P. J. Finglass and L. Coo. Cambridge: 73–86.
Foley, R. (2010) 'The order question: climbing the ladder of love in Plato's *Symposium*', *AncPhil* 30: 57–72.
Fontenrose, J. (1981) *Orion: The Myth of the Hunter and the Huntress*. Berkeley, LA.
Fountoulakis, A. (2013) 'Male bodies, male gazes: exploring *erôs* in the twelfth book of the *Greek Anthology*', in Sanders et al. 2013: 293–312.

Fraser, P. M. (1972) *Ptolemaic Alexandria*, 2 vols. Oxford.
Fraser, P. M. (1996) *Cities of Alexander the Great*. Oxford.
Frijda, N. H. (2007) 'Sex', in *The Laws of Emotion*. Mahwah: 227–57.
Frings, I. (2005) *Das Spiel mit eigenen Texten. Wiederholung und Selbstzitat bei Ovid*. Munich.
Frontisi-Ducroux, F. (1996) 'Eros, desire, and the gaze', in *Sexuality in Ancient Art: Near East, Egypt, Greece, and Italy*, ed. N. B. Kampen, Cambridge: 81–100.
Frost, F. J. (2002) 'Solon pornoboskos and Aphrodite pandemos' *SyllClass* 13: 34–46.
Fulkerson, L. (2005) *The Ovidian Heroine as Author: Reading, Writing and Community in the Heroides*. Cambridge.
Fulkerson, L. (2013) '*Seruitium amoris*: the interplay of dominance, gender and poetry', in Thorsen 2013: 180–93.
Funke, M. K. A. (2013) *Euripides and Gender: The Difference the Fragments Make*. Diss. Washington.
Fusillo, M. (1994) 'Letteratura di consumo e romanzesca', in *Lo spazio letterario della Grecia antica*, eds. G. Cambiano, L. Canfora and D. Lanza, vol. 1.3. Rome: 233–73.
Futre Pinheiro, M. P. (2014) 'The genre of the novel. A theoretical approach', in Cueva/Byrne 2014: 201–16.
Futre Pinheiro, M. P., Skinner, M. B. and Zeitlin, F. I. (eds.) (2012) *Narrating Desire: Eros, Sex, and Gender in the Ancient Novel*. Berlin/Boston.
Gaca, K. L. (2011) 'Girls, women, and the significance of sexual violence in ancient warfare', in *Sexual Violence in Conflict Zones: From the Ancient World to the Era of Human Rights*, ed. E. D. Heineman. Philadelphia: 73–88.
Gaca, K. L. (2014) 'Martial rape, pulsating fear, and the sexual maltreatment of girls (παῖδες), virgins (παρθένοι), and women (γυναῖκες) in antiquity', *AJPh* 135: 303–57.
Gaca, K. L. (2015) 'Ancient warfare and the ravaging martial rape of girls and women: evidence from Homeric epic and Greek drama', in *Sex in Antiquity: Exploring Gender and Sexuality in the Ancient World*, eds. M. Masterson, N. S. Rabinowitz and J. Robson. New York: 278–97.
Gallo, I. (1980) *Frammenti biografici da papiri*, vol. 2: *La biografia dei filosofi*. Rome.
Gallo, I. (1996) 'Biografie di consumo in Grecia: il *Romanzo di Alessandro* e la *Vita del filosofo Secondo*', in *La letteratura di consumo nel mondo greco-latino*, eds. O. Pecere and A. Stramaglia. Cassino: 235–49.
Galoin, A. (2015) *L'iconographie des Amazones dans l'art grec de la fin de l'époque archaique et de la première époque classique*. Marseille.
Gantz, T. (1993) *Early Greek Myth: A Guide to Literary and Artistic Sources*. Baltimore/London.
Garbugino, G. (2014) 'Historia Apollonii Regis Tyri', in Cueva/Byrne 2014: 133–45.
Garin, F. (1914) 'De Historia Apollonii Tyrii', *Mnemosyne* 42: 198–212.
Gaullier-Bougassas, C. (1991) 'Alexandre et Candace dans le *Roman d'Alexandre* d'Alexandre de Paris et le *Roman de toute chevalerie* de Thomas de Kent', *Romania* 112: 18–44.
Giangrande, G. (1990) 'Symptoms of love in Theocritus and Ovid', *Amal* 13: 121–3.
Gibert, J. (1997) 'Euripides' *Hippolytus* plays: which came first?', *CQ* 47.1: 85–97.
Gilbert, P. K. (1997) *Disease, Desire, and the Body in Victorian Women's Popular Novels*. Cambridge.
Gildenhard, I. (2012) *Virgil*, Aeneid *4.1-299: Latin Text, Study Questions, Commentary and Interpretative Essays*. Cambridge.
Gill, C. (2013) 'Philosophical therapy as preventive psychological medicine', in *Mental Disorders in the Classical World*, ed. W. V. Harris. Leiden: 339–60.

Gill, C. (2018) 'Philosophical psychological therapy – did it have any impact on medical practice?', in *Mental Illness in Ancient Medicine: From Celsus to Paul of Aegina*, eds. C. Thumiger and P. N. Singer. Leiden: 365–80.
Giorgianni, F. (ed.) (2006) *Hippocrates: Über die Natur des Kindes (De genitura und De natura pueri)*. Wiesbaden.
Goldhill, S. (1995) *Foucault's Virginity: Ancient Erotic Fiction and the History of Sexuality*. Cambridge.
Goldhill, S. (1998) 'The seductions of the gaze: Socrates and his girlfriends', in *KOSMOS: Essays in Order, Conflict and Community in Classical Athens*, eds. P. Cartledge, P. Millett and S. von Reden. Cambridge: 105–24.
Gow, A. S. F. and Schofield, A. F. (eds.) (1997) *Nicander: The Poems and Fragments*. Bristol.
Graverini, L. (2006) 'Una visione d'insieme', in: L. Graverini, W. Keulen and A. Barchiesi, *Il romanzo antico: Forme, testi, problemi*. Rome: 15–60.
Greene, E. and Skinner, M. B. (eds.) (2009) *The New Sappho on Old Age: Textual and Philosophical Issues*. Cambridge, MA/London.
Griffiths, F. T. (1979) 'Poetry as pharmakon in Theocritus' *Idyll* 2', in *Arktouros: Hellenic Studies Presented to Bernard M. W. Knox on the Occasion of His 65th Birthday*, eds. G. W. Bowersock, W. Burkert and M. Putnam. Berlin: 81–8.
Griffiths, P. E. (1997) *What Emotions Really Are*. Chicago/London.
Grimaldi, W. M. A. (1988) *Aristotle,* Rhetoric *II: A Commentary*. New York.
Gross, D. M. (2007) *The Secret History of Emotion: From Aristotle's* Rhetoric *to Modern Brain Science*. Chicago.
Guardasole, A. (2000) *Tragedia e medicina nell'Atene del V secolo a.C.* Naples.
Guépin, J. P. (1968) *The Tragic Paradox: Myth and Ritual in Greek Tragedy*. Amsterdam.
Hägg, T. (1983) *The Novel in Antiquity*. Berkeley.
Hägg, T. (2009) 'The ideal Greek novel from a biographical perspective', in Karla 2009a: 81–93.
Hägg, T. (2012) *The Art of Biography in Antiquity*. Cambridge.
Hägg, T. and Utas, B. (2009) 'Eros goes east: Parthenope the virgin meets Vāmiq the ardent lover', in *Plotting with Eros: Essays on the Poetics of Love and the Erotics of Reading*, ed. I. Nilsson. Copenhagen: 153–86.
Haley, L. (1924–1925) 'The feminine complex in the *Heroides*', *CJ* 20: 15–25.
Hallett, J. (1990) 'Contextualising the text: the journey to Ovid', *Helios* 17: 187–95.
Hallett, J. (2012) 'Anxiety and influence: Ovid's *Amores* 3.7 and Encolpius' impotence in *Satyricon* 126 ff.', in Futre Pinheiro et al. 2012: 211–22.
Halperin, D. M. (1990) *One Hundred Years of Homosexuality and Other Essays on Greek Love*. London.
Hansen, W. (1998) *Anthology of Ancient Greek Popular Literature*. Bloomington.
Hardie, P. (2003) *Ovid's Poetics of Illusion*. Cambridge.
Hardie, P. (ed.) (2015) *Ovidio, Metamorfosi, vol. VI, libri XIII–XV*. Milan.
Harris, E. M. (2006) *Democracy and the Rule of Law in Classical Athens*. Cambridge.
Harrison, S. J. (2017) 'The chronology of Ovid's career', in *Dicite Pierides: Classical Studies in Honour of Stratis Kyriakidis*, eds. A. N. Michalopoulos, S. Papaioannou and A. Zissos. Newcastle upon Tyne: 188–201.
Harrison, T. (2003) 'The cause of things: envy and the emotions in Herodotus' *Histories*', in *Envy, Spite, and Jealousy: The Rivalrous Emotions in Ancient Greece*, eds. D. Konstan and N. K. Rutter. Edinburgh: 143–63.

Harvey, E. D. (1989) 'Ventriloquizing Sappho: Ovid, Donne, and the erotics of the feminine voice', *Criticism* 31: 115–38.
Hawkins, J. N. (2015) '*Parrhêsia* and *pudenda*: speaking genitals and satiric speech', in *Athenian Comedy in the Roman Empire*, eds. C. W. Marshall and T. Hawkins. London/New York: 43–68.
Heath, J. (1991) 'Diana's understanding of Ovid's *Metamorphoses*', *CJ* 86: 233–43.
Heeg, J. (ed.) (1915) *Galen: In Hippocratis Prognosticum commentaria III (CMG V 9.2)*. Leipzig/Berlin.
Heiberg, J. (ed.) (1921) *Paul of Aegina: Libri I-VI. Pars Prior. Libri I-IV (CMG XI 9.1)*. Leipzig/Berlin.
Heinze, Th. (ed.) (1997) *P. Ovidius Naso, Der XII. Heroidenbrief: Medea an Jason*. Leiden.
Hejduk, J. (2011) 'Phthisical intimacy: Martial 2.16', in *CJ* 106: 223–7.
Henderson, J. (ed.) and North Fowler, H. (transl.) (2005) *Plato I. Euthyphro, Apology, Crito, Phaedo, Phaedrus*. Cambridge.
Henry, M. M. (1995) *Prisoner of History: Aspasia of Miletus and her Biographical Tradition*. Oxford/New York.
Herter, H. (1983) 'Daphne und Io in Ovids *Metamorphosen*', in *Hommages à Robert Schilling*, eds. H. Zehnhacker and G. Hentz. Paris: 315–35.
Herzog-Hauser, G. (1937) 'Die literarische Ausgestaltung der Protesilaus-Mythe', *Annuaire de l'institut de philologie d'histoire orientales et slaves*, vol. 5: *Mélanges Emile Boisacq*. Brussels: 471–78.
Hett, W. (ed. and transl.) (1957) *Aristotle VIII: On the Soul, Parva naturalia, On Breath*. Cambridge.
Heyworth, S. J. (2016) 'Authenticity and other textual problems in *Heroides* 16', in *Latin Literature and its Transmission*, eds. R. Hunter and S. P. Oakley. Cambridge: 142–70.
Hindley, C. (1994) 'Eros and military command in Xenophon', *CQ* 44: 347–66.
Hindley, C. (1999) 'Xenophon on male love', *CQ* 49: 74–99.
Hindley, C. (2004) '*Sophron erôs*: Xenophon's ethical erotics', in Tuplin 2004: 125–46.
Hinds, S. (1993) 'Medea in Ovid: scenes from the life of an intertextual heroine', *MD* 30: 9–47.
Hobe, S. (2018) *Hippocratic Medicine in Aristophanic Comedy*. Diss. Freiburg.
Hofmann, H. (1985) 'Ovid's *Metamorphoses*: carmen perpetuum, carmen deductum', *PLLS* 5: 223–42.
Hollis, A. (1994) 'Rights of way in Ovid (*Her.* 20.146) and Plautus (*Curculio* 36)', *CQ* 44: 545–9.
Holmes, B. (2008) 'Euripides' Heracles in the Flesh', *ClAnt* 27: 231–81.
Holt, P. (1981) 'Disease, desire, and Deianeira: a note on the symbolism of the *Trachiniae*', *Helios* 8: 63–73.
Holwerda, D. (1977) *Scholia Vetera in Nubes (Scholia in Aristophanem, pars I fasc. III 1)*. Groningen.
Holzberg, N. (1992) 'Der Äsop-Roman. Eine strukturanalytische Interpretation', in *Der Äsop-Roman. Motivgeschichte und Erzählstruktur*, eds. N. Holzberg, A. Beschorner and S. Merkle. Tübingen: 33–75.
Holzberg, N. (1995) *The Ancient Novel: An Introduction*. London/New York.
Holzberg, N. (1999) 'Apollos erste Liebe und die Folgen. Ovids Daphne-Erzählung als Programm für Werk und Wirkung', *Gymnasium* 106: 317–34.
Holzberg, N. (2002) *The Ancient Fable: An Introduction*. Bloomington.
Holzberg, N. (2003) 'The genre: novels proper and the fringe', in Schmeling 2003a: 11–28.

Hubbard, T. K. (1998) 'Popular perceptions of elite homosexuality in democratic Athens', *Arion* 6: 48–78.
Hubbard, T. K. (2006) 'History's first child molester: Euripides' *Chrysippus* and the marginalization of pederasty in Athenian democratic discourse', in *Greek Drama III: Studies in Memory of Kevin Lee (BICS Supplement 87)*, eds. J. Davison, F. Muecke and P. Wilson. London: 223–44.
Hubbard, T. K. (2011) 'Athenian pederasty and the construction of masculinity', in *What is Masculinity? Historical Dynamics from Antiquity to the Contemporary World*, eds. J. H. Arnold and S. Brady. Basingstoke: 189–225.
Hubbard, T. K. (2015) 'Diachronic parameters of Athenian pederasty', in *Diachrony: Diachronic Aspects of Ancient Greek Literature and Culture*, ed. J. González. Berlin/Boston: 363–89.
Hunt, J. (ed. and transl.) (1971) *The Aegritudo Perdicae, Edited with Translation and Commentary*. Ann Arbor.
Hunter, R. (1999) *Theocritus: A Selection: Idylls 1, 3, 4, 6, 7, 10, 11 and 13*. Cambridge.
Hunter, R. (2009) 'Fictional anxieties', in Karla 2009a: 171–84.
Hunter, R. (2013) 'Greek elegy', in Thorsen 2013: 23–38.
Hunter, V. (1989) 'The Athenian widow and her kin', *Journal of Family History* 14: 291–311.
Huss, B. (1999a) 'The dancing Sokrates and the laughing Xenophon or The other *Symposium*', *AJPh* 120: 381–409.
Huss, B. (1999b) *Xenophons Symposion: Ein Kommentar*. Stuttgart/Leipzig.
Hutchinson, G. O. (2001) *Greek Lyric Poetry: A Commentary on Selected Larger Pieces*. Oxford.
Huxley, G. (1965) 'Xenomedes of Keos', *GRBS* 6: 235–45.
Ierodiakonou, K. (2014) 'On Galen's theory of vision', in *Philosophical Themes in Galen*, eds. P. Adamson, R. Hansberger and J. Wilberding. London: 235–47.
Ingalls, W. (2001) '*Paida nean malista*: when did Athenian girls really marry?', *Mouseion* 1: 17–29.
Ingleheart, J. (2012) 'Ovid's *scripta puella*: Perilla as poetic and political fiction in *Tristia* 3.7', *CQ* 62: 227–41.
Jacobson, H. (1974) *Ovid's Heroides*. Princeton.
Jäkel, S. (1979) 'The *Aiolos* of Euripides', *Grazer Beiträge* 8: 101–18.
Jasnow, R. (1997) 'The Greek Alexander Romance and Demotic Egyptian literature', *JNES* 56: 95–103.
Jedrkiewicz, S. (1989) *Sapere e paradosso nell'antichità: Esopo e la favola*. Rome.
Jenkins, I. (1983) 'Is there life after marriage? A study of the abduction motif in vase-paintings of the Athenian wedding ceremony', *BICS* 30: 137–45.
Johne, R. (2003) 'Women in the ancient novel', in Schmeling 2003a: 151–207.
Johns, C. (1982) *Sex or Symbol: Erotic Images of Greece and Rome*. Austin.
Jouan, F. (1966) *Euripide et les légendes des chants cypriens des origines de la guerre de Troie à l'Iliade*. Paris.
Jouan, F. and van Looy, H. (eds.) (1998) *Euripide: Fragments*, vol. 1: *Aigeus-Autolykos*. Paris.
Jouan, F. and van Looy, H. (eds.) (2000) *Euripide: Fragments*, vol. 2: *Bellérophon-Protésilas*. Paris.
Jouanna J. (2000) 'Maladies et médecine chez Aristophane', in *Le théâtre grec antique: la comédie*, eds. J. Jouanna and J. Leclant. Paris: 171–95.
Jouanna J. (2012) 'Hippocratic medicine and Greek tragedy', in *Greek Medicine from Hippocrates to Galen: Selected Papers*, ed. P. van der Eijk. Leiden/Boston: 55–80.
Jouanno, C. (2002) *Naissance et métamorphoses du Roman d'Alexandre. Domaine grec*. Paris.

Jouanno, C. (2005) 'La *Vie d'Ésope*: une biographie comique', *REG* 118: 391–425.
Jouanno, C. (2009) 'Novelistic lives and historical biographies: the *Life of Aesop* and the *Alexander Romance* as fringe novels', in Karla 2009a: 33–48.
Kahn, C. H. (1987) 'Plato's theory of desire', *The Review of Metaphysics* 41: 77–103.
Kaimio, M. (2002) 'Erotic experience in the conjugal bed: good wives in Greek tragedy', in Nussbaum/Sihvola 2002: 95–119.
Kampen, N. (ed.) (1996) *Sexuality in Ancient Art*. Cambridge.
Kanellakis, D. (2020) 'Sacrifice, politics and animal imagery in the *Oresteia*', *C&M* 68: 37–69.
Kanellakis, D. (forthcoming) 'Seminal figures: Aristophanes and the tradition of sexual imagery', in *Sex and the Ancient City*, eds. A. Serafim, G. Kazantzidis and K. Demetriou. Berlin/Boston.
Kannicht, R. (1995) 'Fragmenta Euripidea. Aus der Arbeit an der Edition der Tragikerfragmente', *Jahrbuch der Heidelberger Akademie der Wissenschaften für 1994*: 25–9.
Kannicht, R. (ed.) (2004) *Tragicorum Graecorum Fragmenta*, vol. V.1–2. Göttingen.
Kapparis, K. (2017) *Prostitution in the Ancient Greek World*. Berlin/Boston.
Kappelmacher, A. (1909) 'Zu den Kretern des Euripides', in *Zur fünfzigsten Versammlung deutscher Philologen und Schulmänner in Graz 1909*. Graz: 26–37.
Karla, G. A. (2001) *Vita Aesopi: Überlieferung, Sprache und Edition einer frühbyzantinischen Fassung des Äsopromans*. Wiesbaden.
Karla, G. A. (ed.) (2009a) *Fiction on the Fringe: Novelistic Writing in the Post-Classical Age*. Leiden.
Karla, G. A. (2009b) 'Fictional biography vis-à-vis romance: affinity and differentiation', in Karla 2009a: 13–32.
Karla, G. A. (2012) 'Folk narrative techniques in the *Alexander Romance*', *Mnemosyne* 65: 636–55.
Kaster, R. A. (2005) *Emotion, Restraint, and Community in Ancient Rome*. Oxford.
Kazantzidis, G. (2014) 'Callimachus and Hippocratic gynaecology: absent desire and the female body in «Acontius and Cydippe» (*Aetia* fr. 75.10–19 Harder)', *Eugesta* 4: 106–34.
Kazantzidis, G. (2018) 'Between insanity and wisdom: perceptions of melancholia in the pseudo-Hippocratic *Letters* 10-17', in *Mental Illness in Ancient Medicine: From Celsus to Paul of Aegina*, eds. C. Thumiger and P. N. Singer. Leiden/Boston: 35–78.
Kazimirski, A. B. (1875) *Dictionnaire Arabe-Français*. Cairo.
Keilen, S. (2013) 'The sense of a poem: *Ovids Banquet of Sence* (1595)', in Butler/Purves 2013: 155–65.
Keith, A. M. (1995) 'Corpus eroticum: elegiac poetics and elegiac puellae in Ovid's *Amores*', *CW* 88: 27–40.
Kenney, E. J. (1969) 'Ovid and the law', *YClS* 21: 242–63.
Kenney, E. J. (1970a) 'Notes on Ovid III. Corrections and interpretations in the *Heroides*', *HSCPh* 74: 169–85.
Kenney, E. J. (1970b) 'Love and legalism: Ovid, *Heroides* 20 and 21', *Arion* 9: 388–414.
Kenney, E. J. (1979) 'Two disputed passages in the *Heroides*', *CQ* 29: 394–431.
Kenney, E. J. (ed.) (1996) *Ovid*, Heroides *XVI–XXI*. Cambridge.
Keulen, W. (2006) 'Narrativa "di confine"', in L. Graverini, W. Keulen and A. Barchiesi, *Il romanzo antico: Forme, testi, problemi*. Rome: 179–92.
Keuls, E. C. (1985) *The Reign of the Phallus: Sexual Politics in Ancient Athens*. New York.
Kilmer, M. (1993) *Greek Erotica on Attic Red-Figure Vases*. London.

Kline, A. S. (transl.) (2000) *Ovid: The Metamorphoses: A translation into English prose*, 2nd edition. Retrieved from https://www.poetryintranslation.com/klineasovid.php
Kline, A. S. (transl.) (2001) *Ovid: The Love Poems. The Amores, Ars Amatoria and Remedia Amoris*. Retrieved from https://www.poetryintranslation.com/klineaslovepoems.php
Knox, P. E. (1986) *Ovid's* Metamorphoses *and the Traditions of Augustan Poetry*. Cambridge.
Knox, P. E. (2002) 'The *Heroides*: elegiac voices', in *Brill's Companion to Ovid*, ed. B. W. Boyd. Leiden/Boston: 117–39.
Knuuttila, S. (2004) 'Emotions in ancient philosophy', in *Emotions in Ancient and Medieval Philosophy*. Oxford: 5–110.
Konstan, D. (1994) *Sexual Symmetry: Love in the Ancient Novel and Related Genres*. Princeton.
Konstan, D. (1998) 'The *Alexander Romance*: the cunning of the open text', *Lexis* 16: 123–38.
Konstan, D. (2006a) *The Emotions of the Ancient Greeks: Studies in Aristotle and Classical Literature*. Toronto.
Konstan, D. (2006b) 'The concept of "emotion" from Plato to Cicero', *Méthexis* 19: 139–51.
Konstan, D. (2018) *In the Orbit of Love: Affection in Ancient Greece and Rome*. Oxford.
Konstantakos, I. M. (2006) 'Aesop adulterer and trickster. A study of *Vita Aesopi* ch. 75–76', *Athenaeum* 94: 563–600.
Konstantakos, I. M. (2009) 'Nektanebo in the *Vita Aesopi* and in other narratives', *C&M* 60: 99–144.
Konstantakos, I. M. (2010) 'Aesop and riddles', *Lexis* 28: 257–90.
Kortekaas, G. A. A. (2004) *The Story of Apollonius King of Tyre: A Study of Its Greek Origin and an Edition of the Two Oldest Latin Recensions*. Leiden.
Kortekaas, G. A. A. (2007) *Commentary on the* Historia Apollonii Regis Tyri. Leiden.
Kosak, J. (2004) *Heroic Measures: Hippocratic Medicine in the Making of Euripidean Tragedy*. Leiden.
Krappe, A. H. (1927) *Balor with the Evil Eye: Studies in Celtic and French Literature*. New York.
Kraut, R. (2008) 'Plato on love', in *The Oxford Handbook on Plato*, ed. G. Fine. Oxford: 286–310.
Kuhlmann, P. (2002) 'Die Historia Apollonii regis Tyri und ihre Vorlagen', *Hermes* 130: 109–20.
Kuhlmann, P. (2005) 'Akontios und Kydippe bei Kallimachos (67–75 Pf. 2) und Ovid (*epist.* 20–21): eine romantische Liebesgeschichte?', *Gymnasium* 112: 19–44.
Kühn, K. (ed.) (1827) *Galen: De Praenotione ad Posthumum liber (XIV)*. Leipzig.
Kurke, L. (2011) *Aesopic Conversations: Popular Tradition, Cultural Dialogue, and the Invention of Greek Prose*. Princeton.
La Penna, A. (1962) 'Il romanzo di Esopo', *Athenaeum* 40: 264–314.
Labate, M. (1977) 'La Canace ovidiana e l'*Eolo* di Euripide', *ASNP* (ser. III) 7: 583–93.
Labbe, J. M. (2000) *The Romantic Paradox: Love, Violence and the Uses of Romance, 1760-1830*. Basingstoke.
Lacey, W. K. (1968) *The Family in Classical Greece*. Ithaca, NY.
Laird, A. (2005) 'Metaphor and the riddle of representation in the *Historia Apollonii regis Tyri*', in *Metaphor and the Ancient Novel*, eds. S. Harrison, M. Paschalis and S. Frangoulidis. Groningen: 225–44.
Laks, A. and Most, G. W. (ed. and transl.) (2016) *Early Greek Philosophy*, vol. 3, pt. 1. Cambridge, MA.
Lami, A. (2007) 'Lo scritto ippocratico sui disturbi virginali', *Galenos* 1: 15–59.
Lanata, G. (1966) 'Sul linguaggio amoroso di Saffo', *QUCC* 2: 63–79.
Lang, P. (2009) 'Goats and the sacred disease in Callimachus' *Acontius and Cydippe*', *CPh* 104: 1–85.

Langslow, D. R. (1999) 'The language of poetry and the language of science: the Latin poets and "medical Latin"', in *Aspects of the Language of Latin Poetry*, eds. J. N. Adams and R. G. Mayer. Oxford: 183–225.
Lape, S. (2001) 'Democratic ideology and the poetics of rape in Menandrian comedy', *ClAnt* 20: 79–119.
Lardinois, A. (1996) 'Who sang Sappho's songs?', in *Reading Sappho: Contemporary Approaches*, ed. E. Greene. Berkeley, LA/London: 150–72.
Laskaris, J. (2016) 'The eyes have it', paper given at the conference *Bodily Fluids/Fluid Bodies in Greek and Roman Antiquity*, July 2016, Cardiff University.
Lear, A. and Cantarella, E. (2008) *Images of Ancient Greek Pederasty*, Los Angeles.
Lefteratou, A. (2018) *Mythological Narratives: The Bold and Faithful Heroines of the Greek Novel*. Berlin.
Leitao, D. (2002) 'The legend of the Sacred Band', in Nussbaum/Sihvola 2002: 143–69.
Lindheim, S. H. (2003) *Mail and Female: Epistolary Narrative and Desire in Ovid's* Heroides. Madison.
Liviabella Furiani, P. (2001) 'L'amore e gli affetti familiari nel *Romanzo di Alessandro*', *Lexis* 19: 245–66.
Livrea, E. (2016) 'Novità su Saffo nella poesia alessandrina: la chiusa del fr. 31 V. e due letture ellenistiche dell'ode', *Eikasmos* 27: 57–71.
Lloyd, G. E. R. (2003) *In the Grip of Disease: Studies in the Greek Imagination*. Oxford.
Lloyd, G. E. R. (2007) *Cognitive Variations: Reflections on the Unity and Diversity of the Human Mind*. Oxford.
Lloyd, M. (1992) *The Agon in Euripides*. Oxford.
Lloyd-Jones, H. (1963) Review of '*The Oxyrhynchus Papyri. Part 27* by E. G. Turner, John Rea, L. Koenen, José Maria Fernandez Pomar', *Gnomon* 35: 433–55.
Loraux, N. (1987) *Tragic Ways of Killing a Woman*. Cambridge/London.
Louden, B. (2006) *The Iliad: Structure, Myth, and Meaning*. Baltimore.
Ludwig, P. (2007) 'Eros in the *Republic*', in *The Cambridge Companion to Plato's* Republic, ed. G. R. F. Ferrari. Cambridge: 202–31.
Luppe, W. (1982) 'Die Hypotheseis zu Euripides' *Alkestis* und *Aiolos* P.Oxy.2457', *Philologus* 126: 10–18.
Lye, S. (2018) 'Gender in Hesiod: a poetics of the powerless', in *The Oxford Handbook of Hesiod*, eds. A. C. Loney and S. E. Scully. Oxford: 175–89.
Lyne, R. O. (1979) 'Seruitium amoris', *CQ* 29: 117–30.
Lyne, R. O. (1998) 'Love and death: Laodamia and Protesilaus in Catullus, Propertius, and others', *CQ* 48: 200–12.
MacAlister, S. (1996) *Dreams and Suicides: The Greek Novel from Antiquity to the Byzantine Empire*. London/New York.
Magnani, M. (2018) 'L'*Eolo* di Euripide e le genealogie degli Eoli', *Paideia* 73: 511–27.
Mair, A. W. and Mair, G. R. (eds.) (1921) *Callimachus: Hymns and Epigrams; Lycophron*. Cambridge, MA.
Makowski, J. F. (2014) 'Greek love in the Greek novel', in Cueva/Byrne 2014: 490–501.
Masters, S. (2012) *The Abduction and Recovery of Helen: Iconography and Emotional Vocabulary in Attic Vase-Painting c. 550–350 BCE*. Diss. Exeter.
Mastronarde, D. J. (ed.) (2002) *Euripides: Medea*. Cambridge.
Mattern, S. (2008) *Galen and the Rhetoric of Healing*. Baltimore.

Mattern, S. (2015) 'Galen's anxious patients: *lypē* as anxiety disorder', in *Homo Patiens: Approaches to the Patient in the Ancient World*, eds. G. Petridou and C. Thumiger. Leiden: 203–23.

Matthey, P. (2011) 'Récits grecs et égyptiens à propos de Nectanébo II: une réflexion sur l'historiographie égyptienne', in *L'oiseau et le poisson: Cohabitations religieuses dans les mondes grec et romain*, eds. N. Belayche and J.-D. Dubois. Paris: 303–28.

Matthey, P. (2016) 'Le retour du roi. Littérature "apocalyptique" égyptienne et construction du *Roman d'Alexandre*', in *Alexandrie la Divine: Sagesses barbares. Échanges et réappropriation dans l'espace culturel gréco-romain*, eds. S. H. Aufrère and F. Möri. Geneva: 145–90.

Matthey, P. (2017) 'The once and future king of Egypt: Egyptian "Messianism" and the construction of the *Alexander Romance*', in *Beyond Conflicts: Cultural and Religious Cohabitations in Alexandria and Egypt Between the 1st and the 6th Century CE*, ed. L. Arcari. Tübingen: 47–72.

Mayer, M. (1885) 'Der *Protesilaos* des Euripides', *Hermes* 20: 101–35.

Mayor, A. (2014) *The Amazons: Lives and Legends of Warrior Women Across the Ancient World*. Princeton.

Mazzini, I. (1990) 'Il folle da amore', in *Il poeta elegiaco e il viaggio d'amore: dall' Innamoramento alla Crisi*, eds. S. Alfonso, G. Cipriani, P. Fedeli, I. Mazzini and D. Tedeschi. Bari: 39–84.

Mazzini, I. (2012) 'Malattia melancolica da amore tra poesia e medicina nel tardo antico: *Aegritudo Perdiccae (Ae.P.)*', *Medicina nei Secoli Arte e Scienza* 24.3: 559–84.

McKeown, J. C. (ed.) (1987) *Ovid, Amores I: Text and Prolegomena*. Liverpool.

McNamara, L. (2016) 'Hippocratic and non-Hippocratic approaches to lovesickness', in *Ancient Concepts of the Hippocratic*, eds. L. Dean-Jones and R. M. Rosen. Leiden/Boston: 308–27.

Mederer, E. (1936) *Die Alexanderlegenden bei den ältesten Alexanderhistorikern*. Stuttgart.

Merkelbach, R. (1977) *Die Quellen des griechischen Alexanderromans*, revised edn. in collaboration with J. Trumpf. Munich.

Merkle, S. (1996) 'Fable, "anecdote" and "novella" in the *Vita Aesopi*. The ingredients of a "popular novel"', in *La letteratura di consumo nel mondo greco-latino*, eds. O. Pecere and A. Stramaglia. Cassino: 209–34.

Mette, H. J. (1963) 'Euripides, *Kreter*', *Hermes* 91: 256.

Miller, H. W. (1944) 'Medical terminology in tragedy', *TAPhA* 75: 156–67.

Mimidou, E. N. (comm. and transl.) (2013) *Ευριπίδη Αἴολος*. Athens.

Mitchell-Boyask, R. (2008) *Plague and the Athenian Imagination: Drama, History, and the Cult of Asclepius*. Cambridge/New York.

Mitchell-Boyask, R. (2012) 'Heroic pharmacology: Sophocles and the metaphors of Greek medical thought', in *The Blackwell Companion to Sophocles*, ed. K. Ormand. Chichester: 316–30.

Morales, H. (2008) 'The history of sexuality', in Whitmarsh 2008: 39–55.

Morales, H. (2009) 'Challenging some orthodoxies: the politics of genre and the ancient Greek novel', in Karla 2009a: 1–12.

Morgan, J. R. and Stoneman, R. (eds.) (1994) *Greek Fiction: The Greek Novel in Context*. London/New York.

Mossman, J. (ed. and transl.) (2011) *Euripides: Medea*. Warminster.

Most, G. W. (1995) 'Reflecting Sappho', *BICS* 40: 15–38.

Most, G. W. (2013) 'Eros in Hesiod', in Sanders *et al.* 2013: 163–74.

Mülke, C. (1996) 'Ποίων δὲ κακων οὐκ αἴτιός ἐστι: Euripides' *Aiolos* und der Geschwisterinzest im klassischen Athen', *ZPE* 114: 37–55.
Müller, C. W. (2006) *Legende – Novelle – Roman: Dreizehn Kapitel zur erzählenden Prosaliteratur der Antike*. Göttingen.
Müller, G. (1951) 'Interpolationen in der *Medea* des Euripides', *SIFC* 25: 65–82.
Müller, S. (2008) 'Asceticism, gallantry, or polygamy? Alexander's relationship with women as a *topos* in medieval romance traditions', *The Medieval History Journal* 11: 259–87.
Müller, S. (2012) 'Stories of the Persian bride: Alexander and Roxane', in *The Alexander Romance in Persia and the East*, eds. R. Stoneman, K. Erickson and I. Netton. Groningen: 295–309.
Munding, M. (2011) 'Alexander and the Amazon queen', *Graeco-Latina Brunensia* 16: 125–42.
Murgatroyd, P. (1975) '*Militia amoris* and the Roman elegists', *Latomus* 34: 59–79.
Murgatroyd, P. (1981) '*Seruitium amoris* and the Roman elegists', *Latomus* 40: 589–606.
Murgatroyd, P. (2000) 'Petronius, *Satyricon* 132', *Latomus* 59: 346–52.
Murray, A. (ed. and transl.) (1925) *Homer: Iliad*. Cambridge.
Nagy, G. (2015) 'Once again *this* time in Song 1 of Sappho', *Classical Enquiries*, 5 Nov. 2015.
Nawotka, K. (2017) *The Alexander Romance by Ps.-Callisthenes: A Historical Commentary*. Leiden.
Neri, C. (2017) 'Afrodite violenta (Sapph. fr. 26 = "Kypris poem")', *Eikasmos* 28: 9–21.
Nicoll, W. S. M. (1980) 'Cupid, Apollo, and Daphne (Ovid, *Met.* 1.452ff.)', *CQ* 30: 174–82.
Niedenthal, P. M. and Ric, F. (2017) 'Theories of emotion', in *Psychology of Emotion*. New York/London: 1–25.
Nikolaidis, A. (1985) 'Some observations on Ovid's lost *Medea*', *Latomus* 44: 383–7.
Nussbaum, M. C. (1989) 'Beyond obsession and disgust. Lucretius' genealogy of love', *Apeiron* 22: 1–59.
Nussbaum, M. C. and Sihvola, J. (eds.) (2002) *The Sleep of Reason: Erotic Experience and Sexual Ethics in Ancient Greece and Rome*. Chicago/London.
O'Connor, J. F. (1974) *Disease Imagery in Aeschylus and Sophocles*. Diss. Ohio.
O'Hara, J. (1993) 'Medicine for the madness of Dido and Gallus: tentative suggestions on *Aeneid* 4', *Vergilius* 39: 12–24.
O'Neill, K. (2005) 'The lover's gaze and Cynthia's glance', in Ancona/Greene 2005: 243–68.
Obbink, D. (2009) 'Sappho fragments 58–59: text, apparatus criticus, and translation', in Greene/Skinner 2009: 7–16.
Obbink, D. (2016a) 'The newest Sappho: text, apparatus criticus, and translation', in Bierl/Lardinois 2016: 13–33.
Obbink, D. (2016b) 'Ten poems of Sappho: provenance, authenticity, and text of the new Sappho papyri', in Bierl/Lardinois 2016: 34–54.
Obdrzalek, S. (2010) 'Moral transformation and the love of beauty in Plato's *Symposium*', *JHPh* 48: 415–44.
Ogden, D. (1996) *Greek Bastardy in the Classical and Hellenistic Periods*. Oxford.
Ogden, D. (1997) 'Rape, adultery and the protection of bloodlines in classical Athens', in Deacy/Pierce 1997: 25–41.
Oranje, H. (1980) 'Euripides' *Protesilas*, *P. Oxy.* 3214, 10–14', *ZPE* 37: 169–72.
Otis, B. (1970) *Ovid as an Epic Poet*, 2nd edn. Cambridge.
Pachoumi, E. (2012) 'Eros as disease, torture and punishment in magical literature', *SO* 86: 74–93.
Padel, R. (1992) *In and Out of the Mind: Greek Images of the Tragic Self*. Princeton.

Paduano. G. (2005) 'L'apologia di Pasifae nei *Cretesi*', in *Euripide e i papiri*, eds. G. Bastianini and A. Casanova. Florence: 127–44.
Page, D. (1955) *Sappho and Alcaeus: An Introduction to the Study of Ancient Lesbian Poetry*. Oxford.
Page, D. (1967) 'Notes on Euripides' *Cretans*, and Sophocles' *Theseus*', *PCPhS* 13: 32–4.
Palmer, A. and Kennedy, D. (eds.) (2005) *Ovidii Nasonis* Heroides *with the Greek Translation of Planudes*, 2 vols. Oxford.
Panayotakis, S. (2006) 'The logic of inconsistency: Apollonius of Tyre and the thirty-days' period of grace', in *Authors, Authority, and Interpreters in the Ancient Novel: Essays in Honor of G. L. Schmeling*, eds. S. N. Byrne, E. P. Cueva and J. Alvares. Groningen: 211–26.
Panayotakis, S. (2007) 'Fixity and fluidity in *Apollonius of Tyre*', in *Seeing Tongues, Hearing Scripts: Orality and Representation in the Ancient Novel*, ed. V. Rimell. Groningen: 299–320.
Panayotakis, S. (2012) *The Story of Apollonius, King of Tyre: A Commentary*. Berlin.
Papademetriou, J.-T. A. (1997) *Aesop as an Archetypal Hero*. Athens.
Papademetriou, J.-T. A. (2009) 'Romance without *erôs*', in Karla 2009a: 49–80.
Papanghelis, Th. (1987) *Propertius: A Hellenistic Poet on Love and Death*. Cambridge.
Papanghelis, Th. (2009) Σώματα που αλλάξαν τη θωριά τους. Athens.
Parrott, W. G. (1991) 'The emotional experiences of envy and jealousy', in *The Psychology of Jealousy and Envy*, ed. P. Salovey. New York: 3–30.
Peponi, A.-E. (2004) 'Initiating the viewer: deixis and visual perception in Alcman's lyric drama', *Arethusa* 37: 295–316.
Perrin, B. (ed. and transl.) (1920) *Lives. Demetrius and Antony. Pyrrhus and Caius Marius*. Cambridge, MA.
Perry, B. E. (1933) 'The text tradition of the Greek Life of Aesop', *TAPhA* 64: 198–244.
Perry, B. E. (1936) *Studies in the Text History of the Life and Fables of Aesop*. Haverford.
Perry, B. E. (1952) *Aesopica: A Series of Texts Relating to Aesop or Ascribed to Him or Closely Connected with the Literary Tradition that Bears His Name*. Urbana.
Perry, B. E. (1960) 'The origin of the Book of Sindbad', *Fabula* 3: 1–94.
Perry, B. E. (1962) 'Demetrius of Phalerum and the Aesopic fables', *TAPhA* 93: 287–346.
Perry, B. E. (1964) *Secundus the Silent Philosopher: The Greek Life of Secundus Critically Edited and Restored so Far as Possible Together with Translations of the Greek and Oriental Versions, the Latin and Oriental Texts, and a Study of the Tradition*. Ithaca.
Perry, B. E. (1966) 'The Egyptian legend of Nectanebus', *TAPhA* 97: 327–33.
Perry, B. E. (1967) *The Ancient Romances: A Literary-Historical Account of Their Origins*. Berkeley.
Pervo, R. I. (1998) 'A nihilist fabula: introducing *The Life of Aesop*', in *Ancient Fiction and Early Christian Narrative*, eds. R. F. Hock, J. B. Chance and J. Perkins. Atlanta: 77–120.
Philippides, K. (1996) 'Canace misunderstood: Ovid's *Heroides* XI', *Mnemosyne* 49: 426–39.
Phillips, D. D. (2018) '*Moicheia* and the unity of Greek law', paper presented at the Classical Association of the Middle West and South Annual Meeting. Albuquerque.
Pierce, K. F. (1997) 'The portrayal of rape in New Comedy', in Deacy/Pierce 1997: 163–84.
Pinault, J. R. (1992) *Hippocratic Lives and Legends*. Leiden.
Polito, R. (2016) 'Competence conflicts between philosophy and medicine: Caelius Aurelianus and the Stoics on mental diseases', *CQ* 66: 358–69.
Pomeroy, S. B. (1994) *Xenophon* Oeconomicus: *A Social and Historical Commentary, with a New English Translation*. Oxford.

Pratt, N. T. Jr. (1943) 'The Euripidean *Medea* 38-43', *CPh* 38: 33-8.
Preston, K. (1916) *Studies in the 'Sermo Amatorius' of Roman Comedy*. Diss. Chicago.
Primmer, A. (1976) 'Mythos und Natur in Ovids "Apollo und Daphne"', *WS* 10: 210-20.
Puche López, M. C. (1997) *Historia de Apolonio rey de Tiro*. Madrid.
Raeder, J. (ed.) (1926) *Oribasius: Synopsis ad Eustathium (CMG VI 3)*. Leipzig/Berlin.
Rawles, R. (2011) 'Eros and praise in early Greek lyric', in *Archaic and Classical Choral Song: Performance, Politics and Dissemination*, eds. L. Athanasaki and E. Bowie, Berlin/Boston: 139-59.
Reardon, B. P. (1991) *The Form of Greek Romance*. Princeton.
Redondo Moyano, E. (2012) 'Space and gender in the ancient Greek novel', in Futre Pinheiro *et al.* 2012: 29-48.
Reckford, K. J. (1974) 'Phaedra and Pasiphae: the pull backward', *TAPhA* 104: 307-28.
Redfield, J. (1982) 'Notes on the Greek wedding', *Arethusa* 15: 181-201.
Rehm, R. (1994) *Marriage to Death: The Conflation of Wedding and Funeral Rituals in Greek Tragedy*. Princeton.
Rimell, V. (1999) 'Epistolary fictions: authorial identity in *Heroides* 15', *PCPhS* 45: 109-35.
Rivier, A. (1975) 'Euripide et Pasiphaé', in *Études de littérature grecque*, eds. F. Lasserre and J. Sulliger. Geneva: 43-60.
Robiano, P. (2003) 'Maladie d'amour et diagnostic médical: Érasistrate, Galien et Héliodore d'Emèse, ou du récit au roman', *Ancient Narrative* 3: 129-49.
Robson, J. (2013a) 'The language(s) of love in Aristophanes', in Sanders *et al.* 2013: 251-66.
Robson, J. (2013b) *Sex and Sexuality in Classical Athens*. Edinburgh.
Roisman, H. M. (2006) 'Helen in the *Iliad*: causa belli and victim of war: from silent weaver to public speaker', *AJPh* 127: 1-36.
Roscalla, F. (2004) '*Kalokagathia* e *kaloi kagathoi* in Senofonte', in Tuplin 2004: 115-24.
Rose, H. J. (1925) 'The bride of Hades', *CPh* 20: 238-42.
Roselli, A. (2008) '*Suntonos phrontis* e malattia d'amore nei testi medici greci da Galeno agli *Ephodia*', in *Une traversée des savoirs: Mélanges offerts à Jackie Pigeaud*, eds. P. Heuzé, Y. Hersant and E. van der Schueren. Quebec: 391-404.
Rosen, D. (2018) 'Santa Fe High School shooting: an incel killing?', *CounterPunch*: 25 May 2018.
Rosen, R. M. (2013) 'Galen, Plato and the physiology of *erôs*', in Sanders *et al.* 2013: 111-28.
Rosenmeyer, P. (1996) 'Love letters in Callimachus, Ovid and Aristaenetus, or the sad fate of a mailorder bride', *MD* 36: 9-31.
Rosivach, V. J. (1998) *When a Young Man Falls in Love: The Sexual Exploitation of Women in New Comedy*. London.
Rossiaud, J. (1984) *La prostituzione nel Medioevo*. Rome.
Rouse, W. (ed. and transl.) (1992) *Lucretius: De Rerum Natura*. Cambridge.
Roy, J. (1991) 'Traditional jokes about the punishment of adulterers in ancient Greek literature', *LCM* 16: 73-6.
Rudd, N. (ed.) (1989) *Horace, Epistles Book II and Epistle to the Pisones ('Ars Poetica')*. Cambridge.
Rudolph, K. (2016) 'Sight and the presocratics: approaches to visual perception in early Greek philosophy', in *Sight and the Ancient Senses*, ed. M. Squire. London/New York: 36-53.
Ruiz de Elvira, A. (1991) 'Laodamía y Protesilao', *CFC(L)* 1: 139-58.
Ruiz Montero, C. (2014) 'The Life of Aesop (rec.G). The composition of the text', in Cueva/Byrne 2014: 257-71.

Ruiz Montero, C. and Sánchez Alacid, M. D. (2003) 'El retrato de Esopo en la *Vita Aesopi* y sus precedentes literarios', in *Lógos hellenikós: Homenaje al Profesor Gaspar Morocho Gayo*, ed. J. M. Nieto Ibáñez. León: 411–22.

Ruschenbusch, E. (1966) *Solonos Nomoi: Die Fragmente des Solonischen Gesetzeswerkes*. Wiesbaden.

Russell, J. A. and Lemay, G. (2000) 'Emotion concepts', in *Handbook of Emotions*, 2nd edn., eds. M. Lewis and J. M. Haviland-Jones. New York/London: 491–503.

Rynearson, N. (2009) 'A Callimachean case of lovesickness: magic, disease, and desire in *Aetia* frr. 67-75 Pf.', *AJPh* 130: 341–65.

Ryzman, M. (1992) 'Oedipus, nosos, and physis in Sophocles' *Oedipus Tyrannus*', *AC* 61: 98–110.

Sabatakakis, G. (ed. and transl.) (2007) Ευριπίδης: Κρῆτες. Athens.

Sallares, R. (1991) *The Ecology of the Ancient Greek World*. London.

Sanders, E. (2013) 'Sexual jealousy and *erôs* in Euripides' *Medea*', in Sanders *et al.* 2013: 41–58.

Sanders, E. (2014) *Envy and Jealousy in Classical Athens: A Socio-Psychological Approach*. New York.

Sanders, E. (2016) 'Persuasion through emotions in Athenian deliberative oratory', in *Emotion and Persuasion in Classical Antiquity*, eds. E. Sanders and M. Johncock. Stuttgart: 57–73.

Sanders, E. (2021) 'Love, grief, fear, and shame: Medea's interconnecting emotions in Book 3 of Apollonius' *Argonautica*', *G&R* 68: 45–60.

Sanders, E., Thumiger, C., Carey, C. and Lowe, N. (eds.) (2013) *Erôs in Ancient Greece*. Oxford.

Sansone, D. (2013) 'Euripides, *Cretans* frag. 472e.16—26 Kannicht', *ZPE* 184: 58–65.

Sassi, M. M. (1978) *Le teorie della percezione in Democrito*. Florence.

Scafuro, A. C. (1997) *The Forensic Stage: Settling Disputes in Graeco-Roman New Comedy*. Cambridge.

Scarcella, A. M. (1993) *Romanzo e romanzieri: Note di narratologia greca*, vol. 1. Naples.

Schindler, D. C. (2007) 'Plato and the problem of love: on the nature of eros in the *Symposium*', *Apeiron* 40: 199–220.

Schmeling, G. (1988) *Historia Apollonii Regis Tyri*. Leipzig.

Schmeling, G. (1999) 'The History of Apollonius King of Tyre', in *Latin Fiction: The Latin Novel in Context*, ed. H. Hofmann. London/New York: 119–29.

Schmeling, G. (ed.) (2003a) *The Novel in the Ancient World*, revised edn. Leiden.

Schmeling, G. (2003b) 'Historia Apollonii Regis Tyri', in Schmeling 2003a: 517–61.

Schmid, W. and Stählin, O. (1940) *Geschichte der griechischen Literatur*, vol. I.3: *Die klassische Periode der griechischen Literatur (Die griechische Literatur zur Zeit der attischen Hegemonie nach dem Eingreifen der Sophistik)*. Munich.

Schmidt, M. (1992) 'Daidalos und Ikaros auf Kreta', in *Kotinos: Festschrift für Erika Simon*, eds. H. Froning, T. Hölscherand and H. Mielsch. Mainz/Rhein: 306–11.

Schmitzer, U. (1990) *Zeitgeschichte in Ovids Metamorphosen*. Stuttgart.

Scholtz, A. (2007) *Concordia discors: Eros and Dialogue in Classical Athenian Literature*. Washington, DC.

Schubart, W. and von Wilamowitz-Moellendorff, U. (1907) *Berliner Klassikertexte, Heft V, Griechische Dichterfragmente: Teil 2, Lyrische und dramatische Fragmente*. Berlin.

Seaford, R. (1987) 'The tragic wedding', *JHS* 107: 106–30.

Sedley, D. (1992) 'Empedocles' theory of vision in Theophrastus' *De sensibus*', in *Theophrastus: His Psychological, Doxographical and Scientific Writings*, eds. W. Fortenbaugh and D. Gutas. New Brunswick: 20–31.
Séchan, L. (1953) 'La légende de Protésilas', *BAGB* 12: 3–27.
Segal, C. P. (1965) 'The tragedy of the Hippolytus: the waters of ocean and the untouched meadow. In memoriam Arthur Darby Nock', *HSCPh* 70: 117–69.
Sharpsteen, D. J. (1991) 'The organization of jealousy knowledge: romantic jealousy as a blended emotion', in *The Psychology of Jealousy and Envy*, ed. P. Salovey. New York: 31–51.
Shaver, P., Schwartz, J., Kirson, D. and O'Connor, C. (1987) 'Emotion knowledge: further exploration of a prototype approach', *Journal of Personality and Social Psychology* 52: 1061–86.
Shiota, M. and Kalat, J. (2018) 'The nature of emotion', in *Emotion*, 3rd edn. Oxford: 2–38.
Showerman, G. (ed.) (1977) *The Heroides; The Amores*, 2nd edn. revised by G. P. Goold. Cambridge, MA.
Simon, E. (2004) 'Daidalos–Taitale–Daedalus: Neues zu einem wohlbekannten Mythos', *AA* 2: 419–32.
Simpson, M. (1971) 'Why does Agamemnon yield?', *PP* 26: 94–101.
Singer, P. N. (ed.) (2014) *Galen: Psychological Writings. Avoiding Distress, Character Traits, The Diagnosis and Treatment of the Affections and Errors Peculiar to Each Person's Soul, The Capacities of the Soul Depend on the Mixtures of the Body*. Cambridge.
Singer, P. N. (2017) 'The essence of rage: Galen on emotional disturbances and their physical correlates', in *Selfhood and Soul: Essays on Ancient Thought and Literature in honour of Christopher Gill*, eds. R. Seaford, J. Wilkins and M. Wright. Oxford: 161–96.
Skinner, M. B. (2005) *Sexuality in Greek and Roman Culture*. Oxford.
Small, H. (1996) *Love's Madness: Medicine, the Novel, and Female Insanity, 1800-1865*. Oxford.
Soble, A. (2008) *The Philosophy of Sex and Love: An Introduction*, 2nd edn. St. Paul.
Sobol, V. (2009) *Febris Erotica: Lovesickness in the Russian Literary Imagination*. Seattle.
Soleil, D. (2010) 'Les mots d'Aristophane et les mots d'Hippocrate: encore une fois sur le vocabulaire médical d'Aristophane', *Lucida Intervalla* 40: 25–42.
Sommerstein, A. H. (ed. and transl.) (1982) *Aristophanes: Clouds*. Warminster.
Sommerstein, A. H. (ed. and transl.) (2008) *Aeschylus: 2. Agamemnon, Libation-Bearers, Eumenides*. Cambridge, MA.
Sommerstein, A. H. (2020) 'Women in love in the fragmentary plays of Sophocles', in *Female Characters in Fragmentary Greek Tragedy*, eds. P. J. Finglass and L. Coo. Cambridge: 62–72.
Sontag, S. (1978) *Illness as Metaphor*. New York.
Spatharas, D. (2019) *Emotions, Persuasion, and Public Discourse in Classical Athens*. Berlin/Boston.
Spentzou, E. (2003) *Readers and Writers in Ovid's* Heroides: *Transgressions of Genre and Gender*. Oxford.
Spoth, F. (1992) *Ovid's Heroides als Elegien*. Munich.
Squire, M. (2016) 'Introductory reflections: making sense of ancient sight', in *Sight and the Ancient Senses*, ed. M. Squire. Oxford/New York: 1–35.
Stadter, P. (1989) *A Commentary on Plutarch's* Pericles. Chapel Hill.
Stafford, E. (2013) 'From the gymnasium to the wedding: Eros in Athenian art and cult', in Sanders *et al.* 2013: 175–208.

Stark, I. (1989) 'Strukturen des griechischen Abenteuer- und Liebesromans', in *Der antike Roman: Untersuchungen zur literarischen Kommunikation und Gattungsgeschichte*, ed. H. Kuch. Berlin: 82–106.
Stehle, E. (2008) 'Greek lyric and gender', in *The Cambridge Companion to Greek Lyric*, ed. F. Budelmann. Cambridge: 58–71.
Stephens, S. A. (2003) 'Fragments of lost novels', in Schmeling 2003a: 655–83.
Stephens, S. A. (2014) 'The other Greek novels', in Cueva/Byrne 2014: 147–58.
Stephens, S. A. and Winkler, J. J. (1995) *Ancient Greek Novels: The Fragments*. Princeton.
Sternberg, R. J. and Weis, K. (eds.) (2006) *The New Psychology of Love*. New Haven/London.
Stoneman, R. (1991) *The Greek Alexander Romance*. London.
Stoneman, R. (2007) *Il romanzo di Alessandro*, vol. 1. Milan.
Stoneman, R. (2008) *Alexander the Great: A Life in Legend*. New Haven/London.
Swift, L. (2016a) 'Visual imagery in parthenaic song', in Cazzato/Lardinois 2016: 255–87.
Swift, L. (2016b) 'Poetics and precedents in Archilochus' erotic imagery', in *Iambus and Elegy: New Approaches*, eds. L. Swift and C. Carey. Oxford: 253–70.
Swift, L. (2019) *Archilochus: The Poems*. Oxford.
Szalc, A. (2014) 'Kandake, Meroe and India – India and the Alexander Romance', in *Alexander the Great and Egypt: History, Art, Tradition*, eds. V. Grieb, K. Nawotka and A. Wojciechowska. Wiesbaden: 377–90.
Szepessy, T. (1985–1988) 'The ancient family novel (a typological proposal)', *AAntHung* 31: 357–65.
Tallis, F. (2004) *Love Sick: Love as a Mental Illness*. London.
Taplin, O. (1986) 'Fifth-century tragedy and comedy: a *synkrisis*', *JHS* 106: 163–74.
Taplin, O. (1992) *Homeric Soundings: The Shaping of the Iliad*. Oxford.
Thesleff, H. (1978) 'The interrelation and date of the *Symposia* of Plato and Xenophon', *BICS* 25: 157–70.
Thomas, C. M. (1998) 'Stories without texts and without authors: the problem of fluidity in ancient novelistic texts and early Christian literature', in *Ancient Fiction and Early Christian Narrative*, eds. R. F. Hock, J. B. Chance and J. Perkins. Atlanta: 273–91.
Thompson, E. A. (1947) *The Historical Work of Ammianus Marcellinus*. Cambridge.
Thompson, P. A. M. (1989) *Ovid, Heroides 20 and 21: A Commentary with Introduction*. Diss. Oxford.
Thompson, W. E. (1967) 'The marriage of first cousins in Athenian society', *Phoenix* 21: 273–82.
Thompson, W. E. (1972) 'Athenian marriage patterns: remarriage', *California Studies in Classical Antiquity* 5: 211–25.
Thornton, B. S. (1998) *Eros: The Myth of Ancient Greek Sexuality*. Oxford.
Thorsen, T. S. (ed.) (2013) *The Cambridge Companion to Latin Love Elegy*. Cambridge.
Thorsen, T. S. (2018a) 'Intrepid intratextuality: the epistolary pair of Leander and Hero (*Heroides* 18–19) and the end of Ovid's poetic career', in *Intratextuality and Latin Literature*, eds. S. Fangoulidis and S. Harrison. Berlin: 257–72.
Thorsen, T. S. (2018b) 'The second Erato and the deeper design of Ovid's *Ars amatoria*: unravelling the anti-marital union of Venus, Procris and Romulus', in *Vivam! Estudios sobre la obra de Ovidio / Studies on Ovid's Poetry*, eds. L. Rivero, C. Álvarez, R. M. Iglesias and J. A. Estévez. Huelva: 141–67.
Thorsen, T. S. (2019) 'Cydippe the poet', *CJ* 115: 129–45.
Thorsen, T. S. (2020) 'Blindness and insight. Emotions of erotic love in Roman poetry', in *Reading Roman Emotions*, eds. H. von Ehrenheim and M. Prusac-Lindhagen. Stockholm: 117–30.

Thorsen, T. S. (forthcoming) 'Oenone (*Her.* 5), Acontius (*Her.* 20) and the Ovidian *seruitium amoris*', *ICS*.
Thumiger, C. (2013) 'Mad *erôs* and eroticized madness in tragedy', in Sanders *et al.* 2013: 27–40.
Thumiger, C. (2017) *A History of the Mind and Mental Health in Classical Greek Medical Thought*. Cambridge.
Thumiger, C. (2018) 'Liebe als Krankheit', in *Parlare la medicina: fra lingue e culture, nello spazio e nel tempo*, eds. N. Reggiani and F. Bertonazzi. Florence: 253–73.
Thumiger, C. (2020) 'Therapy of the word and other psychotherapeutic approaches in Ancient Greek medicine', *Transcultural Psychiatry* 57(6): 1–21.
Thumiger, C. (forthcoming) 'Information and history of psychiatry. The case of the disease *phrenitis*', in *Information and the History of Philosophy*, ed. C. Meyns. Routledge.
Tilg, S. (2010) *Chariton of Aphrodisias and the Invention of the Greek Love Novel*. Oxford.
Tonelli, N. (2015) *Fisiologia della passione: poesia d'amore e medicina da Cavalcanti a Boccaccio*. Florence.
Toohey, P. (1992) 'Love, lovesickness, and melancholia', *ICS* 17: 265–86.
Toohey, P. (2004) *Melancholy, Love, and Time: Boundaries of the Self in Ancient Literature*. Ann Arbor.
Tralau, J. (2017) 'Cannibalism, vegetarianism, and the community of sacrifice: rediscovering Euripides' *Cretans* and the beginnings of political philosophy', *CPh* 112: 435–55.
Tredennick, H. (transl.) (1990) *Xenophon: Conversations of Socrates*, revised by R. Waterfield. London.
Tuplin, C. J. (ed.) (2004) *Xenophon and His World: Papers from a Conference Held in Liverpool in July 1999*. Stuttgart.
Turyn, A. (1929) *Studia Sapphica*. Leopolis.
Valtadorou, A. S. (2018) 'Hippolytus' neglect of *eros*: a dialogue between Euripides' drama and Sarah Kane's *Phaedra's Love*', *New Voices in Classical Reception* 12: 69–87.
Valtadorou, A. S. (2020) '*Erôs* in pieces (?): tragic *erôs* in Euripides' *Andromeda* and *Antigone*', in *Greek Drama V: Studies in the Theatre of the Fifth and Fourth Centuries BCE*, eds. C. W. Marshall and H. Marshall. London/New York: 115–28.
van Dijk, G.-J. (1995) 'The fables in the Greek *Life of Aesop*', *Reinardus* 8: 131–50.
Wack, M. F. (1990) *Lovesickness in the Middle Ages: The Viaticum and its Commentaries*. Philadelphia.
Walcot, P. (1978) 'Herodotus on rape', *Arethusa* 11: 137–47.
Walsh, P. (ed. and transl.) (1982) *Andreas Capellanus: On Love*. London.
Waterfield, R. (ed.) (1990) '*The Dinner-Party*: Introduction', in *Xenophon: Conversations of Socrates*, transl. H. Tredennick. London: 219–26.
Waterfield, R. (2004) 'Xenophon's Socratic mission', in Tuplin 2004: 79–113.
Webster, T. B. L. (1967) *The Tragedies of Euripides*. London.
Wehr, H. and Cowan, J. W. (1976) *Arabic English Dictionary of Modern Written Arabic*. Ithaca, N.Y.
Weinreich, O. (1911) *Der Trug des Nektanebos: Wandlungen eines Novellenstoffs*. Leipzig.
Weinreich, O. (1931) *Fabel, Aretalogie, Novelle: Beiträge zu Phädrus, Petron, Martial und Apuleius*. Heidelberg.
Weis, K. and Sternberg, R. J. (2008) 'The nature of love', in *21st Century Psychology: A Reference Handbook*, vol. 2, eds. S. F. Davis and W. Buskist. Los Angeles: 134–42.
Wells, M. (2007) *The Secret Wound: Love-Melancholy And Early Modern Romance*. Stanford.

Wender, D. S. (1974) 'The will of the beast: sexual imagery in the *Trachiniae*', *Ramus* 3: 1–17.
Wenkebach E. and Pfaff F. (eds.) (1956) *Galen: In Hippocratis Epidemiarum librum VI commentaria I-VI (CMG V 10.2.2)*. Berlin.
West, M. L. (1997) *The East Face of Helicon*. Oxford.
West, M. L. (ed. and transl.) (2003a) *Homeric Hymns, Homeric Apocrypha, Lives of Homer*. Cambridge, MA.
West, M. L. (ed. and transl.) (2003b) *Greek Epic Fragments*. Cambridge, MA.
Wheeler, S. M. (1999) *A Discourse of Wonders: Audience and Performance in Ovid's* Metamorphoses. Philadelphia.
Whidden, C. (2007a) 'The account of Persia and Cyrus's Persian education in Xenophon's *Cyropaedia*', *Review of Politics* 69: 539–67.
Whidden, C. (2007b) 'Deception in Xenophon's *Cyropaedia*', *Interpretation* 34: 129–56.
White, H. (2006) 'Further notes on Ovid's *Heroides*', *Minerva(vall)* 19: 193–8.
Whitmarsh, T. (ed.) (2008) *The Cambridge Companion to the Greek and Roman Novel*. Cambridge.
Whitmarsh, T. (2011) *Narrative and Identity in the Ancient Greek Novel: Returning Romance*. Cambridge.
Whitmarsh, T. (2018) *Dirty Love: The Genealogy of the Ancient Greek Novel*. Oxford.
Willetts, R. F. (1967) *The Law Code of Gortyn*. Berlin.
Willi, A. (2003) *The Languages of Aristophanes: Aspects of Linguistic Variation in Classical Attic Greek*. Oxford.
Williamson, M. (1998) 'Eros the blacksmith: performing masculinity in Anakreon's love lyrics', in *Thinking Men: Masculinity and Its Self-Representation in the Classical Tradition*, eds. L. Foxhall and J. Salmon. London: 71–82.
Wills, J. (1990) 'Callimachean models for Ovid's Apollo-Daphne', *MD* 24: 143–56.
Wilmanns, W. (1901) 'Alexander und Candace', *Zeitschrift für deutsches Altertum und deutsche Literatur* 45: 229–44.
Winkler, J. J. (1985) *Auctor & Actor: A Narratological Reading of Apuleius's* Golden Ass. Berkeley.
Winkler, J. J. (2002) 'Double consciousness in Sappho's lyrics', in *Sexuality and Gender in the Classical World: Readings and Sources*, ed. L. K. McClure. Oxford: 38–71.
Wisse, J. (1989) *Ethos and Pathos from Aristotle to Cicero*. Amsterdam.
Wohl, V. (2002) *Love among the Ruins: The Erotics of Democracy in Classical Athens*. Princeton.
Wolff, É. (2001) 'Les personnages du roman grec et l'*Historia Apollonii regis Tyri*', in *Les personnages du roman grec. Actes du colloque de Tours*, ed. B. Pouderon. Lyon: 233–40.
Woodford, S. (2009) 'Daedalos and Ikaros on an Apulian fragment newly acquired by the British Museum', *BICS* 52: 93–101.
Wyke, M. (1987) 'Written women: Propertius' *scripta puella*', *JRS* 77: 47–61.
Xanthaki-Karamanou, G. and Mimidou, E. N. (2014) 'The *Aeolus* of Euripides: concepts and motifs', *BICS* 57: 49–60.
Yatromanolakis, D. (2008) *Sappho in the Making: The Early Reception*. Cambridge, MA/London.
Zadorojnyi, A. V. (1999) 'Sappho and Plato in Plutarch, *Demetrius* 38', in *Plutarco, Platón y Aristóteles*, eds. A. Pérez Jiménez, J. García López and R. M. Aguilar. Madrid: 515–32.
Zafiropoulos, C. A. (2015) *Socrates and Aesop: A Comparative Study of the Introduction of Plato's* Phaedo. Sankt Augustin.

Zimmermann, B. (1992) 'Hippokratisches in den Komodien des Aristophanes', in *Tratados Hipocráticos (Estudios acerca de su contenido, forma e influencia): Actas del Vlle Colloque international hippocratique*, ed. J. A. López Férez. Madrid: 513–25.

Ziogas, I. (2016) 'Love elegy and legal language in Ovid', in *Wordplay and Powerplay in Latin Poetry*, eds. P. Mitsis and I. Ziogas. Berlin: 213–40.

Index Locorum

Passages which are simply cited as *similia*, rather than commented upon, are not indexed.

Achilles Tatius
1.9	11
4.9	11 n.36

Aegritudo Perdiccae
19–276 (*sel.*)	42–43

Aeschines
1.15–17	94
1.107	94
1.115	91
1.158	99
2.153–5	94
19.229	91

Aeschylus
Agamemnon
414–19	28
895–950	85
1625–7	87

Alcman
1 *PMG*	51–2
3 *PMG*	52
28 *PMG*	48 n.1
59a *PMG*	4, 55

Alexander Romance
1.3–3.33 (*sel.*)	167–9

Amphis
fr. 23 K-A	91

Anacreon
68 *PMG*	4
413 *PMG*	55
459 *PMG*	52

Andocides
1.124–9	89

Anthologia Palatina
5.64	9
5.168	10
12.13	10
12.106	10
12.127	10
12.150	10
12.159	10

Archilochus
193 W	4
196 W	4, 53
196a W	95, 104

Aretaeus of Cappadocia
Chronic Diseases
3.5.4–11	15 n.55

Aristophanes
Acharnians
524–37	92
526–34	89
848–9	97

Birds
285–6	97
793–6	97

Clouds
1079–82	97
1371–2	72

Ecclesiazusae
877–1111	95
912–13	95
914	96
919–20	96

Frogs
1043–56	66

Knights
1280–9	91

Lysistrata
327–35	95 n.29
1085–8	8

Thesmophoriazusae
343–5	97

Wasps
87–9	8

Wealth
87–92	8
155–7	99
168	97
726	8

Aristotle
Nicomachean Ethics
1118b8–11	103
1148b	9

On the Generation of Animals
747a14–20	39

On the Soul
418a27–419b4	29 n.16

On Dreams
460b1	31

Poetics
1448a–1453a (sel.)	177

[Problems]
879b–80a	9 n.28
954a32–4	15 n.55, 34

Rhetoric
1370a16–25	103
1370b19–29	31 n.20
1372a23–4	97 n.36
1385a23	103
1391a15–19	97 n.36
1392a23	103

On Sense and the Sensible
439a6–440b25	29 n.16

Caelius Aurelianus
On Chronic Diseases
5.7	39

Callimachus
Aetia
fr. 1.2	143
fr. 67	140, 144
fr. 73	140–1
fr. 75	144, 147, 156

Epigrams
46	10

Hymns
4.31	144

Catullus
51	27
65–8	12

Chariton
1.1	11

Cicero
Tusculan Disputations
4	12

Cratinus
Dionysalexandros
17–18	87
fr. 81 K-A	97
fr. 259 K-A	89

Ctesias of Cnidus
688F1.23 *FGrH*	98

Demosthenes/Demosthenic corpus
19.196–8	94
21.46–50	94
23.55–6	94
40.51	91
[48.]53–5	91
[59.]41–2	92
[59.]55–8	88
[59.]64–70	92
[59.]72–84	88

Dinarchus
1.23	94

Eupolis
fr. 171 K-A	98
fr. 267 K-A	89

Euripides
Aeolus
fr. 26	68–70

Alcestis
348–54	80

Index Locorum

Andromache
293–300   87
Cretans
fr. 472   73–6
fr. 472b   73–6
fr. 472e   73–6
Helen
639–41   79
722–5   79
Hippolytus
38–40   6–7
241   6–7
337–8   74
612   151
764–6   6–7
935–1088   75
1213–48   74
1274   6–7
Medea
16   6
37–41   71
1021–80   6
1364   6
Protesilaus
fr. 646a   78
fr. 647   78
fr. 653   79
fr. 655   77
fr. 656   78
fr. 657   81
Scyrians
fr. 682   70 n.23
Stheneboea
fr. 661   66
Theseus
fr. 388   66 n.3
Trojan Women
929–31   75

Galen
Commentary on Hippocrates' Prognosticon
18b K.   15, 35
On Crises
9.696.16 ff. K.   35
On Prognosis
14.625 ff. K.   15, 35

Gorgias
Encomium of Helen
18   63
19   16 n.62

Hellanicus
4F29 *FGrH*   87

Heliodorus
3.5   11
3.10–11   11
4.5   11

Hermippus
fr. 47 K-A   90

Herodotus
1.1–5   92
1.8   104 n.17
3.80.5   93
6.62   104 n.17

Hesiod
Theogony
120–1   4, 53
585–9   4
Works and Days
57–8   4
65–6   4
90–104   4
696–8   85 n.5

Hippocratic corpus
On Semen
1.1   38–9

History of Apollonius
1–49 (*sel.*)   171–3

Homer
Iliad
1.348–50   3
2.698–702   76
3.39–45   87
3.441–6   3
9.342–3   3
12.157   62

17.55	62	4.1030–1170	12
18.80–99	3	4.1037–1287	119
24.28–30	87	4.1058–72	32, 119

Odyssey

Lynceus of Samos

4.259–64	3	Ath. 13.584b	92
10.1–12	68		
17.386	49		
18.201–5	3		
20.79–83	3		

Lysias

1.8	104 n.17
1.16	69 n.22

Horace

Epodes

		1.32–3	96 n.33, 113
		3.5	104 n.17
11.1–2	13	4.8	104 n.17
11.17	13	6.62	104 n.17

Odes

1.33.1–4	13

Machon of Sicyon

Satires

frr. 6–7 Gow	92

1.2	13
2.7	13

Magical Papyri

PGM IV.352–4	16

Ibycus

		PGM IV.1405–13	15
286 *PMG*	4 n.11	*PGM* IV.1530–1	16
287 *PMG*	52–3, 104	*PGM* VII.886–9	15

Isaeus

Martial

6.21	88	2.26	14

Isocrates

Menander

Epitrepontes

8.8–39 (*sel.*)	5–6	136–7	90

Kolax

Life of Aesop

117 ff.	90

30–141 (*sel.*)	166, 175–6

Oribasius

Synopsis for Eustathius

Longus

2.7.7	11	8.8	36–7
4.27–8	11		

Ovid

Lucian

Ars Amatoria

Amores

		1.29–30	120
9	97–8	1.35–40	121

Toxaris

1.37	152

39	93	1.171–2	121 n.7
		1.351–98	131

Lucretius

1.437–68	131

De rerum natura

		2.251–8	131
3.147–8	31	3.1–2	121
3.154–6	31		

Heroides	
3.154	139
4.3	151
20.1	147
20.3	151
20.6	141
20.8	150
20.21–4	140
20.27–32	140
20.34	137
20.37	151
20.38	150
20.41	140
20.44	147
20.47–8	151
20.53–64	141
20.55–60	141
20.60	147
20.66	140
20.67	139
20.68	150
20.69	139
20.75–86	138
20.79–80	139, 151
20.117–18	149
20.117–20	141
20.129–30	146
20.143–50	139
20.174	151
20.181	147
20.189–96	148
20.207	141
20.225	150
20.233–5	155
21.7–12	151
21.9–248	153
21.31–8	149, 155
21.37–8	141
21.52	145
21.53–64	141, 149
21.55–8	137
21.115–16	150
21.117–20	152
21.125–32	152
21.129–44	151
21.135–44	151–2
21.143–4	149

21.155–72	141–2
21.173–82	151
21.181–2	151
21.189–202	142–3
21.213–22	150
21.214	147
21.219–20	146
21.221–2	143
21.241–2	156
21.245–6	156
21.247–8	136, 155
61–2	70
Metamorphoses	
1.4	123, 148
1.452–567	119, 124–30
1.468–73	125
3.341–510	123
6.424–674	123
6.455–7	126
6.458–60	127
6.465–6	127
6.469–70	129 n.26
6.478–82	127
6.490–3	128
6.512–52	129 n.26
7.1–99	123
8.17–151	123
9.450–665	123
10.298–502	123
14.698–761	130–3
Remedia Amoris	
1–4	124–5 n.18
11–12	124–5 n.18
15–20	124–5 n.18
15–18	131
43–4	121
49–50	13, 122 n.12
55–68	122, 129, 133
75–8	128
135–6	126
135–50	132
151–63	132
169–98	132
199–200	126
213–48	132
291–356	127, 132
441–88	132

489–522	132	573d	8–9
579–608	132	*Symposium*	
621–42	132	180d-e	8–9
643–8	132	*Timaeus*	
757	13	86c3–d1	30

Parthenius
Love Romances
34   87

Paul of Aegina
III.17   37

Pausanias
1.23.2   93
2.20.2   94
8.5.12   94

Petronius
Satyrica
126–35   14

Pherecrates
fr. 164 K-A   98

Pindar
Isthmian Odes
2.35–45   145
Pythian Odes
2.21–48   86

Plato
Cratylus
420a-b   62
Laws
636b-c   9
874c   94
Menexenus
236b   89
Phaedrus
244a–257b 104
249d–257b 9
253b   9
251a-c   30
Rhepublic
439d   8–9
515c   8–9

Plautus
Mercator
471 ff.   11 n.38

Plutarch
Alcebiades
39.1–4   98
Demetrius
38   103 n.13
Pericles
24.2   89
24.9   86 n.10, 89
25.1–2   89
32.1   90
37.2–5   89
Solon
23.1   94
23.2   96

Propertius
1.10.14–20   12

Sappho
1 L-P   54–5, 61–2
31 L-P   4–5, 25–6, 53, 61, 63, 103
47 L-P   62
58 L-P   57–9
94 L-P   61
96 L-P   62
130 L-P   4, 55, 62
Kypris poem 59–63

Seneca
Epistles
9.11   12
On Anger
2.20.1   12
2.36.5–6   12

Sophocles
Antigone
635–765	75
1231–9	71 n.32

Oedipus Rex
60	6
61	6
150	6
170	6
217	6
303	6
307	6
1061	6
1293	6

Trachiniae
248–78	86 n.10
813–91	71

Statius
Thebaid
2.247	144

Terence
Eunuch
1026 ff.	11 n.38

Theocritus
Idylls
2.76–110	27
2.82–95	10
11.1–3	10

Theognidea
1249–53	55–6
1353–4	56 n.10

Theopompus, comic
fr. 22 K-A	90

Theopompus, historian
115F213 *FGrH*	91

Thucydides
6.13	5, 104 n.17
6.24	5, 104 n.17
6.54 ff.	104 n.17
6.54.3–4	93

Tibullus
1.1.55–8	12

Vergil
Aeniad
4.65–7	13
4.697	13

Eclogues
6.3–5	123 n.15
10.55–61	13

Xenophon
Constitution of the Lacedaemonians
2.12–13	112 n.48

Cyropaedia
1.4.28	110 n.39
4.6.11	114
5.1.12	116
5.1.3	114
5.1.5	114
5.1.8–10	115
5.1.14–16	115
5.1.18	115
6.1.31–6	116
6.1.41	116
6.1.47	116
6.4.3	116
6.4.6	117
7.3.9	117
7.3.14	117

Hellenica
4.8.39	117 n.57

Hiero
3.6	96 n.34

Memorabilia
1.2.22	113
1.2.30	112
1.3.8–11	112
1.3.10	112 n.49
1.3.12	112
1.3.13	112–13, 115
2.2.4	85
2.6.28	114
2.6.32	112
3.11	105

Oeconomicus
12.14	113

Symposium
1.2	106–7	4.53–4	108
1.8–10	106–7	7.2–3	108
1.11–12	107, 116	7.5	108
2.1	107	8.1	112
2.2	108	8.2–3	107
2.15–16	108	8.12–16	113–14
2.22	108	8.19–21	113–14
3.1	108	8.23	112–13
3.13	116	8.25	113
4.12	107	8.42	116
4.14–16	111	9.3–5	108–9
4.21	111	9.7	108–9
4.22	31 n.18, 110		
4.23–5	110	**Xenophon of Ephesus**	
4.28	108	1.5	11

Index Nominum et Rerum

Terms which are vastly used throughout the book (e.g. love, *erôs*, cupid, sex, passion, desire, pathology, disease, illness, lovesickness, medicine, genre, body), names of ancient authors and titles of their works (for which see the *index locorum*) and names of literary characters (except for some famous mythical figures) are not indexed.

abduction 16, 58–9, 172, 189
abuse 9, 83, 94, 98
Achilles 3, 11, 16, 121 n.10, 139
acrobats 107–8, 110 n.36
adolescent/*adulescens* 11–12, 47, 56–7, 95 (see also: young/youth)
adoption 88–9
adultery/adulterer 13, 21, 74, 83, 85, 87, 92, 96–111, 137 n.6, 159, 161, 169, 170, 172, 175–6
Aeneas 13, 28 n.15
Agamemnon 3, 6, 85–7
agôn 68, 75
agony 10, 116, 118
Ajax 76, 86, 93
Alcibiades 97–8, 110 nn.35–6, 186
Amazon 16, 121, 168
Anaxarete 119, 123, 130–3
anger 1 n.1, 12, 19, 30, 34, 40, 102 nn.7–8, 124, 139 n.17, 174, 183
animal 72–4, 82, 125, 166 n.17
antidote (see: remedy)
Antigone 70–1, 75, 89
anus/anal 9, 98
anxiety/anxious 5, 14, 32, 34, 43, 62, 83, 85, 89, 99–100, 146
aphrodisiac 1 n.1, 13–14
Aphrodite 3–4, 6, 10, 28, 50–1, 55, 58–62, 69, 73, 75, 78, 79, 80 n.78, 86–7, 108, 112 n.45, 182 (see also: Venus)
Apollo 20, 49, 69, 119, 123–30, 132–3, 136, 149
Aretaeus 15, 40 n.48, 43
arrow 61, 121 n.9, 124–5, 128, 133, 190
Artemis 3, 94, 135, 146 (see also: Diana)
Asclepius 7 n.22, 8
Aspasia 86 n.10, 89–90, 92
Athena 69, 86, 144 n.31

attraction/-tive/-ness 4, 19, 20, 62, 74, 84, 87, 97, 99, 100, 102–6, 108–9, 110 n.37, 113–14, 116–18, 141, 161, 164
audience 4, 7 n.22, 11 n.39, 13, 20, 27 n.14, 46, 63 n.22, 65, 67, 70–3, 76, 82, 96, 177

Barthes 24, 45
bastardy 69, 88–9, 169
Bellerophon 66–7
bestiality 20–1, 73, 159, 166 n.17, 176
betrayal 6, 12 n.41, 28, 123, 125 n.18, 143
blame 3, 42, 75, 99, 115, 140
blood 15, 41, 189
brain 37–8
Briseis 3, 139
brothel 85, 88–9, 91–2, 94, 100, 172

Caelius Aurelianus 38, 43
cancer 1 n.1
Cassandra 6, 70, 87, 93
choral poetry 47–9, 51, 56–7, 59
choregos 52, 56
chorus 5, 51, 69, 73, 75–6, 87, 177
Circe 14, 86, 123
Clytaemnestra 6, 67 n.8
comedy/comic 8, 11–14, 20, 40, 83, 86 n.10, 87, 89–92, 94–5, 97, 104, 112 n.47, 120, 123, 130 n.27, 165, 174, 177
complexion 26, 41, 146
crime 11, 93, 97 n.36, 122, 124 n.18, 150, 172–3, 174
crying 44, 68, 116, 118, 133, 169, 176 (see also: tears)
cure (see: remedy)
curses 15–16, 86, 190 (see also: spells)
Cyrus 110 nn.36 and 39, 114–16

Daedalus 72–3
daimôn 15, 112
dance/dancing 15, 35, 48–9, 58, 107–9
Daphne 20, 119, 123–30, 133
deceit/deception 11–12, 31, 46, 72, 115 n.55, 129, 138, 140, 147–8, 150–1, 164, 169, 181
Deianira 70–1
deictics 20, 48, 51, 54–5, 63
Delphi 174–6
democracy 5, 8–9, 83, 85, 95 n.30, 99
devotion 19, 78, 80–1, 83, 85, 91, 126 n.22, 161
diagnosis 11, 15, 26, 35, 43, 45 n.62, 103 n.13
Diana 126 n.22, 136, 147–8, 151, 172 (see also: Artemis)
didactic 8, 20, 120, 123, 130, 167, 170–1
Dido 13–14, 28 n.15, 42, 122
Dionysus 49, 73 n.41, 89, 108
disguise 113, 168–70
dithyramb 49
dolor 31–2, 119, 122, 188–9
door 130–1, 146
dreaming 12, 23, 31 n.19, 38–9, 97–8

ejaculation 32, 39, 80 n.78
elegy 12–14, 20, 47, 49, 55–6, 120, 123–4, 126–7, 130–1, 135, 137 n.6, 138–9, 140, 161
encomiastic poetry 5, 29, 63
Epicureans 12, 33, 119
epigram 9–10
epithumia 8, 102 n.8, 103
Erasistratus 35, 42, 186
erastês 8, 12, 106 n.26, 112 n.48 (see also: homosexuality, pederasty)
erômenos 5, 12, 106 n.26, 107 n.28
euphemism 108, 176
exhibitionism 21, 159, 175–6
eyes 10–12, 16, 23, 26, 28–31, 35–9, 42, 44, 47, 50, 53, 63, 74, 90, 101, 103, 106–7, 110–11, 126–8, 141, 143–4, 146, 181, 188 (see also: vision)

fainting 10, 31, 41
fear 10 n.34, 15, 29 n.17, 30–1, 36, 93, 102 n.8, 115, 138–9, 145, 147–9, 153, 185
female/feminine/-nity/effeminate 3–5, 9, 12 n.40, 13, 15, 47, 50, 56–7, 59, 62, 65–9, 71, 76, 83, 85–6, 89, 91, 93 n.22, 95 n.28, 98–9, 104 nn.15–16, 107, 120, 124, 148, 166 n.17, 193
fever 35, 104 n.18, 142, 149, 185
fire/flame/burning 4, 9–10, 13, 15–16, 26, 33, 41–2, 69, 103, 110–12, 115, 117–18, 125–8, 130, 132 n.33, 141, 184–8, 191
flirt 101, 167
friend/-ship 4, 12–14, 19, 53, 101, 102 n.8, 107, 114–15, 143, 175, 180, 186, 190
furor 7 n.21, 13, 32, 42–3, 119, 127, 130, 137, 141

Galen 15, 29 n.16, 33–40, 43
gaze 4–5, 10, 12–14, 16, 20–21, 27 n.10, 30, 50–3, 56–7, 63, 104 n.18, 106–7, 115, 127–8
gender 3 n.7, 13 n.43, 48, 56, 83–4, 100
genitals 9 n.28, 74 n.45 (see also: penis, vagina)
gestures 107, 109, 118, 128

Hades 66, 70 n.27, 78–9, 86
heart 3–4, 10, 15, 25–6, 32, 36, 40–1, 45, 54–5, 58, 61–2, 74, 101, 103, 104 n.18, 108, 110, 118, 126–8, 153, 180–1, 185–91
Hector 77, 87
hêdonê 8
Helen 3, 16, 27–9, 51, 63, 74, 79, 87, 89, 92, 122, 181
Hellenistic poetry 2, 9, 27, 119
Heracles 71, 76, 86
hetaera 91, 93, 105, 106 n.26 (see also: *pornai*, prostitute, whore)
heterosexual 9, 20–1, 48, 57, 59, 66 n.5, 83–7, 92, 98–9, 101, 105, 109 n.33, 114, 118, 159, 161, 165–6
hierarchy 4 n.9, 5, 8, 13 n.43, 67
Hipparchus and Hippias 93
Hippocrates 7, 14–15, 33–4, 38–9, 41 n.52, 42–3, 50–1

Index Nominum et Rerum — **231**

Hippolytus 6, 7, 27, 66–7, 74–5, 86, 151
homosexual/-erotic 9, 16 n.61, 20, 48, 57, 59, 98–9, 100–1, 104–5, 107, 109–12, 166 (see also: *erastês*, pederasty)
hubris 20, 93–4, 144–5, 147–8
hunting 104, 124–6
hymenaios 42, 142

Icarus 73
iconography 16, 51 n.4
identity 1, 74, 129, 159, 164, 170, 178
image/-ing/-ery 2, 5, 16, 23, 25–39, 41–2, 45, 67, 73–4, 80 nn.79–80, 103, 110–11, 127–8, 141, 143–4, 146–7, 165, 172
immunity 115, 129
impotence, sexual 14
incest 6, 20–1, 68 n.13, 70, 81, 159, 171–3, 176
infection 2, 11, 16, 21, 156
injury 12, 67, 74, 119, 138, 189 (see also: wound)
innovation/invention 2, 19, 99, 128, 136 n.5, 146 n.38, 154 n.3, 157, 160, 162, 171
insomnia 15, 30–1, 36, 41, 44
intertextuality 3 n.7, 27–8
Iphis 20, 119, 123, 130–3
irony/-ic/-ically 8, 13, 105, 101, 125–6, 128, 139, 147, 150, 156

Jason 6, 10, 70
jealousy 5–6, 102 n.4, 104 n.16, 118–19, 123, 186
joke 8–9, 98 n.39, 107–8, 164, 174–5

kinaidos 8, 97
kiss 11, 80, 108–10, 112–14, 117, 127, 143, 186

Laodamia 71, 76–82
laugh/laughter 14, 25–6, 44, 101, 103, 191
law/(un)lawful/legal 12 n.39, 29 n.17, 71, 81, 85, 88–97, 140, 151–2, 169, 171
libido 50, 87
longing 3, 23, 24 n.4, 28, 39, 61, 66, 102 n.8, 110, 118, 183
loyalty/fidelity 3 n.7, 96, 160–1

lust 36–7, 87, 93, 99, 102, 104, 127, 129 n.26, 151, 169, 172, 175–6

madness/maddened/madly/*mania* 5–13, 27, 29 n.17, 32, 35, 42–4, 74, 104 n.16, 111, 117–18, 130, 141, 182, 185–6, 188
magic/-cal/-cian 14–16, 27, 146 n.24, 164, 168–9 (see also: sorcery, spells)
malakia 5
manliness/masculinity/manhood 5, 11, 83–6, 92, 98, 100, 124
marriage/married 3 n.6, 11–14, 34 n.26, 44 n.60, 49, 66–8, 70–2, 77–9, 81, 83–9, 94–8, 100, 101, 104–5, 109–10, 135–7, 140, 142, 146, 147, 149–50, 152–6, 161, 167, 169, 171, 173, 192 (see also: wedding)
Medea 6, 10, 14, 71, 104 n.16, 120, 122–3, 189
melancholy/black bile 3 n.2, 11 n.38, 15, 34, 40–1, 43, 45
melos 48–50
memory 33, 37, 45, 84–5
Menelaus 28, 79, 87, 122
mental/mind 3 n.2, 4–5, 7, 10, 15, 19, 29, 30–3, 36–8, 40, 44–5, 50, 53, 61–3, 88, 110–12, 118–19, 123, 135, 151, 153, 176, 179–80, 184, 191–3
metaphor 1, 4–5, 7 n.21, 9 n.27, 11 n.37, 19, 30, 46, 53, 74, 103–4, 110–11, 118–19, 133, 143, 147
Minos/Minotaur 73–6
miser 42, 119, 131, 142, 146 n.35, 149, 155, 190
misogynous 4 n.9, 14 n.51, 174
mistress 12, 60, 89, 119, 132, 139, 191
money 19, 90–2, 97, 99, 104 n.17, 111, 113, 118, 170, 172, 183–4, 193
monogamous 159, 161, 171
mourning 3, 131, 175, 191

naked 11, 175
Narcissus/narcissism 3, 14
narrate/-ive/-tor/-tion/-tology 1–5, 10–11, 16, 20–1, 24, 37, 39–40, 49, 51, 53–4, 56, 58–9, 73, 75, 77, 92, 102, 124,

127 n.24, 130, 135, 149, 157, 159–73, 175–8
nausea 60–2, 184
necrophilia 6, 21, 159, 176
nosos/νοσῶ 6, 14, 16 n.62, 29 n.17, 66, 67 n.6, 74, 116, 182, 184–6
nymphomania 14, 21, 159, 175–6

oath 75, 136, 140, 148, 151, 153, 156
obsession/-ive/-ed 3, 13, 20, 32, 37, 44, 86, 89–90, 112, 117, 128, 132–3, 135, 137, 140, 149, 156
Odysseus 3, 86, 167
Oedipus 6
Omphale 86, 89
oracle 7, 125 n.19, 136
oratory/rhetoric 5–6, 20, 63, 71, 81 n.82, 83, 87–8, 90–2, 94–5, 102 n.8, 104, 122–3, 186
Oribasius 15, 36–7

pain 3–4, 6, 9, 13, 32, 60–1, 69, 74, 102, 104 n.18, 112, 119, 122, 155, 182, 190–1
Pandora 2–4
panic 26, 173
paralysis 26, 91, 103
Paris 3, 27–8, 63, 75, 87, 89, 98, 122
partheneion (Alcman) 48, 51–3, 56–7
Pasiphae 72–6, 82, 122, 145
Paul of Aegina 15, 36–7, 38 n.42, 43 n.59
pederasty 8–10, 20, 55, 83, 85, 98–9, 104, 161, 166 (see also: *erastês*, homosexual)
Penelope 3, 14, 86
penetration 9, 12, 50, 71
penis 14, 38 (see also: genitals)
Penthesilea 16–18, 121, 152
perfume 89, 98–9, 108, 142
Persephone 70 n.27, 86
persuasion 54, 68, 88, 113–14, 129, 152, 179, 182
Phaedra 7, 14, 27 n.14, 67, 73–4, 122, 151
phantasising/*phantasia*/-*sma* 33, 37, 39 45–6, 128
pharmakon (see: remedy)
philia 3, 102, 114, 117–18
Philomela 122, 126–9

phrenes 5 n.13, 110
plague 7, 89 n.13, 174
poison 12, 144–6, 167 (see also: potion)
Polyphemus 123, 129 n.26
pornai 85, 91 (see also: hetaera, prostitute, whore)
Poseidon 66, 72–5, 144 n.31
potion 11 n.36, 27 (see also: poison)
pregnant 68–70, 94, 96 n.33, 97, 168
pride/proud 3, 6, 91, 102 n.8, 105, 115, 124, 132, 150, 190
prostitute/-tion 9, 11, 89–92, 95–6, 99, 172 (see also: hetaera, *pornai*, whore)
Protesilaus 65, 67, 71, 76–82
puella 13, 121, 122 n.12, 125 n.18, 130–1, 151–2, 191
pulse 15, 30, 35, 43, 50, 62, 186
punishment 42, 70, 72, 78, 86–7, 93–4, 98–9, 126, 135, 144–5, 148, 150, 174
Python 124–6

rape/-ist 8, 11, 21, 69 n.22, 81, 83, 85–6, 92–6, 98–100, 104, 151–3, 156, 159, 161, 172, 176 (see also: violence)
remedy/cure/*pharmakon*/antidote 5–6, 8, 10–13, 15, 35, 42, 96 n.33, 121 n.10, 128–131, 185
revenge 3–4, 6, 42, 97, 102 n.7, 119, 123, 125
rhetoric (see: oratory)
ritual 7 n.22, 9, 16, 20, 48–51, 54–7, 63, 79, 93, 168
romantic 5, 8, 10, 12, 19, 21, 37, 46, 96, 102, 123, 136 n.2, 165–8, 171–2, 174, 177, 179
Romantic(ism) 1, 48

sacrifice 30, 42, 72, 75, 161
sadomasochism 3
satire 13–14, 91
Scylla 122–3
sedative 9 n.27, 12
seduction 1 n.1, 11 n.39, 52, 67, 69 n.22, 81, 83, 85–8, 95 n.30, 96–8, 104, 113, 161, 168–9, 175–6
semen/sperm 9 n.28, 38–9

Index Nominum et Rerum — **233**

shame/-ful 5, 7, 10 n.34, 35, 44 n.60, 84, 97, 102 n.8, 116–18, 122, 126, 142, 150, 170–1
silent/-ence 7, 43, 97 n.36, 106–7, 118, 132, 143, 170–1, 182, 184
slave/-ery 5, 11–12, 44 n.60, 46, 81, 85, 86 n.10, 90, 93 n.22, 94–5, 104 n.18, 108 n.30, 111–12, 116–18, 138–9, 161, 174–5, 184, 191
sleep 14–15, 35, 37, 39, 42, 52–3, 69, 80, 108, 111, 116, 128, 143, 169, 184
smile 26, 54, 62, 101, 107
Socrates 9, 62, 85, 101, 104–8, 110–15, 117
solitude 24, 132
Solon 85, 88, 94, 96
Soranus 42, 193
sorcery 135, 144–6 (see also: magic, spells)
soul 6, 8–9, 12, 29 n.17, 30–1, 36, 38 n.43, 41, 43–4, 46, 106–7, 109, 112–14, 116–18, 153, 184–5, 190
spells 15–16, 27, 146 (see also: curses, magic, sorcery)
statue 20, 28, 65, 67, 76–8, 80
Stheneboea 66–7
Stoics 12, 29 n.16
suffering 2–7, 9, 11–12, 24, 26–7, 29 n.17, 30–2, 34–7, 39, 43, 45–6, 60–1, 63, 74, 76, 100, 104 n.17, 107, 109, 125 n.18, 131, 133, 135, 139, 141, 143, 148, 150, 156, 171, 174, 185, 191–2
suicide 3, 6–7, 10–11, 13–14, 42, 45, 67, 69–71, 78, 81, 117, 131
sweating 26, 30–1, 33, 36, 104
sword 68, 70–1, 78, 108, 144, 151
symptoms 2, 5, 10–11, 14–15, 19, 23, 25–7, 30–3, 36–7, 42, 44, 61–3, 69, 74, 101, 103–4, 111, 113, 116, 118, 123, 126–7

tale 25 n.4, 36, 135–6, 149, 159, 163–4, 166, 168–70, 175–6, 178
Tauropolia 94
tears 1, 15, 36, 131, 138, 142–3, 172 (see also: crying)
Telchines 135–6, 143–7, 157
Tereus 122–3, 126–7, 129 n.26
Theseus 66 n.3, 75, 86

thumos 5 n.13, 19
Tithonus 58–9, 86
torture 13, 86, 126, 138, 173
touching 19, 26, 38, 42, 108–9, 115, 117, 127, 138, 142–3, 146, 154–6, 186, 192
trembling 4, 25–6, 30, 33, 47, 55, 62, 180
tyranny/tyrant 8–9, 93, 99, 104 n.17, 110 n.36, 184, 191

vagina 4 (see also: genitals)
Venus 32, 42, 120, 126, 189–90 (see also: Aphrodite)
victim 3–4, 12 n.40, 16, 29 n.17, 92, 94, 96 n.33, 97, 132, 145
violence 3 n.7, 10, 83–4, 87, 93, 95 n.30, 97, 101, 104 n.16, 105, 118, 123, 137, 151–2 (see also: rape)
virginity 3 n.6, 10 n.33, 11, 34 n.26, 74, 84, 143, 149–51, 153–4, 172, 192
virility 79, 124, 175
vision/visual/-ity 4 n.9, 12, 20, 23, 25–33, 36–8, 41, 45–6, 51 nn.4–5, 74, 94, 109, 111, 117, 169 (see also: eyes)

war 3, 5, 16, 26 n.8, 76–7, 89–93, 99, 104 n.17, 121 n.9, 124–5, 132, 135, 145, 167, 168–70, 189
weakness 7, 30–1, 35–6, 40, 42, 86 n.9, 97, 145
weapon 121 n.9, 122 n.12, 124, 150, 152
wedding/wedlock 70–1, 78–9, 86, 136, 141–2, 156, 169 (see also: marriage)
whore 91–2, 170 (see also: hetaera, *pornai*, prostitute)
wound/*vulnus* 13, 16, 32–3, 83–4, 113 n.50, 119, 121, 125, 128, 133, 150, 182, 185, 191 (see also: injury)

youth/-ful 9 n.27, 11, 58–9, 62, 66 n.5, 87, 97, 99–100, 104 n.15, 108–9, 110, 113–14, 117–18, 161, 163, 167, 182, 184, 186

Zeus 4, 8–10, 48, 66 n.3, 68 n.13, 72–3, 93, 144–5

www.ingramcontent.com/pod-product-compliance
Lightning Source LLC
Chambersburg PA
CBHW050522170426
43201CB00013B/2052